The Theatres and Performance Building

Rob Firman

AuthorHouse™
1663 Liberty Drive
Bloomington, IN 47403
www.authorhouse.com
Phone: 1-800-839-8640

First published by AuthorHouse 12/16/2011

ISBN: 978-1-4678-8573-7 (sc)

Printed in the United States of America

author HOUSE®

Cover photograph: Wales Millennium Centre Donald Gordon Theatre; Sarah J Duncan

For Xavier

it's the same sky wherever we are
and wherever our journeys take us

This book is one of one hundred and eleven
copies printed in February 2012 in celebration of
the survival of 111 buildings that are, or were,
used for the presentation of live entertainment
in South Wales at the time this book was
conceived and written

Number 24/111

to PJ

Plenty of scope in here to
keep you busy replacing
seats for many years......
Good luck & best wishes
R

Rob Finnis
March 2012

About the Author

Rob Firman BSc(hons) BArch RIBA, Chartered Architect

I entered the world in the long cold winter of 1963 in Sanderstead in Surrey, moving to East Yorkshire at the age of 3 and thus I now consider myself a Yorkshireman through and through. I was a student at the Welsh School of Architecture in Cardiff from 1981 to 1986.

My first job on leaving School of Architecture with a Distinction in my higher degree was as an Assistant Architect on the Symphony Hall and International Convention Centre Project in Birmingham, working for the Cardiff based Practice Percy Thomas Partnership. From 1986 to the opening of the building in 1991 I fell in love with buildings for the performance arts, qualified as an Architect and had become Project Architect for the delivery of 8 of the auditoria in that building along with all of their front and back-of-house support accommodation. I now have 25 years experience in arts and culture projects, and have worked both domestically and internationally.

I returned to Cardiff in 1998 to join the team of Architects at Percy Thomas Architects to design and deliver the Wales Millennium Centre in Cardiff Bay. From 1999 I was the Project Director and Executive Architect for the entire project and as well as creating the concept for the design of the main auditorium (now known as The Donald Gordon Theatre) I wrote the Strategic Client Brief for all of the accommodation provided on the site for 7 of Wales' leading arts organisations. From 2000 until leaving Percy Thomas in 2007 I was Project Director for the Hoddinutt Hall development for the BBC National Orchestra and Chorus of Wales also constructed on the Wales Millennium Centre site.
I was delighted to win an RIBA Award and Royal Eisteddfod Gold Medal amongst many other awards for the Wales Millennium Centre in Cardiff and am proud to have contributed to such a landmark in the development and future opportunities for the arts in Wales. I believe passionately that buildings serving the arts should engage directly with the local community and, as such, opportunities to enhance economic development and regeneration have been paramount in all of my work.

On leaving Percy Thomas Architects, or Capita Architecture as that Practice had by then become, I joined the Cardiff Studio of Austin-Smith:Lord and their team of incredibly talented theatre design specialists. While I was immersed in the design and delivery of the WMC project, Austin-Smith:Lord designed and delivered the Riverfront Arts Centre in Newport (opened 2004) and designed the new Theatre Severn in Shrewsbury (opened 2009) and a new Concert Hall for Guildford in Surrey (opened 2011).

My initial role was to assist in the development of the design of a major new cultural project in Abu Dhabi and I assumed responsibility for leading the team of Architects designing the three theatres that were central to the entire development. That project succumbed to the global economic crisis in 2009-10 and on finding myself between projects I began the journey of discovery that has led to this book.

I live in St Fagans on the western edge of Cardiff with my faithful old dog and cat and am considering exploring the rest of Wales and recording the Theatres and Performance buildings of mid and North Wales as a companion volume to this one.

Contents

All photographs by the author unless otherwise identified

Acknowledgements

First thanks must go to my employer Austin-Smith:Lord LLP and especially Cardiff Studio Principal Martin Roe for their unstinting support thrroughout the time it has taken to gather the information in this book.

Then, thanks must go to Mhora Samuel, Jason Barnes and Fran Birch at the Theatres Trust without whose enthusiasm for my fledgling idea in the summer of 2010 the road-trip might never have started. By allowing me to name them as supporters of my adventures they have opened many doors for me and I hope my contribution to the Theatres Trust Database and Image Library in some way returns the favour.

I am of course eternally grateful to all of the theatre management and staff of the venues visited whose generosity with their time and information about their buildings has been invaluable. There are simply too many of them to mention individually but I hope they remember my visit and know how they have helped me.

I'm grateful too for the work of the local historians and website owners and contributors whose work has been vital in piecing together histories for the venues, to colleagues and friends in the Architectural fraternity who have allowed me to use images of their work and to the photographers of buildings I haven't been able to photograph myself. I hope I have given all sources credit in the appropriate place and apologise unreservedly for any I've not included or mentioned.

The whole exercise would not have been possible in the first place had it not been for those ambitious and enlightened individuals and groups who commissioned this amazing cultural heritage asset over the last 150 years and I hope I have served their legacy well with my accounts of their work.

And finally, sincere and heartfelt gratitude to Ian Pepperell and John Rudge whose faith in my ability as a young aspiring Architect back in 1986 set me on this journey 25 years ago and to Keith Vince, first a mentor then companion and friend on many of my career experiences and without whom I'd have made many more mistakes and had a lot less fun.

Introduction

The idea

As an Architect specialising in the design of buildings for the Performing Arts I am passionate about being involved in the conservation and future success of all Theatres. Being based in South Wales has presented me with an opportunity to explore a resource possibly unique in the United Kingdom and in 2010 I decided to find out what I could about all of the buildings used for performing arts across South Wales.

Desk-top research is all well and good but it can't beat visiting and experiencing buildings, their settings and meeting their staff to understand them properly. Despite that certain knowledge, the first step had to be to conduct a desk-top study into what information currently exists about the Theatres in Wales. The database I now have and the information gathered together in this book has been pieced together from several sources and I've added to it by simply driving past theatres not discovered in the desk study as I've travelled around. Once I had established where all of the buildings were the road-trip commenced, the purpose and methodology being to take a photographic record of each one and make an assessment of the economic and physical health of the venue.

The timing

In the 15 months from the end of June 2010 to September 2011 I have visited 111 buildings that are currently used for live theatrical and other performing arts events or were once theatres or performance venues but are now mothballed, derelict or have been converted to a different use and from my starting point in Cardiff I've covered over 3,500 miles.

Eagle-eyed readers may spot my trusty companion on this adventure featuring throughout this book and with whom I've discovered some epic driving experiences on surely some of the best mountain passes anywhere. Whenever it has been possible I've parked my old car outside the venues I've visited as a way of proving I'd been there in my photographic record.

The aim was to complete all visits within as short a period of time as possible so that all assessments and records I made were contemporaneous. Having eventually taken more than a full year to complete my odyssey I hope my findings can still be considered contemperaneous.

The area covered

There was never any intention (in the beginning at least) to visit every theatre and performance building in the whole of Wales, for no other reason than ease of access. This may yet follow as I have no reason to suspect that the quality of buildings and the history and cultural heritage they represent might be any less impressive through mid and north-Wales.

Being based in Cardiff however, it made sense to restrict my visits to those venues close enough to visit within a maximum 2 hours drive and so the area selected reached from Monmouth in the east to Milford Haven in the west and from Brecon in the north to Barry in the south.

This area covers the most densely populated areas of Wales and takes in the County areas of Monmouthshire, Newport, Torfaen, Caerphilly, Blaenau Gwent, Rhondda Cynon Taff, Merthyr Tydfil, Cardiff, Vale of Glamorgan, Bridgend, Neath Port Talbot, Swansea, Powys, Carmarthenshire and Pembrokeshire. The gazetteer later in this book is structured in sections relating to each County for ease of reference.

Definition of buildings selected for visit

All of the buildings identified in this book were originally constructed as a place for live entertainment and had an auditorium with a stage at that time, or were constructed for some other use but have been converted into performance spaces since their construction. I have not included purpose built cinemas although there were a great number constructed in this region over the same period as that covered by this assessment of the theatre buildings, but where theatres have been converted to cinema use after their initial construction I have included them.

There were (and still are) many other buildings in this region constructed as Miners' or Workmen's Institutes and with large function rooms or ballrooms but if they did not have an auditorium with stage built initially or subsequent to their opening I have not included them here.

The caveat

Whilst every endeavour has been made to locate, visit and research every extant venue in the area covered there are quite possibly other buildings I have not discovered and any omissions are entirely unintentional.

On a great many of the days I've travelled to and between the theatres I've visited I've found buildings I hadn't come across in the desk-based research and during many hours surfing the internet for snippets of historical information about one building I've stumbled upon sources that have led to the discovery of others I hadn't driven past. I will be delighted to include any venues I've not included here in any future editions of this book.

Similarly a great deal of effort has gone into researching the histories of these buildings but I accept there may be errors in some of the dates and descriptions of events or identities of owners. I sincerely hope any such errors don't detract from the underlying story behind our wonderful theatres.

All opinions and observations contained in the descriptions of the buildings that follows are entirely those of the author and it has not been my intention to cause any concern by expressing my views, particularly in respect of my perception of the condition or general health of these buildings and venues. It is however my intention to 'say it as I see it', as both an Architect with a knowledge of this building typology and as a committed supporter of those who endeavour to provide opportunities for audiences to experience live entertainment.

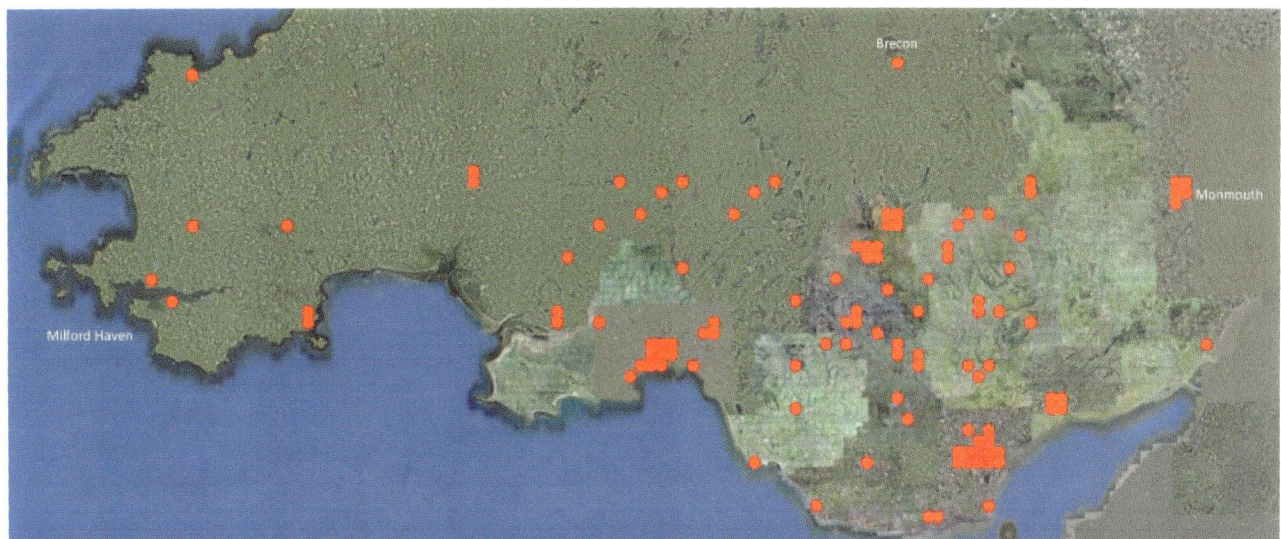

Locations of all buildings visited

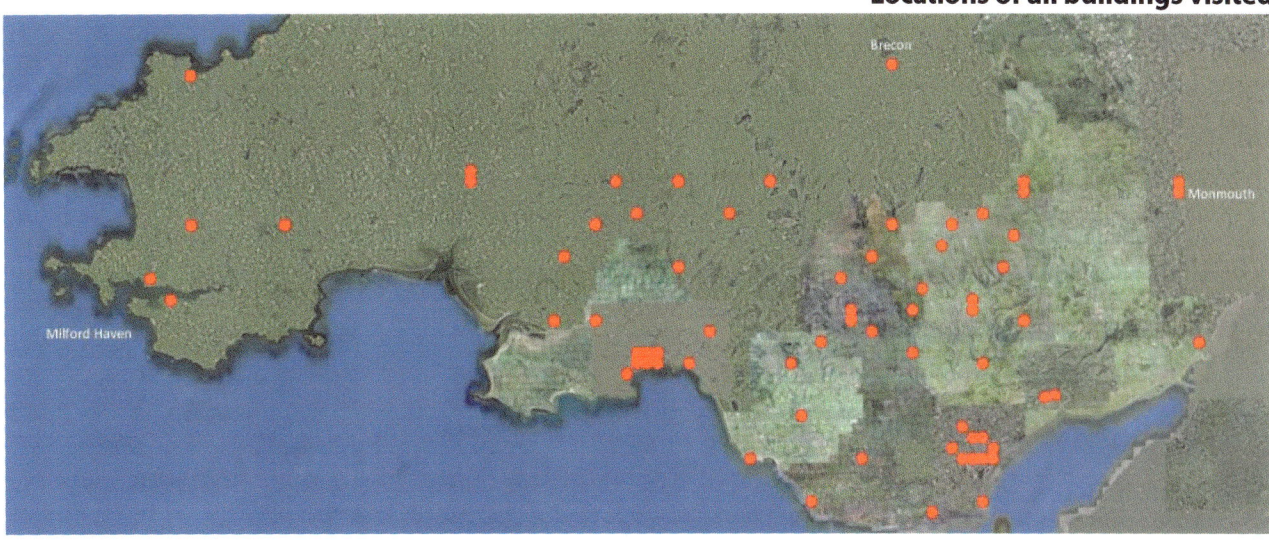

Locations of operational theatre and performance buildings visited

Impressions and Findings

Summary of findings so far

The most surprising finding so far is that there are so many buildings in this relatively small geographical area. Included in this book are assessments of 111 extant buildings that are or have been used for theatre and other performing arts presentation during their life. Although up to date information about auditorium capacity hasn't been possible to ascertain for every venue it is realistic to suggest that these buildings contain a collective total of something in the order of 57,000 seats. The population of the area covered is approximately 1,883,250 (based on mid 2008 census figures), giving us an approximation of 1 seat being available for every 33 men, women and children in the region. This represents an enormous asset by any standards and access to the performing arts is surely beyond most people's expectations.

Yet this is only about two-thirds of the theatres that have ever existed in this region and Darwinian processes of extinction of the weak and those who can't adapt to changes in audience expectations and tastes are fully functioning still - in the time I've been visiting these buildings several more have been mothballed or closed completely and there remain only 69 venues surviving and endeavouring to provide live performance entertainment.

I think the people of Wales ought to be taking this precious cultural heritage asset much more seriously and taking affirmative action to preserve and sustain it. I hope that this book raises public awareness of this incredible collection of buildings that fundamentally exist only for their benefit and that it provokes a debate amongst those in positions of power and influence who might be able to join together to find the solutions to the five questions that I have distilled my thinking down to and that seem to me, in no particular order of importance, to be the at the root of any future strategic thinking and planning for the Performing Arts in this region:

How many theatres do we want (or need) in (South) Wales?

How many more theatre buildings do we allow to disappear?

How do we decide which ones we should keep and which ones we allow to die?

How do we pay to maintain and sustain the ones we want to keep?

Should we be building any more new theatre buildings in (South) Wales until we've fixed the ones we've already got?

Theatre Buildings At Risk

Sadly, not all of the 111 buildings I have visited are open for business and my visits have established that there are currently 21 buildings standing derelict or unused and 16 more are no longer operating as buildings for the performing arts.

The Theatres Trust is The National Advisory Public Body for theatres and a statutory consultee on planning applications affecting land on which there is a theatre. Their remit covers theatre buildings old and new, in current use, in other uses or disused. It was established by The Theatres Trust Act 1976 to promote the better protection of theatres. In 2006 The Theatres Trust published the first Theatre Buildings At Risk Register (TBAR) in response to growing public interest in theatres, to identify important theatres, and to create a Risk Register to work alongside similar lists held by other organisations and Local Authorities.

The first three TBARs identified only the 10 theatres across the whole United Kingdom considered to be most at risk and no theatres in Wales were included. In 2009 the format was changed to identify theatres at 'High', 'Medium' and 'Low' risk of loss. Five theatres in the region covered by this book featured on the 2009 TBAR with The Gwyn Hall, Neath, Palace Theatre, Swansea and Patti Theatre, Craig-Y-Nos listed as 'High' risk, the Theatre Royal, Barry as 'Medium' risk and Philharmonic Hall, Cardiff as 'Low' risk.

At that time the decision to resurrect the renovation of the Gwyn Hall, Neath had not been made and it was standing derelict after the fire of 2007, the Palace in Swansea had already been standing derelict for 2 years and there was concern that the owner of the Patti Theatre wasn't investing as much as was needed in the restoration and maintenance of the venue given its Grade 1 listed status. The Theatre Royal in Barry had yet to close and the Philharmonic in Cardiff had only just closed for business.

In 2010 the format of the TBAR changed again and comprised separate lists for each Country in the UK. There were 5 theatres considered at risk in Wales, and all of them were in the region covered by this book. The Gwyn Hall, Neath had been removed (as the renovation project had recommenced), as had the Philharmonic Hall, Cardiff (although by then it had stood unused for over a year) but the Palace Theatre, Swansea, Patti Theatre, Craig-Y-Nos and Theatre Royal, Barry remained. Two buildings were listed for the first time in 2010 - The Town Hall, Pontypridd (unused since 1984) and Thear Elli, Llanelli (considered under threat by the proposals to construct a new 500 seat theatre elsewhere in the town).

The presence of only 5 buildings considered at risk in the whole of Wales suggests a degree of detachment from this region by the body set up specifically to preserve and protect the theatre buildings of the entire United Kingdom.The publication of the 2010 TBAR coincided with the start of the road-trip that has led to this book and I was immediately curious to establish whether it was a full reflection of the condition and prospects of the buildings in South Wales.

Two of those buildings listed in 2010 are in private ownership and both owners expressed dismay at being on the TBAR to the author – one because it caused potential damage to his business and the other because he has made considerable progress towards establishing funding and planning for the restoration and re-opening of his building over the next few years. As a result of actually visiting all of the theatre buildings in this region it is clear to me that the Theatres Trust had overlooked others and some of those are the most serious cases of buildings under threat.

In the 2011 TBAR the number of venues considered at risk in Wales was increased to 10 with 6 of them being in South Wales.Once again the Palace, Swansea and Theatre Royal, Barry were listed and Pontypridd Town Hall also remained listed for a second time. The future of the Palace, Swansea nd Town Hall, Pontypridd do remain uncertain but it sadly seems inevitable that the Theatre Royal, Barry won't be on the 2012 TBAR as it is scheduled for demolition in the spring of 2012.

Both the Patti Theatre, Craig-Y-Nos and Theatr Elli have been removed because they are both no longer considered under immediate threat and both are currently operational. This means that 3 theatres in this region have been added to the list that weren't considered at risk the year before. The 3 new additions are Parc Hall, Cwmparc near Treorchy which was mothballed in December 2010 as a result of declining audiences and funding, the De Valence Pavilion, Tenby which was closed and placed on the open market in August 2010, and St Donats Arts Centre over concerns for its future.

I still don't believe the list is comprehensive but it reflects those venues in most dire straits for now.

I don't want to appear too critical of the Theatres Trust - they have been extremely enthusiastic supporters of my endeavour - and by contributing to the complete updating of both their on-line Theatres database and Image Library I believe that future TBARs will more accurately represent the number of truly endangered theatre buildings in this region.

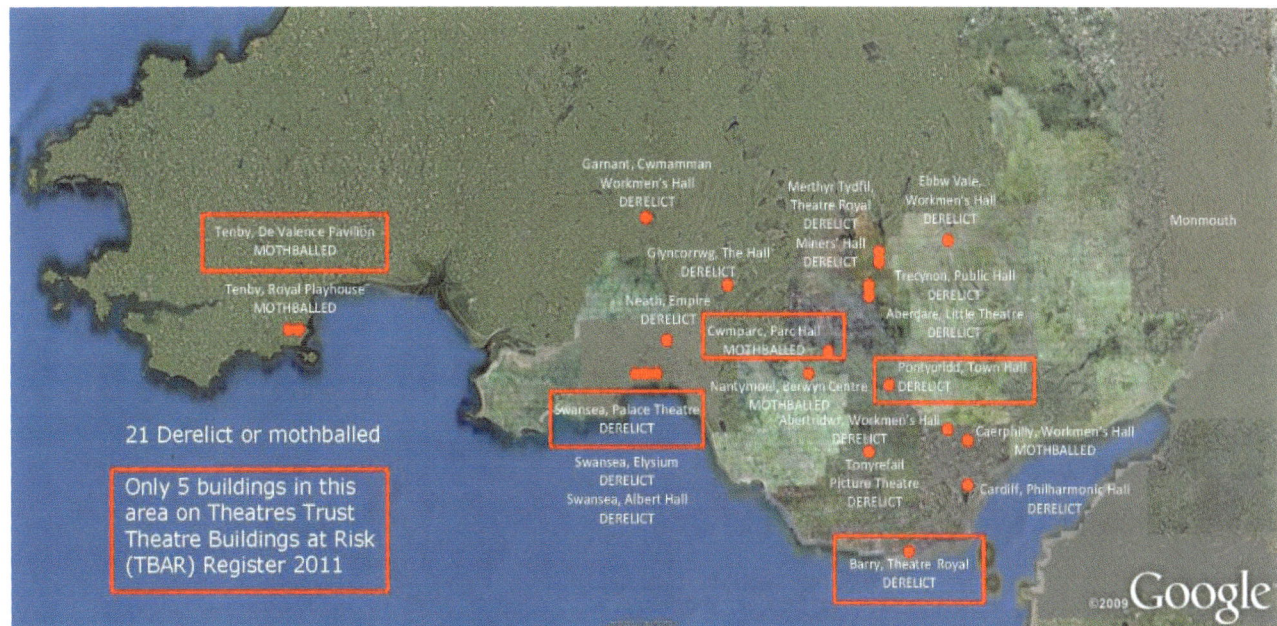

Locations of derelict and mothballed Theatre buildings in 2011

It is my assessment that in the period of time covered by this road-trip there are up to 8 more buildings currently operating as performance buildings that are in serious danger of being lost in the near future.

As my research into extant venues has progressed I have also identified a further 47 theatre buildings across this region that have been lost through demolition (predominantly since the Second World War).

I have no doubt that there are may other lost buildings that I have not been able to find any references to in my research. Whilst compiling my research and findings into this book it seemed appropriate to include them in this record. The decline in our theatre stock has obviously been happening for a long time and shows no tangible sign of slowing.

In about half the time we have been building theatres in Wales about one third have already been permanently lost and if those currently standing derelict or mothballed are added to this total, 40% have gone. Surely the time has come for a serious debate about the extent of the theatre buildings estate in Wales (and South Wales in particular) because, it seems to me this rate of decline is excessive.

Listed Buildings

It is perhaps surprising that not all of the 111 extant theatre buildings have listed status given their individual and collective importance to the development of the culture of South Wales but one reason for this might be that so few people are fully aware of the scale and beauty of the theatre buildings estate?

Of the 111 buildings described in this book 35 are listed buildings with only one theatre (the Adelina Patti Theatre at Craig-Y-Nos castle) and one concert hall (The Brangwyn Hall in Swansea) being listed Grade 1 (buildings of National importance). Five theatre buildings are listed Grade 2* and all of the other listed buildings are Grade 2.

The Palace Theatre, Swansea

Possibly the most endangered theatre building in Wales and one of the most endangered Victorian buildings in the entire United Kingdom.

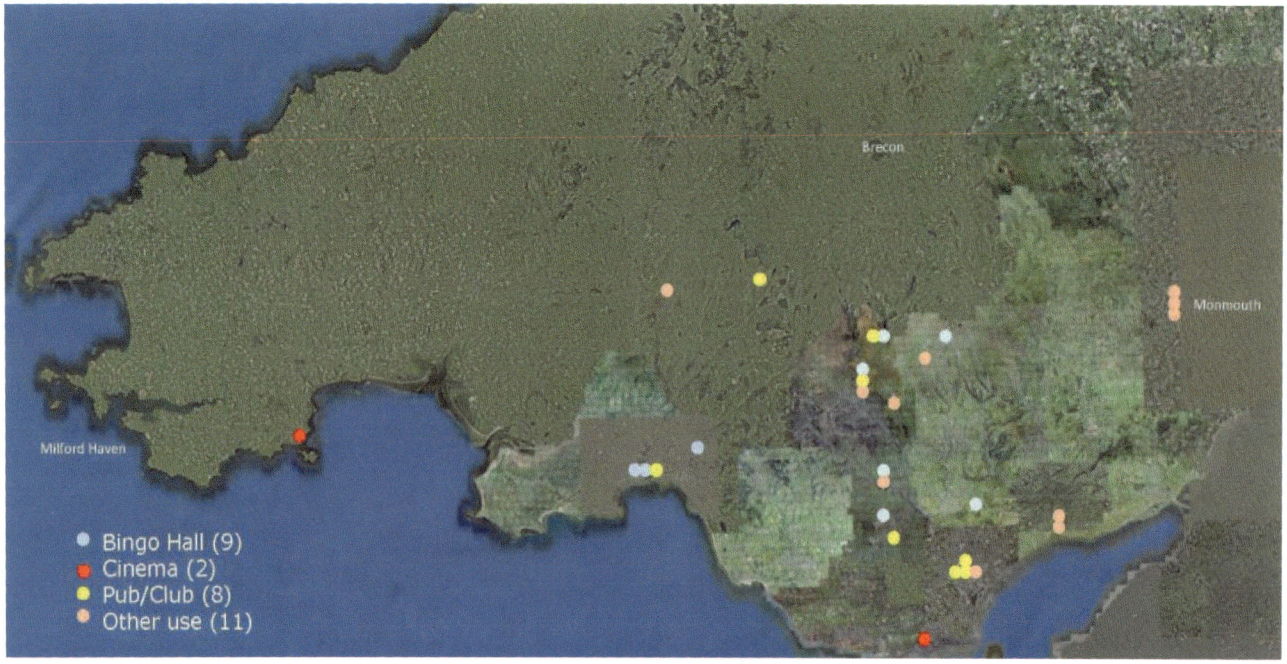

- Bingo Hall (9)
- Cinema (2)
- Pub/Club (8)
- Other use (11)

Locations of Theatre buildings converted to other uses

The Adeline Patti Theatre, Craig-Y-Nos

Listed Grade 1 and a National treasure

The Theatre Royal, Merthyr Tydfil

Listed Grade 2 but derelict

Of those 35 listed buildings only 23 are currently operating as theatres or buildings for live performance so we have 'protected' less than a quarter of the theatre buildings that remain and this makes the remaining unlisted ones extremely vulnerable to redevelopment for other uses or worse, demolition should they become derelict.

It must be said however that listing is not necessarily a guarantee of protection as 11 of the listed buildings have been converted to other uses already and 8 of those are now standing derelict along with 1 listed theatre building that is standing derelict too. So, one third of those extant theatre buildings that have been listed are standing derelict and must surely be at risk of demolition, especially in the uncertain economic times that currently prevail.

Clearly then, listing is not a panacea or a guarantee of survival and despite being part of quite a small group within the context of the overall number of buildings that exist there are as many venue managers who regard operating a listed building to be a hindrance to development of their venues as there are those who see it a valuable recognition of the significance of their buildings.

Those who regard it as a hindrance often cite difficulties with the process of securing Listed Building Consent to make changes to the building fabric with delays incurred by that statutory approval process sometimes meaning the loss of funding for projects. This may still occur in individual situations but it is clear from many examples found on this trip that through appropriate consultation with Cadw before and during the planning and execution of a project excellent results can be achieved and our theatre buildings sensitively brought up to 21st Century standards.

Ownership of theatre buildings

The origins of the majority of the performance venues of the South Wales Region fall into three broad categories.

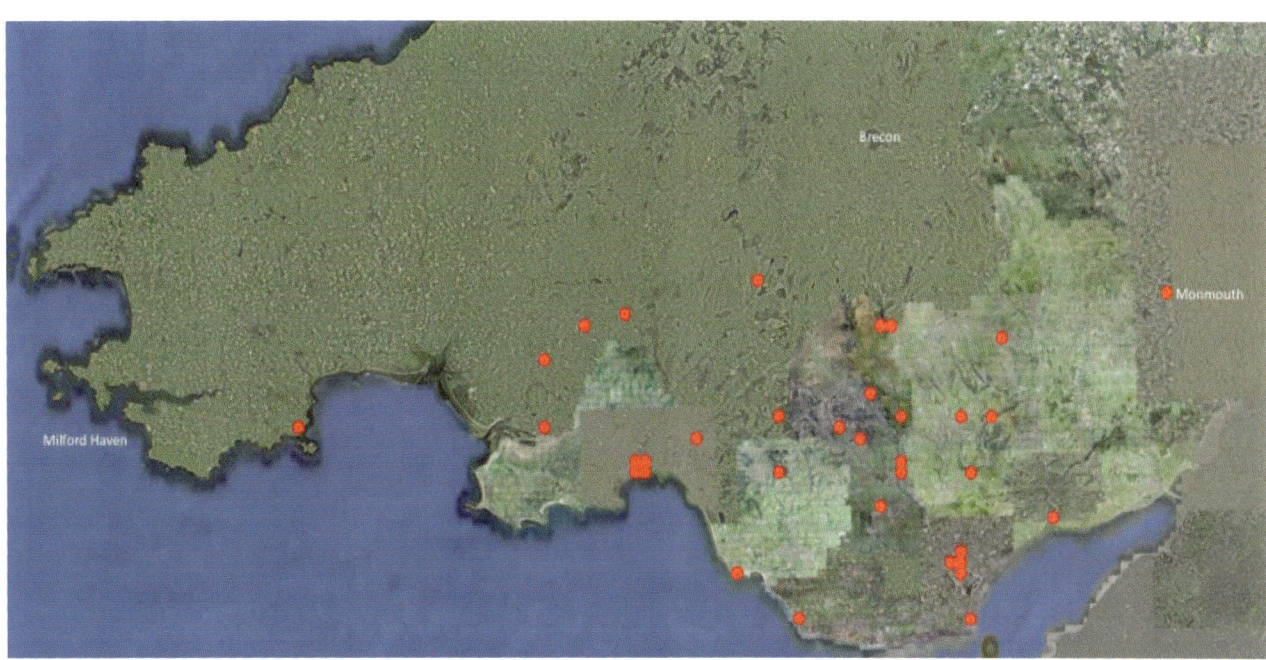

Locations of Listed Theatre buildings

In the first category are those built by the communities of miners and iron and steelworkers for themselves, often using their own money from the 'penny in the pound' wage deduction savings scheme paid into the communal building fund.

Where did these largely uneducated men find the ambition to make so many unique buildings from? I have nothing but admiration for the sheer guts and astonishing vision of the people who raised the money and commissioned buildings like the Park & Dare in Treorchy, the Memo in Newbridge and The Miners' Theatre in Ammanford.

The second group of venues was built by wealthy individuals or by Local Authorities including Maesteg Town Hall (built by a prosperous Authority in the thriving market town in 1881) Parc Hall in Cwmparc near Treorchy (gifted by Lord David Davies of Llandinam, owner of the Ocean Coal Company to his workforce in 1908), and The Adelina Patti Theatre at Craig-Y-Nos built in 1891 to enable the opera diva to entertain her house guests.

The third group is a comparitively recent addition to the estate insofar as its origins are in the education sector and are theatres providing both academic facilities for students entering the world of performing arts and venues for audiences drawn from communities local to the facility.

Irrespective of ownership or origin there are common histories to the vast majority of the buildings in the first two categories. In very large part, these buildings were created by local people for their local community and in their early years the buildings provided a place for education as well as entertainment and social gathering.

Many were converted to cinema use either initially on the advent of moving pictures or when 'talkies' came along as the management and communities they served aspired to avail themselves of the latest technology and social trends and they were hugely successful throughout the middle years of the 20th Century. After the Second World War the rise of alternative forms of entertainment, especially television in the home, saw many venues seek additional or entirely new revenue streams so they became Bingo Halls or drinking establishments and then those businesses failed and many buildings became neglected and ultimately dis-used and derelict. It appears that the larger the venue, the more susceptible to dereliction and oblivion. Many extraordinary buildings have been demolished as lost causes but over the last 15 to 20 years there are clear signs that some of the survivors have been returned to the purpose for which they were originally created and are once again at the heart of their communities and thriving.

The majority of currently operating theatres are now in the care of Local Authorities. Some are owned, managed and operated directly (31) while others are operated by charitable trusts or management companies granted long leases whilst the local authority retains responsibility for repair and maintenance of the building fabric (10). Some are owned and operated by entirely independent charitable trusts (31) and there are indications that more will follow this route as Local Authority budgets get increasingly stretched by the prevailing austerity measures resulting from the financial crisis of 2008-09. Some remain in private ownership (29) though only 2 of those are actually operating as

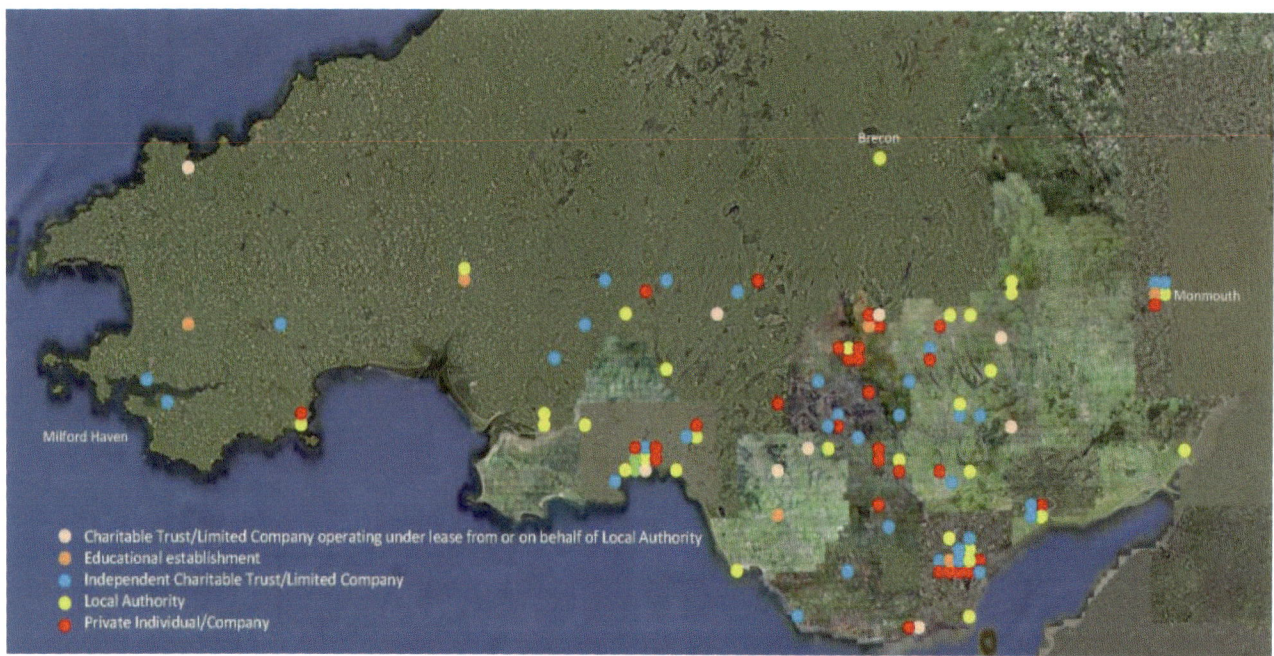

Ownership of surviving Theatre buildings

performance venues – the rest have been converted to other uses and the rest (8) are established within educational establishments. Some have become essential stops on National and International tours and others are focused on serving their immediate local communities.

Artistic offering and shared intelligence

Today there are further issues that separate the venues into different groups, in addition to who now owns, manages or operates them, and those are the various approaches to the nature of use and shows or events that sustain them.

These different approaches are producing a range of levels of support and success. Some venues receive substantial financial support (through direct or external funding) while others appear to have less external support and find it difficult to plan for their long term future. Those in independent or private ownership seem to be struggling most of all to sustain their businesses and some are resorting to non-theatrical events and activities to create essential revenue.

What appears to have been happening in respect of artistic offering is that a large proportion of the surviving venues currently compete with each other for audience and this approach is potentially a threat to some of extinction because a venue a few miles away is better supported, more comfortable for the audience or easier to access by touring companies pressed for time between appearances. There is an apparent collective attitude of ignoring the mobility of audiences in this day and age which is rooted in the past and surely needs to better recognised.

An organisation called Creu Cymru was established by the sector in 2001 to help overcome such issues. Across the whole of Wales only 44 venues are members. Of those 44, 29 in the region covered by this book are members leaving 40 other operational venues unconnected to the support and market intelligence Creu Cymru exists to provide.

Creu Cymru does appear to restrict its membership in its statement that *'membership is open to all arts centres or theatres in Wales that are professionally managed and which host professional performances'.* There is no mention on its website of the other venues managed by amateurs, volunteers from communities or otherwise deemed by implication 'unprofessional' and of course a great number of them do host 'professional' performances by touring theatre and performance companies. Surely there is an opportunity to use Creu Cymru to connect more venues and even in times when its own funding is increasingly stretched it must surely pursue a wider membership across Wales much more vigorously than it has so far achieved?

In 2009 Creu Cymru commissioned a response to the Arts Council of Wales' paper 'Striving to Excel'. Written by Elan Closs Stephens it was entitled 'A Position Paper on Theatres and Arts Centres Across Wales'. At risk of 'cherry-picking' extracts from a comprehensive paper, it makes a number of interesting observations that seem to me to have been taken forward with only limited success in the 2 years since its publication.

It observes that *'the sector* (performing arts) *has not been viewed in the past as a strategic partner for ACW* (Arts Council of Wales)*, capable of offering discussions on art forms and audiences. Whilst ACW has recently agreed art form strategies there is no strategic plan for the curatorial leadership and business development of theatres and arts centres'*

Further to this *'The sector would wish to be recognised in developmental terms as a single organisation and to grow its ambitions – and those of the Arts Council - through the development of a recognised network'* and *'the sector wishes to argue for enhanced and accelerated shared services, marketing opportunities and programming co-operation.'*

So why does the 'sector' know so little about its own extent and why do the 'professional' venues appear to wilfully ignore the 'non-professional' ones? Surely it must learn to speak with one voice, representing the entire 'sector' or 'industry' in order to exert influence over decision making made by those outside the day-to-day fight for survival undertaken by the majority of venues?

The paper develops the theme of a wider network by stating *'Central to the discussion of a network would be the development of a map showing the interconnectivity of centres and where shared services or programme development already exists. This would corroborate or challenge the interconnectedness of the network and would highlight good practice. There is already much good work that needs to be understood and built upon. Such a map might also lead to discussions as to the inter-relatedness of local and regional centres and whether this might lead to the development of clusters.'*

As far as I have been able to ascertain, the map in the Introduction to this book is the only one in existence that actually locates all extant theatre buildings in South Wales (and should the second companion volume to this one ever be realised there will be a similar map for North and Mid-Wales). Perhaps Creu Cymru, or the Arts Council of Wales, will use it to start the process of establishing 'interconnectivity advocated by Creu Cymru's paper?

The paper refers to the existence of an initiative called 'ArtsConnect' and claims that its work so far has been *'One area of fruitful collaboration'.*

ArtsConnect is a 'project' or 'initiative' established in the autumn of 2007 with the aim of ensuring that local arts services in the region of South-East Wales will be more efficient and effective. Its central theme is that by integrating provision, services will be good value for money and audiences, participants and other stakeholders and customers will benefit from high quality and cost effective services. It is supported by the Arts Council of Wales and the Welsh Local Government Association and initially comprised almost all local authorities in the region as 'partners' including Blaenau Gwent, Bridgend, Caerphilly, Merthyr Tydfil, Monmouthshire, Rhondda Cynon Taff and Torfaen.

At the time of writing it is due to be implemented (before September 2011) but whether or not it will be as successful in achieving its aims is already suspect as several of the original 'partners' have withdrawn and only a small core of already well organised local authorities with a significant estate of performance buildings remains involved.

Surely at some risk now are the ambitions to achieve effectiveness gains at a Regional level including artistic programming, marketing, event management, arts development, approach to sponsorship and external funding, procurement, shared expertise and a single point of contact/box office for all involved venues?

Certainly the aspiration it had of creating equal access and spread of resources across the region (which are uneven) can no longer be achieved and there is a serious risk, it seems to me, of it creating 'haves' and 'have nots' in the areas within and without the collaborative partnership. It has undeniably already failed to progress the idea that the 'sector' might one day speak with a single voice to the Arts Council of Wales or the Welsh Government.

A significant other risk that an initiative such as ArtsConnect poses to the community of performing arts is that it may result in a further shrinking of the number of operating venues (as those outside this network find it impossible to compete with the larger network of well supported and organised venues) or it may ensure the survival of a number of venues that would otherwise fail and disappear if not brought under the aegis of this new group. Surely time would be better spent ending the prevailing thinking at a myopic level of individual buildings or small groups of publicly owned venues considering only their own concerns and extend awareness, engagement and future planning to the entire region.

Whilst it is inevitable that to do so will involve strong Political leadership and perhaps the emergence of a 'champion' from within the sector who has the respect and authority to speak on behalf of all involved in the operation of theatre buildings, there is no doubt that unless the sector finds a way of becoming whole instead of fractured, of working together rather than against each other the future will mirror the past.

There is no reason to believe that theatre as an art form, and as a form of public entertainment, will not continue to thrive in Wales and it is right that the majority of funding is focussed on the companies who create the art. It is also an unavoidable truism that some current theatrical work can happen in places and spaces that are very far removed from enclosed buildings and auditoria (perhaps the grandest and most successful recent example being the production of 'The Passion' in Port Talbot at Easter 2011 involving the actor Michael Sheen and National Theatre Wales with a host of local people involved directly in supporting roles and in making the production happen). But not all theatrical and performing arts productions can happen without theatre buildings, and we have surely now reached the point where it is the buildings that need attention.

General appraisal of the condition of the buildings

There have been 5 fairly well defined periods of activity in theatre building construction in (South) Wales – the Victorian/19th Century period (pre-1900), the Edwardian/pre-war period (1900-1914), the Inter-war period (1918-1939), the post-war/late 20th Century period (1945-1999) and the post-Millennium/21st Century period (2000 onwards).

The statistical analysis of construction of buildings in these periods reveals that of the 111 buildings that are or once were theatres and performance venues in this region, the largest number by far were constructed in the 19th Century (34). Of these only 17 remain in theatre use in 2011. In the Edwardian/pre-war period a further 20 theatre buildings were constructed and only 9 of those remain in use as theatres. Between the two World Wars, 22 more theatres were opened and 16 of those remain in theatre use. 25 were built in the second half of the 20th Century and 24 of those survive and since the commencement of the 21st Century 8 new venues have been added and all are still in operation (including Y Ffwrnes in Llanelli currently under construction and plans under development for a new venue in Merthyr Tydfil). Clearly the pace of construction of new venues has not kept pace with the rate of closure and demolition of older ones, particularly over the last 50 years.

Any theatre that ends up derelict is a tragedy and I was surprised to find any at all in this country renowned the world over for its cultural heritage. However there are 19 that I've found so far that would appear to be on the brink of disappearing for good. To bring these venues back into viable use will take incredible energy and funds that may be difficult to find. There have been many theatres in Wales lost over recent decades (47 are described at the end of this book) and the risk of losing more is ever present. During this trip I have found some perilously close to oblivion for reasons as diverse as fear of imminent structural collapse through lack of investment in maintenance to simply being unable to programme events that attract audiences. I wonder how many will be left if I repeat this road trip in 2020.

Of course the vast majority of buildings that have already been demolished and those standing derelict now failed as commercial businesses before their fabric began to deteriorate (only 9 of these 47 'lost' buildings disappeared as a result of fire damage or structural collapse) but there is a powerful relationship between maintenance of building fabric and commercial success that cannot be ignored.

If a building is well cared for and maintained, whatever its age, it is far easier to retain an audience than it is if it is allowed to start looking scruffy or even unclean. If the audience sees the building they are using being uncared for they are likely to start to feel that they are not cared about by the owner/operator either and will start to decline in number. Ultimately, if not lost to live performance as audience members completely they will take their business to another venue that does appear to care.

It is a vicious downward spiral from that point forward that can probably only be arrested by substantial capital investment in a major refurbishment of the venue supported by intensive and sustained (expensive) marketing to attract the departed audience back. This is not always successful. This inescapable fact of life is not however one that is uniformly respected by all of the current group of theatre building owners and operators. These are uncertain economic times and all of the signs are that for the foreseeable future funding streams that boomed with the creation of the National Lottery and went crazy around the Millennium are shrinking year on year or disappearing completely to some. As a consequence it is clear that for almost all of the venues visited the majority of any revenue earned or funding granted to them is spent on product (shows) before fabric and general building maintenance and there appear to be no proactive planned maintenance strategies in place in any except the most recently built and well-funded venues.

As a group of building owners and operators, the theatre fraternity generally seems to simply wait till something breaks then fix it if they can afford to. This reactive approach is inevitably resulting (in general) in a steadily deteriorating building stock, getting worse year on year, and time will run out for some of our theatre buildings unless something considered and sustained is put in place soon to ensure they don't disappear through neglect.

In some cases there have been repairs carried out to old buildings that have contributed to their eventual decline. This seems bizarre but particularly in the second half of the 20th Century many fine solid stone-walled buildings have, for example, been covered over with cementitious render in the misguided intention of 'water-proofing' them after some water penetration through the walls may have caused concern. The fact is that this kind of 'repair' has a devastating impact on buildings that used a construction method predicated on the buildings being able to 'breathe' and allowing the passage of some moisture through the construction in both directions (from the outside in but more importantly from the inside out). Re-pointing the stonework and reinforcing the damp-proof courses around windows and doors will almost always solve such problems. Covering the walls with an impermeable layer of concrete render with a synthetic paint covering often applied over that in many coats can certainly enhance the external appearance of a building but it traps moisture inside causing untreatable condensation problems that can destroy a building over a surprisingly short period of time.

There is perhaps an argument that the reason for some of the decay in the fabric of the remaining buildings is poor commercial management of the businesses occupying the buildings and I have already stated that the two symptoms of decline (commercial failure and building deterioration) are inextricably linked. But notwithstanding bad management, is there anything that could be done to alleviate the burden of maintenance and repair from these businesses in the long term to give the buildings the best chance of survival possible?

Before I started this trip I suspected that the majority of the current owners and management of these venues would have concerns about issues such as accessibility and heating, ventilation and general energy consumption worries.

I genuinely thought they would spend more than they do on maintaining their buildings. Almost every place I've visited has things the management would improve about the physical fabric of their venues given creation or receipt of adequate funds. Generally, every venue does what it can to maintain the best possible environment for performers, audience and staff and the vast majority do a great job with the limited means at their disposal.

There are very few of the older venues where front-of-house accessibility is fully in line with current statutory requirements although awareness of the Disability Discrimination Act is widespread and a genuine concern. Indeed a large number of venues are actively making improvements to this aspect of their buildings and sensitively integrating access for all into their facilities.

What did surprise me in many of the older venues I've visited was just how poor facilities back-of-house are. Most productions that were staged in these venues when they first opened were probably either local amateur dramatic, operatic and choral societies or small itinerant travelling companies who simply put up with having to prepare for their performance in whatever spaces were provided. That so many venues still have out-dated and uncomfortable backstage facilities must be an issue to focus some attention on.

Loading bays are frequently presenting operational difficulties (if indeed the venue actually has what we now think of as a loading bay). When first opened, shows presented at the older venues would generally be built as bespoke installations on stage and thrown away afterwards or, if touring across many venues would be delivered on carts or flat-bed trucks with a much higher axle height than today's vans and trucks. Compounding this is an architectural approach that consistently located the auditorium and stage at first floor level and the topography of many sites (many of the buildings visited were constructed on the side of steep hills) so now loading and unloading 21st century visiting shows can be a logistical nightmare, and in many venues probably contravenes manual handling restrictions defined by current Health and Safety legislation. Surely some attention to this could bring longer term benefits to our theatres?

Ultimately it depends on the nature of the products being toured and ticket sales resulting from a potentially wider range and greater availability of shows but, If we can improve loading facilities we could increase the number of shows in a run leading to more revenue for the producers and venues, which ultimately achieves pay-back for the investment and enhances the chances of survival of the venues that take this action.

Proposals

So what do I think could, or should, be done to reverse the decline in the fabric of our theatre buildings and to improve their facilities so that they are all fully accessible, comfortable and can operate to standards expected of any brand new facility?

To my mind, by far the most difficult issue is the generation of funding specifically targetted at maintaining the fabric of these buildings. In any business that occupies buildings there needs to be a line in the operating budget for generally taking care of the building and such allowances almost always exist (even if used entirely to cover the costs of simple regular cleaning or replacing worn out light bulbs). I would venture that it is reasonably safe to cast the allegation however that the majority do not have allowances made for specific building repairs, in a planned and sustained manner year-on-year, let alone stick to those allowances.

There could be any number of reasons for the widespread non-expenditure of revenue income on planned and regular repairs but in general, it is probably also safe to assume that the revenue needed either isn't earned, gets spent in an ad-hoc fashion on emergencies such as unexpected failures of heating boilers, as a result vandalism such as broken windows or graffiti or is diverted to pay for a show that is hoped will increase audience numbers in the short term. Allowances for repairs might be made with the best intentions but the evidence is out there that repair and maintenance are the two expenses that are first to be sacrificed when times get tough. Of course it doesn't help that the cost of repairs (especially to older buildings) can be extraordinarily expensive and things that might have been dealt with in the past by sending one of the resident crew up a ladder now can only be carried out after hiring scaffold and specialist tradesmen. It can also be a perception issue insofar as any money spent on maintenance and repair is like treading water in terms of development of the building - the investment reaps no obvious return, no quantum change in comfort or appearance and after maintenance the building tends to look exactly how we thought it always did - the fear is perhaps that it is dead money and any money spent should be made to give 'a better' return.

The tricky part about my recommendation that follows is that responsibility for maintaining buildings should indeed rest with their owners and management and it is a certain sign of good governance if this vital activity is carried out in a planned and sustained way - a well-maintained building gives out all the right signals to its audience and potential audience and the investment (however imperceptible) pays off in the long term with the establishment of a loyal audience base and sustained desire from producers and presenting companies to visit and perform there. And of course far fewer emergencies that have to be fixed instantly to avoid losing shows or audience or both.

Whilst I have a particular allegiance to and fondness for the Wales Millennium Centre in Cardiff and its management team as the legacy of being its Executive Architect, I can confidently hold it out as an exemplar in this respect. From the outset of that project the Board were insistent on understanding from the Design and Construction team the life-expectancy of the elements that constitute its fabric so that they could anticipate when they would need to spend money on ongoing general maintenance and ultimately replacement. They produced a document as a supplement to their Business Plan and it is now a mature and guiding document that enables the Centre's operational management team to plan 'down-time' for major works and for the financial management (and those external bodies and agencies that help fund it) to see well in advance of when funds will be needed to keep the building looking its best and comfortable for its visitors and staff. Adherence to this plan is regarded as essential and it is never sacrificed to cover the cost of other seemingly higher priorities.

I therefore submit for debate the notion that every theatre building owner or management team should follow this lead and adopt it as a guiding principle that drives their business planning equally as hard as promoting a range of performances and events they think will attract the most revenue income from audiences. Of course this should not be anything new to all bar the least capable of building managers and business plan writers but the fact that so few exist and anecdotal evidence confirms it is the first allowance on most budgets to be spent on something else means this approach of ad-hoc emergency response must change. If it does indeed change and owners and management teams start to become far more proactive in their care of their buildings the decay of our theatre buildings' fabric will gradually be arrested and the experience of operating and visiting these buildings will improve for everybody concerned.

Perhaps, if there was the desire or motivation, organisations such as the Wales Millennium Centre could actively share the methodology they have adopted for the creation of a maintenance plan with associated budget?

My radical proposal for the future funding of the upkeep of our theatre buildings estate follows on from this first step (the creation of planned maintenance strategies with budget costings) but instead of leaving the creation of appropriate funding for ongoing maintenance to each individual venue could we not consider centralising it? There was a time when Politicians used the phrase 'Nationalise' for such approaches but in this case I think 'centralising' better and certainly more altruistic.

The thrust of this idea is that such is the value of this cultural heritage asset to the nation of Wales that in order to guarantee its survival and proper upkeep responsibility for full funding of maintenance be removed from owners and operators and that responsibility be transferred to a central fund that provides access to funding on a grant basis as and when the venue's adopted maintenance plan dictates. The singular condition for accessing funds from this centrally held fund would be the preparation of a properly executed and considered plan that was updated annually to demonstrate 'membership' of the estate. The big question this idea leads to is who or what should hold and administer such a fund and how should the monies be found to cover the costs of this unending future maintenance programme?

Perhaps it is timely that the Arts Council of Wales, having published its strategic funding review in the early summer of 2010, is, at the time of writing, planning to publish its Capital Funding Strategy for the period 2012 -17 following publication of a draft document for consultation in the summer of 2011.

In the Draft for Consultation, ACW seeks answers to several questions including *'Do you think that there are specific actions we could be taking to ensure a more 'joined up' approach through our Capital Strategy?'* . It goes on to say *'We'll need to use our funds astutely to achieve maximum impact from our investment. It's likely, for example, that we'll want to place a greater priority on the refurbishment of existing facilities rather than new build schemes',* and *'A key area of concern is the potential revenue impact of a Capital scheme'.* It's thought provoking and absolutely commendable stuff and it is to be hoped that the response to the consultation process leads to a Strategy for the next five years that truly places the Arts Council of Wales at the heart of strategic thinking across the Performing Arts sector, engaging with the entire fraternity as indeed advocated by that paper prepared on behalf of Creu Cymru in 2009.

One cause for a degree of alarm in the document exists however. The Arts Council of Wales has, as a result of its Revenue funding review of 2010 aligned itself very clearly and powerfully behind the organisations it provides revenue funding to. Quite rightly, ACW must demonstrate to the general public that it spends its money wisely and prudently and quite rightly it has identified what it believes to be the most appropriate companies (and in some cases venues) to provide support to. What is slightly disturbing is the suggestion that the capital Strategy might shadow the Revenue Funded Organisations strategy and focus its capital expenditure on the places where RFOs are based. It seems to me that such an approach denies access to much needed funds to the majority of venues across Wales and, if this is the outcome and direction the Capital Strategy takes, ACW are not the organisation to manage the fund for building maintenance I am suggesting neither will they be the source of the necessary funds.

The Consultation document does set out as one of its scheme priorities maintaining the standard of the (arts) infrastructure. Here it clearly states that *'it's imperative that the range of first class facilities and artworks created* (over the past 14-15 years)*does not deteriorate over the next five to ten years'* and *'A key priority should therefore be to ensure that the value of the capital investment undertaken in creating the arts infrastructure is not lessened by failure to maintain buildings to a high standard or to respond to new opportunities. We need to upgrade and extend facilities that will contribute to the creative and financial success of the organisation and help to ensure future sustainability. A national audit of the condition and ongoing capital needs of facilities supported by the Arts Lottery could form the basis for a national investment plan to ensure that the quality of the arts infrastructure is maintained'.*

Whilst it is clear that currently ACW does not see this priority as applying to the entire estate of theatres and performance buildings in Wales, surely it could be expanded and surely if venues had existing maintenance strategies in place the task of expanding the vision of the Arts Council would be so much easier to achieve?

After I read the Arts Council's consultation paper I was struck by the commonality between some of the things they say and things I have thought about and discussed with many of the theatre building owners and managers I have met during this road-trip. I am encouraged that at least some of the picture is visible and now I hope that some of the research and information in this book might increase the visibility of those venues not on the Arts Council's radar or past investment portfolio and they too will start to advocate or encourage the preparation of a thorough assessment of maintenance requirements and repairs that the entire existing building stock requires.

Ultimately, however, my vision does not have the Arts Council and its capital spending budget at the heart of building maintenance in the future for I believe their role is a different one. Their Consultation document mentions the need to ensure that all of the venues and buildings it provides support to must all become compliant with current legislation and better able to serve audiences and performers for the foreseeable future and I see this as the contribution they should focus most on. It is the Arts Council Capital Strategy that should, in my opinion, help make our venues fully accessible and extend and modernise backstage areas so that they are comfortable work-places for building staff and visiting performers and companies. Perhaps the only area of overlap between enhancement and maintenance seems to me to be in the area of energy consumption or rather the reduction of energy consumption and environmental sustainability of our estate. It is arguable that replacing out-dated and inefficient boilers for example is simply normal maintenance required through the (long) life of these buildings but such is the benefit of installing boilers with 21st Century technology to the reduction in fuel costs being incurred by some venues that Arts Council Capital could, in such instances make a huge difference.

The vast majority of our surviving theatre buildings are in need of an approach which I would advocate should where possible, adopt an approach that aims to create a highly sustainable 'conservation' project, which weighs up the best in sustainable design with the 'right' approach to historic building conservation. These are, of course, not always the best bed-fellows, and a number of decisions will be made during the process which may result in some sort of compromise. In essence, however, design proposals should not put at risk the building's historic fabric, whilst they should aim for the building to be as sustainable as it can be in the future and hence as affordable and easy to run and occupy as reasonably practicable.

It is simply a myth that it is not possible to insulate old buildings and improve their thermal efficiency, but such work needs to be specified and designed by specialists to avoid the risks that are ever present to the integrity of the historic building fabric. The major focus of any sustainability strategy for any of the older theatre buildings should be to create an internal environment which achieves excellent thermal and daylight comfort levels through minimal carbon emissions and capital and operational costs. This must begin with a careful site and programme assessment to understand constraints and opportunities and develop project-specific strategies for energy and sustainability. It involves a close working relationship between architects and engineers and the carrying out of detailed thermal modelling to test a range of passive design solutions for the building to seamlessly integrate the environmental and design strategies. Quantification of energy, carbon and costs throughout the building's lifecycle is an integral part of the process which would allow building owners and operators make informed decisions.

Opportunities in individual buildings might include refurbishment of existing windows, improving insulation in existing walls, floors and roofs and making significant improvements to the air tightness of the building. The approach to servicing the building ought to maximise passive design strategies including natural ventilation and daylighting before low carbon systems and then renewable energy generation are considered. Passive ventilation should be encouraged in as many areas as possible, with efficient active systems for any high use areas (such as the auditoria).

Overall this should be addressed by adoption of an integrated energy strategy which utilises cost-effective energy efficiency measures to reduce demand in the first place (therefore reducing capital costs of required renewable energy) and careful combination of relevant technologies for each individual location, all the while considering operational and maintenance issues.

Water use can be reduced through the specification of highly efficient fixtures and fittings, which are usually the most cost effective solution with further consideration given to rain water harvesting and grey water recycling for use in sanitary fittings if desired. Water meters could be installed to ensure that water consumption can be monitored and therefore reductions in water consumption can be encouraged. Consideration may be given to the installation of leak detection systems as well as sanitary supply shut offs to reduce the impact of major leaks in the buildings as well minor leaks in toilet facilities that may otherwise remain undetected.

With the possible exception then of installation of new technologies to reduce future running costs, I still maintain that the planning and budgetting for general repairs and maintenance has to be driven by the venues themselves. I return then to the question of centralising funds from which venues could draw-down monies when they need to and how would the money be raised?

We can look to other parts of the United Kingdom for precedents to this situation. An assessment of the physical condition of theatre buildings in the west end of London was carried out by The Theatres Trust in 2003 ('Act Now! Modernising London's West End Theatres', a Report by The Theatres Trust). In the conclusions of that report, it was estimated that a capital investment approaching £250million would be needed to be spent by 2018 to bring the 40 commercially owned theatres in London's West End up to modern standards comparable with those in the subsidised sector (which have had access to funding from the National Lottery and its derivative funds since its launch in the 1990s).

The Report referred to The Wyndham Report of 1998 which established that VAT receipts from ticket sales in the Theatre sector in London alone amounted to over £48million every year – nearly three times the amount the report identified as being necessary to be spent each year on repair and renovation of the theatre buildings. Perhaps it will take a substantial increase in the devolved powers of the Welsh Government from Westminster for them to make a business case for redirecting tax income back into the maintenance of our theatre building stock but my feeling is that it is likely that the figures needed to get the Welsh theatre buildings estate up to current standards will be of a similar order to those identified in London and it could be an avenue to be explored in the future?

So perhaps we'll have to wait a while before the (Welsh) Government steps in and provides the funds by 'recycling' tax income, and perhaps the Government is not the best administrator of funding for the purpose of general repair and maintenance anyway. The problem with all organisations susceptible to the political cycle of election and personality changes at Ministerial level is that their planning tends to focus on what they can be seen to achieve within a single period in office rather than take a longer term view, just in case they don't get re-elected and the strategy for preserving and protecting the theatre estate is one that will need above all else to be (very) long term and, if I'm honest, is probably not a significant vote-winning policy.

The most viable and sustainable source of monies to create the fund I am suggesting is to apply a levy on ticket prices so that the money is raised from the venues and the audiences who use them. Figures published recently by The Arts Council of Wales suggest that up to 80% of the entire population of Wales attends or participates in live theatre events at least once a year.

The nature and scale of both venues and events this audience attends of course varies tremendously across the country and ticket prices vary accordingly. Some might therefore argue that only the largest venues, in the metropolitan areas, that can promote and present well-known artists and shows and consequently charge higher ticket prices should be the source of any 'ticket levy' income but I absolutely disagree. For any such scheme to succeed it must be subscribed to by every venue whatever its scale and whether the tickets are sold for the Welsh National Opera at the Wales Millennium Centre in Cardiff or a local Youth Theatre Group performance in one of the community focussed venues in the valleys the levy should be exactly the same. And to achieve this consistency across all venues the levy cannot be a large sum of money, this much is obvious.

If we consider the measured size of the audience using the theatres in Wales as recorded by the Arts Council we find that for a nation with a population in the order of 3 million people, 2,400,000 people visit the theatre at least once every year. Even a modest levy such as 25 pence on the price of every ticket sold would raise £600,000 every year given this size of audience and when it is quite difficult to find anything else you can buy for 25p, and especially when that modest sum would do a whole industry so much good this seems to me like a good place to start.

Finally then, and on the basis that such a fund is viable, there is the issue of who or what administers the fund once it is established and receiving income from the ticket levy and by definition becomes a focus and representative of its member venues.

I have already explained that I do not believe this is a role for either the Arts Council of Wales or for the Welsh Government and I would certainly advocate removing any administrative group from any political cycle. One established body stands out for me as potential independent holders of the role of administrator but I don't know enough about their constitutions to be able to say with any confidence that they are suitable - that is Cadw, the Welsh Government funded agency that exists to preserve and protect the built heritage and historical landscapes of Wales.

This organisation already deals with funding through grant aid repairs to listed buildings of all types so it has an organisation in place that is used to assessing funding applications and managing a budget.

If, as a result of further consideration it is thought that engaging this body as quasi-estate-managers of the theatre buildings of Wales would be inappropriate then a new Charitable Trust would be the second option with Trustees appointed to a managing Board composed of respected individuals from within the theatre management, operation and perhaps design fields. One can imagine a Board of Trustees featuring members drawn from a range of organisations, perhaps including Cadw (for knowledge of listed buildings and their specific requirements), The Theatres Trust (for knowledge of issues associated with preservation and protection of theatres across the UK), the Welsh Local Government Association (since so many theatres are currently in Local Authority ownership), The Arts Council of Wales (to manage the interface between that organisation's capital funding strategy and the mission of this new Trust), The Theatre Managers Association (for insight into the issues that concern venue managers most), Creu Cymru (for knowledge of the whole network of venues), The Welsh Association of Performing Arts (for their knowledge of venue facilities) and say 3 others drawn from the private sector, perhaps with a recognised interest in the performing arts as patron or donor.

Supported by construction industry and facilities management professionals this Board would be responsible for the development of the fund and dispersal of grants for specific maintenance and repair projects based on the individual maintenance plans that each member venue would be required to prepare.

Which brings me neatly to the other aspect that allies itself to natural building decay forming the deadly partnership that leads to oblivion - the widely variant backgrounds, standards and capabilities of theatre management and their teams across the region. There will be some who read this with indignation and others perhaps who recognise the issues and want help to improve but whether they perceive themselves to be 'professional' or 'amateur', exemplary managers and custodians of their buildings or hopelessly out of their depth, I believe all have something they can share with their peers and certainly all can learn from each others successes and mistakes to raise their collective performance and avoid further building failure through poor management.

In its document 'A Position Paper on Theatres and Arts Centres across Wales'. Creu Cymru also picked up on this issue and advocated *'Development of Leadership within Theatres and Arts Centres and Succession planning through the development of young managers'* going on to state *'Individuals can be developed through mentoring and twinning'* and *'The sector might benefit therefore from a leadership programme ... geared to the needs of Wales with opportunities for sharing examples of work with the other devolved nations and the smaller European nations'*; *'Theatres and arts centres, especially those attached to Local Authorities, might also benefit by looking at the opportunities on networks such as Public Service Management Wales where the annual Summer School puts its emphasis on developing leadership skills.'*

Beyond the central role of administering the maintenance fund, it is relatively easy to imagine the organisation I am suggesting is created expanding its remit quite quickly to include issues such as venue management training or mentoring to help individual venue managers who may not have a 'professional' background work better and smarter. Mentoring by individuals from other venues might help some people improve their understanding of fundamental activities that will assist their venue's survival in the long-term including for example promoting events, improving efficiency and profitability, obtaining external grant funding for projects and the like.

Ultimately I know and understand that any such change will require a huge leap of faith from the people currently engaged in management of our theatre buildings and a major change in attitude to their peer group from competitor to collaborator across the public, private and independent sectors. Much easier said than done perhaps but hopefully food for thought.

One final idea that has evolved as I have travelled around the country driven by the impression that the current venues tend to compete with one another for audience and product a lot of the time is that perhaps now this record is available for all interested parties to access and refer to, the information in this book could be used to reinforce the work and membership of Creu Cymru and perhaps 'centres of excellence' can be identified or established in strategic geographic locations that specialise in one particular art form as some undoubtedly could. Indeed, Creu Cymru already recognises this is a potential criticism of the sector and has proposed '*As arts centres and theatres work more closely together, and as a map of collaboration and interconnectivity is developed, there is a strong argument for moving away from broad remit requirements to an acknowledgement that theatres may specialise both in artforms and in audience development. Some theatres are better placed to develop social inclusion or Welsh language work just as some arts centres might provide dance opportunities whilst others build a reputation for modern music.*'

For example, we could have a number of state-of-the-art dance centres to support the burgeoning dance organisations across the valleys, complimenting and working with centres focussing on drama, opera, musical theatre and live music. There would be no reason why all venues that currently present a wide range of events and art forms shouldn't continue to do so but tours could be directed to those centres of excellence for the benefit of both the interested audience and the performers. Creu Cymru has advocated '*The Sector believes that theatres and arts centres have a strong curatorial role in providing a mixture of experiences including loyalty to existing companies and the promotion of new work.*' and '*The sector is well placed to discuss the range of products available to audiences, the size and frequency of the offer, and the development of audiences over time.*'

If we don't start to think around corners or outside the box or whatever modern cliché applies like this and simply allow Darwinian evolutionary processes to run their course many more venues will fail and die.

Theatre people are used to adopting a 'make do and mend' approach to their venues but this may not be sustainable for several of the venues visited so far. If nothing else we need to take the management and governance of our venues across the piece, quantity of product available for presentation in all of our theatres, maintenance of their fabric and opportunities to reduce their energy consumption seriously now or we risk losing more venues over the next decade.

It would be a wonderful outcome if we are able to use the information I have gathered together in this book to contribute to the essential future decision making that will extend the life or even ensure the survival of all extant venues.

The Political background

However ideological, evangelical even, that I have become about the need to do something to prevent further decline of our theatre buildings estate, I am of course acutely aware that in the end politics (and politicians) will inevitably come to bear on the issue and will need to be properly addressed at many levels from small, local community councils right up to the office of the Welsh Government's Minister for Housing, Regeneration and Culture.

There is no doubt that some very difficult decisions lay ahead regarding the future of the theatre building stock in this country and many of those decisions will be taken by the principal public funding bodies that have become so important over the last few decades – the Welsh Government and the Arts Council of Wales. The Local Authorities across this region that have invested so much energy in human and financial resources are also funded through the Welsh Government so ultimately the buck stops at the door of the Welsh Minister whose portfolio includes responsibility for the Culture and Heritage of our Nation.

In its 'One Wales' policy published in June 2007 the Welsh Assembly Government stated its aim that '*high quality cultural experiences are available to all people, irrespective of where they live or their background*' and set targets to be achieved by 2010. One of the targets set was '*to ensure first rate accessible facilities exist throughout Wales*' and it stated that '*the major opportunity for Wales over the next decade lies in developing the infrastructure of our cultural assets and trying to make them sustainable in the longer term*'. In one of the few mentions of buildings in the document, it also states '*we should review the stage capacity in Wales, looking at the condition and standard of theatre buildings and equipment, identify the gaps in provision and remedy them*'. In their own progress update published in June 2010 there is no mention of any progress made towards achieving these objectives.

Despite this it is obvious that the Welsh Government does recognise the potential of this cultural heritage asset and does whatever is possible to make it a priority.

In a letter from the then Minister Alun Ffred Jones AM setting out the Arts Council of Wales remit for 2010 -11 the following statement was made:

'*The development of our arts venues in Wales is continuing, notwithstanding the absence of Lottery funding for capital investment. In the past twelve months, I have seen very effective use made of capital across Wales; we must continue to ensure that capital investments in arts buildings mesh effectively with other Welsh Assembly Government strategic investment priorities, in order to maximise the funding potential. I look to the Council to work alongside major investors to ensure that funds invested in arts venues, whether for refurbishment or new builds, are being duly maximised, and that value for money is tested and achieved.'*

In response the Arts Council of Wales stated the following:

'Some parts of the cultural sector form significant tourism attractions, generating demand for transport, accommodation, catering and other tourism-related business. But they also help put Wales on the international map. Our cultural landmarks don't just define the image of Wales; they are big business in their own right'.

'We believe that the arts in Wales are suffering from significant under investment. In 2008, direct Assembly Government spending through the Arts Council on the arts accounts for just 0.2% of the Government's total budget – or less than a single calendar day of Assembly Government expenditure'.

'The 'do nothing' option – presiding over a downward spiral of decline – is no option at all'.

In advance of the National Assembly for Wales Elections in 2011, the Wales Association For The Performing Arts (WAPA) published a 6 point manifesto document that was sent to every candidate, urging them all to pledge their support for protecting and enhancing the arts in Wales.

They quoted some impressive statistics on Employment (more than 27,700 people work in the creative and cultural industries in Wales, across 1,482 businesses), Economy (those 1,482 businesses contribute £1.03 billion GVA to the Welsh economy) and Investment (every £1 invested in the arts contributes a further £2 to the economy).

Whilst not directly mentioning the buildings in which our substantial body of artistic endeavour and creativity is performed, the message is clear that those with direct or indirect responsibility for the sustenance of our performance venues understand that without the buildings future investment in the arts will be of little value at worst and diminished at best.

So is there any evidence in the venues I've visited of these targets and policy objectives being realised and delivered? Broadly the answer to this question is yes, but it's a qualified yes because it is by no means certain that it's happening because of government action or intervention. High quality cultural experiences are definitely being provided right across this region of Wales but they could be improved still further, with a focus on the building stock.

I submit that perhaps the results of my research and road-trip could now be used to help in the prioritising of commitments.

It represents what I feel is the information about the theatre buildings estate that will be of most interest to people reading this book but behind it there is a large body of detailed information that hasn't found its way into print yet.

At the very least and even in this form it provides the Welsh Government, Arts Council of Wales and other agencies with a database of venues that they would otherwise have had to pay someone to create and it could easily be be used to drive the delivery (albeit after it was first promised) of that *review the stage capacity in Wales, looking at the condition and standard of theatre buildings and equipment, identify the gaps in provision and remedy them.*

Delivering against that commitment might deliver something akin to the strategic thinking I have advocated in these pages and could sit well with the WG's ongoing support for capital projects to protect employment in the construction industry in Wales during these uncertain economic times. As ever, one suspects that the benefits of a strategic investment of any kind in this remarkable cultural and heritage asset could have spin-off effects across a wide spectrum of our society and economy.

Future prospects?

There is absolutely no doubt that the performing arts in Wales will continue to provide wonderful, innovative and inspiring entertainment to its audience whatever the economic circumstances that prevail. The performing arts are simply too far entrenched in our Nation's collective and individual psyche to be derailed by a lack of political support or external funding.

Even as I travelled around this region discovering the range of fascinating buildings used to accommodate live performances there were five fully funded new-build and restoration projects under design or construction which will reinforce the estate when they are opened for business over the next two years.

The new venues are:

The Gwyn Hall, Neath, for Neath Port Talbot County Borough Council designed by Holder Mathias Architects of Cardiff (completion 2011)

Y Ffwrnes, Llanelli, for Carmarthenshire County Borough Council designed by Lawray Architects of Cardiff (completion 2012)

Sherman Cymru, Cardiff, for Sherman Cymru designed by Capita Architecture of Cardiff (completion 2012)

The Memo, Newbridge, for the Friends and Trustees of Celynen Colliery Institute and Memorial Hall designed by Alwyn Jones Architect of Taffs Well (completion 2013), and

Merthyr Tydfil Arts Centre, for Merthyr Tydfil Housing Association (with Chapter Ltd and Merthyr College) designed by Austin-Smith:Lord Architects of Cardiff (completion 2013).

And during the course of my travels the amazing new facilities at the Royal Welsh College of Music and Drama in Cardiff and the Sony Theatre in Bridgend both opened. Clearly this is not a time for doom and gloom in the arts fraternity as surely these major investments demonstrate powerfully how seriously the provision of high quality venues for audiences and performers is still being taken in this nation.

I remain convinced however that replacing older venues with new ones is not sustainable in the long term and that it is vital that we do not forget those buildings that already exist, cemented at the heart of the communities and audiences they serve yet so often feeling isolated from their peer group and continually staving off extinction in a hand-to-mouth existence.

As well as quite rightly focussing on their locality, every single one of the existing theatre buildings in (South) Wales also has the opportunity to serve people from the entire region and they offer many different choices of scale, intimacy, history and delight. It is remarkable how few of them are well-known and how little attention they receive for they truly represent an astounding collection of buildings tracing the trends and developments of theatre practice over the last 150 years. It is surely not beyond the capacity of this energetic emerging nation to celebrate its cultural heritage more and to acknowledge the asset it possesses?

At this time when regeneration of communities and well-being of individual citizens are hot topics in political circles, in our midst is a collection of buildings that with increased care, maintenance and organisation can provide so much towards the achievement of such aspirations. I truly hope that something is done with this remarkable estate as a whole entity, that the current custodians of these wonderful and historically important buildings and those who perform in them and visit them as members of audiences soon stop taking them quite so much for granted and that together, all interested parties find a single strong voice to state their case for protection and investment.

I look forward to the day when there is an established Arts Festival in Wales that exploits every one of these builidngs in a concentrated period of time (say every four years?) showcasing the Nation's heritage and cultural talent to the world with confidence and in a spirit of collective pride. All it needs is a collective will and it could surely happen.

The Theatres and Performance Buildings

The following Gazetteer of surviving theatre and performance buildings in South Wales is intended to provide a source of basic information about each of the venues I have visited.

I have included (where possible to establish) details of the current ownership and operating organisation, the age of the buildings and their original Architect and Builder.

I have researched as far as time has allowed the histories of each venue, in an attempt to catalogue significant events, alterations to the building and changes of ownership.

I've also included a subjective description of the buildings, written from the point of view of an Architect interested in theatre buildings, and in this description identified the condition of the building fabric in general terms and an assessment of each venue's economic/commercial well-being.

Finally I have included details of the audience capacities of each venue and dimensions of the performance area where such details are available or have been possible to obtain.

The gazetteer is structured to follow the geography of the Counties visited from east to west with the towns where the venues exist arranged alphabetically and then, where a town contains more then one venue, those venues also arranged alphabetically.

Monmouthshire

Abergavenny
    The Borough Theatre
    The Melville Theatre
Chepstow
    The Drill Hall
Monmouth
    The Blake Theatre
    The Savoy

The Borough Theatre, Abergavenny

Organisation: Monmouthshire County Council

Address: Cross Street, Abergavenny, Monmouthshire NP7 5HD

Construction/Opening: 1869-1871

Architect: Wilson & Wilcox, Bath

Builder: unknown

Current Owner: Monmouthshire County Council

History/previous names & ownership

In 1620, a new timber-framed market house was erected in the middle of Cross Street in front of the site of the present Market Hall. By 1794 this was causing so much congestion in the town that Improvement Commissioners ordered it to be demolished and a new market to be erected (on the present market and Town Hall site). This market was designed by John Nash (not yet famous as George IV's architect) and opened as a modest Market House in 1795 followed by a Market in 1825. By the middle of the 19th century it was decided that a covered market was desirable, and this, with the Town Hall in front, in the style of the continental Hotel de Villes, was completed in 1871.

It was designed as a multi-purpose building to provide municipal offices and a council chamber, a general market, an assembly room, the corn exchange and the poor law offices. The tower clock was presented by Crawshay Bailey the ironmaster who lived at Maindiff Court, Llanfoist and is inscribed 'Gilbert and Bland, Croydon 1871'. The northern clock face is said to have been painted black to commemorate the death of Prince Albert, but he died in 1862 so this may simply be popular myth.

The building now housing the Borough Theatre was originally known as the Market Hall & Assembly Room. It had an orchestra and seating for 600 people when it was converted into a theatre in 1906. It was at this time that the balcony was inserted.

The Town Hall building (including the Borough Theatre) was listed Grade II on 2nd November 1971.

In 1990, extensive renovations designed by Architect Colen Lumley were carried out including replacement of the audience seating (and consequent reduction in seating capacity) installed onto a new fixed stepped floor constructed over the original flat floor, an orchestra pit was created, the stage extended into auditorium to improve performance depth, architectural features installed over new side lighting positions and over stage (allegedly to restrict loading on the original roof structure) and ventilation units installed in the auditorium and over the stage. Ownership transferred from Abergavenny Town Council to the Monmouthshire County Council Unitary Authority in 1994. In 1996 the audience Foyer was extended into the rear of the original stalls area (under the theatre balcony).

Description

The building is an imposing example of Victorian neo-gothic architecture in the heart of Abergavenny and the theatre shares the building with a thriving market hall and offices of the Town Council.

The exterior fabric appears to be well maintained and is principally dressed Old Red Sandstone with Bath limestone ashlar dressings and natural slate roofs.

Entry into the theatre is directly from the street into a compact ticket office area leading to a steep staircase and access to the theatre (and council offices) above and staff office accommodation adjacent. Access to the auditorium for audience members with movement disabilities is via the market hall and a goods lift located at the interface between public areas and backstage.

All other audience members must use a long and steep staircase leading up to the theatre on the second floor of the building. Those seated in the balcony have a further full storey height staircase to navigate. For the last 15 years the audience foyer has been extended into what was the original stalls level under the balcony (providing a crush bar) but until then was simply a large landing on the staircase (still used when the auditorium has a full audience).

The auditorium is dominated visually by the original and beautiful Victorian roof structure and additions installed in the 1990 refurbishment, including perforated metal faced baffles over side-lighting positions in the auditorium and a proscenium header panel of the same finish. The current audience seating was installed in 1990 onto a stepped floor built over the original flat floor, the stalls area now extending up to the underside of the original heavily decorated balcony front. There is no direct connection between stalls and balcony within the auditorium. The seats are showing signs of distress in the upholstery. Removable seats at the front of the room liberate space for a compact orchestra pit and create wheelchair positions near the front on house left.

A sound and lighting control room has been created at the rear of the balcony and facilities exist for in-room mixing. Follow-spot positions at the rear of the balcony have been raised from their original positions to prevent conflict with audience members seated in the back rows.

There is no flytower over the stage and rigging of scenic effects and production lighting is seriously compromised by the presence of 'architectural' baffles suspended across the stage right to left. Wing space is extremely limited as the stage extends to the building envelope and a narrow crossover has been constructed against the rear wall to facilitate movement from the dressing rooms located at stage right across to the stage left entry point. There are significant areas of distressed stonework around the stage area presumed to be as a result of water ingress through the solid walls.

There are several well appointed dressing rooms, all but one having access to daylight and a connection between backstage and front-of-house was created in the 1990 renovations.

Loading and unloading for visiting shows is tortuous and indirect. Equipment cannot be delivered directly to the backstage area by vehicle and has to be taken either through the market hall or through the adjacent pub yard to reach a goods lift and travel up to the stage at second floor level. The goods lift has a 'top-hat' section but anything larger than 8 feet in length has to be manhandled up two steep and long flights of stairs.

Underneath the dressing rooms and accessible via the market hall is a small rehearsal room known as the Corn Exchange. In itself it is a room of simple beauty with rooflights and a good floor. It is heavily used by community groups and provides additional chorus or dance troupe changing space when the need arises.

Auditorium Capacity: Original capacity approximately 600, reduced during extensive renovations in 1990 by reduction in size of stalls area and replacement of original seats to current capacity of 338 – approx 220 on stalls (variable depending on extent of disabled seating positions and presence of orchestra pit) and 120 on the balcony

Stage details:

Performance space – width – 11.5m (including wings)
Performance space – depth – 6.7m (excluding apron)
Depth of apron – 1.5m
Wing space (Right and Left) – 1.5m SR, 1.4m SL
Proscenium height/width – height - 4.53m; width - 8.6m
Orchestra pit (maximum no of players) - 14
Height from stage floor to grid – 5.5m
Rake - Yes, gradient 1:25

The Melville Theatre, Abergavenny

Organisation: Monmouthshire County Council

Address: The Drama Centre, Pen-y-Pound, Abergavenny, Monmouthshire NP7 5UD

Construction: 1898 (as a school) **Opening:** 1998 (as a theatre)

Architect: E. A. Johnson, Abergavenny

Builder: unknown

Current Owner: Monmouthshire County Council

History/previous names & ownership

Built as King Henry VIII Grammar School in 1898, and extended in 1904 to designs drawn up by the original Architect, the building was used as a school until closure in 1962.

At that time the building was taken into the ownership of Monmouth District Council and creation of 'The Drama Centre' began. Gwent Theatre became the resident theatre company some time after that. The Drama Centre was listed Grade II on 20th October 1995.

The Melville Theatre was officially opened by Glenys Kinnock MEP on 11th September 1998 and the theatre is named in honour and dedicated to the memory of Melville Thomas, founder of Gwent Theatre.

In 2010 the Arts Council of Wales announced withdrawal of grant funding to Gwent Theatre and the future of the resident company at the Melville was put in doubt although the Company's intent is clearly to remain based at the building. The building owner announced their intent to maintain the theatre facility in the same year but with a new focus on Youth Theatre, Dance and Community use.

Description

The building containing The Melville is very typical of Edwardian school architecture having a vaguely ecclesiastical appearance and quite grand pretensions.

It is located in between residential and commercial districts of the town set back from the road with a well maintained lawned garden to the front and a large car park to the rear.

The building envelope comprises stone walls – predominantly pennant or similar - with sandstone/bath stone features around windows, doors and to gables and chimneys. It has a slate roof. Detailing is in a Victorian gothic style. The building is single storey.

Entry to the front is up 4 shallow steps and separate provision for access for people with movement difficulties is made from the rear car park. The original school entrance hall is used as the theatre foyer and the walls are hung with many examples of Gwent Theatre show memorabilia and posters.

The auditorium is a converted school hall (or large classroom) and all wall surfaces have been painted black, with all original windows also blacked out from the inside. The original parquet floor remains and extends through the area used for performance as well as under the installation of audience seating that is formed on shallow stepped timber risers with a carpet finish. A suspended ceiling has been installed and a significant suspension grid for curtain tracks, performance lighting and sound system has been hung below that.

There is no stage machinery and no fixed proscenium. The stage area is level with the auditorium floor giving great flexibility in the arrangements of staging that can be offered. The performance area is limited by the building envelope and consequently there is no wing space other than that created by the installation of perimeter black drapes. There is no capacity for flying.

A small sound/light control box has been constructed at the rear and in one corner of the audience seating area.

There is no adjacent support accommodation to the performance space – dressing rooms are at the opposite end of the spine corridor that bisects the building and loading into the theatre space is through the building main entrance doors and through the foyer/entrance hall. Accommodation for Gwent Theatre dominates the building – offices and meeting rooms to the rooms at the front and a bar area to the rear along with some space used by local dance troupe 'DanceBlast' and a careers advisory service office maintained by the local authority.

Auditorium Capacity: 75

Stage details:

Performance space – width – variable
Performance space – depth – variable
Depth of apron – n/a
Wing space (Right and Left) – none
Proscenium height/width – n/a
Orchestra pit (maximum no of players) – n/a
Height from stage floor to grid – not available
Rake – None

The Drill Hall, Chepstow

Organisation: Chepstow Town Council

Address: Lower Church Street, Chepstow NP16 5HJ

Construction: 17th or 18th Century (as an industrial building) **Opening:**1920 approx (as a theatre)

Architect/Builder: unknown/unknown

Current Owner: Monmouthshire County Council

History/previous names & ownership

It is believed the building was constructed in the 17th or 18th Century as an industrial building, probably a mill, and it was thought to have been used for the production of linen or ropes.

Sometime in the 19th Century through to the end of the First World War at least it was adopted for use by the Monmouthshire Regiment and became the Drill Hall.

The Officers and Men of E Company, the 1st Battalion of the Monmouthshire Regiment held their last parade here on 5th August 1914 before leaving for the western front and the hall is now preserved in commemoration of their sacrifice.

Sometime soon after the end of the First World War it began use as a theatre and community hall. Little is known of the history of the hall through the 20th Century.

It is assumed that in the mid 1990's the building was taken into ownership of the new Unitary Authority of Monmouthshire County Council and in 2008 management responsibility was passed to Chepstow Town Council.

Description

The Drill Hall is a deceptively low-key single storey building located at one edge of a large municipal surface car park, not far from the river, town museum and castle. Its appearance does nothing to suggest its origins or current use.

Constructed of random light coloured local stone with expressed mortar pointing and punctured by regular windows with red brick surround detailing along all of its exterior walls. It has a pitched slate roof with two ridge ventilation cowls.

Entry is through a small lean-to porch up a gentle ramp from the car park and directly into the large hall space. The hall has a flat, timber floor with a raised stage at one end comprising modular units that offer some flexibility in the staging of events. There is no suspended ceiling and the hall is open to the underside of its roof over both the audience and performance area giving it a reasonable volume and apparently a good acoustic for orchestral, choral and unamplified musical performance. Some decorative hangings are suspended over the audience area between and from the metal lattice roof trusses. Audience seating is provided by loose chairs giving further flexibility for audience capacity and arrangement up to a maximum of 250 for theatrical events. Storage of the loose chairs for events in the round or needing large clear flat areas is a problem.

Extensive rigging facilities have been installed around and over the stage and there is a painted 'proscenium header' panel suspended at the stage front edge although there is no fixed proscenium and drapes are used to create a frame when needed. A further mural has been painted by a local artist on the rear stage wall. Wing space is reasonable and variable depending on the use of proscenium drapes. There are two good sized and well furnished dressing rooms at stage level, both with en-suite facilities and loading is directly onto stage via two sets of double doors – in the building envelope and onto stage itself. At the rear of the audience area is a separate room used for catering and for large meetings and a kitchen/licensed bar area opens directly off this space. It is used as a foyer bar during shows. Audience toilets are provided, including provision for disabled visitors on the opposite side of the hall from the main entrance.

This is a thriving facility entrenched in its community and extremely popular for a wide range of events from Theatre through choral concerts, live rock acts, wedding parties (the building has a civil license) and book signings to cinema and community functions. It is generating sufficient revenue to enable the management committee to consider building works to further improve the facilities in the future.

Auditorium Capacity: 250

Stage details:

Performance space – width – 9m
Performance space – depth – 6m
Depth of apron – n/a
Wing space (Right and Left) – variable
Proscenium height/width – h: 2.6m; w: 11.4m
Orchestra pit (maximum no of players) – n/a
Height from stage floor to grid – 3.5m (max)
Rake – None

The Blake Theatre, Monmouth

Organisation: Monmouth School Enterprises Ltd

Address: Almshouse Street, Monmouth, Monmouthshire NP25 3XP

Construction: 1961 (as a School Hall) **Opening:** 2005 (as a theatre)

Architect: unknown

Builder: Davlan

Current Owner: Monmouth School

History/previous names & ownership

The building now housing the Blake Theatre was built as Monmouth School Hall in 1961.

In 2005 the current building was constructed as a purpose built theatre within and around the existing School Hall (as part of wider refurbishment of the Monmouth School estate). The new theatre was funded by and named after Bob Blake, an old Monmothian who attended the school between 1938 and 1946. It is used as a venue for performances by both the boys' and girls' schools of Monmouth, and by external performers. It was officially opened by HRH Prince Edward, Earl of Wessex on 22nd April 2005. It had cost approximately £1.1million.

Auditorium Capacity:

500 (for theatrical events),

600 maximum (for school assemblies)

Stage details:

Performance space – width – 14m (including wings)
Performance space – depth – 6.9m
Depth of apron – n/a
Wing space (Right and Left) – variable
Proscenium height/width – height: 4m; width: 12m
Orchestra pit (maximum no of players) - 20
Height from stage floor to grid – 4m
Rake – None

Description

The building has a prominent location on a bend in one of the main access roads to the town centre from the nearby A40 dual carriageway and was part of a wider refurbishment of the adjacent Monmouth School estate.

The building is effectively a new envelope and interior constructed in and around the original concrete frame of the 1961 building it replaced.

The main front entrance is in a pointed arch curtain-walling glazed opening extending to the first floor of the foyer space and cut into the gable wall. The roof is a single pitch extending the full length of the building and gives no indication of the scale of the auditorium and ancillary accommodation inside.

Entry is into a generous foyer space containing box office and a large bar used for public performances. The original axial entrance into the auditorium has been blocked up and a new access corridor added to the original building as an extension along the main street frontage side elevation.

The auditorium entrance is adjacent to the stage at the front of the room and is level with the front entrance to the building. The auditorium is a large though simple space, quite wide and open to the underside of the roof giving a considerable volume and apparently very good acoustics for orchestral music.

Small audience balcony boxes have been constructed on either side of the room with the intention of creating an environment recognisable as a theatre and they are successful in this regard. Access to them is unusual insofar as it is from the stage.

Audience seating is on a single motorised retractable unit and affords a capacity of 500 for theatre events. This is increased to 600 for School assemblies. There is a projection/sound and light control room at the back of the audience seating and space for in-room mixing desks immediately in front of it.

An orchestra pit is provided in front of the stage with clever lift up cover panels that form the pit rail when raised and thereby eliminate the need for storage when the pit is in use. It can accommodate 20 musicians.

The stage is large both in width and depth and whilst there is a fixed proscenium it too is very wide and drapes are used to vary the width to suit different events and performances. There is no flytower and rigging height is limited by the original roof trusses that have been retained throughout. There is decent wing space even with the wide proscenium arrangement and this can obviously be improved still further by reducing the proscenium width.

Loading for visiting shows is not ideal – trucks must park on the adjacent busy road and equipment and scenic effects carried in through a side door into the auditorium before lifting onto stage.

There are 2 large and well appointed dressing rooms below stage level but storage is extremely limited.

The theatre operates on a part-time basis and provides a range of shows and a film club, as well as being available for hire for community groups seeking a professional venue for their production.

The School underwrites the theatre operation and uses the auditorium for full school assemblies and for examinations.

There is a conscious attempt not to compete with the Savoy Theatre in its programming and the venue is making a reputation for live screenings of performances from The New York Metropolitan Opera amongst other venues. It appears to have become a successful and viable operation.

The Savoy, Monmouth

Organisation: The Savoy Trust

Address: 18 Church Street, Monmouth, Monmouthshire NP25 3BX

Construction/Opening: 1851

Architect: J. F. Rogers

Builder: unknown

Current Owner: Private individuals

History/previous names & ownership

In 1751 The Bell Inn originally standing on this site is believed to have commenced presenting artistic performances and they have been continuous on the same site ever since. The site is believed to be the oldest site of theatrical performance in Wales.

In the 1830's the Flannel Exchange and Assembly Rooms were built at the Bell Inn site with the current building replacing it in 1851. It was opened as the New Theatre (but was also known as The Bell Assembly Rooms and The Theatre Royal around this time).

In 1875 the building was converted to 'The Rinkeries' roller skating venue and then in 1910, Frank Colbourne converted it to a picture house and reopened it as the 'Living Picture Palace & Rinkeries' – Monmouth's first cinema venue. For some time in 1911 it was used as a place of worship. In 1917 the entrance was moved to its current location in Church Street (although it is not clear where the original entrance was). In the period 1917 to 1927 it is understood to have changed hands several times but was primarily used for cinema presentations.

In 1927 the building was totally rebuilt by the Albany Ward Company and added to its provincial cinema circuit. It was renamed 'The Picture Palace'. In 1928 it was purchased by Provincial Cinematograph Theatres Ltd and re-named 'The Savoy Theatre'.

From 1928 to the 1950's there were many changes of hands and periods of closure until it was purchased by the grandfather of the current owners.

In 1987 the building was refurbished and re-opened as 'The Magic Lantern Theatre' and operated under that name until 2004 when a Lease was acquired by the Savoy Development Trust and a major programme of restoration commenced. The Trust renamed the building The Savoy Theatre.

The building was listed Grade II* on 2nd September 1989.

In 2009 after a period of financial difficulty The Savoy Trust replaced The Savoy Development Trust as lease-holder, and a further programme of repair and restoration commenced, principally to the building envelope but including dressing room upgrades and construction of a demountable stage apron over the original orchestra pit.

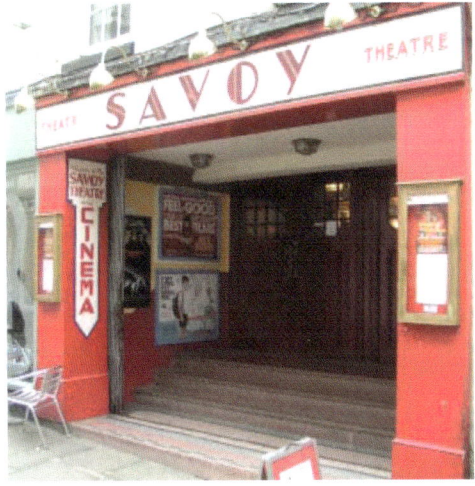

Description

The theatre is located on a pedestrianised street in the town centre and occupies part of a typical and well proportioned town house building to the front with an attached larger building to the rear containing the theatre auditorium. The front elevation of the building is rendered and painted white but the sides are exposed original brickwork and it has a slate roof. There is no access to the rear of the building apart from down a narrow alleyway to one side – the other side is bounded by a churchyard and another property and the rear is enclosed by two further properties.

The main entrance is of similar scale to the adjacent shop unit and there are two residential flats on the first and second floors above the shop and theatre entrance understood to be in the same ownership as the theatre.

Entry into the theatre foyer is up shallow steps into a small ticket desk and foyer area. There are clear signs of the building's multiple ownerships and uses over its lifetime having an impact on finishes and decorations in this foyer area but it retains many of its original Victorian features, mouldings, cornices and extrovert decorations and finishes in general.

The auditorium stalls entry is another few steps above the foyer level and is at the rear of the room under the single upper balcony. The auditorium is a jewel of a room and a fine example of a theatre of this age. The walls are generally plain and decorated a warm red but have feature mouldings and painted medallions that are both well preserved and spectacular. There is an area of water ingress in the external wall house left near to the proscenium wall that is suspected to be due to faulty/broken rainwater goods and is targeted for repair in the near future subject to availability of funds. The ceiling is a single span gentle arch again animated by highly decorated and elegant mouldings.

The stalls seating is set on a single slope down to the pit rail and appears relatively new – the seats are in good condition. There is a semi-permanent apron recently constructed over the original orchestra pit installed to improve the area of the performance space as the current operators try to increase theatrical events over previous focus on cinema. The proscenium is flamboyantly bounded by classical pilasters and mouldings and the house curtain is an elegant deep red with gold embroidery.

The film projection room is at the rear of the stalls and some seats have recently been removed from the back rows to create a permanent in-room sound and lighting control desk position.

There is a single balcony which in addition to containing approximately a third of the audience has the unusual feature of 3 private boxes right at the rear that can still be used by small groups or families. Modern ventilation units have been installed above the boxes on the balcony and at high level at the rear of stalls to supplement the original moulded grilles set throughout the ceiling (served by cowls on the roof ridge).

There is no foyer serving the balcony audience save for a narrow corridor and there is no access to the upper area for visitors with movement disabilities. Wheelchair positions are provided at the front of stalls but access is via a narrow alleyway to the side of the building and entering through a fire door. Given the constraints of the building there seems little prospect that this could be improved.

The stage area itself is very compact and there is no flytower. The original roof structure is exposed above the stage and restricts the height of scenic effects and lighting bars. At some point electric winches have been installed to the lighting bars but their cables are insufficiently long to achieve the maximum possible 'flying' height. The winches might be moved higher up the stage left wall to overcome this.

Loading of incoming scenic effects and equipment is very restricted – there remain a large set of 'elephant doors' some distance above the stage level in the external wall that open into the adjacent narrow alleyway but these are unused. Any visiting show with equipment now enters through the front-of-house and through the auditorium and the current operators generally avoid booking events that use their own material or equipment.

There are 3 well appointed dressing rooms below and behind the stage (refurbished between 2004 and 2009 from total dereliction) with a well used green room area.

Auditorium Capacity:

The original capacity is not known but is presumed reduced when the current relatively modern audience seating was installed. Current capacity is 380 comprising 260 at stalls, 120 on balcony.

Stage details:

Performance space – width – 11.2m (including wings)
Performance space – depth – 5.4m (excluding stage thrust)
Depth of stage thrust –2.3m; width - 3.43m
Wing space (Right and Left) – SR - 2.25m; SL - 2.25m
Proscenium height/width – height: not known; width - 6.7m
Orchestra pit (maximum no of players) - 12
Height from stage floor to grid – no grid
Rake – Yes, slope 1:44 (2.3%)

Newport

Newport

    The Dolman Theatre

    The Riverfront Theatre and Arts
    Centre

The Dolman Theatre

Organisation: Newport Playgoers Society; Dolman Theatre registered Charity

Address: Unit 21, Emlyn Square, Kingsway Shopping Centre, Newport, Gwent NP20 1HY

Construction/Opening: 1967

Architect/Builder: unknown/unknown

Current Owner: Newport Playgoers Society

History/previous names & ownership

The theatre was purpose built in 1967, following a re-development of Newport Town Centre, which included the demolition of the previous theatre used by the Newport Playgoers Society, known as The Newport Little Theatre, and housed in a converted church in nearby Dock Street. The theatre is named after the president of the Society who secured the long lease on the land and paid for the construction of the building.

In 2000 the original Green Room was converted to The Studio and some consequential front-of-house alterations were carried out.

5 years later the theatre's main entrance was relocated from inside the Kingsway Shopping Centre to its current location as part of a UBS funded redevelopment of the shopping centre and adjacent retail units.

Description

An unexpectedly large theatre building given it is owned by an amateur dramatic society, located adjacent a recently renovated but largely empty shopping centre.

The exterior is fairly typical of the building's age though it does have some quality features and detailing. Facades are of a dark coloured brick and there are elements of exposed concrete frame, punched horizontal windows to the backstage areas and small areas of curtain wall glazing to the studio and main entrance. The entire envelope appears to be in good condition and well maintained.

The main entrance and box office was originally accessed through the adjacent shopping centre but was moved some 5 years ago to its current location and the theatre is now completely independent of its neighbour.

The new entrance was created in a space originally occupied by an advice centre and the works included the provision of a contemporary steel and glass staircase connecting the entrance at street level to the foyer inside at first floor level. A decent management office space has also been created behind the box office desk.

A trophy cabinet containing prizes won by the Newport Playgoers Society in amateur theatre festivals and competitions is well-stocked and resides under the new stair.

The main foyer area is at first floor level and is a large and spacious double-height volume, significantly bigger than would ordinarily be expected of a venue of this nature. It contains a large wet bar, audience WCs and accesses to the main theatre auditorium and studio space and has a direct link through the backstage areas to the stage door. On one wall there are carved stone features that were rescued from the demolition of the Lyceum Theatre in Newport (demolished in 1967 and a former home to the Newport Operatic Society who now perform at the Dolman).

The auditorium seating is arranged in straight rows on a fairly steep rake with some loose seats in 'boxes' against each side wall near the front of the room. There are technical balconies above these boxes containing in-room mixing and control positions and equipment. There are further, enclosed control/projection rooms at the rear of the auditorium at its highest point.

The auditorium itself is very plain with simple, straight and single colour painted blockwork walls, carpet to the floor and a suspended lay-in grid tile ceiling. The applied technical balconies and recessed lighting positions and slots in the ceiling achieve a real sense of theatre however.

There is a hydraulic forestage lift which creates an orchestra pit or a forestage extension but for some time it has not been used to accommodate additional audience seating as a result of some health and safety concerns about the lift's operating mechanism.

The stage is flat and is very large and has a full flytower within which flats up to 20 feet high can be fully flown out. There are generous wings and a crossover at the rear. The structural proscenium opening is also extremely large for a theatre of this size and the legs are adjustable giving the venue a very flexible width and allows it to accommodate the needs of any visiting show or event.

Beyond and adjacent to the stage and at the same floor level are extensive storage and workshop areas and a get-in with good access for visiting vehicles. The threshold of the loading doors is however quite high but this is really the only (minor) criticism of what is a well laid out and expansive backstage that would be the envy of many a newer venue.

There are 6 dressing rooms, 4 of which have full en-suite facilities and all of which have windows and are well furnished and equipped. There are 4 quite large rehearsal rooms that are used extensively by the many community and amateur groups that consider this theatre their home.

A 60 seat studio space easily accessed from the foyer is a popular venue for experimental and youth theatre work and provides further rehearsal space for larger shows. It has the benefit of access to daylight which increases its popularity for rehearsal use.

This is a thriving amateur theatre and claims to be one of the largest little theatres in the country. It is used by a large number of local amateur companies and presents a wide range of shows year-round. A 'gentleman's agreement' with Newport City Council has been made such that the Dolman has undertaken not to present touring professional companies and this means that there are only very occasional overlaps in product and competition for audience between the two Newport venues has been all but eradicated leaving both venues to be very successful.

The success of this theatre is all the more remarkable when it is considered that there are only two full-time employees and the entire operation is dependent on volunteers and members to sustain it.

It is a very impressive operation and must be one of the best laid out and equipped theatres in Wales, particularly in respect of its excellent backstage support accommodation.

Auditorium Capacity:

400 in the main theatre auditorium; 60 in The Studio

Stage details:

Performance space – width – 12.2m
Performance space – depth – 9.75m
Depth of apron –2.6m (6.4m wide)
Wing space (Right and Left) – variable
Proscenium height/width – height:6.1m; width: 12.2m
Orchestra pit (maximum no of players) – 24
Height from stage floor to grid – 6.7m
Rake – None

The Riverfront Theatre and Arts Centre

Organisation: Newport County Borough Council

Address: Kingsway, Newport NP20 1HG

Construction/Opening: 2004

Architect: Austin-Smith:Lord LLP, Cardiff

Builder: E Turner and Sons

Current Owner: Newport County Borough Council

History/previous names & ownership

The need for an arts and entertainment facility in Newport was first identified by the former Newport Borough Council as far back as 1983. Local group Arts Focus joined forces with the council to support the proposals.

In 1995, the council allocated resources to the development of a theatre and arts centre in Newport and applied for funding towards the development of the project.

In 1999, the Arts Council of Wales announced that Newport had been awarded a lottery grant of £8.5m towards the building of the centre. The balance for completing the theatre and arts centre came from the council. The brief called for a 'landmark' building, comprising two theatre spaces, one seating 500 with proscenium arch and fly tower and another seating 150 in a flexible form, a dance studio, recording studio, art gallery, function room, workshop spaces, crèche, shop, café, bar and ancillary spaces.

When plans for the theatre and arts centre were first unveiled, Newport City Council called on the public to suggest names for the venue. 400 suggestions were received with the riverside location inspiring the vast majority of the suggestions. This list was whittled down to ten top names, which were put out to the public vote. The people of Newport voted for the locational name, The Riverfront, for their arts centre.

Whilst building The Riverfront, in July 2002 the remains of a mediaeval ship were discovered in what is now the orchestra pit in the main auditorium. The Newport Mediaeval ship is one of the most important recent archaeological maritime discoveries and is the most complete example of a vessel which sailed in the 1400s. Around 25 metres long and dating from 1465, the find was considered to be as important as the discovery of the Mary Rose. The Welsh Assembly Government awarded a grant towards the construction of the basement display for the mediaeval ship. During its six month excavation, a new exhibition space was designed and built beneath the foyer, to house and display the discoveries, presenting the ship's unearthing, its history and eventually the fully conserved ship.

The project was completed in October 2004 for a value of £15 million.

Photographs courtesy of Austin-Smith:Lord LLP

Description

The site is prominent, allowing panoramic and long distance views to and from the centre of Newport and offering the first 'framed' view past the ruin of Newport Castle from trains arriving in South Wales. It is bounded on one side by the tidal river Usk and on the other by a major arterial road. The orientation of the building on the site addresses these views and takes into consideration both riverside and city centre pedestrian and vehicle access.

The three performance spaces are treated as independent entities in the architectural composition. Their plan and three dimensional form and those of the ancillary and foyer spaces form a solid-void-solid rhythm which helps reduce the scale of the building, relates it to the neighbouring urban grain and makes it 'legible'. The three main forms are clad in vitreous enamel steel and lighting is placed around the building projecting, at night, ever-changing colour onto the elevations. There is a dark coloured brickwork plinth containing the ancillary accommodation wrapped around and connecting the upper auditorium forms. Linking the three major spaces together is a transparent, double height foyer which unifies the individual elements and provides a beacon to draw people in. The foyer is open, bright and fresh, containing the ticket office, a café, artwork and a buzz of activity.

Once inside the main auditorium, the freshness of the foyer gives way to a warmth which indulges all the senses - the colour of aubergine, the sight of rich chocolate coloured wood and the touch and smell of leather. Like the building's exterior, the main auditorium is asymmetric. At just under 500 seats, it is intimate, and the stalls and upper tier are connected on one side with a bank of seating adding to the feeling that the audience is contained in a single space rather than separated into two or more groups by the more usual vertical arrangement of balconies. Indeed it is this arrangement of the audience which is the most prominent feature of this room – the walls and ceiling are understated and simply decorated. The stage is large and there is a full flytower, a forestage elevator offering flexibility of audience capacity (30 seats are lost when it is used as an orchestra pit or forestage extension) and loading for visiting companies is directly from a good sized truck bay immediately adjacent. Backstage accommodation is well thought out and there areseveral dressing rooms, all with en-suite facilities and windows. There is ample storage near the stage and workshop spaces.

The Studio space is a simple square on plan and has a flat floor and retractable bleacher seating. A balcony wraps around the entire space providing audience and technical circulation although the balcony over the stage end of the room does present staging limitations. It follows the colour theme established by the main house of rich, dark warm colours. High level technical access bridges are exposed in the room but it feels more like a performance space than working/rehearsal room. The Dance Studio is excellent, both in scale and character and has a large corner window affording dramatic views over the river and flooding the space with high quality light.

This has become an extremely successful venue since its opening and is well supported by the Council and the local community and audience.

Auditorium Capacity:

493 (Main House)

comprising 286 on stalls and 207 on balcony

128 (Studio)

Stage details:

Performance space – width – 11m
Performance space – depth – 14m
Depth of apron – 1.1m
Wing space (Right and Left) – SR - 4.1m; SL - 4.8m
Proscenium height/width – height 6.5m; width 11.4m
Orchestra pit (maximum no of players) – 30 max
Height from stage floor to grid – 17.4m
Rake - None

Torfaen

Blaenavon
The Workmen's Hall
Cwmbran
The Congress Theatre

Workmen's Hall, Blaenavon

Organisation: Blaenavon Workmen's Hall

Address: High Street, Blaenavon, Pontypool NP4 9PT

Construction: 1893-94 **Opening:** 1895

Architect: E. A. Lansdowne, Newport

Builder: unknown

Current Owner: Torfaen County Borough Council

History/previous names & ownership

In 1891, the Blaenavon Workmen's Institute purchased a parcel of land on Waun Field from the Blaenavon Company for the sum of £600 for the purpose of building a Workmen's Hall. The Blaenavon Company was so impressed with the workers' aims of self-improvement that it donated some £800 to the cause. Bleanavon Workmen's Hall was built between 1893 and 1894 and opened on 7th January 1895 by Cllr. Robert William Kennard, the son of the chairman of the Blaenavon Company. The Original cost of the building was £9,000 and like many valley institutes its creation was funded by the Blaenavon Workmen's Institute, who collected a weekly deduction of a halfpenny from its members' wages – employees of the Blaenavon Company. Many local workers also undertook voluntary building work and when it was completed it was the largest building in town and the most important to the local community.

Originally the hall housed a library, newspaper room, magazine room, recreation room, billiard room and committee rooms on the ground floor and a very large theatre on the first floor that was used for concerts, bazaars and political meetings. It was later converted to cinema use and an additional cinema space was added during the early twentieth century, showing the first 'talkies' by the 1930s.

The rise of radio and television meant that people were less willing to regularly participate in community activities for their recreation. Cecil Northcote, the secretary of the committee, reported in 1959 that cinema audiences at the Workmen's Hall had fallen by more than a half since the early 1950s. Unable to meet the costs of operating the Recreation Grounds and the swimming pool at Coed Cae that the Institute also owned, the Workmen's Hall transferred the facilities to the Blaenavon Urban District Council in 1961. Similarly, the Workmen's Hall library was taken over by Monmouthshire County Council Library Service in 1954 and was moved to Park Street in the early 1980s.

By 1984 the Workmen's Hall faced numerous challenges. The cost of much needed repairs was well beyond the means of the committee. There were even concerns that the magnificent hall might have to be demolished due to serious structural problems. The building was sold to Torfaen Borough Council, who closed the hall for several years while extensive maintenance took place.

The renovated Blaenavon Workmen's Hall reopened on the 7th of January 1995 to mark the centenary of the building's original opening. The Workmen's Hall was listed Grade II on 2nd September 1995.

Since that time it has been operated by a voluntary committee, which has worked hard to ensure that the Workmen's Hall is once again the focal point of community activities. The cinema has been reopened, regular concerts are held in the theatre and a number of local groups and societies continue to use the on-site conference facilities.

Description

This is a truly wonderful building that is the manifestation of incredible ambition in those responsible for commissioning it. In many ways similar to the Park & Dare in Treorchy in scale and grandeur but perhaps even more flamboyant in its architecture.

Located on one of the main roads into the town and surrounded by workers' housing it dominates its immediate environment from its elevated position on a hillside.

The external envelope combines rubble stone with brickwork panels and dressed stone features around openings and on each of the many gables and dormers on the roof line. The main entrance is grandly pronounced in the architecture at the top of a flight of steps with a classical swagger of dressed stone articulating the central of 3 arched openings.

Notwithstanding the sloping topography of the site these steps make accessibility an issue that can only be overcome by providing a route through the building from the higher access points at the rear.

Somewhat disappointingly a rather institutional 'Welcome to Blaenavon Workmen's Hall' sign of white plastic has been placed in the arched glazed overpanel above the entrance doors and surely could be provided in a more sympathetic way outside the building.

On the side of the building that appears to be the rear (if a freestanding building can actually have a rear face) the detailing is much less flamboyant and two wings extend from the main body of the building. In this section of the building the Local Authority occupies some office space.

Entry through the front doors is into a generously proportioned reception area (unusual for such buildings) with a ticket desk/reception point offset to one side but immediately in front of the doors. To the left of the reception a corridor leads to the small cinema and the billiard room. The cinema has 60 seats and a fixed stepped raked floor. The seats appear relatively recent and it is a comfortable and practical space. The billiard room contains one snooker table still but is mostly used for meetings and conference events.

To the right of the reception a wide flight of stairs leads up to the auditorium on the first floor, again unusual insofar as there isn't a symmetrical approach to the main space in the building. There is a large lobby area with decorative terrazzo floor at the top of the stairs with photographs of past committee members and portraits of local dignitaries which reinforce the sense that this was and remains a community focussed building.

The auditorium is entered through a bar area and large sound and light lobbies at each corner of the rear stalls. It is a very large room and easy to imagine the original capacity of 1500 people, perhaps less easy to imagine how small an audience of 400 as current capacity might appear. The stalls has a flat floor and loose seats while the single balcony retains its original fixed seats on a stepped tier. If the exterior rivals the Park & Dare for architectural ambition, the auditorium is very different and has a restrained and stripped-down feel being much more practical than flamboyant.

The walls are plain with a dusky pink painted plaster finish, articulated by large windows on both sides and projecting structural piers supporting the main roof trusses. The roof structure is exposed within the room with the ceiling panelled with raised timber mouldings. The original ventilation grilles are retained but are now un-used and new ventilation grilles have been integrated sensitively across the room. Several large feature light fittings are suspended from the ceiling but do not appear to be original. Performance lighting bars are suspended across the room.

The stage has a proscenium but again it is plainly detailed with simple shallow pilasters to the sides and a horizontal cornice panel across the top. The stage itself is large and has generous wing space. There is no apron or orchestra pit and although there are plentiful suspension and rigging points over the stage there is no capacity for flying. Dressing rooms for performers are provided behind the stage and at stage level. There is no direct route to the outside from the stage so loading/unloading of visiting shows has to be done from the yard at the 'rear' of the building with manual handling to reach the stage at first floor level.

This appears to be a venue that isn't quite living up to its potential with a slightly ad hoc and irregular approach to programming. The voluntary committee currently managing the venue would benefit from some professional assistance to increase the usage of this incredible building.

The building fabric is being maintained in excellent condition and clearly being one of the most important community buildings within a World Heritage site must ensure its future upkeep is to high standards.

Auditorium Capacity:

Main Hall: Original Capacity 1500; current capacity 400

Cinema: 60

Stage details: Not available

The Congress Theatre, Cwmbran

Organisation: Congress Theatre Company (Charitable Trust)

Address: 50 Gwent Square, Cwmbran, Gwent, NP44 1PL

Construction/Opening: 1974

Architect: Gordon Redfern, Chief Architect, Cwmbran Development Corporation

Builder: unknown

Current Owner: Prudential Insurance Company

History/previous names & ownership

The theatre was constructed in 1972-74 with the intent that it would be used as a multi-function space and lecture hall within the surrounding large town centre shopping centre development. In the late 1970's a permanent stage was installed with consequent modifications made to backstage access.

In 1993-94 the Front-of-House facilities were extended as part of an upgrade of the town centre shopping centre fabric. In the late 2000's the Foyer was redecorated, a platform lift installed to facilitate access for all to first floor, the box office extended and a sliding folding wall installed between auditorium and foyer space to meet fire regulations.

Description

The building is located in the heart of a large commercial shopping centre development on the edge of a large public space to the front and the town bus station to the rear. The shopping centre is on top of extensive car parking (provided free to customers) so this venue has excellent audience accessibility and prominence in its environment. It is a simple rectangular building, concrete framed and faced with plain render. The principal elevation features the theatre sign and sculptures of 'Dai' and 'Myfanwy' either side of a large clock. The auditorium is at first floor level and the ground floor has a reasonable foyer and box office/reception area. The remainder of the ground floor at the front is occupied by a large retail unit. To the front/main aspect the brutalist architecture has been softened slightly with a vaguely pagoda-like timber roof parapet. The band stand immediately outside the front doors is privately owned and the theatre does not have access to use it for performances. The side elevations are blank and the rear to the bus depot features a stage door access point and loading doors to the stage (set approximately 3.5m above the street level). Loading of incoming shows has to take place amongst the movements of local buses and relies entirely on manual handling in the absence of a backstage goods lift. Frequently visiting shows are instructed to minimise the size of scenic effects and equipment so that it can be man-handled up the stage door staircase to stage level.

The auditorium is very plain and still bears characteristics of a lecture room rather than a performance space. There is a fine timber dance floor extending under the entire extent of audience seating and stage but the stage and later apron addition are fixed and only the first 10 rows of seats are retractable thus limiting the available dance floor area. Tea dances are held regularly however without compromise to the event. The stage apron is removable to create a small orchestra pit (used approximately 4 times each year) and a semi-permanent proscenium has been constructed recently from black serge faced rigid flats. There is very little wing space either side of the stage and it is not a large performance area at all. There is no flytower and whilst well equipped with lighting and suspension bars, scenic effects can only move sideways – height to rigging points/bars is about 5m.

The foyer space is a single large room at first floor level used more frequently for community events than by theatre audiences. It contains a licensed bar and refreshments counter and loose seating and tables. It is extensively used and can be connected directly to the auditorium by retracting a sliding/folding wall between the two spaces.

Backstage facilities are very good – there are 5 large well appointed dressing rooms with windows and washing facilities for performers and a large and comfortably appointed green room. Access for performers is either from the stage door at the rear of the building or through front-of-house and there is an excellent direct connection from the green room into the foyer space.

The loading bay remains at the original auditorium flat floor level so to compound the difficulties of loading from the street level below more lifting is required once the equipment is inside the building. The loading bay doubles as an equipment store and is cramped.

Auditorium Capacity:

Original capacity 324, reduced by 12 to accommodate permanent in-room sound mixing desk to current capacity of 312, comprising 134 on retractable bleacher and 178 fixed seats

Stage details:

Performance space – width – 14m

Performance space – depth – 7.52m

Depth of apron – 2m

Wing space (Right and Left) – variable

Proscenium height/width – no fixed proscenium

Orchestra pit (maximum no of players) - 12

Height from stage floor to grid – 5.18m

Rake - None

Caerphilly

Bedwas
The Workmen's Hall
Blackwood
The Little Theatre
The Miners' Institute
Caerphilly
Workmen's Hall
Newbridge
The Memo

The Workmen's Hall, Bedwas

Organisation: Bedwas Workmen's Hall Committee

Address: Newport Road, Bedwas, Caerphilly, NP1 8BJ

Construction/Opening: 1923

Architect/Builder: unknown/unknown

Current Owner: Bedwas, Trethomas & Machen Community Council

History/previous names & ownership

The person who was mainly behind the construction of this building was the Secretary of the Federation in the Bedwas Lodge in the colliery after the members had decided to build the hall for the benefit of themselves and their children. The first secretary and general manager of the Workmen's Hall was W.H.Milson. Opened in 1923, the hall's construction was funded by a penny a week contributions from miners, public funds and donations from charities plus a grant from Sir Samuel Instone the controlling shareholder of Bedwas Navigation Colliery (1921) Ltd. Six foundation stones were laid on January 13th by local dignitaries including W. H. LeGrand Chambers, Director of the Bedwas Navigation Colliery. On the ground floor there was a billiard room, and a dance hall with the main hall located on the first floor. The dance hall closed in the 50s and then became a meeting chamber and was used for other uses.

The Workmen's Hall was the local Cinema from before the 'Talkies' came into being and live concerts, theatrical shows, and dances were frequently held there. It quickly became the place where meetings and conferences were held and much of the historic Trade Union activity of that time was organised there. It ceased being a cinema in the 1960s and returned to being a community hall.

The building was listed Grade II on 2nd August 1999.

Storm damage to the roof and vandalism to the envelope was repaired in 2009 with grant aid from Caerphilly County Borough Council.

In 2010 it was decided that the building was in need of major refurbishment. After a strong local campaign it was awarded £40,000 from the Big Lottery Fund's Peoples Millions television programme after winning a public vote and the funds were used to modernise the hall's theatre facilities for community use early in 2011.

Description

The Workmen's Hall is located on the edge of the town on a road presumably once much busier before the near-by by-pass was constructed. There is a single storey prefabricated library building on one side and Bedwas Adult Education Centre offices on the other (occupying some of the original ground floor Institute rooms) with a large surface car park and recreation ground to the rear, sharing access with Bedwas High School.

The building is set back from the road with a small forecourt given over to visitor and staff parking and this position allows the full scale of the building to be appreciated for it is a surprisingly large building.

The front elevation is 3 storeys high and constructed in a classical style built from red brick with dressed stone features including 4 full-height pilasters surmounted with a pediment over the central pair. A large bay window projects at first floor between the central pilasters.

The sides and rear elevations are relatively plain and entirely red brick. Both side elevations have 4 semi-circular windows at high level into the upper part of the Hall within and at the rear there is a two storey lean-to containing the backstage accommodation. The roof is slate and there are two quite ornate ridge ventilator cowls.

The main entrance is on the central axis of the building and entry is via 2 sets of 4 shallow steps through a pair of large glazed doors into the entrance hall. The entrance hall is spartan in the extreme and quite tall and narrow. There are opposed staircases leading immediately up to the auditorium but the floor is plain tiled and the walls painted plaster with no features and no signage. Signage of course isn't really necessary since the only place its possible to go is upstairs from this point. Access therefore for people with movement limitations is extremely inhibited and it is difficult to imagine how this might be overcome given the constraints of the building layout.

At the first floor there is a reasonably large ante-room area which is located behind the large bay window and consequently a bright and comfortable space. There is an impressive model of the local colliery head in the window bay and on the wall next to the doors leading into the auditorium a commemorative carved marble plaque recording the opening of the building and original members of the building committee and trustees.

Large double doors lead directly into the rear stalls of the auditorium which is a carpeted, flat floored area under the balcony. The rear stalls is raised above the main floor of the hall by a further 3 shallow steps and there is an open wrought iron balustrade between the upper and lower parts of the stalls floor. The main floor is large and has a sprung timber floor. Moving from the raised stalls out into the main floor area reveals just how large this room is – it is a very tall space surmounted by a single curved vault ceiling with feature moulding ribs springing from pilasters on the side walls and large plaster grilles at the centre for extraction of warm air.

The side walls are elegantly proportioned with the pilasters standing on a dado plinth (containing radiators) and the panels between them decorated with further raised mouldings. The high level window openings have faux balconies under their cills and are also picked out with highlight mouldings around their perimeter. All of the mouldings are painted a dark red in contrast to the base cream colour of the majority of the wall surfaces, and the balcony front reverses this with the dark red as its base colour and feature mouldings highlighted with the cream.

The proscenium wall is highly unusual insofar as the original ornate plaster moulding pilasters and feature panels have been almost entirely obscured by a much later installation of metal framework supporting drapes and the (currently dysfunctional) cinema screen motor and rigging. This forward proscenium has been used for many years and there are no plans to return to using the original proscenium wall.

The upper audience balcony is reached from a further pair of symmetrically opposed stairs leading from the ante-room at stalls level up to a simple, small landing at second floor level and directly into the back row of the audience seating. It is quite steeply raked so sightlines are very good although, as it retains the original 1920s seats, legroom is a bit restricted. Behind the balcony is the original cinema projection room now unused.

The stage is very large and slopes gently down towards the audience through the proscenium line and onto an unusually large forestage apron. There is no flytower but such is the height of the building to the underside of the roof over the stage that limited flying is possible and the entire stage area is served by an extensive suspension bar and rigging installation. This is a very well equipped stage despite the absence of any stage machinery.

Immediately behind the stage and several steps below it are 3 large and well appointed dressing rooms with windows and access to backstage toilets and a green room equipped with kitchen facilities. If a 'star' dressing room is ever required a small management office in the backstage corridor is adapted. There is access to the backstage area via a stage door in the side of the building and access onto the stage from either side and at the centre of the upstage wall.

The building fabric appears to be well-maintained despite evidence that the roof and original windows are in need of some remedial works or replacement at some point. Certainly the interior is in immaculate condition.

The management committee is clearly very enthusiastic about the Hall and passionate about sustaining it as a facility for the local community and wider area in the long term. They are aware of initiatives such as the Arts Council of Wales backed 'Night Out' scheme and have hosted performances by National Theatre Wales.

Primary users are the local schools and Rotary Club and sell-out shows produced by both are not uncommon suggesting it has a loyal audience to support its survival.

Auditorium Capacity: 540

Stage details: not available

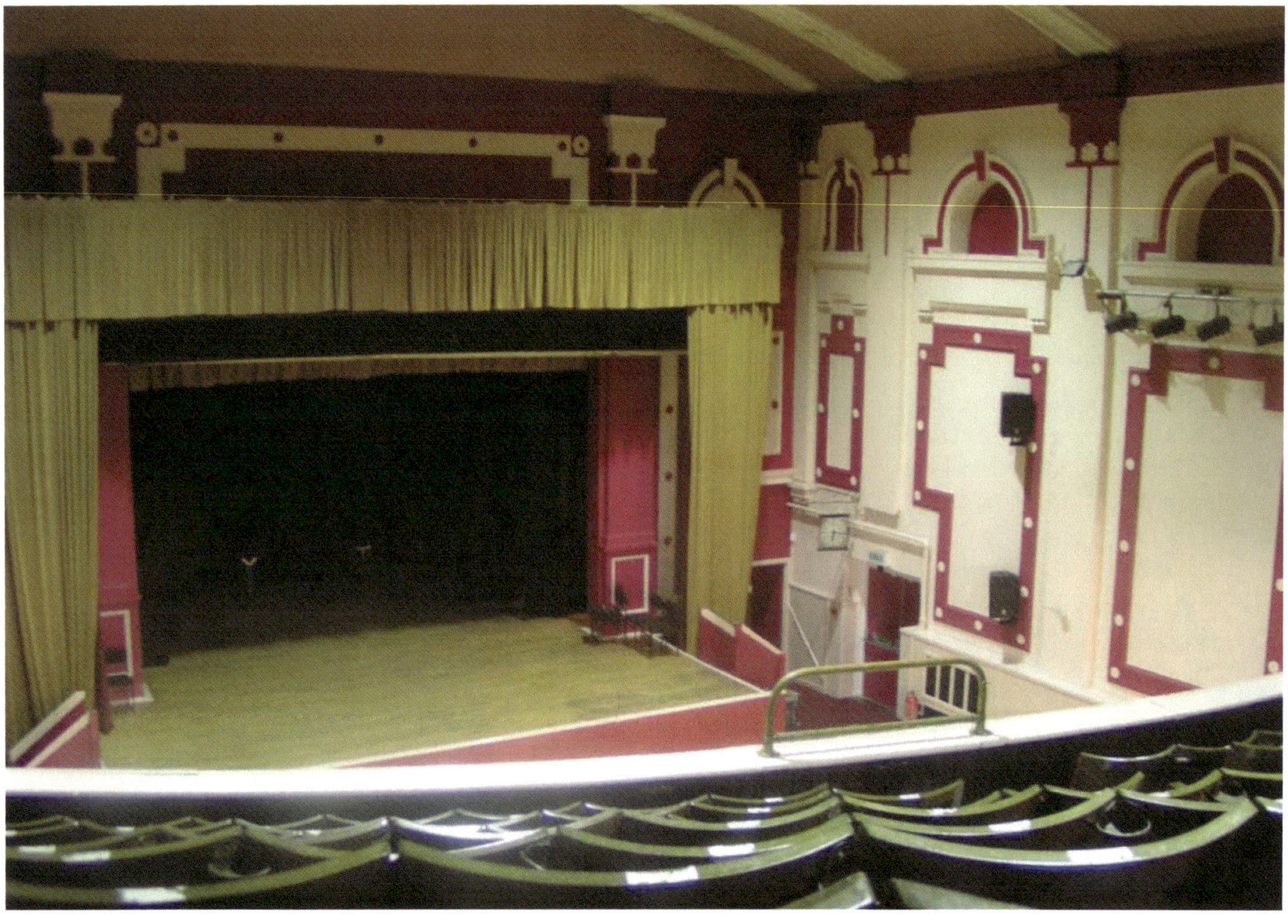

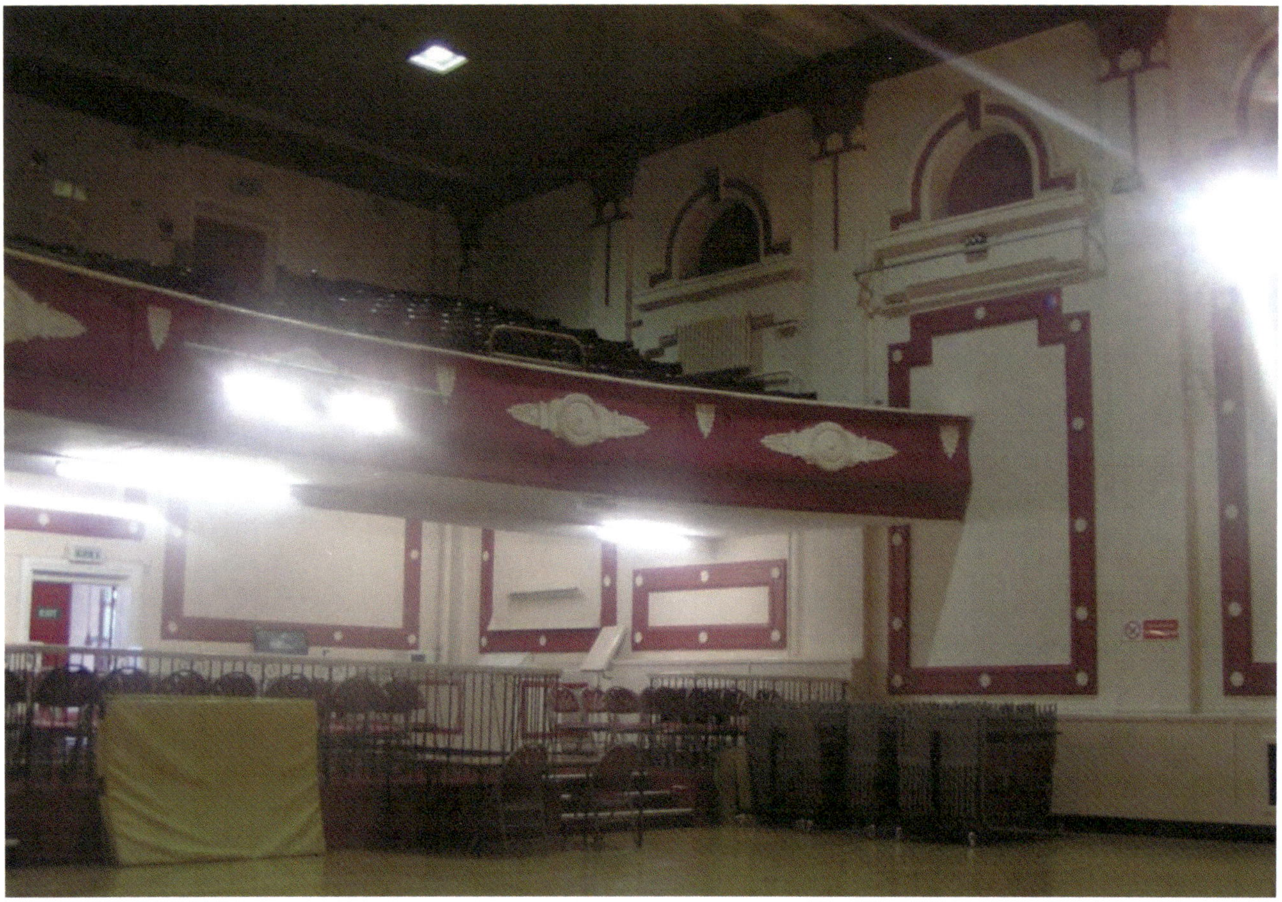

The Little Theatre, Blackwood

Organisation: Blackwood Little Theatre

Address: Woodbine Road, Blackwood NP12 1QJ

Construction: 1904 (as Primitive Methodist Church)
Opening: 1956 (as a theatre)

Architect: R. L. Roberts, Abercarn

Builder: unknown

Current Owner: Blackwood Little Theatre

History/previous names & ownership

The building was constructed as a Primitive Methodist Church in 1904, witnessed by a large number of foundation stones around the main front entrance and along the side of the building. The church was closed as a place of worship before the Second World War and the building taken over by the UK Government Ministry of Supplies. It was used throughout the Second World War and beyond as a regional storage depot.

In 1948 the building was purchased by the organisation that was to become Blackwood Little Theatre Company and members set about converting it into a theatre themselves. It was opened as theatre in 1956 and has remained in use ever since.

Major internal alterations to the interior were carried out by company members in 1995-96 following receipt of substantial capital grants from The Arts Council of Wales and other agencies. The works carried out included the removal and replacement of the auditorium floor, installation of central heating throughout the building, construction of a technical control room, office and storeroom over the original church balcony, creation of the Davenport Suite bar area at first floor level over the entrance, installation of disabled WC facilities and improvements to the entrance area, box office/reception and audience toilets. Dressing rooms and storage areas were created in the original Sunday School annexe building behind the stage.

Auditorium Capacity: 150

Stage details:

Performance space – width – 9m (including wings)
Performance space – depth – 7.92m
Depth of apron – n/a
Wing space (Right and Left) – SR - 1.5m; SL - 1.5m
Proscenium height/width – height unknown; width 6m
Orchestra pit (maximum no of players) – n/a
Height from stage floor to grid – 3.65m
Rake - None

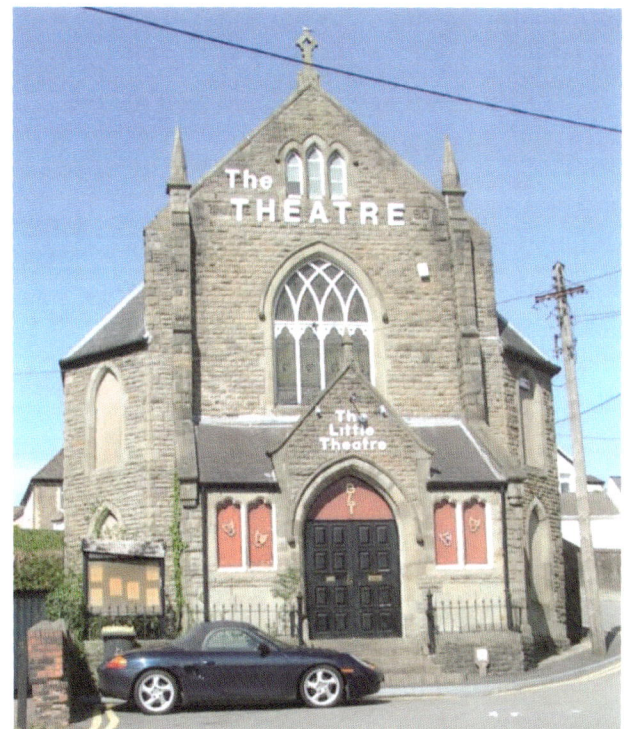

Description

The Little Theatre is located close to the main road through the town centre and is visible from it standing on an elevated site on the axis of Woodbine Road and terminating the view from below. It is unmistakably of ecclesiastical origin with touches of gothic detailing and features in its dark stone facades. The main frontage is quite tall and narrow with a centrally positioned main entrance porch under a gable end framed with buttresses with a large stained glass window immediately above and the original carved building name above that (although it is now largely obscured by 'The Theatre' sign). Finally, very close to the top of the wall a group of 3 pointed arch windows.

To the sides of the entrance the building footprint increases to follow the site boundary and each side has 5 double stacked windows (blocked up many years ago and probably before the building was converted to theatre use) originally serving the areas inside that are at ground floor level and on the balcony above. The majority of the side and rear elevations are now finished in grey render though it is not known if this was the original wall finish. The building has a steeply pitched slate roof.

The entrance is up 5 steps directly from the street outside and into a small porch area that leads into an unexpectedly large reception/box office space containing access to the auditorium and audience WCs. A pair of staircases either side of the main entrance within the porch lead up to a well equipped lounge bar (named the Davenport Suite) that serves as a clubroom for the theatre company and a foyer for audiences.

The auditorium is also surprising insofar as expectations are that the a space will be much less a theatre than an obviously converted church. This is very much a theatre first however and evidence of its origin though present are vestigial rather than overt. The original upper balcony front is retained and expressed in the wall under the high-level technical box and the original delicately detailed cast iron columns that supported the balcony are visible in alcoves in the rear wall of the auditorium. The most obvious remnants of the church space are the high ceiling, or rather the volume under the ceiling that lines the steeply pitched roof and the blanked off windows at high level along both sides of the room.

Entry to the auditorium is at the rear and it has a flat carpeted floor with rescued seats from an old derelict theatre arranged in staggered rows with quite wide aisles to each side. There are no overt architectural features other than those already described and the space is simply decorated in mid and dark green paint over plain plaster.

The technical control box created by the theatre company over the original balcony is reached via a narrow stair leading up from the first floor bar and has an excellent view over the audience to the stage. It is very well equipped and has windows that can be opened to improve audibility for sound mixing.

The stage is the full width of the original building and a proscenium arch has been created to provide decent wing space either side. There is no capacity for flying due to the nature of the ceiling and roof structure above the stage but there is extensive coverage by suspension bars and rigging points and a clear height of around 3.6m.

Behind the stage (which is quite deep) there is a range of rooms created within what was originally the Sunday School annexe of the church, At stage level there is a large storage area for scenery flats and props with 2 good sized dressing rooms above it and a further dressing room and costume store above that. A stage door immediately off stage left provides access for performers and equipment.

The building is not used on a full-time basis and there are clear signs of the envelope suffering with water ingress noticeable in several areas, especially around the entrance porch which is on the most exposed side of the building. The Little Theatre Company presents 3 or 4 shows each year with a pantomime at Christmas and the venue is actively promoted for use by visiting companies and for one-off performances by stand-up comedians and the like with a view to maximising revenue income. The Company is a member of the Little Theatre Guild and tours productions throughout the UK.

The venue has a high standard of equipment and facilities especially considering that it receives no external funding and this is a testament to the enthusiastic and talented company members and leadership. Unlike some other Little Theatre Companies, the Blackwood Company seems able to generate lasting interest and involvement from local young people and frequently sells out its shows. On current performance it will sustain itself long into the future.

The Miners' Institute, Blackwood

Organisation: Caerphilly County Borough Council Directorate of Education and Leisure

Address: High Street, Blackwood, Caerphilly NP12 1BB

Construction/Opening: 1925

Architect: F Beaton (Islwyn Borough Council)

Builder: unknown

Current Owner: Caerphilly County Borough Council

History/previous names & ownership

The final stones on the front of the original building were laid on 4th December 1925 and it was originally opened as a single storey snooker hall, known as The Miners' Welfare Institute. The building was owned by The Coal Industry Social Welfare Organisation and managed by Oakdale Colliery Miners' Institute and had been paid for by Oakdale Colliery miners at the rate of 3d a week each deduction from their wages.

In 1936 two further floors were added to the building to include the stage, auditorium, dance floor, reading room, library, ladies room and rehearsal rooms for local societies. Original events staged in the building included tea dances, snooker/billiards, reading groups, rehearsals and union meetings for local miners. The building was re-named Blackwood Miners' Institute. At some point the building ownership changed to the Trustees of Oakdale Colliery Miners' Institute.

The building fell in to disrepair in the 1970s/1980s with the pit closures and in 1989 the trustees sold it to Islwyn Borough Council who promised to make it available for community use.

The building was reopened by Lynne Vaughan in February 1992 as a community arts and entertainment venue following funding from Islwyn Borough Council and the Welsh Office and ownership of the building passed to Caerphilly County Borough Council.

The building was listed Grade II* on 31st May 2002.

In late June 2011 Caerphilly County Council announced a £750,000 programme of repairs and renovations. The work will include making the building envelope weathertight, the replacement of the roof, defective floors and 200 of the auditorium seats. The reception area will be redecorated and energy efficient technologies will be incorporated. The main facade will be cleaned and the lesser hall demolished to improve vehicle access to the rear of the building. All works will be overseen by Caerphilly County Architects.

Auditorium Capacity: Original: unknown

Current: 395 (comprising 156 on the stalls flat floor, 183 on stalls raked seating and 56 on balcony);

The ground floor second space has a capacity of approximately 150 in theatre style but is more frequently used for rock gigs where capacity is much increased for standing audiences.

Stage details:

Performance space – width – 8.1m
Performance space – depth – 6m (including apron)
Depth of apron – variable - 0.85m - 1.85m
Wing space (Right and Left) – SR - 1.3m; SL - 1.3m
Proscenium height/width – height 4.2m; width 7.18m
Orchestra pit (maximum no of players) – n/a
Height from stage floor to grid – 5.04m
Rake - Yes – 1:24 slope

Description

The Miners' Institute building is situated immediately on the back of the pavement of the main through road in Blackwood and stands relatively alone. It is a 3 storey frontage of stone but the stone does not extend far around the sides where it is replaced as the envelope finish by grey render.

The building has a flat roof behind a parapet (which at the time of writing had been causing problems with water ingress) while the auditorium that was added 10 years after completion of the Institute has a slated pitched roof. Minor problems of water ingress are reported at the junction of the 2 buildings but should be overcome by the planned works to replace the roof finishes.

The main entrance is on the central axis of the building and entry is into an elegant foyer space, grander than the majority of similar buildings of a similar age, both in terms of space and décor which has a classical theme. During the renovations in the early 1990's a ramped access was added to one side of the main frontage to afford access to visitors with movement impairment and who can't enter up the main steps. A front-of-house lift was installed at the same time.

The foyer contains symmetrical staircases that access the auditorium, dance studio and several function rooms and administration offices above, a box office and access directly into the original snooker room (now used as a second performance space, venue bar and by many local community groups) and a small and apparently un-used cafeteria/restaurant area.

The auditorium is largely as original apart from the removal of original seats and their replacement with retractable bleachers during the 1990's. It has a sprung flat floor and a single longitudinal barrel vault ceiling with feature rib details. Walls and ceiling are painted a dark purple and original windows into the auditorium have all been bricked up.

The original balcony was retained albeit with much reduced seating capacity and the balcony front was heavily modified to suit revised sightlines from the audience seating. A well-equipped sound/light and projection control room was installed (although no longer used for cinema due to advent of DVD and Sky Movies and the like)

The stage is raised on a modest riser with small apron and is well equipped despite having no fly tower. There is no orchestra pit.

Access for loading and unloading is relatively good insofar as it is afforded level from the adjacent small car park/ loading yard. It is directly into the auditorium rather than the stage but this does not appear to cause any operational difficulties.

There are 4 dressing rooms, 2 large ones for chorus use and 2 smaller ones closer to the stage for principals.

There is a very good dance studio on the top floor of the Institute building with fully sprung floor, full height wall mirrors and barres. This is apparently well used by local community dance groups but is one of the rooms worst affected by water ingress on the inside of the front elevation of the building.

The original snooker room on the ground floor was gutted in the 1990's renovations and a bar installed along with new vinyl tiled floor, suspended ceiling and décor. It is equipped with removable staging and has performance lighting positions in the ceiling.

It is heavily used by community groups, provides the foyer bar facility for performances in the main auditorium and is used for rock gigs and events where ticket sales for shows in the main space are low.

Workmen's Hall, Caerphilly

Organisation: Trustees of Caerphilly Workmen's Hall

Address: 20, Castle Street, Caerphilly CF83 1NY

Construction: 1924-25; **Opening:** 1925

Architect/Builder: unknown/unknown

Current Owner: Trustees of Caerphilly Workmen's Hall

History/previous names & ownership

Foundation stones were laid on 5th April 1924 by Mr B. M. Williams, manager of the Senghenydd and Aber Valley Co-Operative Society, Mr Charles Mason, South Wales Representative of the Industrial Welfare Society and Mr Robert Bassett on behalf of the Caerphilly Miners. The building was opened in 1925 and contained a large theatre auditorium used for cinema presentations from the outset. Originally the proscenium was 18 feet wide although it was later expanded for Cinemascope to 34 feet. Attached to the auditorium was a reading room, workingmen's club, snooker hall and lecture room. The reading room and other institute offices were very small, being located at the rear of the hall in a block that backed up to the screen. The institute possessed a separate back entrance which did not connect with the front entrance. The most popular welfare facility was the reading room which displayed a range of daily newspapers and magazines.

Whilst operating as the Workmen's Hall Cinema there was a neon sign over the Castle Street entrance. It was said to contain some of the most uncomfortable seats in cinema history. The front rows of the stalls area were formed of metal framed seating with wooden backs and bases. They were replaced with more comfortable, albeit secondhand seating after the introduction of part time bingo. The cinema closed as a full time operation during the late-1960's but there were occasional film shows throughout the 1970's.

The Workmen's Hall and Institute was listed Grade II on 11th October 1995.

In 2009 the building was placed on the open market for sale and around that time plans were prepared for the conversion of the building into a memorial tribute/museum for comedian Tommy Cooper who was born in Caerphilly. Those plans have not been realised. The backstage part of building now appears to be occupied by a Gymnasium but the remainder is currently un-used and subject to ongoing discussions with the Council regarding its possible regeneration and reopening as a local cultural centre and venue.

Description

The Workmen's Hall occupies a prime site directly opposite Caerphilly Castle and occupies a large area connecting down a low hill to Bedwas Road at the rear (where the entrance to the Institute was located).

The exterior is constructed entirely of red brick and whilst there are some feature details in the brickwork it is a comparitively plain building. The entrance on Castle Street is framed by a pair of doric columns and presumably leads almost directly into the auditorium.

Photographs of the interior show it to be a much more elaborate and flamboyant auditorium than the exterior would suggest with a single audience balcony, shallow barrel vaulted ceiling and significant use of decorative mouldings to the ceiling and side walls. It seems to be a rather beautiful space.

It is to be hoped that a way of resurrecting this auditorium as a place of live entertainment can be found before it succumbs to the ravages of neglect and consequent decay.

Auditorium Capacity: 600

Stage details: not available

Interior photograph: www.ciswo-services.org.uk

The Memo, Newbridge

Organisation: Trustees of Celynen Collieries Institute & Friends of Newbridge Memorial Hall

Address: High Street, Newbridge, Caerphilly, NP11 4FH

Construction/Opening: 1924

Architect: E.D.T. Jenkins

Builder: Ewart Evans

Current Owner: Trustees of Celynen Collieries Institute & Friends of Newbridge Memorial Hall

History/previous names & ownership

The Institute designed by Architect R. L. Roberts was opened at a cost of £6,000 and contained a library, reading room and billiard room. The Memorial Hall was added in 1924 at a cost of £10,000 and opened containing a ground floor Ballroom with auditorium above. The auditorium was built as a theatre and cinema. Both buildings were owned and managed by Celynen Collieries Institute. In 1949 the Ballroom stage was modified and a curved front added and in the 1950's the entrance to the Memorial Hall was modified and extended to provide audience WCs.

During the 1960's an extension link block was added to join the original Institute and Memorial Hall buildings together and the library, reading room and billiard room were adapted for use as a drinking club. The Ballroom was modernised and significantly redecorated. In 1970 a new ticket desk was constructed in the Memorial Hall main entrance and the original art deco desk on the first floor was abandoned. In 1972 the Cinema was closed and the Memorial Hall left derelict. It remained unused and derelict to 2010. In 1984 the Drinking Club went bankrupt and the entire Institute fell into disuse.

The Institute was listed Grade II and the Memorial Hall Grade II* on 17th March 1999 and during that year the downstairs seats in the auditorium were removed and stacked on the upper balcony to facilitate filming of scenes for the Sara Sugarman film "Very Annie Mary".

In 2003 the Institute and Memorial Hall were placed on its list of significant buildings requiring the protection of the state by Cadw and in 2004 they were saved from demolition by a local action group and the Trustees of Celynen Collieries Institute and Friends of Newbridge Memorial Hall took responsibility for the buildings, The Memo came second in the 2004 BBC 'Restoration' programme.

In 2009-10 Architect Alwyn Jones of Taffs Well developed designs for a scheme for refurbishment of the Institute and Memorial Hall and the replacement of the 1960's extension and was appointed in late 2010 to execute the refurbishment project in 2 phases with completion planned for 2013. The proposed scheme seeks to repair and restore the building's existing interior and the exteriors of both the Memorial Hall and Institute will be restored to their original appearance, with the complete removal of the external suspended fire escape gantry from the east elevation. All electrical, heating and hot and cold water services and sanitary fittings will be removed and replaced.

Within the auditorium 'soundproof' linings and secondary glazing will be installed to the original windows, the 'modern' flat ceiling panels will be removed and replaced with a lath and plaster ceiling with relief panels and retaining the vents and ribs of the original, and the original floor will be retained after cleaning and repair. New auditorium seating will be installed at stalls level and a mixture of new seats and refurbished originals will be installed on the balcony. A new technical area will be created at the rear of the balcony for in-room sound and light system control. All existing stage equipment will be removed and new lighting, cinema screen, curtain tracks and rigging installed, supported on a new structure at high level over the stage. A new stage extension/apron with storage within will be created.

Description

The Institute stands in a prominent position in the centre of Newbridge with a small memorial garden and car park adjacent. The Memorial Hall stands some distance away from the main road and on first approach is largely hidden from view. Originally two completely separate buildings a poorly designed and constructed link building was built in the 1960's to provide new toilet facilities and access between the Institute and Memo.

At around the same time the original Institute entrance was bricked up and a large bar installed in the hall serving what was the reading room on one side and the billiard room on the other. The Institute became a drinking club.

The Institute is a brick and stone construction with plentiful large sash windows into the communal rooms within. It appears in fairly good condition although some ill-advised and poorly executed 'maintenance and repair' are evident, especially on the stone window surrounds. On the upper floor the original Library remains in virtually original appearance but is suffering from significant neglect and water ingress through the roof. The adjacent function room has been heavily 'modernised' over time and very few original features remain. The Memorial Hall is constructed of brick to the main frontage with grey render to all other elevations. It has been un-used since 1972 and although various emergency repairs have been effected it stands in a state of significant distress. The majority of the original windows have been boarded up following vandalism to the glazing and significant vegetation has grown up over the flank walls. The rain water goods do not collect water and there are several areas of damage or slippage to the roof slates.

An unpleasant extension was added to the front entrance of the Memo in the 1950's to provide ground floor WCs and the original hardwood grand entrance doors were replaced with domestic scale glass doors. All of these problems are due to be addressed in the forthcoming restoration works, with the intent to return the building to its original grandeur.

On the ground floor of the Memo building is a large ballroom with a highly regarded and original 1920's dance floor. This room has also been heavily 'modernised' over time concealing many of its original art deco details and features, including the original ceiling now hidden by a suspended lay in grid tiled secondary ceiling. A bar has been installed into this space too. The ballroom is actively used for regular tea dances and music events and has two stages – one used by bands, the other by DJ's.

A short flight of stairs leads up into the backstage area where there are 2 dressing rooms under the stage of the main auditorium. One of these features a remarkable collection of original show-posters and theatre memorabilia. Each dressing room originally benefitted from a pair of high level windows (actually set at pavement level outside such is the level difference across the site) but these have long since been blocked up.

The main auditorium is spectacular and remarkably preserved intact in original condition albeit clearly having suffered from lack of maintenance and uncontrolled environmental conditions. It is for this reason that is regarded as one of the most significant art deco rooms in the UK. It is a time-capsule and the forthcoming restoration will create a space of some beauty again.

It is a rectangular auditorium with a single upper balcony. The stalls floor is quite steeply raked and whilst the original floor remains, the seats were removed by a film company in the 1990's and are stacked without consideration of their value in disregarded piles on top of the upper balcony seating.

The ceiling is a single longitudinal barrel and features moulded plaster ribs and ornate ventilation (extract) grilles. The original light fittings are all still within the space although only 2 remain hanging.

The walls feature ornate panelling, important art works and decorative screens over the windows to provide black-out for the film screenings for which it became most heavily used. Several films and TV shows have been made in the auditorium since it fell into disuse and each have left a mark on it, either by over-painting areas of the walls (especially around the proscenium), removing the seats, light fittings and even fixing fake paintings over the original art work. It is the intention of the forthcoming restoration project to completely return the room to its original condition and appearance.

The original projection room remains (albeit not accessible due to asbestos contamination) and still contains the original film projectors.

There is no dedicated foyer space to the auditorium and two staircases that served the auditorium lead directly upwards from the entrance hall on either side of the building. The stairs are in bad condition. On the first central landing of the stairs stands the original art deco ticket desk, of striking curved hardwood and glass. This was replaced by a less elegant desk in the main entrance hall shortly before the building was closed and again this will be addressed in the forthcoming works.

The 1960's link building is constructed of grey brick and concrete and contains stairs (but no lift) and a small foyer area (with bar) that serves the ballroom only. It is due to be removed as part of the forthcoming works and replaced with something more elegant.

69

Auditorium Capacity:

Originally 700-800, capacity after current renovation and restoration project will be 376 (comprising 292 on stalls and 84 on the circle (of which 40 will be refurbished original 1925 seats)

Stage details:

Performance space – width – 15.2m (including wings)
Performance space – depth – 5.75m
Depth of apron – 1.2m
Wing space (Right and Left) – 3.5m each side
Proscenium height/width – height 5.05m; width 8.15m
Orchestra pit (maximum no of players) - n/a
Height from stage floor to grid – 6.25m to stage ceiling
new grid to be installed below this level
Rake – None

Blaenau Gwent

Abertillery
The Metropole Cultural & Conference Centre

Brynmawr
The Market Hall

Ebbw Vale
The Beaufort Theatre

Tredegar
The Little Theatre

The Metropole Cultural & Conference Centre, Abertillery

Organisation: Blaenau Gwent County Borough Council

Address: Mitre Street, Abertillery, Blaenau Gwent NP13 1AL

Construction/Opening: 1892

Architect: Alfred Swash, Newport

Builder: unknown

Current Owner: Blaenau Gwent County Borough Council

History/previous names & ownership

Built by local businessman Charles John Seaborne as The Metropole Theatre and Dance Hall in 1892, Mr Seabourne remained in ownership and managerial control of the venue until selling it to Blaenau Gwent District Council in 1952. Ownership passed to Blaenau Gwent County Borough Council on the formation of the Unitary Authority in 1994.

In 1997 it fell into disrepair and closed due to structural failure. Around that time the Dance Hall was converted to use as the local Museum and from 1999 to 2006 Simon Jennings, Architect (of Blaenau Gwent County Borough Council in-house Architects) led the complete refurbishment and restoration of the theatre with the primary focus on providing community theatre space and a regional conference venue.

As part of the works, the auditorium was reduced in length at stalls level by the introduction of a foyer bar area at the rear of the original stalls level, and in width by the introduction of circulation corridors and meeting rooms at first floor level. All of the original audience seating was replaced and stalls seating replaced with a retractable bleacher unit. New decorations and finishes were applied throughout and the auditorium roof structure exposed as an architectural feature.

Auditorium Capacity:

Original : 800; 1967: 645; Current capacity is 216 (comprising 98 on retractable seating, 118 on fixed balcony seating)

Stage details:

Performance space – width – 9.75m
Performance space – depth – 9.3m
Depth of apron - n/a
Wing space (Right and Left) – 4.57m each side
Proscenium height/width – height 7m; width 7m
Orchestra pit (maximum no of players) – n/a
Height from stage floor to grid – 5.79m
Rake – Yes, slope 1:20

Description

The building is located in the heart of Abertillery town centre in a prominent location. It is well served by adjacent surface car parks and a nearby multi-storey that provides free parking to visitors.

The extensive building renovations of 1999-2006 have been carried out to a high standard and the building is now in extremely good condition. The external envelope is finished with a white render and has prominent venue signage on its exposed flanks and front elevation. A new meeting room constructed at roof level is clearly contemporary but sits well with the massing of the original Victorian elevations. Prior to the most recent renovations the ground floor Dance Hall beneath the theatre was refurbished and converted to use as the local Museum and has its own independent access.

Entry is via a small lobby into a reception area nestling alongside the auditorium and stage, and leads immediately into the auditorium stalls at the front of the room. Circulation to the foyer bar area and first floor balcony feels a bit squashed into the available space and is neither intuitive nor direct but is well signed. If the support accommodation isn't especially successful in either theatre planning or architectural terms, the auditorium is a good example of a sensitive upgrade combining original structure and features with contemporary detailing, décor and fittings and equipment. The Victorian cast iron structural columns are retained and exposed throughout and the original roof structure has been exposed too in its bare natural timber state. The auditorium has warmth and character.

The original raked stage is large and has been retained as original albeit with extensive technical equipment and finishes upgrades. Loading is directly onto stage through doors set at truck bed level and reached via the car park to the front of the building.

As should be expected from comparatively recent design and construction work, access throughout the building is very good.

This is a successful and well supported venue and whilst not promoting theatrical events widely or frequently has established itself as a community resource and viable conference and meetings venue.

Market Hall, Brynmawr

Organisation: Blaenau Gwent County Borough Council

Address: Market Square, Brynmawr NP3 4AJ

Construction/Opening: 1894

Architect/Builder: unknown/unknown

Current Owner: Blaenau Gwent County Borough Council

History/previous names & ownership

As early as 1844 a Market Hall was built in Brynmawr and after various alterations was replaced by a new and larger hall in 1894 constructed on land donated by the Duke of Beaufort. The new hall was built at the public expense at a cost of £2,500 and was opened in February 1894 by a civic ceremony and lunch to which two hundred guests were invited. The original Market Hall clock was presented by Mr Charles Morley esq, Member of Parliament for Breconshire. In its original form the New Market Hall could hold at least 1,500 people.

The Market Hall has been used as a cinema since the early 1900's and has undergone many architectural changes throughout the 20th century. In 1937 it was known as the Town Hall Cinema and had an auditorium with 800 seats. It has a 35 feet wide proscenium, a 30 feet deep stage and three dressing rooms. Around this time there was a major alteration and renovation of the front elevation (the appearance of the building at that time now recorded on mural on side of building on approach to the town centre). Prior to the Second World War boxing matches were staged in the Hall. In the early 1950's it was re-named Market Hall Cinema. In 1957 Brynmawr Amateur Operatic Society first performed in the building and has done so ever since.

In the 1970's the building was given an overhaul in an attempt to modernise it, and the original facade was covered up with profiled metal sheeting. Up until this time, the flat floor of the hall was used for a weekly market but after this renovation the market was moved into what was originally the backstage area and the theatre/cinema stage/screen moved to its current location.

The exterior of the building was again renovated in 2008, with funding from the Welsh Assembly. The steel cladding on the front was removed and stonework and masonry cleaned and re-painted. Improvements included new windows and doors, improved lighting and signs at the entrance, a new fire escape and front canopy and the refurbishment of the building's original clock.

Description

The building stands in the centre of Brynmawr in a very prominent location, with a large public square in front of it. The building is part of a larger group of connected buildings that include the town library and Workmen's Institute. The front elevation has been much changed over the life of the building, most significantly when the original stone façade was covered by an extension that provided an enlarged projection room (apparently the original façade was retained and although covered now by internal wall linings the original stone work and foundation stones are accessible from within the projection room).

Since then it has been altered at least twice and currently has a soft-grey render coating over the majority of the elevation and original windows have been replaced with contemporary metal framed windows, albeit of a similar size and appearance to the originals. The side and rear elevations retain the original rubble stone walling with relatively recent openings formed in each side to create emergency escape doors from the auditorium. The building has a slate roof.

Entry is on the level from the public square and directly through automatic opening glass doors into the small foyer area that contains staff accommodation, a ticket desk and audience toilets. A central door opens into a short staircase that leads directly into the upper section of the auditorium via a slightly off-set vomitory. Access to the front of the auditorium is provided on either side and there are several spaces available for wheelchair users on the flat floor in front of the stage. The auditorium is compact and much reduced in size from the original hall as the stage is now approximately in the centre of the original – relocated when the market was moved out of the theatre into the original backstage area. Capacity has also been significantly reduced over time, most recently by the introduction of fixed audience seating on a single raked tier. The internal decoration is quite plain and there is no proscenium frame – instead where lobbies have been created to emergency exit routes either side of the stage the side walls are canted in to meet the stage/screen opening and a rich red drape creates a horizontal top to the stage/screen opening under the curved ceiling.

The walls are painted pink and there are feature mouldings creating panels on the stage and side walls painted white to contrast with the walls. The mouldings appear to be original as they are crudely bisected by a dado rail and handrail against the side walls where the tiered seating was installed. The original single barrel-vault ceiling has been covered with a lay-in grid tiled suspended ceiling that follows the original curve and was presumably installed in an effort to improve the thermal or acoustic performance of the hall. It appears incongruous now however, an appearance exaggerated by the functional lighting bars suspended beneath and through this added layer.

The Market Hall Cinema is one of the few publicly owned cinemas in the country. It shows first run films 7 days a week but is also used for one week in each year (around Easter time) for shows presented by the Brynmawr Amateur Operatic Society. Occasionally choral performances are also staged. As there are no dressing rooms in the theatre the adjacent library is closed for the week of the live performances and is used as dressing rooms and performer green room. The building envelope is in good condition but there are areas inside the building that are in need of some maintenance.

Budget constraints appear to be limiting the extent of regular maintenance possible but there are no concerns for the future of the building as it is well used by audiences and well supported by the Local Authority as part of its group of 3 venues across the County.

Auditorium Capacity:

Original: >1500; 1937: 800; current 350

Stage details: Not available

The Beaufort Theatre, Ebbw Vale

Organisation: Blaenau Gwent County Borough Council

Address: Beaufort Road, Beaufort Hill, Ebbw Vale, Blaenau Gwent NP23 5QQ

Construction/Opening: 1908

Architect/Builder: unknown/unknown

Current Owner: Blaenau Gwent County Borough Council

History/previous names & ownership

Constructed by The Beaufort Cinema and Billiard Hall Company in 1908 and named Beaufort Cinema and Billiard Hall, it operated in this guise until the 1960's when it was sold to Blaenau Gwent District Council and converted to theatre use. It is presumed that at that time the original brickwork building envelope was over-clad with profiled metal sheeting, the billiard room was converted to current ballroom use, an extension was added at ballroom (ground floor) level to provide licensed bar facilities, the safety curtain was removed and the permanent stage apron installed.

In the 1990's ownership passed to the new Unitary Authority of Blaenau Gwent County Borough Council and it underwent a further upgrade including construction of a new extension to front-of-house providing larger foyer and ticket office accommodation, improved office space for staff and conversion of the original projection room into a sound and lighting control room at first floor level. The original auditorium seating was replaced with a consequent reduction in audience capacity and new stage equipment and ventilation and house lighting was added to the auditorium.

Its future is currently uncertain as proposals have been made to build a new theatre on the site of the abandoned British Steel works in the valley adjacent to Ebbw Vale town which would replace the Beaufort and lead to its demolition.

Description

The theatre stands at the top of a hill in the small community of Beaufort some 2 miles from Ebbw Vale and as such has a prominent location. There is a significant level difference across the site that was exploited by the original Architect such that the ballroom (originally the billiard hall) is directly under the theatre auditorium and can be independently accessed from the lower level.

There are busy roads on three sides of the building and a large car park for users on the other (at the lower level). The main entrance is at the highest point of the site and has been extended to improve audience and staff facilities. The exterior of the building at street level has been substantially improved to the front with the application of bright rendered panels and venue signage but the remainder of the building lurks under the cover of a grey coloured profiled metal cladding system conveying the appearance of a warehouse or industrial building. Lower levels of the external walls have been vandalised by graffiti artists and where exposed the original concrete appears to be seriously distressed and in need of maintenance and repair.

The entrance area contains a sweet shop and ticket desk and leads directly into the rear of the auditorium, to a steep and narrow staircase connecting the theatre to the ballroom and bar below, and to the staff offices and control room on the first floor. The auditorium is plain and has no distinguishing architectural features apart from the single span timber board clad curved ceiling. The floor is a single continuous (and steep) rake down to the stage but as a result audience sightlines are very good throughout. New seating was installed in the 1990's and is in very good condition. The ventilation and heating systems reportedly present no problems with over-heating or cold. The stage area is small and has a surprisingly tiny fixed but unembellished black painted proscenium frame. There is no flytower and restrictions imposed by the exposed roof structure above the stage have reduced suspension height to only 16' with a venue imposed limit on height of scenic effects and equipment of just 12'. There is no wing space worth the name to stage right and stage left is open to the loading bay area.

There are 3 dressing rooms below stage (accessed via steep staircases only) which are well appointed and do have access via their linking corridor to both sides of the stage above. There is no route through the building from backstage areas to front-of-house apart from passing through the auditorium.

The ballroom at ground floor is large and can accommodate up to 120 people in a theatre style seating arrangement. It is heavily used by the local community for a wide range of events and is in good decorative order. It connects to a freestanding building 'extension' of unknown age linked to the original structure by a small passageway and housing the licensed bar serving all building users – at 2 storeys below the auditorium entrance/exit it is not especially convenient and some event interval times have to be extended to allow patrons time for refreshments and the long climb down and back upstairs.

The ballroom has a mezzanine space used for small meetings and as a dressing room for musicians performing in the ballroom on the small permanent stage that has been built in one corner of the larger room. The mezzanine space has an adjacent kitchen area but it is not operational and would require a significant and expensive upgrade to comply with current food-handling regulations.

Auditorium Capacity: Original: unknown; Current: 338 on a single fixed raked floor.

120 people in theatre style in ground floor ballroom.

Stage details:

Performance space – width – 8.53m
Performance space – depth – 5.79m
Depth of apron – 1.2m
Wing space (Right and Left) – SR = none, SL = directly into loading bay and consequently large
Proscenium height/width – height 3.66m; width 4.27m
Orchestra pit (maximum no of players) – n/a
Height from stage floor to grid – approx 4.88m (venue places limit of 3.66m on height of any scenic effects)
Rake – Yes, slope unknown

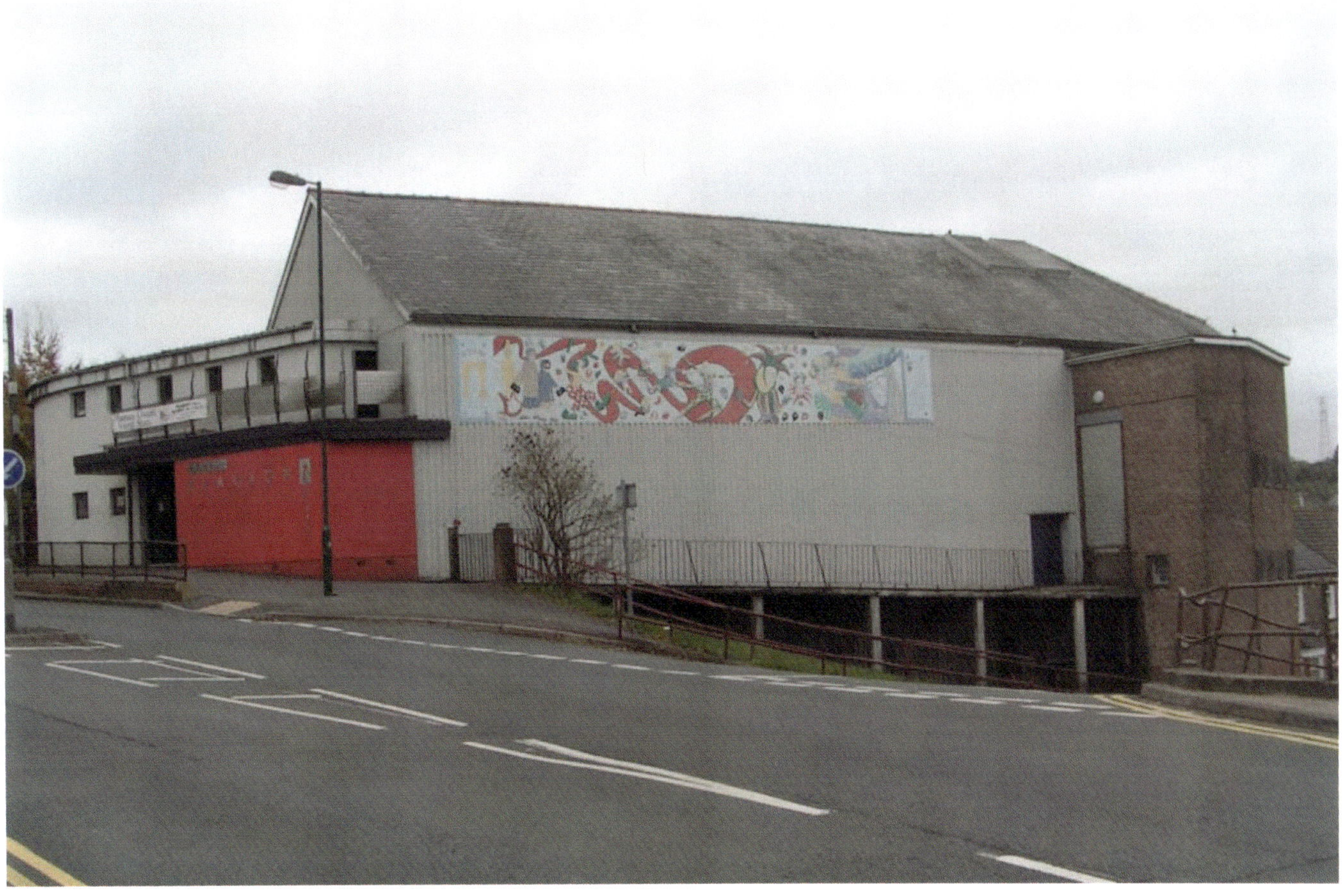

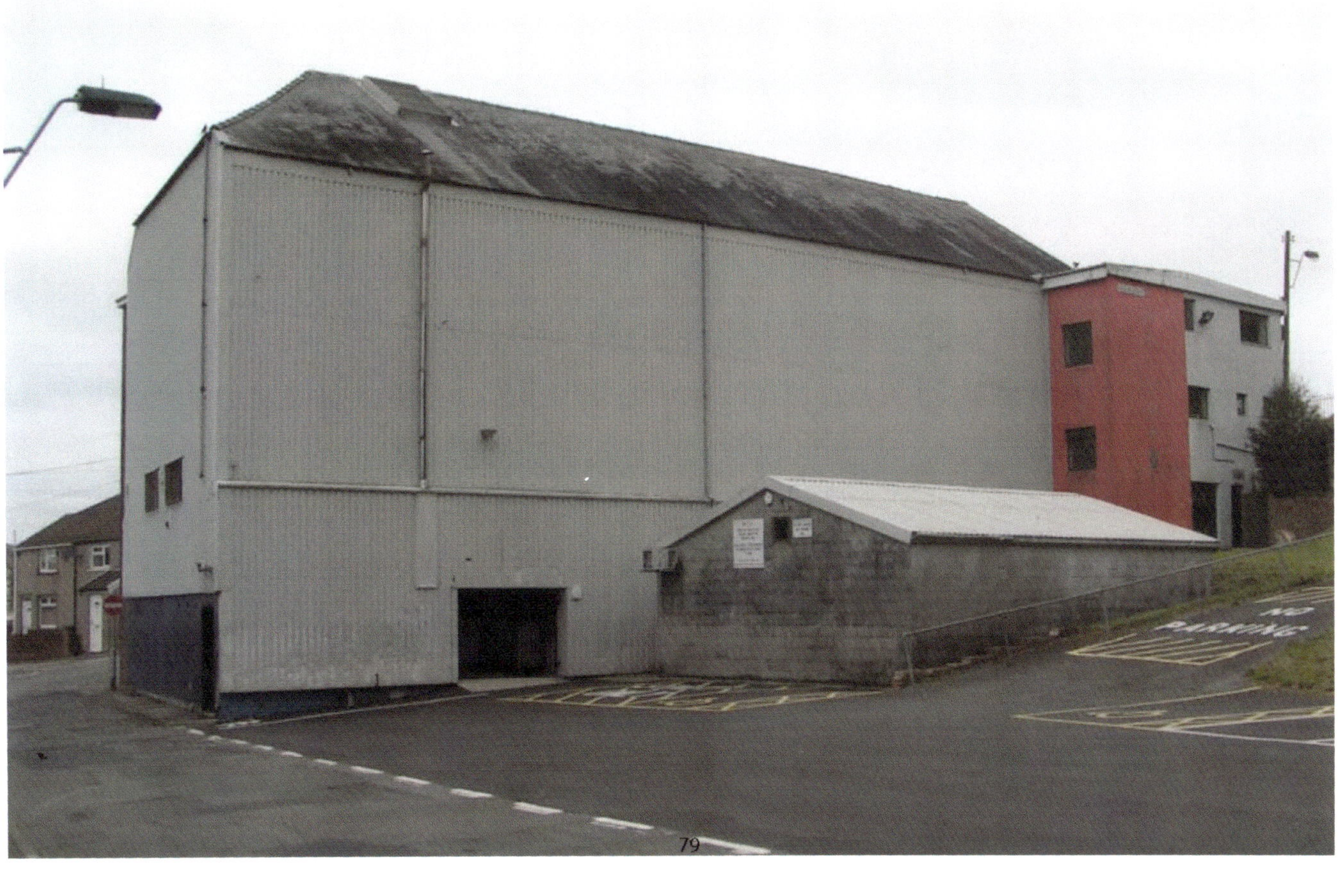
NO
PARKING

The Little Theatre, Tredegar

Organisation: Tredegar Thespian Players (Tredegar Little Theatre)

Address: Upper Coronation St, Tredegar NP22 3YA

Construction/Opening: 1962

Architect/Builder: unknown/unknown

Current Owner: Tredegar Thespian Players (Tredegar Little Theatre)

History/previous names & ownership

The Tredegar Thespian Players Society was founded in 1945 by a small group of drama enthusiasts, with rehearsals held in a room at the rear of the Castle Hotel, Tredegar under the control of the first producer John Morris. Initial performances were held at the Workmen's Hall, but soon it was decided to enter drama festivals which were held annually at up to thirty different venues across South Wales.

Then in 1956, the players felt a need for a home of their own, and nine members made personal loans of £180 each for the purchase of the derelict pub, "The Freemasons' Vaults" in Coronation Street. For the next six years, members shared the work of refurbishing the building, whilst continuing to travel to drama festivals. Their prize monies augmented grants from Tredegar Urban District and Monmouthshire Councils and one for £700 from the Caoustie Gulbenkian Foundation. On 30th October 1962, The Little Theatre opened with a performance of "Serious Charge" by Philip King. In the ensuing years, the theatre has seen a diversity of productions, including plays, serious, romantic, comic and farcical. Music Hall and variety shows are also presented.

In 1996 the Theatre received an Arts Council of Wales grant to upgrade the theatre with new seating, electrics, a balcony bar, hearing loop system and wheelchair access.

Following receipt of a capital grant from Blaenau Gwent County Borough Council in 2010 the building fabric was renovated including construction of a new roof and total re-rendering of the external walls Further renovations included upgrade of the dressing rooms and a general overhaul and redecoration of the auditorium.

Description

The Little Theatre is located very close to the main square at the heart of the town centre although is actually tucked away behind the large library building in a small street shared with the town's Fire Station and some residential buildings so it is necessary to know where it is rather than to rely on simply walking past. It does however have a significant presence on the street where its main frontage is located by virtue of projecting from the surrounding buildings right to the back of the pavement and having good, clear signage on the facades.

It appears as though a single storey building but is quite high and has a pitched roof giving it more height and visibility. The walls are only punctured by doors, the main entrance on the corner visible from the approach from the town centre and various emergency exits and other access points. There are no windows at all. The external walls are all finished cream render which is well detailed and overall the building envelope appears very crisp. The main entrance is at pavement level and leads into a small entrance lobby with stairs leading immediately up to the balcony and doors leading directly into the rear of the auditorium stalls. There are 2 large and modern audience toilets off the lobby area.

The auditorium occupies the full width and height of the building at the entrance end and is a simple rectangle in plan. There is an off-centre aisle leading to the stage. Seating under the balcony is set on a shallow raised dais but all seats are arranged with no offset from row to row and consequently some sightlines are restricted. Upward sightlines in particular are limited due to the depth of the low balcony overhang and height of the stage riser. Otherwise the stalls floor is flat. The balcony is quite small and only accommodates about 20 loose seats. Downward sightlines from the rear of the balcony are also quite limited. Behind the balcony there is an open sound and light mixing/control position and at the top of the stairs there is a small licensed bar servery. The auditorium walls are quite plain but have a high dado with timber panelling below and an ornate cornice top moulding. Performance lighting is suspended from the roof structure over the audience. The stage is high in relation to the audience and extends the full width of the building too such that there are no wings at all and scenery or drapes are used to create very limited circulation space for actors on the sides.

There is a proscenium but it is almost as wide as the stage and quite high such that the top is difficult to see. The stage is quite deep in comparison to its width but is limited by the junction of the auditorium roof with a higher part of the building to the rear of the site. This higher building accommodates a large backstage space used variously for cast gathering, green room and for the creation of scenic effects. A stage door leads to stage left at the rear and is at pavement level outside meaning that accessibility to the stage itself is remarkably good. However, the dressing rooms are located both above and below stage via narrow and steep stairs. There are 3 dressing rooms, one of which having direct access to toilet facilities and all of which also serve as storage areas for the extensive collection of props, costumes and scenic effects held by the Company.

The building is clearly well maintained although the interior is in need of upgrade to catch up with the recent improvement to the appearance of the envelope. There are some signs of moisture penetration, or perhaps more likely internal condensation on one of the interior walls backstage which could be a result of the render treatment to the envelope or simply be coincident with the junction between the two levels of roof of the building.

The Company is similar to many other Little Theatre and Amateur Dramatic Groups insofar as it finds it increasingly difficult to attract and retain new members and volunteers but the small core group that seems to drive it have awareness of the building's potential and ambitions to increase its flexibility and attractiveness to a wider range of events and activities to sustain it in the long term. The Little Theatre Company stages 3 or 4 plays each year plus a pantomime and encourages use of the building by other Companies whenever possible.

Auditorium Capacity:

142 comprising 122 on stalls and 20 on balcony

Stage details:

Performance space – width – 15.24m
Performance space – depth – 5.18m
Depth of apron – n/a
Wing space (Right and Left) – none
Proscenium height/width – not available
Orchestra pit (maximum no of players) - n/a
Height from stage floor to grid – not available
Rake – None

Merthyr Tydfil

Merthyr Tydfil
    The Myfanwy
    The Old Town Hall Arts Centre

The Myfanwy Theatre

Organisation: Merthyr Tydfil College

Address: Merthyr Tydfil College, Ynysfach Road, Merthyr Tydfil   CF48 1AR

Construction: 1952 (as a College); **Opening:** 2008 (as a theatre)

Architect: Yorke, Rosenberg & Mardall, London

Builder: unknown

Current Owner: Merthyr Tydfil College

History/previous names & ownership

The original College Hall which The Myfanwy now occupies was constructed in 1952 and was converted to a new flexible theatre space in 2008 with a new foyer created in the entrance hall of the existing college building.

Auditorium Capacity: 275

Stage details: Not available

Description

This theatre is a small multi-function space located on the first floor of a1950s College building with no external visibility whatsoever. The auditorium is a converted College Hall, rectangular in shape and set with retractable bleacher seating and demountable staging.

All of the internal walls are painted out black, the original Hall windows have been blocked up and it has a sacrificial black lino floor throughout. It is a very black black-box space!

There is insufficient height for flying but significant rigging points are provided across the stage area and throughout the auditorium for scenic effects, drapes (to form proscenium when required) and performance sound and lighting installations.

The audience foyer was created within the original double height college entrance hall by filling in a floor void and is served by a bar and cloakroom. There is no on-site Box Office and audience WCs are provided by general college provision in the vicinity.

There is a boiler room backstage which causes significant overheating problems in the workshops and technical areas that support the auditorium space (and cannot be turned off because of demand from other college courses). A fitness gym directly above the auditorium occasionally causes noise break-in problems. There is no mechanical ventilation to the auditorium.

The retractable bleacher seating is motorised but very heavy and due to the location of the existing door into the college hall, split into two blocks of audience separated by a wide aisle on the auditorium centreline which is considered not ideal for either audience or performers.

The theatre is the primary space serving the academic drama course at Merthyr College so the focus is on teaching students. Some public performances are promoted including drama and dance, live rock music and awards ceremonies for students, plus cabaret and jazz evenings. It was designed as a multi-function space but the conversion of the original College Hall is regarded by the operators as a 'make-do-and-mend' approach and several limitations to ambition prevail.

Replacement of the auditorium with a purpose designed space is in planning stages and will be available from 2013-14 as part of the ongoing conversion of Merthyr Tydfil Town Hall into an Arts Centre. On completion of the replacement theatre space, the current building containing the Myfanwy Theatre space is expected to be demolished to be replaced with a brand new College complex as part of what is to be known as the Merthyr Learning Quarter.

The Old Town Hall Arts Centre

Organisation: Chapter Arts Ltd/Merthyr College

Address: High Street, Merthyr Tydfil   CF48 1AR

Construction: Original Building: 1896-98; Arts Centre: planned for 2012 - 2013

Opening: Original building: 1898; Arts Centre planned for summer 2013

Architect: Original building: E.A Johnson, Abergavenny; Conversion to Arts Centre: Austin-Smith:Lord LLP, Cardiff

Builder: Original building: Harry Gibbon, Cardiff

Current Owner: Merthyr Tydfil Housing Association

History/previous names & ownership

The Old Town Hall was built when Merthyr Tydfil was the largest town in Wales. The Old Town Hall was an important symbol of civic pride, and its ambitious design reflects the aspirations of the age. It originally housed both the council offices and the law courts and police cells. A powerful and colourful late Victorian composition of mixed features, its style is generally described as French Renaissance.

The building was listed Grade II on 22nd August 1975 and subsequently upgraded to II* on 29th March 2011 by virtue of being regarded an exceptional example of a late 19th Century Municipal Building.

Merthyr Tydfil Council operated from the building until 1989. Following its demise as the seat of local government in 1989, the building became the privately owned Zone nightclub. The interior was adorned in garish colours: purples, pinks, oranges and turquoise, which jarred with the delicate decoration of the original design. A private sector consortium which subsequently purchased the property raised expectations in the local community with an ambitious plan for its restoration. However, its failure to deliver any results because of financial difficulties intensified doubts about future development and highlighted the importance of commercial viability over well intentioned but highly fanciful altruism.

The freehold interest in the site was acquired by Merthyr Tydfil Housing Association in August 2007 by which time the building was derelict and in need of substantial repair. Proposals for the Arts Centre project were produced by Powell Dobson Architects of Cardiff and were granted planning permission in February 2011. In March 2011 Austin-Smith:Lord Architects of Cardiff were appointed to propose certain variations to the design, resulting from changes to the brief and the inclusion of Merthyr College to the end user team, and then to further develop the scheme.

All images courtesy of
Austin-Smith:Lord LLP
Architects

The Project comprises the general repair and refurbishment of the Victorian building structure and fabric to provide a community based creative industries centre catering for visual, performing and media based arts together with provision of spaces for performance, exhibiting, production and sale; together with associated office space and café/catering facilities.

Demolition of a central core toilet block in the courtyard will allow the provision of new café and performance area with a contemporary glazed roof over. The courtyard presents an ideal space for small presentations of drama, music recital, lectures, local civic events and choral evenings. The room will combine the informality and excitement of an outdoor gathering with the convenience of being warm and weather proof.

There will be three venues within the Arts Centre, located within the original County Court House. The spaces will be flexible studios, for use for drama or music performances, rehearsal, film screenings, talks, conferencing, seminars, and exhibitions.

A revised Planning Application for the revised scheme was submitted in June 2011 and it is anticipated that a contractor will be appointed to commence construction and restoration early in 2012.

Auditorium Capacity:

Venue 1: 150; Venue 2: 55; Venue 3: 55;   Courtyard: 120

Rhondda Cynon Taff

Aberdare
The Coliseum
Cwmaman
The Institute
Cwmparc
Parc Hall
Penrhiwceiber
The Institute
Pontypridd
The Muni Arts Centre
The Town Hall
Ton Pentre
The Phoenix Centre
Trecynon
Public Hall
Treorchy
Abergorky Hall
The Park & Dare Theatre
Tylorstown
Welfare Hall

The Coliseum, Aberdare

Organisation: Rhondda Cynon Taff County Borough Council Cultural Services

Address: Mount Pleasant Street, Trecynon, Aberdare, CF44 8NG

Construction/Opening: 1938

Architect/Builder: unknown/unknown

Current Owner: Rhondda Cynon Taff County Borough Council

History/previous names & ownership

The Coliseum was purpose built as a Theatre and opened on 17th September 1938 for the Trecynon Welfare Committee who had purchased the site in 1926. It was built as a replacement for the old Trecynon Public Hall which dated from 1902 although the Public Hall has survived. It has been more or less untouched for the last 70 years with only minor changes to its appearance and size although for a period it was known as the New Welfare Hall. At some point the original Safety Curtain with its painted mural of the Festival of Britain was encapsulated to prevent asbestos migration. The mural still exists but is not visible and wasn't replicated on the new covering.

From 1989 ownership was vested in Cynon Valley Borough Council. In 1990 there was extensive renovation work carried out to the building envelope and in 1995 a fairly substantial extension was built to the side of the original building providing additional front of house facilities. Both phases of redevelopment works were carried out to designs by Kirkham, Williams & Lewis Architects. At this time the auditorium seating was replaced and capacity reduced. The Cynon Valley Museum & Gallery, Aberdare holds archive records of the original theatre construction and significant events and has the original box office kiosk as exhibit following its removal to increase public foyer space.

On the formation of the unitary authorities in Wales, ownership passed to Rhondda Cynon Taff County Borough Council and it has been operated by RCT Theatres under the aegis of Cultural Services to this date.

Description

The Coliseum is a freestanding purpose built theatre located in a largely residential area with a large surface car park adjacent. The front elevation is finished in coloured render, whilst one side and the rear elevation are exposed pennant stone, all surmounted by a slate roof. There are painted timber windows to the majority of openings (although there are not many that haven't been crudely blocked up in the past) with large glazed doors to the front entrance installed during the 1995 extension and front-of-house upgrade works.

Steps and a ramp provide access to the small ground floor foyer directly off the street. The original central freestanding box office kiosk was removed in 1995 and replaced with new open desk to one side with a sweet shop opposite inside the entrance extension. The audience foyer leads directly through central doors and a few steps into the dress circle and access to stalls is via a corridor and steps to house left and via the bar and stairs/lift to house right (the bar and lift access were installed in 1995 serving stalls but no disabled access is available to the dress circle). Doors between the foyer and auditorium are original 1938 hardwood glazed doors with brass ironmongery.

There is evidence of substantial water ingress in the passage to auditorium house left – the suspected cause is either vegetation on the roof, a blocked gutter or failure of a blocked up original window.

The auditorium is in a striking art deco style with plaster 'acoustic' nodules as features on the side walls and applied plaster ribs which emphasise the proscenium. The only works carried out in the auditorium in 1995 was the replacement of the audience seats (which reduced capacity by over 100) and basic redecoration.

There is no mechanical ventilation in the auditorium – the original building relied on fresh air 'chimneys' either side supplemented by fans. Now one side has been blocked up completely and the fan has broken on the other meaning ventilation during performances is a problem. It suffers from the perennial old theatre building problem of being too hot in summer and too expensive to heat properly in winter (although the aged boilers were replaced in the summer of 2010 as part of an energy saving initiative by the owner/operator and hopes are that this will solve this problem).

There is a small sound/light/projection control room at the rear of the dress circle/balcony and a permanent in-room mixing desk position at the back of stalls. There is no supplementary ventilation in the control room.

The stage is well equipped and has a full flytower and mid-height fly-galleries (although access to these is from on-stage via vertical ladders, only one of which has safety hoops). Loading is directly from outside (in the adjacent car park) via a single set of metal doors. The loading dock is at an unsatisfactory height for contemporary vehicles and several steps below stage level so loading takes place using a long metal ramp which is pushed out of the stage onto the back of trucks.

There is a permanent orchestra pit capable of accommodating approximately 20 musicians (though it is rarely used to capacity) and a stage extension is available to cover it when needed. Backstage access for performers is via an un-manned stage door well below car park level and only accessible via steps. There is no direct connection between front and back-of-house within the building.

There are 3 substantial dressing rooms below stage, with opening windows, but access to stage and orchestra pit is via narrow steep stairs.

The new 1 and 2 storey extension built in 1995 is finished in coloured render to match the original frontage and contains a large bar with adjacent fully equipped kitchen (seldom used), front-of-house access to the auditorium for people with movement disabilities, audience toilets, a large function room (without windows or straightforward access so also seldom used), a smaller function room (used by a toddlers playgroup amongst other local groups) and a workshop space that was unfinished.

This is a successful venue operated by an enthusiastic team and supported well by the Local Authority as part of their portfolio of 3 venues. With some further investment to complete the fitting-out of the extension and consideration given to back-stage access this could be an excellent venue for the next century.

Auditorium Capacity:

Original capacity is believed to have been over 700 but capacity was reduced in 1995 after the fitting of replacement audience seats to the current 588 – 347 at stalls, 241 on dress circle/balcony.

Stage details:

Performance space – width 9.9m
Performance space – depth 5.85m
Depth of apron – 2.85m
Wing space (Right and Left) – SR – 1.1m; SL - 1m
Proscenium height/width – height 6.6m; width 7.8m
Orchestra pit (maximum no of players) - 20
Height from stage floor to grid – 12m
Rake - None

The Institute, Cwmaman

Organisation: Cwmaman Institute

Address: Alice Place, Cwmaman, Rhondda Cynon Taff CF44 6NS

Construction/Opening: original building 1891-92, rebuilt 2001

Architect: 1892 building: Thomas Roderick of Clifton Street, Aberdare; 2001 rebuild: Gareth James of The James Partnership, Cardiff

Builder: 1892 building: Powell and Mansell, Cardiff; 2001 rebuild: unknown

Current Owner: Cwmaman Institute

History/previous names & ownership

The Institute was established in 1868 originally as a reading room, in a rent-free house donated by the Cwmaman Coal Company. Very soon a library was added, providing a place where local people could read books and children could be educated. Local-working men had ambitions to create a much-needed Institute and a campaign to raise funds to establish a suitable building began. In 1884, a committee of officials at Cwmaman Colliery started a scheme whereby a half penny in each pound was deducted weekly from the wages of workmen at the colliery and the movement to establish a purpose-built Public Hall & Institute was born.

The building was formally opened by Lord Aberdare on the 25th January 1892 as the Cwmaman Colliery Workmen's Institute and Hall and included a public hall with seating for 700, reading rooms, a billiard room and a caretaker's cottage. The Original building was largely destroyed by fire in 1896 but was restored and reopened in 1897. In 1906 a second (lesser) Hall was added to the original building then in 1925 a single storey extension was also added. Public Cinema facilities were added in 1954 and the building became a licensed premises in 1967.

However, the fate of the Institute was inextricably linked to the demise of coal mining in the Cynon Valley. With the closure of local collieries from the early 1960s onwards, the Institute found it harder to raise local funding and commitment. The fabric of the building began to deteriorate during the 1960s and 1970s, while at the same time, membership of local groups and societies grew and there was new interest in maintaining the building as a community centre for Cwmaman.

Extensive external restoration works were carried out in 1992-93 and then almost the entire building was demolished to allow the construction of the new building behind the retained façade on Alice Place in the late 1990's. The building reopened in 2001.

Description

This is a new building constructed behind the original street façade of a Victorian Miners' Institute. The retained original façade is of pennant stone with feature detailing in red brick, whilst all of the new building envelope is finished in buff brick with blue metal windows/curtain walling and a slate roof. The building provides its local community with a contemporary version of an old Miners' Institute comprising bar, lounge (used for regular acoustic/unplugged music performances) and function rooms with a dedicated theatre auditorium and concert room for larger scale performances and events. In the tradition of Welsh Miners' Institutes, the entrance foyer is small but is a light and airy double height space benefitting from the retained windows in the original façade. There is a small Box Office and Sweet Shop at the entry level.

Auditorium Capacity: Original: 700.

Current: 300 (200 at stalls, 100 on balcony)
Concert Hall: 250 approx

Stage details: Not available

The Theatre has 300 seats with 200 on a raked stalls floor and 100 on a stepped balcony with smaller subdivided sections forming box-like enclosures to the rear of the balcony. The auditorium walls are finished in blue–painted plaster with veneered timber feature panels applied to accentuate the proscenium and provide a degree of sound absorption on the back wall behind the audience. The ceiling is white painted plaster and the floors are carpeted throughout. The auditorium is air-conditioned although utilises a top-down supply system which causes cold air dumping issues occasionally for occupants of seats against the side walls. This is seen by the management as a major design failure.

There is an orchestra pit/forestage elevator giving flexibility to the stage size and performance type without impacting on audience capacity. The stage is well equipped, with full flying, a rear-stage area and decent wing space. Access for loading is directly from the adjacent road and there is an un-manned stage door in this location too. The Stage Door provides the entry point for visitors using the Institute bar and Lounge facilities such that the 'main entrance' to the building is only open when there is an event on in the theatre auditorium. There are 3 dedicated dressing rooms available for adults with a separate children's dressing room, all located one storey below stage and none of them having access to daylight. All levels of the building are however fully accessible and well served by lifts and ramps at floor level changes. There are plentiful WCs and shower facilities for performers at this level.

Adjacent to the dressing rooms are 2 large function rooms connected/separated by a sliding/folding acoustic panelled wall. Both rooms have wonderful views through large windows to the mountains and forestry that surround the site. These rooms are well used by the community. Above the function rooms is a large space known as the 'concert hall'. This room has a raised stage and a ballroom dance floor and a large bar servery as well as spectacular views through large windows over the surrounding landscape. For orchestral concerts it can seat an audience of approximately 200. This room is popular with the local community for wedding receptions and conference events and is served by an adjacent fully equipped kitchen. Both the function rooms and concert space are finished simply with white painted plastered walls and suspended mineral fibre ceiling tiles in an exposed grid. All spaces are mechanically ventilated and have ample performance lighting and sound system installations.

The rebuilt Institute opened with 15 full-time staff but now operates with 3 full-time and approximately 20 part-time staff. Revenue funding is a major concern. The theatre is rarely used either for visiting shows or cinema events and the centre appears to sustain itself by sales of alcohol from the bars and lounges, local community group use and small scale local meetings/business conferences.

Photograph: www.cwmamaninstitute.com

Parc Hall, Cwmparc

Organisation: Cwmparc Community Association

Address: Parc Road, Cwmparc, Treorchy CF42 6LD

Construction/Opening: 1908

Architect/Builder: unknown/unknown

Current Owner: Cwmparc Community Association

History/previous names & ownership

The Cwmparc Miners Institute building was constructed at some point in the late 19th Century but no information survives to confirm the actual date of construction.

In 1908 the Park & Dare Workmen's Hall was built as an extension to the original Institute by mining entrepreneur David Davies of LLandinam and was operated and managed by the Park & Dare Miners Welfare Institute. A commemorative plaque survives in the auditorium with the following dedication (translated from the original welsh):

'Respect this, for respect is owed. This plaque was placed to show the ages to come: the hall was given for free by David Davies YSW.AS Llandinam in 1874. After this, there was an extensive conversion for it to be a reading place, by the Ocean Company in 1880. By blessing the righteous, the city is praised'

There is no available information about the building apparently constructed in 1874 (unless this is in fact the original Institute and this plaque was moved into the 'new' auditorium in or around 1908). The current building has an inscription above the main entrance giving a date of 1908. The Hall is believed to have been built as a theatre for the choirs and theatre groups from the workers and families of the Parc and Dare mining community and preceded the later Park & Dare Theatre in the centre of Treorchy by 5 years.

Both the Institute and Hall were closed for beneficial use and left derelict at a date presumed to be around the early 1980's or coincident with the Miners' Strike until it was purchased by the local community under the guise of the Cwmparc Community Welfare Association and re-opened after extensive renovations. In 1988 the boiler block was rebuilt to its original external dimensions and in 1990 an extension was added to the Welfare Hall to provide improved fire escape and toilets.

In October 2010 it was announced by the Management that the Hall was to be mothballed because of lack of income and it closed in December 2010. The Institute remains open and continues to provide services to the community.

Description

The building is located on a fork in the main road through Cwmparc and is deceptively low-key.

The Theatre (originally named Park & Dare Workmen's Hall) was added to an original Miners' Institute building in 1908 and provides the primary 'front door' to the venue directly on the front elevation as the visitor approaches the building.

There is very little evidence on the outside of the building of the presence of a theatre and the building appears very low because the entrance is some distance below pavement level due to the lie of the land. The theatre building is constructed of red brick with sandstone features and detailing and the front entrance is an unusual half octagon. The roof is of welsh slate. Above the main entrance there is a low porch surmounted by a semi-circular gable with sandstone orb and inset panel with the name of the building and date of opening inscribed.

There are large hardwood framed windows either side of the entrance doors and along the rear elevation but it would appear that any windows on the street frontage were blocked up and the street frontage wall covered with render at the time of the 1987 renovations.

The original Victorian Institute building is built of local stone with red brick feature detailing and is 3 storeys tall (the lower floor effectively below street level because of the sloping site). It now consists of various rooms serving the local community including a café (not open at the time of writing), computer room, offices for development and management staff, a large hall at first floor level used by community groups and for evening classes and meetings, toilets, and a photographic dark room. There is no lift at present within the building and disabled access to the upper floor is via the 'side' entrance and stair lifts installed in 2009.

On entering the theatre building there is a small holding area containing a licensed bar in place of the original ticket desk. It is a double height volume separated from the auditorium beyond by an elaborate hardwood framed glazed screen wall. Entry into the auditorium is either side of the bar counter into the rear of the audience seating area. The auditorium is a real surprise. Despite the 1987 renovation of the building it has survived largely in its original form (albeit with fewer fixed seats, non-original colour scheme (presumed) and a 'new' lacquered timber strip ceiling).

The audience seating area steps gently down to a large area of flat parquet flooring in front of the stage – approximately 120 of the original seats remain. Large windows on house left afford spectacular views across the valley and have had roller blinds fitted over them to provide a degree of black-out for theatrical performances.

The stage is raised above the floor by approximately 800mm, the original stage construction being an unusual 'U' shape with a central area presumably left open to accommodate an orchestra. This 'cut-out' can be filled with removable rostra units to extend the stage up to and beyond the proscenium.

The proscenium is modestly decorated with a small painted plaster moulding and there have been additions to the pros wall decoration made by the current owner/management that are clearly not original.

The ceiling is of lacquered timber strips (presumed not original) supported by timber beams/joists exposed below the soffit and at their junction with the auditorium side walls.

The most striking feature of the auditorium is the glazed screen wall at the rear of the audience seating – a full height delicate hardwood framed glazed delight and extremely unusual.

A permanent PA system and fixed lighting bars have been sympathetically installed into the room.

There is no flytower over the stage but rigging bars have been installed to allow the suspension of drapes and fixed scenic effects as well as visiting company/band sound systems and performance lighting.

Behind the stage there are various rooms providing limited storage (primarily of the loose auditorium chairs) and accommodation for technical crew and visiting performers. There are no dedicated dressing rooms per se. It is possible to move between the auditorium and original Institute building through the backstage area.

This is a jewel of an auditorium sadly unheard of in the wider region and even disregarded by much of its local community. Attempts to create a reputation as a venue for up and coming bands to play live have been made with some success but have recently been abandoned due to a run of poor ticket sales and loss-making promotions.

There is intent to commence operating a time-bank credit system in the near future to try to encourage more engagement by the local community but if this is unsuccessful the future of this venue seems bleak.

Financial difficulties and withdrawal of funding for an Arts Development Officer mean that a decision to mothball the theatre from December 2010 was taken in October (although it will still be available for hire by community groups or external promoters)

Auditorium Capacity:

Original capacity was 300, reduced in 1987 during extensive renovations.

Current capacity is 240 (120 fixed seats, 120 loose seats)

Stage details:

Performance space – width – 7.5m
Performance space – depth – 4m
Depth of apron – variable (rostra units) - 1.2m
Wing space (Right and Left) – not available
Proscenium height/width – not available
Orchestra pit (maximum no of players) – n/a
Height from stage floor to grid – no grid
Rake - None

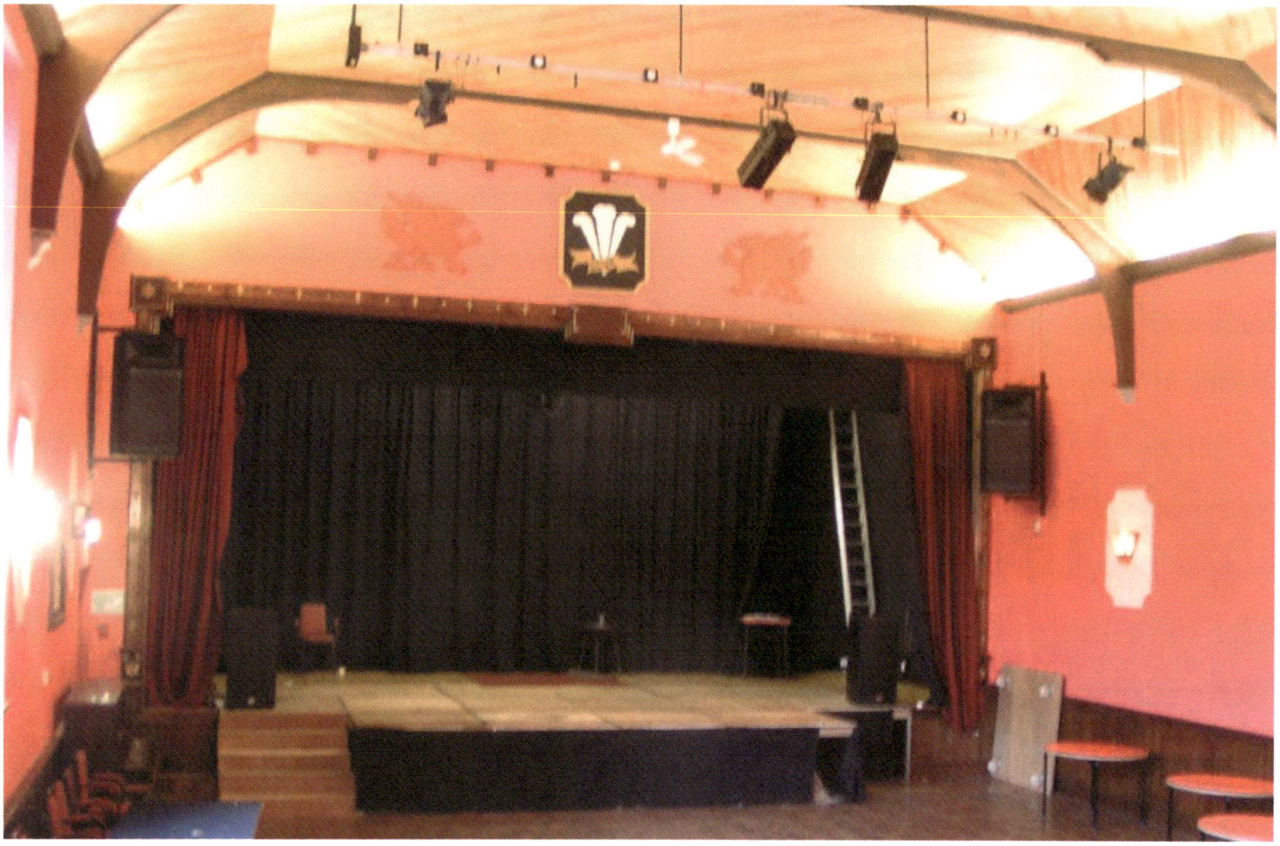

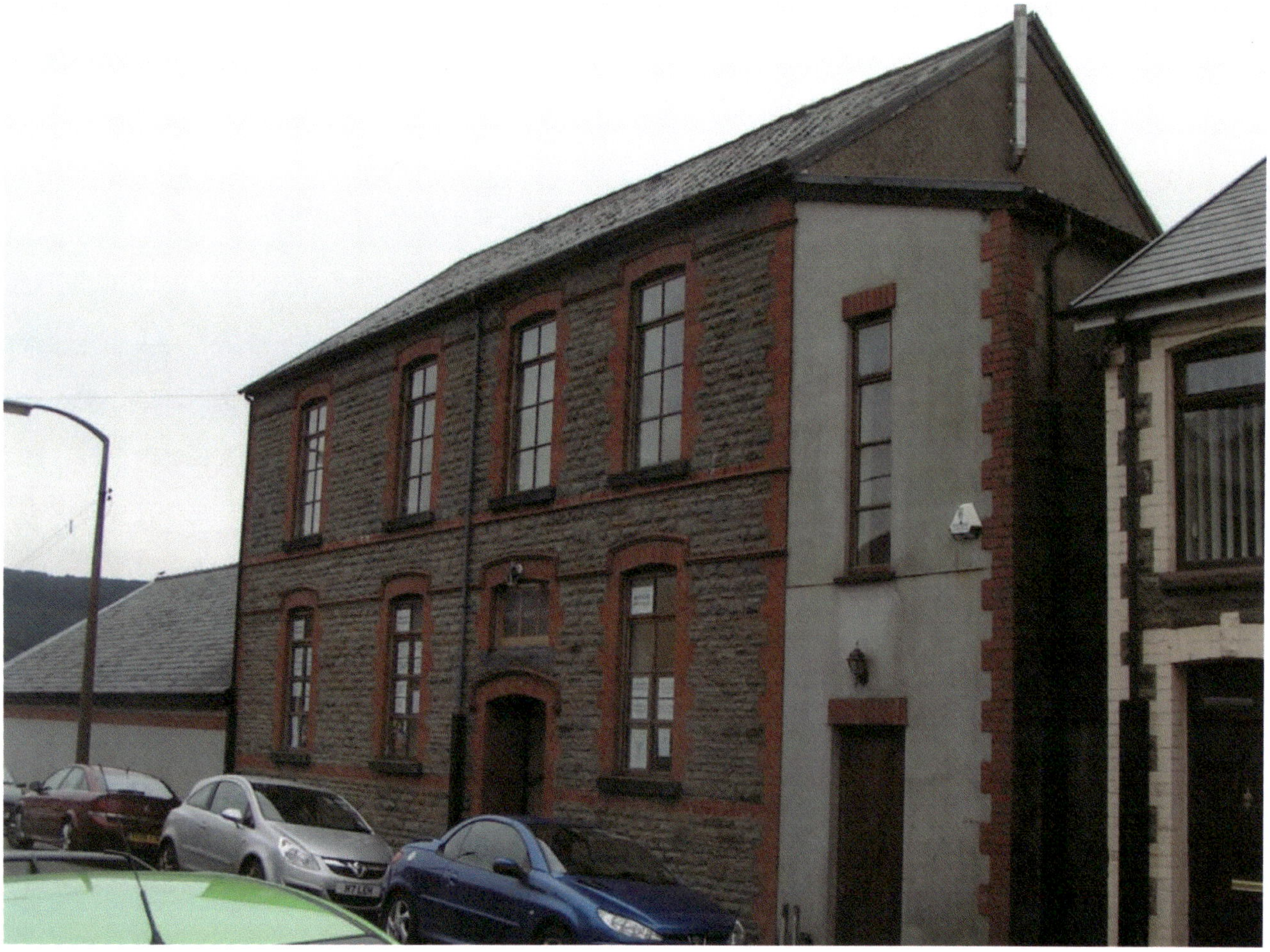

The Institute, Penrhiwceiber

Organisation: Penrhiwceiber Institute & Community Society

Address: 35 Penrhiwceiber Road, Penrhiwceiber, Mountain Ash CF45 3SP

Construction/Opening: 1887-88

Architect: Edward H Bruton, Cardiff

Builder: unknown

Current Owner: Penrhiwceiber Institute & Community Society

History/previous names & ownership

Penrhiwceiber Workmen's Hall and Institute has its origins at the turn of the 20th Century. Land was conveyed to the organisation as far back as 1892 and under the Friendly Society Act of 1896 the trustees registered their society on 2nd June 1900. The society held leasehold and freehold ownership of several parcels of land which included a library and reading room. The current hall located at Penrhiwceiber Road was built in 1887-88 and was paid for by local miners by deduction of wages. Ownership was vested in the Penrhiwceiber Colliery Miners' Institute Trustees. The new building contained a theatre auditorium above a large Committee Room, Library and Snooker Room with smaller reading rooms and a dressing room for use by performers. The building was opened as the Penrhiwceiber Miners' Institute and Public Hall but has been commonly known as Ceiber Hall by the local community throughout its life. From 1964 to 1993 it was more formally known as Penrhiwceiber Workmen's Hall and is now known as Penrhiwceiber Institute.

In 1900 the original building was extended to designs by Morgan and Elford Architects.

At some time in the early 20th Century a projection room was constructed at the back of the balcony, cantilevered out over the pavement and providing a unique architectural feature that distinguishes the hall from all of its peers. The Hall was used primarily as a cinema until 1964 when that use ceased and the Trust ended its relationship with the Friendly Society and registered with the Charities Commission. The Hall was given over to full-time bingo use until 1992.

According to extracts from the 1968 Annual Report of the Coal Industry Social Welfare Organisation renovations to the foyer were carried out in that year. The Library was converted into a cafeteria and an adjoining smaller room (presumed to have been a Reading Room) converted into a kitchen at some point, possibly around the same time.

In 1992 the Trust was removed from the Charities Commission register and ownership passed to a new Board of Trustees of the Penrhiwceiber Institute and Community Society who have managed and operated the Hall ever since.

The building was completely refurbished in 1992-93 to designs by Architects Community Design Service with funding assistance from Cynon Valley Borough Council, The Welsh Development Agency and Mid-Glamorgan County Council. It also received Urban Programme funding from the Welsh Office as part of the Community Revival Strategy for Penrhiwceiber. The building was listed Grade II on 3rd October 2003.

During the later part of 2010 and early 2011 students of the Interior Design course at the University of Glamorgan based in Cardiff designed and executed a renovation of the foyer and the largest room on the lower ground floor level in advance of a re-launch of the venue with emphasis on local community use. The process was filmed by BBC Wales with weekly reports shown on the consumer programme 'X-Ray'.

Description

Located on the main road through the centre of the village, this building is larger than its neighbours and instantly recognisable because of the projection room extension cantilevered out over the pavement above the main entrance and the yellow paint finish that has been applied over the original stone at some point.

The main frontage features dressed stone over a rough pennant stone plinth and a pair of large windows either side of the centrally located main entrance doors. To the side of the main body of the building is a smaller section with the appearance of a small shopfront and currently providing accommodation for the venue management, Communities First team and desk space for other organisations serving the local community who use the building as a base.

Auditorium Capacity:

Original capacity unknown and has certainly changed by the removal of fixed seats from front half of stalls (date unknown) and the collapse and non-replacement of approximately 12 seats on the balcony (various unknown dates). Current capacity is 300 maximum but is limited to 240 by the management to avoid overcrowding (comprising 104 on balcony and 136 on stalls)

Stage details: Not available

The rough stone plinth extends around the side of the building and due to the topography of the steeply sloping site provides the envelope to the remaining rooms that constituted the original Miners' Institute in a lower ground floor. The side walls of the Hall are painted brickwork above the pennant stone plinth. All of the windows on the side elevation (4 to the Hall and 3 to the lower ground floor rooms) have been blocked up at some point (most likely when the building was used primarily for cinema) and their existence is invisible on the inside of the building. The brickwork walls of the Hall are left unpainted on the rear elevation and the original door (and block and tackle) providing access directly onto the stage from the rear has been bricked up. The accommodation to the rear of the management offices has an untreated render finish to the walls. The roof is welsh slate and features a pair of ridge ventilators over the Hall. The building fabric appears to be in good condition.

Entry through the main entrance with its Victorian Gothic door surround is up one shallow step from pavement level and leads directly into a small foyer/entrance hall containing the original ticket hatch on one side and a single flight of stairs up to the auditorium balcony on the other. This area was redecorated in 2010 and features plain white walls, new slate-effect floor tiles and lighting.

From the entrance hall a shallow ramp leads directly into the rear of the auditorium stalls through a pair of single doors at the end of aisles between fixed audience seating under the balcony and leading to an open flat-floored area in front of the stage that gives the venue useful flexibility in audience size and disposition for different events by the use of loose seats. The auditorium is quite simple and understated in its form and decoration – there is no flamboyance and a real honesty in the use of materials to the walls and ceiling – this is truly a working hall, not a show-off space and it is a simple rectangle on plan.

The floor has sheet linoleum and the original auditorium chairs are simple and functional and their red velour upholstery is the only hint of 'luxury' in the place. The side walls are plain plastered and painted in a soft pink colour throughout over a dado rail with heavily textured and typically Victorian patterned and textured wallpaper between dado and skirting as a hard-wearing surface in the area where the audience comes into contact with the walls most. The wallpaper is used across the stage riser and on the balcony front. The ceiling of the auditorium is lined with painted timber boards following the pitch of the roof and the roof purlins, primary timber beams and metal tie-bars are left exposed in the space, again in an expression of honest functionality rather than for any decorative benefit or purpose.

The original proscenium continues the utilitarian theme with its painted timber panelled surround set at an angle on the sides and flat across the top. The doors leading off stage on both sides represent a small departure from the plain approach everywhere else and are almost playfully set in a quasi-classical frame and portico-like frame overpanel. There is a large curved applied framing feature panel over the proscenium with the name of the hall painted on it, the whole surmounted by a split pediment moulded timber feature at its crown and this appears to have been a later addition, almost certainly not original. The large cantilevered brackets supporting this curved feature on either side of the proscenium have the dates 1888 and 1993 painted on them (the original construction date and most recent restoration date) which suggests this elaborate proscenium frame was a later addition.

There is no orchestra pit and no theatre technical equipment that would support a performance of any size or complexity and the stage is significantly higher than any of the surrounding accommodation making it difficult to access and load scenic effects and equipment onto. Generally any loading is done through the front door of the building and through the auditorium as access to the rear of the building is non-existent due to surrounding residential properties and roads.

As with so many auditoria of this age it is reported to be very cold in winter (despite the 1990's high-level radiant heaters slung below the ceiling) and very hot in summer (the original ventilators at the ridge were decommissioned in the 1993 restoration)

There is a single large dressing room adjacent and slightly below stage level which is split into two by a central curtain when the need arises. This is one of the few rooms in the building that hasn't had its use changed over the life of the building and it also retains its original window with views over the valley beyond. In addition to the stairs leading to the balcony from the entrance hall another flight of stairs connects the stalls level to the balcony on the house right side of the building in an area lying between front and back-of-house. This staircase enters the balcony in the small audience side balcony/open box area on house-right. The original seating on the balcony remains in use but in slightly smaller numbers than originally as prior to the current owners taking control, when seats broke they were simply removed and scrapped rather than being mended or replaced.

Entry to the projection room is via two doors leading into a small curved lobby on each side. Although now glazed the lobbies were originally open balconies. The projection room hasn't been used for cinema for many years but has recently had server racks installed for a surround-sound speaker system and may be used for sound and/or lighting mixing should the frequency of live performances in the auditorium increase.

The lower ground floor accommodates the Institute rooms which are now used to provide facilities for a wide range of community groups. There is a domestic standard kitchen serving a larger room (originally the library and reading room) but it is in need of new equipment to service the ambitions to open a community café facility in the future. The ex-Library room has been redecorated to a high standard by the students of the Interior Design course at the University of Glamorgan. The original snooker room contains 2 original 19th century snooker tables and a small bar area but is not often used for snooker anymore. The original Committee Room holds a collection of photographs of the various Boards of Trustees who have looked after the building during its life but all of the original bespoke furniture that was in the room has long been lost.

Clearly this is a successfully operated and managed venue with an ambitious and enthusiastic management and Board of Trustees aiming to return the Hall to the centre of community life. Innovations such as creating a village Film Festival in 2011 and plans for further developments are tangibly connecting with the community and should ensure its future viability. The auditorium is used for a wide range of events including live performances, cinema and bingo sessions twice a week. Almost every other space in the building is used with the office on Penrhiwceiber Road housing the Penrhiwceiber Community Revival Strategy Group formed in 1997 and The Institute is home to the Ultimate Stage Company - an up and coming Youth stage company that presents two shows each year on the stage in lieu of rent. It is also the home base for the Penrhiwceiber Communities First Partnership Board and Residents and Tenants including Glasbrook Committee, Labour Party, C.I.S.W.O, and various social groups, the local health group has arranged several diabetic clinics in the building, the Police and local AM have held surgeries, and Interlink has provided Grant Advice surgeries. There is a youth club and during school holidays the large rooms on the lower ground floor are given over to a children's play scheme. Revenue funding remains a constant challenge as does the replacement of the older members of the Board of Trustees with younger people who share the current Board's vision.

The Muni Arts Centre, Pontypridd

Organisation: Rhondda Cynon Taff County Borough Council Cultural Services

Address: Gelliwastad Road, Pontypridd, CF37 2DP

Construction: 1895 (as Wesleyan Chapel) **Opening:** 1968 (as Arts Centre)

Architect: Arthur O. Evans, Pontypridd

Builder: unknown

Current Owner: Rhondda Cynon Taff County Borough Council

History/previous names & ownership

Constructed as a Wesleyan Chapel in 1895, the building was a place of worship until closing in 1961. It passed into the ownership of Taff Ely District Council and was converted into a building for entertainment in 1968. A commemorative stained glass window was installed over the entrance doors at this time and the building was re-named 'Municipal Hall'. It was used for dances and musical events.

In 1993 it passed into the ownership of the new Unitary Authority of Rhondda Cynon Taff County Borough Council and was converted into an Arts Centre and renamed The Muni. The building was listed Grade II on 26th February 2001.

Description

The Muni is a typical early 20th Century ecclesiastical building, stone built and with steep slated roof and tower and spire over the main entrance. It is located in a prominent position at the back of pavement on one of the principal arterial roads through the town. The external fabric appears to be in decent condition but on closer inspection there are many minor repairs required to ensure the longevity of the envelope.

Entry through the original main door to the chapel passes under a stained glass panel installed by the Taff Ely Council at some point after the building ceased use as a place of worship, identifying the period 1968 – 1993 as one of some significance although the current building manager was unable to shed any light on it.

A small lobby contains an information board and the Centre's Box Office with Admin office suite immediately behind. Entry into the main part of the building enables the visitor to turn immediately left into the Main Hall, right into the Cafeteria (that serves as the Centre's audience foyer for performances) or carry on upstairs to the Castle Gallery Space, further administration offices and a route to the Main Hall backstage and dressing rooms. It's all rather domestic scale at this point, with all of the circulation contained in a small area and the stairs being quite modest in both width and detail. There is no theatrical flamboyance here.

The Main Hall was the original chapel space, flat-floored and rectangular in plan and quite tall (although it is clear that the current ceiling is unlikely to be the original which may remain in the void above). The chapel pews were removed at the point of deconsecration and a new ballroom dance floor installed. The audience is accommodated on a combination of loose seating and retractable bleacher seating. The bleachers are accessible from the front and rear at first floor level. A large and well equipped stage has been constructed although there is insufficient height above it for flying. It has direct access to a loading area outside (over land that is not owned by the venue) and to the main street to stage right. There is no mechanical ventilation in the main hall (minimal high level extract is installed but is largely ineffectual when the Hall is full) and heating is only by low level domestic scale radiators. It therefore suffers from the stereotypical theatre problem of being too hot in the summer and difficult to keep warm in the winter.

There are 2 dressing rooms backstage with direct access to both stage and front-of-house but not for people with movement limitations. Performers have to cross the stage from the get-in to reach the dressing rooms. A projection/control room is at the rear of the audience seating and an in-room mixing desk position has been created on the top row of bleachers.

The venue is truly multi-functional and its programme includes theatre, stand-up comedy, live music (especially local, emerging rock acts), dances and wedding receptions. The foyer cafeteria is open all day every day and appears well used as a community meeting space. The Gallery space at first floor is tending to become a photographic exhibition gallery and conference space used increasingly frequently by local businesses and associations.

There is definite intent by the management to focus on making the Main Hall venue a significant live music destination – discussions have commenced to increase its licensed capacity and a new fire detection system has recently been installed at the behest of the licensing authority to this effect.

Auditorium Capacity:

352 theatre style

(120 loose seats on flat floor with 232 on retractable

 bleacher seating);

400-450 standing

Stage details:

Performance space – width – 14.9m
Performance space – depth – 9.12m
Depth of apron – n/a
Wing space (Right and Left) – SR: 3.93m; SL: 4.3m
Proscenium height/width – height: 4.87m; width: 6.4m
Orchestra pit (maximum no of players) – n/a
Height from stage floor to grid – 5.2m
Rake -None

The Town Hall, Pontypridd

Organisation: None

Address: Market Street, Pontypridd CF37 2ST

Construction/Opening: 1885

Architect: Thomas Rowlands, Pontypridd

Builder: unknown

Current Owner: The Pontypridd Market Company

History/previous names & ownership

The building was constructed by the Pontypridd Market and Town Hall Company in 1885 on the site of an earlier market and was originally known as The Old Market Hall. Further buildings including Market Chambers and the Market Tavern Hotel were built immediately adjacent over the next 5 years forming an impressive group of civic buildings in the centre of the town.

Throughout the first part of the 20th Century, the auditorium was used for Music Hall shows and as a cinema and the original opulent and highly decorated Victorian interior was replaced with the current art deco inspired decoration in the 1930s.

In the 1950's The Town Hall became landlocked by the over-roofing of the surrounding market, the original bath stone frontage was removed and the Hall's foyers were extended with an example of uncompromising brutalist concrete architecture. Use as a cinema continued along with occasional use for Bingo until 1982 when the Hall was closed and it has remained un-used and derelict since.

The building was listed Grade II on 17th July 1990, by virtue of being part of the curtilage of the Pontypridd Indoor Market. It was not listed in its own right and was considered to have no significant architectural or theatrical merit or value but the listing was amended by Cadw on 26th February 2001 such that it now records the market complex being listed for architectural interest as a late Victorian public building retaining original character and for group value with the Old Market Hall and Market Tavern Hotel.

Description

The building is a major landmark on the town sky-line because of its tall flytower and because it stands on top of the already sizeable market complex. The theatre was closed in 1982 and has been un-maintained for a great many years, the envelope is in an advanced state of decay and the building is overgrown with vegetation in many places. The envelope is almost entirely shrouded in a dark, dirty grey cementitious render of indeterminate age although there are signs that once there were more elaborate treatments and materials. The original Architects drawings illustrate an extremely opulent French renaissance style of architecture with the entire front façade finished in dressed Bath stone. In the 1950's the original spectacular bath stone classical front elevation treatment was removed and a brutalist concrete extension added in its place. Most of the original windows to the upper levels of what was the front-of-house in that extension are now either boarded up or broken. The roof ridge appears to be sagging along its length which implies structural weakness but there are no signs of failure of the slate tiling.

There is no obvious means of access to the building from the market below (a market stall now stands in front of the original front entrance) and whilst there is a pair of covered routes to the building from adjacent streets and built over the surrounding market roof which provided a way in independent of the market they too are now inaccessible. The only remaining access into the auditorium is via what originally served as the stage door, tucked away at the end of one of the alley-type approaches to the market and with no remaining signage or other indication that the securely locked door provides a route into the theatre above.

The architectural features and wall lining of the theatre auditorium are entirely covered with and in some cases fabricated in asbestos based materials and access is not possible without appropriate protective clothing. It is believed that removal of the asbestos would inevitably remove the majority of the existing architectural features but would be an essential precursor to any restoration efforts.

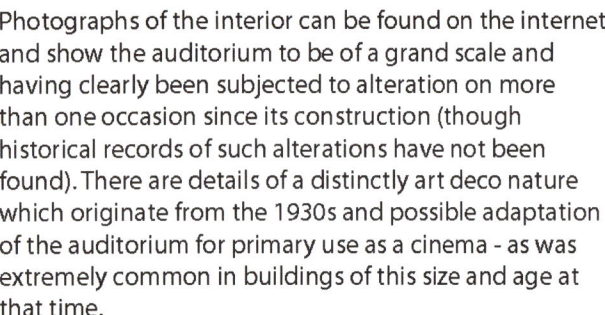

Photographs of the interior can be found on the internet and show the auditorium to be of a grand scale and having clearly been subjected to alteration on more than one occasion since its construction (though historical records of such alterations have not been found). There are details of a distinctly art deco nature which originate from the 1930s and possible adaptation of the auditorium for primary use as a cinema - as was extremely common in buildings of this size and age at that time.

These details include elaborate grilles in the ceiling and a softly curving edge moulding to the central area of the ceiling, both picked out in a starkly contrasting white against the dark blue ceiling, as well as the treatment of the auditorium side walls as they approach the proscenium.

There is a pair of small audience boxes very close to the stage that suggests an earlier more elaborately modelled interior than the slightly austere version that exists to date.

All of the original audience seats appear to be in place although some have clearly suffered damage through the years of neglect. They do not, in general, appear to be beyond repair. They have deep red patterned upholstery over timber seats and backs with what appear to be cast iron side panels.

Whilst the balcony area is relatively clear of debris (one or two ceiling panels appear to have fallen from place), the stalls seating is almost invisible under large piles of debris and detritus and the building appears to have been used for some considerable time as some kind of general store for things too difficult to throw away.

The balcony front is a very simple and plain element, quite close to the proscenium and making the stalls overhang quite deep. The balcony front is elegantly connected to the proscenium following a soft curve around the front of the balcony audience and enclosing at balcony level exits to the stage end of the building on either side of the stage.

There is a cinema projection room at the rear of the balcony, complete with a pair of derelict film projectors and a variety of other projection room ephemera still in place.

Auditorium Capacity:

The original seating capacity is believed to have been over 1700. No changes to capacity are recorded.

Stage details: not available

Interior images courtesy of Adam Slater

The Phoenix Community Cinema and Theatre, Ton Pentre

Organisation: Rhondda Community Development Association

Address: Church Road, Ton Pentre, Rhondda CF41 7EH

Construction/Opening: 1895

Architect: Abel Richards (Institute); Jacob Rees (Theatre)

Builder: Alban Richards

Current Owner: Rhondda Community Development Association

History/previous names & ownership

The Maindy & Eastern Workmen's Institute opened in 1895 at cost of £4,000. The original hall consisted of a ground floor with a news room, refreshment room and caretaker's room and a first floor library and committee room whilst in the attic were two bedrooms and storerooms. The Workmen's Hall/Theatre was constructed as an extension to the original Institute in 1904 to designs by Jacob Rees of Merthyr Tydfil and the original seating capacity given as 630.

In 1908 projection equipment to show silent movies was installed and for an unknown period the Hall was rented out to a private company and it became a full-time cinema.

From 1931 to 1971 the building was operated as a cinema and early in this period there was an upgrade of the cinema equipment to allow playing of talkies. In the period from the 1940's to 1971 the building was known as The Ton Pentre Workmen's Hall.

From 1971 to 1989 following conversion it operated as a bingo hall and in 1989 it was closed and left derelict. The building was rescued by the Rhondda Community Development Association with funding from the European Community and in 1991 it re-opened as The Phoenix Centre after some restoration works had been carried out. The building was listed Grade II on 23rd December 1996.

Description

The original Institute Building is of domestic scale and typical in appearance of large residential properties of its era. The Theatre extension built 10 years later is of much grander pretensions although is rather tucked away down a side street. Both buildings are faced with stone and have slate roofs and, where windows remain they appear to be original. (Many windows to the hall have been blocked up – presumably as part of changes made when the building operated primarily as a cinema). The main entrance to both buildings is now down a side street into the theatre foyer space set between the 2 constructions and is elevated above the pavement limiting wheelchair access. The ground floor cinema/theatre foyer contains a simple box office/refreshments kiosk and symmetrical stairs leading up to the upper balcony of the main hall and the first floor rooms of the Institute (including the original Miners' Library). There is no lift so no access to the upper balcony, library or owner's offices on the first floor for wheelchairs.

The auditorium is rectangular and has something of a chapel feel to it. There is an upper balcony and the balcony front extends along the sides of the room to the proscenium. The decoration is slightly austere with very little in the way of feature mouldings or details and the like. The side balconies feature a single row of timber bench seating rather than individual upholstered seats. The side balconies are supported by slender cast iron columns and the ceiling of the room is carried by trusses supported by buttress brackets projecting into the room from the side walls.

There is no orchestra pit and the stage projects beyond the proscenium. The stage is flat. There is a flytower contained within the volume of the building with full flying capability although currently a more or less permanent cinema screen and sound system is filling most of the available stage area. The screen can be flown out for theatrical events. There is decent wing space either side of the proscenium opening. There is no physical internal connection between front-of-house and back-of-house spaces apart from through the auditorium.

There are small dressing rooms below stage level, accessed via steep and narrow staircases so access for disabled performers is not possible and moving equipment around is difficult. There is no dedicated loading bay or get-in and equipment is brought in via large doors in the rear of the stage leading directly to the adjacent street.

The building is currently in survival mode, barely breaking even by operating as cinema and community venue (eg Bingo for OAP's every Monday afternoon), some office space is currently rented out to a Local Authority Advice Centre and the Resident Performance Company (ARC Entertainers) which has a contract to present 3 shows/year in the theatre.

The owner is a charitable organisation and relies on Grants and revenue from ticket sales to sustain the building fabric and the community facility.

Auditorium Capacity:

Originally 630, presume reduced following conversion to Bingo use, current capacity is 327 total, comprising 215 on stalls and 112 on the upper balcony

Stage details:

Performance space – width – 9m
Performance space – depth – 6.62m
Depth of apron – not available
Wing space (Right and Left) – SR - 2.2m; SL - 2.2m
Proscenium height/width – height - 5m; width 9m
Orchestra pit - None
Height from stage floor to grid – 5.5m
Rake –None

Public Hall, Trecynon

Organisation: Trustees of the Trecynon Public Hall and Library

Address: Mill Street, Trecynon

Construction: 1902 **Opening:** 1903

Architect: C. H. Elford

Builder: D. Tyssul Davies

Current Owner: Trustees of the Trecynon Public Hall and Library

History/previous names & ownership

Construction of the Free Library and Hall in Trecynon commenced with a foundation stone laying ceremony held on 25th August 1902. Stones were laid by D. A. Thomas MP, the Right Honourable Robert George, Lord Windsor, Lord Lieutenant of the County of Glamorgan and Rees Llewellyn esq, Chairman of the Board of Trustees.

Funds for the construction of the Hall came from a variety of sources, including Bwllfa Colliery - £105; Lord Windsor - £50; D A Thomas MP - £50; whilst public subscription raised £180. A commemorative stone was unveiled on the building in November of 1902 expressing gratitude to Andrew Carnegie esq of Skibo Castle, Dornoch, Sutherland who gave £1,500 towards the cost of construction.

The hall was officially opened on 10th March 1903 by Lord Kinnaird and a grand concert was organised.

Little is known of the history of the building through the 20th Century.

In 2009 a funding grant from Rhondda Cynon Taff Council that had previously maintained the operation of the library was withdrawn and since then the library has moved out of the building leaving the ground floor unoccupied. At around this time, the cost of renovating the building was estimated at £300,000 by Trustees.

In October 2010 the Trustees submitted an application to RCT Council for a Premises Licence/Club Premises Certificate for the building but in 2011 it is standing empty and for all intent and purpose is derelict.

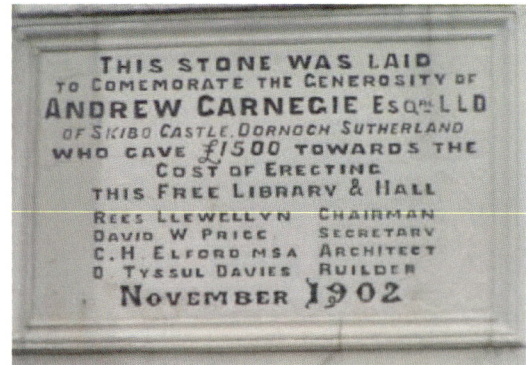

Description

This is a curious little building, located in the centre of Trecynon on the edge of Aberdare.

It occupies a prominent sloping corner site, emphasising the corner by following the site boundary at the back of the pavement which creates an unusual point in the building at the corner.

Architecturally it is unremarkable and has something of a welsh chapel appearance, slightly austere and very functional although the fact that it was part funded by the Carnegie Foundation, the local MP and the Lord Lieutenant of Glamorgan implies that it was considered quite an important building at the time of its conception.

The two facades abutting the adjacent roads and pavements are finished with a sand coloured render while the other two retain the exposed rubble stone of their base construction visible. The building has a pitched slate roof. Foundation stones and a further, later commemorative plaque set in the front elevation record the dignitaries who were involved in its funding and construction.

There are clear signs of recent neglect of the building fabric and the interior that is visible from outside has apparently been stripped of all fixtures and fittings.

Auditorium Capacity: unknown

Stage details: not available

Abergorky Hall, Treorchy

Organisation: Abergorki Community Hall Ltd

Address: 16-18 Bute Street, Abergorky, Treorchy CF42 6DB

Construction/Opening: 1915

Architect/Builder: unknown/unknown

Current Owner: Abergorki Community Hall Ltd

History/previous names & ownership

Abergorki Community Hall was constructed as a Miners' Welfare Hall in 1915 through the "miners' penny" salary sacrifice funding method and contained a theatre/cinema, dance hall, billiard hall and library. It has been known at various times as Gorky Miner's Welfare Institute and Cinema, Abergorky Workmen's Hall and Abergorky Community Hall.

The venue started film shows from around 1924 when being run by Abergorky Workmens Hall Ltd under resident Manager Fred Wiltshire. W.E. Willis had taken over by 1938 when the audience capacity had been reduced to 600 seats. Seating had been reduced to 503 seats by 1951. It was being used mainly for bingo post-1964 and the cinema went out of use in the early 1970's.

Since then the hall has become a base for community businesses and community groups but by the late 1990's the businesses had left. In August 1986 a Planning Application to convert the building into warehouse and retail premises was refused.

The hall has received much renovation and continues to be used as a community centre, the community runs the building to provide classes for the arts, life-long learning, health, fitness and exercise. The hall has a current membership of over 400 people and some of the clubs have existed for over 35 years.

In 2005 redevelopment proposals were drawn up by Lampeter based Architects Hess Kincaid Leach involving the creation of a new entrance atrium and new hall for community use behind the partially retained existing front façade but these plans have not been realised.

Description

A large building though not as large or ostentatious as the Park & Dare in the centre of Treorchy which has a similar audience capacity. Abergorki Hall is easily identifiable by its ruthlessly symmetrical front façade and pair of truncated towers with brickwork pilasters and abstracted Corinthian capitols either side of the central bay (and of course the prominent name signage painted in a rather quirky font on the white panel above the first floor windows). Bizarrely the symmetry disappears immediately behind the front façade as the ridge of the large roof hip is distinctly off-centre.

The front façade is a mixture of materials including red brickwork, grey and white rendered panels and white feature dressings around the window openings. The sides are all faced with grey render and there is a slate pitched roof.

The building is set back from the main road passing through the community of Abergorky on the outskirts of the nearby larger town of Treorchy with the forecourt given over entirely to tarmac and car parking. There appears to be no access to the sides or rear of the building from the front as the building is tightly sandwiched between its neighbours. There is a narrow alleyway to the rear providing access to the stage end of the building and shared with surrounding housing.

There are two entrance doors to the front which suggest that originally one was used to access the hall at first floor level and the other served the ground floor dance hall, billiard room and library. One entrance now appears to be permanently shuttered and the other is approached up a recently added ramp constructed over the original steps.

Entry is into a tiny lobby area containing a large notice board announcing timing of a myriad of community group activities in the building and leading to a long axial corridor on the ground floor and stairs up to the upper levels. There is no sense of grand arrival here.

Whilst there is little evidence that the hall is ever used for live performances it is clearly being well used and the building fabric appears to be fairly well maintained. The redevelopment plans developed in 2005 were quite ambitious and would have been quite expensive but the fact that the operators were prepared to investigate the possibility of revitalising the building so radically bodes well for its long term future in the care of the enthusiastic community that uses it.

Auditorium Capacity: original: 600; current: unknown

Stage details: Not available

The Park & Dare, Treorchy

Organisation: Rhondda Cynon Taff County Borough Council Cultural Services

Address: Station Road, Treorchy CF42 6NL

Construction/Opening: 1895 (Institute) 1913 (Theatre)

Architect: Jacob Rees, Pentre (original Library and Institute); T Owen Rees & Jacob Rees (theatre)

Builder: unknown

Current Owner: Rhondda Cynon Taff County Borough Council

History/previous names & ownership

In 1895 the Workingmen's Library and Institute was opened in Treorchy at an original cost of £4,000 raised from the donation of money from their wages by the miners of the Ocean Coal Company and in 1913 the Theatre building was added to the Miners' Institute. The original plan for the theatre was as a major music hall venue but it began its life as a cinema, with the addition of live performances from local dramatic companies as well as hosting the prestigious annual semi- national Eisteddfod.

The two buildings combined were owned by the Parc & Dare Miners Institute between 1913 and 1926 when the impact of the great depression forced its sale to The Ocean Coal Company. The Coal Company retained ownership of the Institute and Theatre until 1952.

The first 'Talking Picture' was presented in the theatre in 1930 and by 1937 it was operating as a full time cinema, which continued into the 1950's. It had closed as a cinema by 1963.

From 1952 to 1975 the building was owned and operated by the Parc and Dare Lodge of the National Union of Mineworkers who then sold it to Rhondda Borough Council. By 1980 it had re-opened as a cinema again, with 960 seats and occasional stage shows.

Over the next 20 years various alterations were made to the interior décor of the original miners' Institute building including installation of double glazed uPVC windows, a sprung dance floor in dance studio, all manner of surface mounted electrical installations and light fittings and security shutters in lieu of the original Institute building entrance doors. In 1990 the exterior stonework was cleaned and restored.

On the formation of the Unitary Authority, ownership passed to Rhondda Cynon Taff County Borough Council in 1995 and it was renamed The Park & Dare Theatre. The Council remains the owner and manager of the buildings. They were listed Grade II* on 20th December 1996.

In 2003 replacement auditorium seating was installed and the audience capacity reduced by about 40 seats. In 2010 a new steel flytower grid was installed above the existing (and historically significant) timber grid and the crossover gallery within the flytower was removed to increase performance space on the stage.

Description

This is a very grand and large building dominating the skyline of Treorchy and still clearly representing the ambition of the the Miners who built it for their own use to make something really special.

The original Miners' Institute is relatively grand in comparison to other buildings of the same age but is dwarfed by the 1913 Theatre 'extension'. Both are faced with stone to the principal elevations with rendered brick to the less public faces and slate roofs.

The auditorium has stalls and 2 balconies and a seating capacity of 660. The balcony fronts are aligned vertically and feature plaster moulding details of plants and flowers. Remnants of the original gas lamp holding brackets remain. Both balconies extend around the auditorium side walls and meet the proscenium wall creating an intimate environment. The proscenium wall is elaborately detailed.

There is no orchestra pit but a semi-permanent area at the front of the stalls floor is used when required. Occasionally a band is set up in another room in the building with electronic connection to the sound system in the auditorium. A permanent in-room sound and light mixing desk position has been created at the expense of some seats at the rear of stalls, house left.

There is a permanent stage apron extending the performance area (which is severely constrained in depth by the building envelope) and the stage is raked (at a slightly unusual gradient of 1:24). The stage house provides full flying capability significantly improved by the removal of a crossover gallery that once connected the fly bridges to each other, along with the installation of a new steel grid to replace the old timber joist installation in the summer of 2010. A separate (external covered bridge) route is provided around the back of the stage at stage level although this is several metres above the external ground level and is enclosed in a timber clad structure cantilevered off the stage wall.

Large dressing room accommodation is provided in the original Institute building at 2 levels, neither of them the same as stage, and backstage accessibility for people with movement difficulties is severely restricted by the many staircases.

Similarly, loading and unloading of incoming/outgoing sets and equipment is extremely hampered by the many changes of level in the immediate backstage area and the current get-in is via the original pair of entrance doors to the Institute building, again restricted by the central stone column.

A large foyer bar has been created underneath the auditorium and is used for performance events in its own right. It has a small raised stage and sprung dance floor area. Otherwise, as is typical of similar venues, the front-of-house foyer area is minimal and focussed on circulation directly into the auditorium via symmetrically opposed staircases. There is a ticket desk in the entrance area. At some point a small passenger lift has been installed that enables wheelchair users to gain access to the stalls but floor level differences between the original Institute building and theatre extension prevent any access for the disabled to the upper balconies.

A large room in the first floor of the original Institute building is now a Dance Studio and above that is a further event/rehearsal/exhibition space. Neither of these spaces is easily accessed by people with movement difficulties or large pieces of equipment or exhibits. Both spaces have been redecorated and contain no visible original features. The original sash windows have been replaced with double-glazed uPVC windows. Surface mounted small power electrical installations have proliferated in both.

This is certainly one of the most impressive theatre buildings in the region and it is clearly recognised as such by the owner and operator. It presents a wide range of well-attended shows and there is no doubt that the Park & Dare has a secure future.

Auditorium Capacity:

Original capacity believed to have been over 700; 1935: 1100; 1984: 900; 1992: 800; 1994: 803

Current capacity is 666 total, following replacement of seats in 2003 and comprising

323 on stalls; 195 circle; 148 gallery

Stage details:

Performance space – width – 13m
Performance space – depth – 6.1m
Depth of apron – approx 2.5m
Wing space (Right and Left) – SR - 3.55m; SL - 3.44m
Proscenium height/width – height 8.72m (max), 6.1m (min); width 12.95m
Orchestra pit (maximum no of players) – No pit
Height from stage floor to grid – 14.63m
Rake - Yes – 1:24

Welfare Hall & Institute, Tylorstown

Organisation: Tylorstown Welfare Hall & Institute Friendly Society

Address: East Road, Tylorstown CF43 3DA

Construction/Opening: 1933

Architect/Builder: unknown/unknown

Current Owner: Tylorstown Welfare Hall & Institute Friendly Society

History/previous names & ownership

In 1933 the trustees of the friendly society which operates the building signed a conveyance and trust deed for the land on which the hall sits. The Welfare Hall was constructed with funding from local colliery miners wage deductions and contributions from the local community. Originally planned as a theatre with a flat stalls floor to accommodate dance events, cinema equipment and fixed seating was installed during construction and the venue operated primarily as a cinema for the first 50 years of its life. Live shows were presented but only as many as the prevailing legislation allowed before installation of a safety curtain became mandatory.

In the mid-1980's receipt of substantial grant funding from UrbanAid facilitated the complete repair and restoration of the roof, removal of original render from the entire building envelope and replacement with new render and substantial interior modifications including the removal of the fixed seating from stalls to return the venue to its originally intended configuration. The originally installed hardwood parquet floor was found to be too badly damaged to allow it to be left exposed as the stalls floor finish and broadloom carpet was installed. Use of the building became focussed on community activities.

A few years later, in the early 1990's, changes to the Fire Regulations required the re-orientation of one of the original pair of auditorium balcony audience access staircases such that it exited directly to outside. Associated alterations to the foyer space and building envelope were carried out.

The building was listed Grade II on 18th March 1997

Maintenance and repair of the building fabric continued throughout the next 10 years including the replacement of the original main entrance doors with bespoke new doors modelled on the original design and appearance, the refurbishment of the original bespoke security gate/shutter to front entrance and at some time in this period the original 3 dressing rooms behind the stage were converted into offices. In addition to the Hall Management Committee offices, the Communities First organisation funded by the Welsh Government occupies basement (original Miners' Institute) spaces providing additional revenue income to the building.

In 2010 the auditorium balcony was closed to audience access following weather ingress caused by the theft of the lead flashing from the rear of the front façade parapet. This and other repairs are due to be carried out in advance of planned celebrations of the 80th anniversary of the opening of the building in 2013.

Description

The grand classically styled front façade of this building dominates the central residential area of Tylorstown. It is a large building rising from the back of the pavement to almost double the height of the adjacent and surrounding housing. As is generally the case with buildings such as this it presents a fairly narrow frontage to the public domain with the length of the auditorium within perpendicular to the road and extending some distance into the valley behind. Such is the topography of the site that there is a further storey of accommodation below the entrance level.

The front façade is ornately classical in its appearance with bath stone features and red brick infill panels. The remaining walls of the building are finished in plain render with feature pilasters perhaps coincident with the internal structural frame. High level windows are provided on both sides of the building serving the auditorium but on the south side they have been completely blocked up following identification of them being the source of significant weather ingress. Since they were blocked up there have been no further issues of water ingress. The windows on the north elevation remain. There is a simple single pitched slate roof.

The main audience entrance is on the central axis of the building and is via 2 shallow steps and 2 pairs of partially glazed doors directly into a small foyer space containing the original ticket desk (complete with original telephone for internal building communications) and access to audience toilets. Disabled access is not directly possible through the front entrance but can be achieved through a side entrance/fire escape serving the auditorium directly and back-of-house areas.

Originally there were opposing symmetrical staircases leading directly from the foyer/entrance hall up to the balcony above on both sides but changes to fire regulations in the early 1990's required the closure of one of the stairs and its re-orientation such that it now provides emergency exit only from the balcony directly to the outside via doors inserted into the side elevation. Entry into the auditorium is at the rear of the stalls on the level. The auditorium has a flat floor providing excellent flexibility and allowing a wide range of events and shows to be presented in the building. The floor has a carpet finish laid over the original hardwood parquet dance floor that was damaged when the original fixed seating was removed in the 1980's and was considered uneconomic to repair. A licensed bar servery and confectionary sales desk are located either side of the entrance doors at the rear of the room. The auditorium is quite wide in relation to its length, almost square in plan, and the upper balcony projects over approximately one third of the stalls area. The cantilevering beams supporting the balcony are expressed in the ceiling under the balcony and this 'honesty' about the construction lends character to the space.

It is not an extravagantly decorated auditorium but does feature raised plaster mouldings on the balcony front and side walls. From the point at which the balcony front meets the side walls, raised mouldings continue the line of the balcony front to the proscenium which is itself an applied painted raised moulding. A dado rail is fitted to the entire perimeter with contrasting colour decoration below.

Auditorium Capacity:

Originally 600, reduced to 400 on removal of fixed seating to stalls level (comprising 200 fixed seats on upper balcony and 200 loose seats on stalls)

Stage details: Not available

The colour scheme is an interesting combination of pastel pink and green and white evoking the art deco period in which the building was made but contrasting sharply with the classically proportioned and detailed exterior. The windows on the north wall at high level are set between and within further feature mouldings and are covered by deep red coloured curtains. The ceiling is typical of many buildings of this age and origin insofar as it is a single shallow barrel vault spanning the auditorium and featuring contrasting colour mouldings and inset ventilation grilles. Original pendant light fittings remain but are unused due to accessibility issues.

The stage is very shallow but quite wide and has a shallow rake. There is no flytower and rigging over the stage area for production scenic effects and lighting is limited. The building has been primarily used for cinema for the majority of its existence and the management exploited legislation prevailing through the first 50 years of that period by limiting the number of live performances to the maximum number allowed before a fire curtain was required to be installed. There were three performer dressing rooms originally but they have all been converted into offices for the management committee's use. The balcony retains the original 200 fixed seats and the projection room serving the cinema use is at high level at the rear over the entrance hall/foyer. There is no in-room control desk position.

There is no mechanical ventilation and heating is provided by perimeter cast iron radiators. There are no reported difficulties with keeping the room cool in the summer but the cost of maintaining warmth through the winter is causing concern as the cost of fuel rises.

The floor below the auditorium is currently occupied by Communities First – an outreach organisation funded by the Welsh Government. The rooms at this sub-stage level were all originally used by the Tylorstown Miners' Institute and included offices and meeting rooms. Both live theatre and cinema presentations are now infrequent but the building remains able to stage either.

This venue clearly has good local community support and is used for an extremely wide range of events. Prudent stewardship of the building by the Management Committee has ensured the survival of the venue when others in the local area have long disappeared. Its future appears secure.

Cardiff

Cardiff

- Chapter Arts Centre
- The Gate Arts Centre
- Hoddinutt Hall
- Llanover Hall
- Mike Barlow YMCA Theatre
- New Theatre
- Royal Welsh College of Music & Drama
- Sherman Cymru
- St Davids Hall
- Wales Millennium Centre

Chapter Arts Centre

Organisation: Chapter Ltd

Address: Market Road, Canton, Cardiff CF5 1QE

Construction: 1904 - 1907 (as Canton High School) **Opening:** 1971 (as Arts Centre)

Architect: James & Morgan (original school building)

Builder: unknown

Current Owner: Chapter Ltd

History/previous names & ownership

A redundant school building was provided as the site for an ambitious project to create an Arts Centre in Cardiff with workshops, exhibition spaces, theatre and cinema. Chapter Arts Centre opened on March 1st 1971. To create performance and cinema spaces a row of classrooms was fitted out with curtains, screen and some old cinema seats. Improved seating was installed later and subsequently replaced again and the audience benefitted from seats bought from the closed Capitol Cinema on Queen Street, Cardiff.

By 1987 funding was obtained to build a completely new cinema; Chapter One, seating 194. The original cinema was closed and the space re-used. However, a second cinema had been created by a private society and became part of Chapter, as Chapter Two, seating 68 with more basic seating and equipment and catering for a minority audience.

In 2007 the process of completely upgrading the facilities at Chapter commenced and was completed in 2010 to designs by Ash Sakula Architects of London. The design received an RIBA Award in 2010 for the quality of the architectural solution to the transformation. The theatre and cinemas were upgraded but the most significant changes were to the public areas and circulation spaces which now incorporate a visual arts gallery, shop and extensive cafe and bar complete with sheltered external terrace.

Description

There is no doubt that Chapter retains the appearance of the original High School building that it occupies but also no doubt that the recent renovation works have injected a new and distinctive character to the place. On the whole it appears as a bespoke Arts Centre now, emphasised by the bold rooftop graphics, pleasant forecourt garden square and huge visual art installation over the main entrance that is changed twice a year. The main entrance leads into the social heart of the building, conceived and created during the renovations from space that used to be much more cellular and disconnected. Now there is a very large open space with a café/bar server running the length of one wall and rooflights introducing daylight into the deep plan. It always seems to be a heavily used space irrespective of whether or not there are any events being staged for which audiences are gathering. All of the component spaces of the Arts Centre can be accessed from and through this space and whilst being such a large building signage is essential, it is graphically well designed and the building is easy to navigate from the central orientation space.

Auditorium Capacity: 196 (comprising 96 on retractable bleacher unit and 100 loose seats)

Stage details:

Performance space – width – 8.45m
Performance space – depth – 9.75m
Depth of apron – n/a
Wing space (Right and Left) – n/a
Proscenium height/width – n/a
Orchestra pit (maximum no of players) – n/a
Height from stage floor to grid – 3.85m
Rake – none

The 2 cinemas are on the ground floor, with the visual arts gallery, box office and shop and the theatre is on the first floor. The theatre has a decent sized ante-room type audience foyer and gathering space set behind the art installation over the main entrance which impacts greatly on the atmosphere and lighting of the foyer depending on its nature. Audience entry into the theatre is at the rear of the retractable bleacher seating at a higher level then the audience space but access for all is dealt with well.

The auditorium is a simple rectangular 'black-box' flexible space with no notable architectural features to detract from the freedom the space offers for experimental work. The flexible seating allows a range of audience and performance staging configurations to be used and there is a grid of suspension and rigging bars extending over the entire footprint of the room.

The bleacher seating does tend to accentuate the end-stage configuration however and access onto the performance area is focussed at the end opposite the bleachers. Large doors (extra high and wide) lead into a generous corridor off-stage from where access is provided to dressing rooms and a lift for moving equipment and scenic effects down to the truck bay at ground floor level below.

Since re-opening in 2010 Chapter has become even more successful than it was before closing for the the renovation works. The café/bar area in particular has exceeded expectations in respect of its use and popularity with audiences and casual visitors and has generated significant revenue income allowing the venue to expand its range of events and shows presented. The theatre presents around 300 shows a year and is well supported by audiences with the cinemas showing a mix of mainstream films and world-cinema. The gallery presents several themed exhibitions each year. Having just celebrated its 40th birthday, the future of Chapter seems assured.

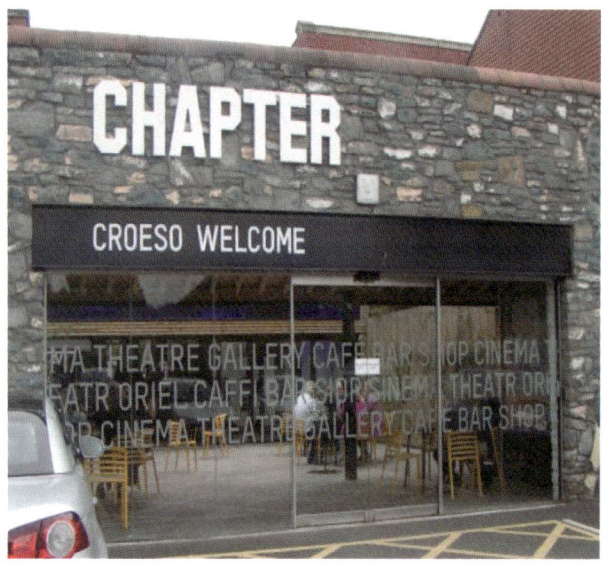

The Gate Arts Centre

Organisation: The Gate Trust (registered charity)

Address: Keppoch Street, Roath, Cardiff CF24 3JW

Construction: 1886 – 1901(original Church Hall and Chapel) **Opening:** 2004 (as Arts Centre)

Architect: J. H. Phillips (original Hall); W. Beddoe Rees, Cardiff with J. H. James (original Chapel);
Rob Cruwys (conversion to Arts Centre)

Builder: unknown

Current Owner: The Gate Trust

History/previous names & ownership

The original building now occupied by The Gate was built in two phases with the Plasnewydd Presbyterian Church Hall opening in 1896 followed 5 years later by the Chapel. It functioned as a church until the end of the 20th Century.

The building was listed Grade II on 9th September 1998.

The Gate Trust purchased the church in 2000 and commenced a four year redevelopment to create the current Arts Centre. The conversion was made possible by funding of £1.2M from the Heritage Lottery Fund, £1.2M from a private individual and £400,000 from the Welsh Assembly Government. The Gate opened its doors in September 2004.

Description

The Gate is located in a quiet residential area though close to one of the major arterial routes through the city. It stands on the corner of a square with recreational facilities in its centre and immediately stands out as a lavish example of Victorian ecclesiastical architecture.

The exterior is largely unchanged from its original church form and all stained glass windows and features remain. The roof appears to have been re-covered and the stone elevations have perhaps been cleaned. Announcing the building's location is an extravagant turret on the corner of the site rising high above the building itself and surrounding two storey terraced housing.

The entry to the building has been changed however and is now located not on the centre of the church but to one side, tucked away and not immediately obvious. The entrance is approached up a gentle ramp from the back of the pavement and access throughout the building has been given consideration and is excellent.

Glazed entrance doors lead into a small reception area and then immediately into two wide corridors leading across the front of the building and down one side towards backstage accommodation and the management offices. The walls of these corridors are generously hung with fine examples of contemporary visual art, emphasising the nature of the centre as being about more than just performance art.

The main auditorium is located at first floor level in the building and audiences approach up a pair of winding staircases to the rear of the balcony area. The auditorium has been created by infilling the void in front of the original upper balcony with a flat floor used heavily as a performance space in its own right, especially for dance shows and drama such as Shakespeare in the round. All of the original balcony pews are retained as the fixed audience seating and loose seating can be laid out on the flat floor for end-stage or proscenium presentations on the small stage area above what would have been the altar position in the church.

The auditorium is quite wide and roughly square in plan form but is a lofty volume with the original roof structure and timber boarding roof lining exposed. The original balcony front is elegant wrought iron and contemporary insertions to meet current legislation are complimentary glass balustrades that focus attention on the Victorian original.

A comprehensive grid of suspension points and lighting positions has been inserted across the entire room in a sensitive manner so as not to detract from the clarity, and indeed beauty of the space.

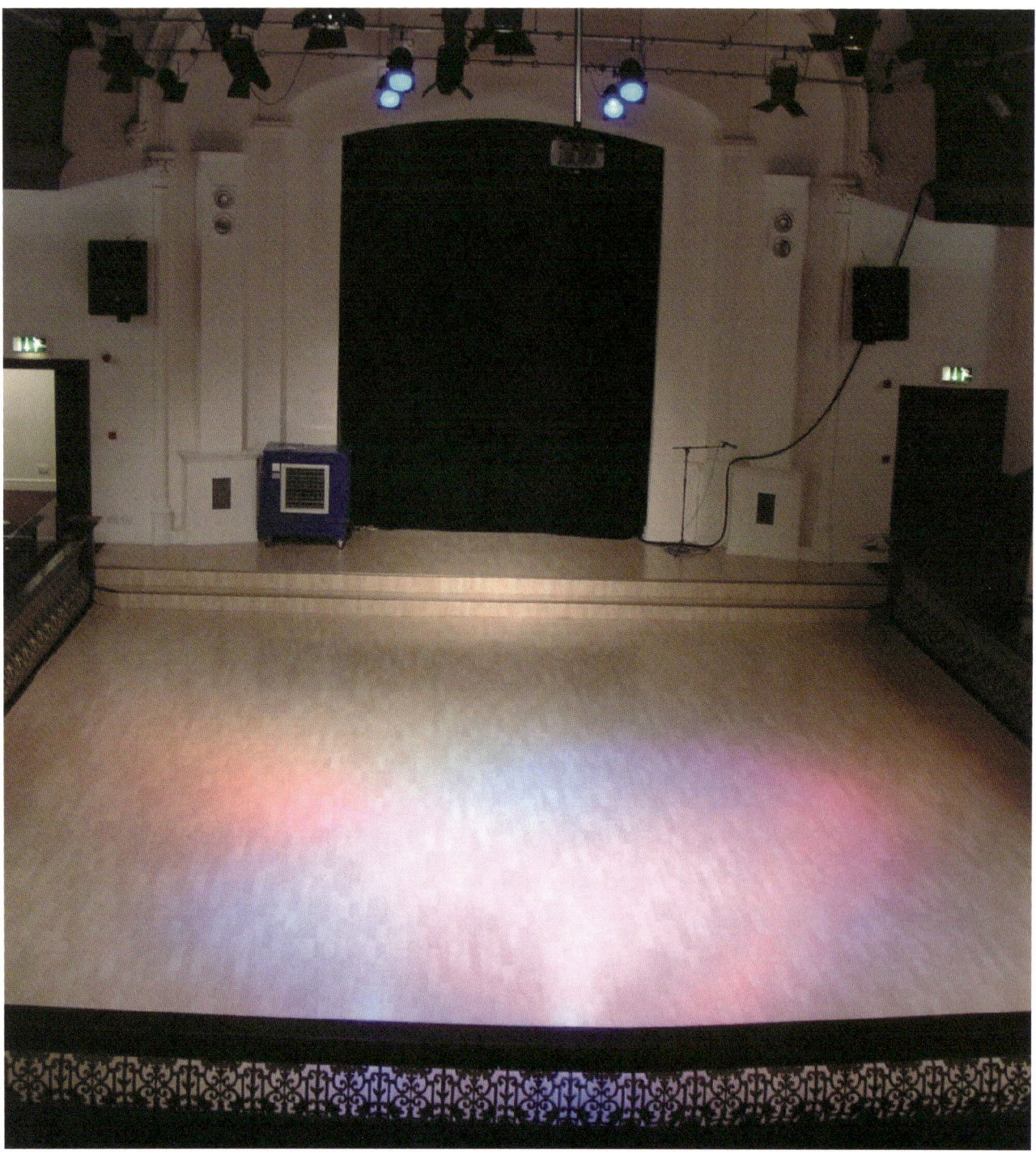

The stage area is slightly raised above the flat floor by shallow steps and the proscenium is an original stone arch of the chapel building. This leaves the stage performance space quite small, both in width and depth and there is very limited wing space or storage at stage level.

Immediately behind the stage and at the same level is a large single dressing room that connects to an even larger space for use by larger performing companies. These spaces are also available for external organisations to hire for conferences and the like. These rooms benefit from a really good quality of light from high level windows and have a character formed by the ceilings following the complex shapes of the underside of the roof in this part of the building.

On the ground floor and underneath the flat floor of the main auditorium is a dance studio accessed directly from the corridor at the front of the building. The studio occupies the original floor of the chapel although a new dance floor has been inserted and it contains the original chapel pulpit and decorated columns supporting the balcony above. One wall has been covered with full height mirrors. It is a stunning, lovely little space and understandably extremely popular with many local groups both for rehearsals and meetings.

This is clearly a highly successful venue, used heavily by local Community Groups and frequently by touring companies as well as for live music events and conferences. The management reports steady and sustained growth in audience numbers and events presented over the last few years and staff numbers have increased to meet the demand.

The building has been beautifully and thoughtfully converted to its current use, retaining the character and special features of the original church whilst injecting the entirely new and fresh personality of a vibrant arts centre. It provides excellent facilities in a very well maintained environment and its future seems assured.

Auditorium Capacity:

350 (comprising 270 on pews and 80 on loose seats on flat floor)

Stage details: Not available

Hoddinutt Hall

Organisation: BBC National Orchestra and Chorus of Wales

Address: BBC Hoddinott Hall, Cardiff Bay, Cardiff, CF10 5AL

Construction: 2007-2008 **Opening:** 2009

Architect: Capita Architecture, Cardiff

Builder: Sir Robert McAlpine Ltd

Current Owner: Lime Property Fund

History/previous names & ownership

Since 1967, the Orchestra had been based in Studio 1 at the BBC Studios in Llandaff, Cardiff, but they had long out-grown this home and a new purpose-built studio was needed.

In 2000 discussions commenced between the Orchestra, BBC Wales and Wales Millennium Centre for the construction of a purpose built facility on the site of the WMC in Cardiff Bay and after funding for the development was secured construction commenced in 2007 and the Hall was launched with an opening festival held Thursday 22nd January to Sunday 1st February 2009, with live performances broadcast on BBC Radio 3. Hoddinott Hall is named after the late Welsh classical composer Alun Hoddinott CBE and was officially opened by the HRH Charles Prince of Wales on 31 January 2009.

Description

Hoddinott Hall is the principal component of what was effectively phase 2 of the development of the Wales Millennium Centre site in Cardiff Bay. Provision was made during phase 1 works to delineate the site for further development in the form of a free-standing slate wall curving around the north of the site to the main vehicular entrance.

The new hall occupies the space between that slate wall (which now forms the external envelope of the second phase development), the main site vehicular entrance and the public concourse at the front of the site.

From the outside of the site little evidence presents itself of the presence of a large Orchestral Rehearsal and Recording Studio within the walls, apart from the top storey which projects above the slate wall parapet clad in waney-edge timber.

The scale of this hidden volume is much more evident from within the site as its sheer vertical inner face rises dramatically opposite the backstage facilities of the theatre contained in the first phase creating a canyon like space between the buildings.

The 'stage door' for Hoddinott Hall sits directly opposite the WMC stage door and the logic of the site layout is clear and well executed. The public/audience access to the Hall is located inside the main WMC building and announced by a large pair of doors using the name Hoddinott in the design of the door ironmongery at first floor in the north concourse.

The Hall is as much (if not more) a place of work for the Orchestra and Chorus as a place of live performance so it is the stage door entry which is most used. A compact reception space with excellent accessibility leads into a lift and stair lobby and initially all circulation is upwards as the main body of the hall is at first floor level, both to accommodate the audience access location and a small visitor car park under the belly of the auditorium.

Large circulation spaces around the platform end of the hall double as gathering and social space for the musicians and lead through very large double doors directly onto the platform area. A separate, less generous route is provided to the second floor for the chorus who are able to access the choir seating from both sides of the room.

The auditorium is a wonderful space both architecturally and acoustically and has received wide praise from the orchestra musicians and staff as well as audiences and critics. It is both surprisingly intimate and cavernous – a contradiction that is quite hard to explain and that is difficult to capture in photographs. Perhaps this feeling is induced by the scale of the orchestra platform and the consequent proximity of the audience to the orchestra or by the relatively small number of audience seats in respect of the volume of the space. The majority of audience seats are fixed on a generous rake providing uninterrupted sightlines to every musician and section of the orchestra and the chorus seating at the opposite end of the room is even more steeply raked and really gives a sense of people wrapping around the orchestra (even though the long side balconies don't contain any audience seating at all and serve an acoustic function whilst containing ventilation systems).

It is an overwhelmingly 'woody' room with a variety of different timber elements and treatments contributing to the overall harmony of the composition. Some timber panels provide reflective surfaces and others 'scattering' surfaces and of course the entire floor is timber (with different species under the strings sections from the remainder to optimise acoustic response). A large organ screen dominates the wall above the orchestra and choir platform, again clad in a timber frame.

The frame of the building is clad throughout with precast concrete panels left exposed in many areas and far from appearing industrial at all give a further richness to the space. The final wall components are the many acoustic panels used for sound absorption and retractable into timber pockets around the room. Over the orchestra an array of height adjustable reflecting panels add to the incredible range of facilities to 'tune' the room to suit the scale of the piece being played or orchestra performing.

One of the early requirements set as an absolute essential was the inclusion of windows into the hall to allow daylight in during day-time rehearsals and the large pair of windows above and behind the audience provide an excellent quality of light into the space.

The orchestra platform is flexible insofar as it can be set to different arrangements using rostrum units and a hydraulic elevator has been added since construction completed to the most frequently modified section and providing an easier method of moving pianos around.

The Hall is the centre of activity for the orchestra but the building contains administrative offices, band rooms, instrument storage and all other spaces creating a self-contained base for the organisation. There is also a 'second' space, named the Grace Williams Room, and used for a wide range of activities including education and outreach, chorus rehearsals, sectional rehearsals for small groups of musicians from the orchestra, and meetings. It contains many of the architectural and acoustic devices and features of the main hall but has a special character of its own. It too is deemed a great success and is very popular.

The orchestra's truck used for touring has its own dedicated bay within the footprint of the building and can also be used by Outside Broadcast Studio vehicles.

This Hall has established itself as one of the pre-eminent Orchestral Rehearsal and Recording Studios in the UK and is widely used for recording by almost all well known recording companies. Live radio broadcasts (primarily to BBC Radio 3) are regular and concerts are generally sold out to a growing and supportive audience.

It is one of the very few venues I have visited where there are only good things said about the design and outcome of the construction process and it is a delight that such a facility exists in Wales.

Auditorium Capacity: 349

Stage details: Not available

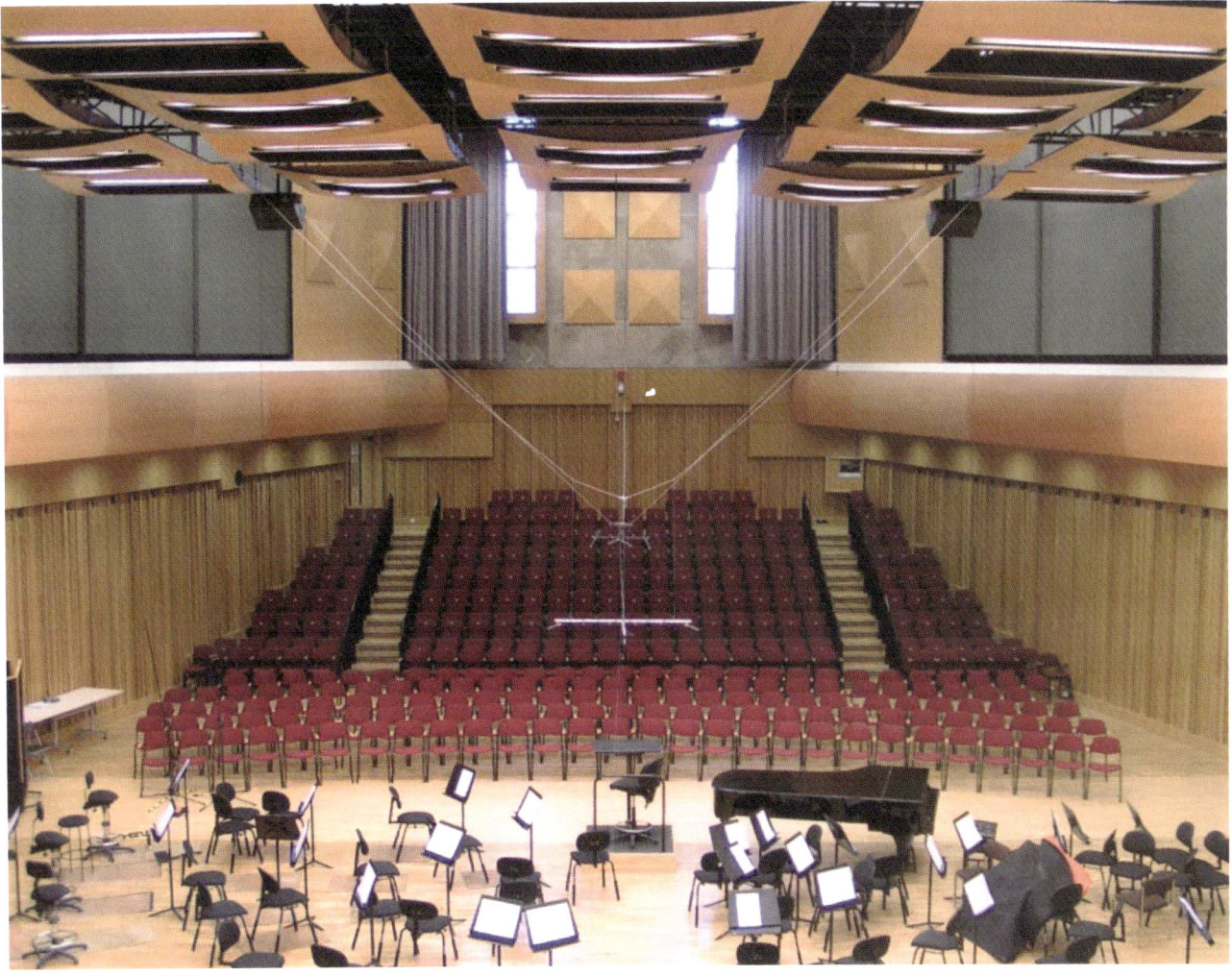

Llanover Hall

Organisation: Llanover Hall Community Arts

Address: Romilly Road, Cardiff CF15 1FH

Construction: approx 1900 **Opening:** 1968 as Arts Centre, 1971 Theatre opening

Architect: unknown

Builder: William Symonds, Cardiff

Current Owner: Cardiff County Council

History/previous names & ownership

17 Romilly Road was built as a private residence by and for William Symonds around the turn of the 19th Century and remained a private residence until 1937.

In 1938 Cardiff City Juvenile Employment Committee purchased a lease on the property with a view to converting the house into a Juvenile Employment Instruction Centre for Girls. On 17th March Cardiff City Council's Director of Education approached the Trustees of the Llanover Estate seeking permission to name the new centre 'The Lady Llanover Hall'. Permission was granted by the Estate to use the name (by then changed slightly to 'Llanover Hall' in 1939 and the new centre opened on 15th June of that year.

From 1941 the Hall was occupied by displaced students from the nearby and partially bombed Canton High School and the school continued to use the building until the 1960s. In 1968 a 'Modern Art Workshop' for young people organised by staff from the local education authority was offered the building having previously been based at two other venues in Cardiff and a year was spent in the repair, painting and refurbishment of the centre for its new use.

The first full-time Director of Llanover Hall was appointed in 1971. The aim of the centre was to provide young people with the opportunity to pursue their interests in the arts to whatever level they themselves felt appropriate. A variety of arts workshops were organised, taking place 5 evenings a week and the Cardiff Youth Orchestra, Brass Band and Action Pie Theatre Company became resident at the centre. The first Artist in Residence (Steve Benbow, Photographer) was appointed and the gallery created in 1977 followed in 1978 by the appointment of the second Artist in Residence (Tony Goble) who later became the centre's first Gallery Director.

In 1987 the Education Department of South Glamorgan was reorganised bringing the Adult, Youth and Community branches of the service under the umbrella of 'Community Education'. The Centre opened its doors to people of all ages and abilities and the programme was expanded to include daytime classes and increase the reputation of the County's Youth Theatre which was by now based at the centre. The professional Theatre Company WOT Theatre also became resident at the centre at this time. Llanover Hall Community Arts was formed in 1993 with the purpose of keeping the Centre open when it was threatened with closure due to cutbacks in the Local Education Authority budget.

The Charity obtained a £50,000 grant from The Foundation of Sports & the Arts in 1995 and the Centre embarked on a programme of expansion offering 50 workshops each week in subjects including printing, painting, drawing, photography, ceramics, batik, drama, youth theatre, dance, picture framing and arts classes for adults with learning difficulties. A new computer studio was added in September 1995.

In 1998 the Charity secured a Lottery grant of £398,000 from the Arts Council of Wales to build the West Wing along with a new entrance, meeting room and disabled toilets, A new lift was installed serving all floors, two new studios were constructed and many of the workshops were refurbished. The upgraded and renovated building was reopened in 2000 by Godfrey Thomis, Chairman of the Llanover Advisory Board, John O'Neil, Trustee of Llanover Community Arts, Sybil Crouch, Chair of the Arts Council of Wales and Nicola Heywood-Thomas, Television presenter.

A grant was obtained in 2010 to carry out a Feasibility Study for Youth Enablement of the performing arts space. The aim was to include a 2nd studio, new changing rooms, new lighting, and new sound equipment and a launch event was held in April 2011 to celebrate the refurbishment of the theatre space.

Description

The Arts Centre is located in a leafy street in one of the suburbs of Cardiff and occupies a large 3 storey house typical of the area and era when this part of the City was being developed for residential use. The original building has clearly been much extended and altered over its life but retains much of its origin as a private family house both in its exterior appearance and internal layout.

The main building is principally a red-brick built structure with some feature stone dressing around windows and doors and contrasting buff brick sections on the large chimneys. There is some red clay tile hanging in the gables and black and white timbered panels very typically Victorian. It has a slate roof. The new extension mimics the original in use of materials but doesn't attempt to replicate any of the Victorian detailing flourishes.

The main entrance is through a small garden via a ramp and into a shallow glazed lean to which also contains a small gallery area. There is a reception in the hallway which also accommodates some management office space and from this entrance hall a large staircase leads up to other offices and facilities.

The theatre is at the back of the site and occupies what is understood to have been an outbuilding within the garden of the original house. From the outside it has a barn-like appearance although it could have been used for parking vehicles at some stage. The area between the theatre and road is now used for staff car parking but also provides very good access for visiting companies directly to the theatre stage area.

Following a narrow corridor from the reception area to the theatre there are numerous rooms and studios to each side and the walls are generously hung with contemporary visual art everywhere. Immediately before entering the theatre two good-sized spaces can be used for audience gathering at events or for rehearsals and warm-up or meetings. There is no foyer in the normal sense but it is easy to imagine the combination of these two spaces with their recent installation of a glazed rooflight, contemporary furnishings and light, crisp décor working well in lieu of a foyer.

The auditorium is entered close to the rear and has an entirely flat slightly sprung timber floor throughout. It is a simple rectangular shape with the pitched roof structure exposed and the volume extends up to the underside of the roof. Both walls and ceiling are painted dark grey/black and there are no expressed architectural features. It feels like a much larger space than it is. There are large windows along both of the long sides of the room providing an excellent quality of light for daytime events and with black-out drapes available to cover them over for performances.

The audience can be arranged in a wide variety of configurations but for the majority of events loose seats are arranged on portable riser units at the entry end leaving the opposite end as an end-stage arrangement. There is no fixed proscenium and drapes are used to create one if required. The stage is not raised above the audience so performances can be very intimate.

The whole room is covered by a network of suspension bars and rigging points but there is no mechanical stage equipment. There is a sound/lighting control box open to the room and situated at high level in the wall opposite the stage area.

At the rear of the stage area every available space is used for storage of equipment, props and scenic effects and two dressing rooms with washing facilities have been constructed for use by performers.

This is clearly an extremely successful venue, with events taking place throughout every day and at least 5 evenings every week. It is remarkable that it doesn't have a higher profile.

The building fabric is well maintained with ongoing general upgrades of the facilities being carried out as funds allow. In 1998 Cardiff County Council confirmed that would commit to supporting the centre for 25 years but there is no reason to doubt, based on its current level of activity and wide appeal that it will continue to be successful well beyond 2023.

Auditorium Capacity: 100

Stage details: Not available

Mike Barlow YMCA Theatre

Organisation: Cardiff Players/YMCA Players

Address: The YMCA, The Walk, Cardiff CF24 3AG

Construction: 19th Century (as a Convent School) **Opening:** 1981 (as a theatre)

Architect/Builder: Cardiff Players/YMCA Players

Current Owner: Cardiff YMCA

History/previous names & ownership

The building containing this theatre was originally constructed as Our Lady Convent School in the 19th Century (actual date of construction is unknown).

In 1978 Cardiff YMCA was forced to move out of its original facilities on Station Terrace to liberate the site for development of the Capitol Shopping Centre and the organisation moved to take over the by then disused school buildings. In the same year the Cardiff Players Amateur Dramatic Society were invited to move into space originally occupied by science laboratories within the school and started the process of converting it to a new theatre themselves. The first production in the new Theatre was "Bedroom Farce" By Alan Ayckbourn performed in October 1981.

The theatre was formally renamed in November 2010 as the Mike Barlow YMCA Theatre in recognition of the actor/director and administrator who was the driving force within the YMCA Players society for almost 40 years.

Description

The Cardiff YMCA is situated in a largely commercial district with University buildings close by too. It occupies a corner site and a building originally constructed as part of a Convent and School complex although at first glance there is little to suggest that it is a Victorian building, let alone a school. Clearly there has been significant alteration to the original over time and most striking amongst those changes are the red metal framed windows, with those to the ground floor of one wing of the building blacked out, and the cream render applied to the entire building envelope. All that appears to remain of the original features and appearance of the building is the cast iron rainwater goods and the initials OLCS (Our Lady Convent School) carved above one of the entry doors.

The theatre occupies space above the original double height gymnasium of the school so is effectively at second floor and there is nothing on the exterior of the building to suggest a theatre is within. The building is entered on the internal corner through a glazed lobby on the level from a small garden forecourt. The reception is primarily organised to serve the functions and activities of the YMCA and there is no box office operation serving the theatre at all. Access to the theatre is via narrow stairs (or lift) shared with the other accommodation in the building and on arrival at the second floor there is no tangible audience space prior to entering the auditorium. There is a suite of meeting rooms available however and used for small conferences and the like and there are plentiful toilets close to the theatre.

The auditorium is entered at the rear on house left and is arranged as a single fixed stepped rake down to the stage at the opposite end of the room. Sightlines are very good from all seats. The audience seats were rescued from the Capitol Theatre on Queen Street in Cardiff prior to its demolition to make way for a shopping centre and are as original (and very comfortable). There is a control box at the rear on house right. There are 4 large windows in the house left wall with black-out facilities and the remaining walls and the ceiling are plain plaster painted a deep blue.

The stage is surprisingly large and surrounded by dark stained timber strip cladding to create the proscenium, supplemented by deep red house cloths. Wing space is generous too but there is limited headroom due to the presence of the original roof structure exposed above the performance area and there is no capacity for flying. There are plentiful rigging, suspension and lighting points over the stage however and it is well equipped. Behind the stage is a large store containing scenery flats and props and small space used for workshop activities. There is a single dressing room below the theatre on a mezzanine level of the theatre fire escape stair which is not ideal but presents no operational difficulties since it is firmly in the back-of-house area of the theatre and allows complete privacy for performers.

The Mike Barlow Theatre is remarkable for its lack of visibility coupled with its obvious success as a venue popular with a wide range of organisations that use it for their regular presentations. The resident company (the Cardiff/YMCA Players) present five shows every year and several other local groups occupy the theatre regularly enabling it to present a wide-ranging and regular series of events. The management is keen to exploit the potential of the theatre even more and are actively seeking ways of increasing its use for even more performances but also for related activities such as conferences. This venue has a lot of potential and its future would appear to be secure.

Auditorium Capacity: 139

Stage details:

Performance space – width – 8.83m (including wings)
Performance space – depth – 5.18m
Depth of apron – 1.52m
Wing space (Right and Left) – 1.52m and 1.22m
Proscenium height/width – height unknown; width 6.09m
Orchestra pit (maximum no of players) – n/a
Height from stage floor to grid –not available
Rake – None

The New Theatre

Organisation: Cardiff County Council

Address: Park Place, Cardiff CF10 3LN

Construction/Opening: 1906

Architect: Ernest Runtz, Runtz and Ford, London

Builder: unknown

Current Owner: Cardiff County Council

History/previous names & ownership

The New Theatre was opened on 10th December 1906 by Sir Herbert Beerbohm Tree and the first performance was a production of William Shakespeare's "Twelfth Night". Seating for 1,570 was provided in orchestra, circle and balcony levels.

The first film was shown in the theatre in 1917 and in 1931 structural alterations were made to allow the theatre to show films more frequently and it became primarily used for cinema with occasional music hall and live shows. In 1935, live theatre returned full-time under the direction of Prince Littler. In 1956 the Redford family sold the theatre to Stoll Theatres Corporation for £20,000 and in 1961 an application for its demolition was submitted to Cardiff City Council. A Preservation of Use Order was issued and in September of that year it was sold to Mecca Ltd.

In 1963 Cardiff City Council negotiated a seven year lease and The New Theatre Trust was formed to manage the building. In 1969 the Council purchased the Theatre aided by grants from The Arts Council and the Welsh Office and in 1970 it was closed for renovation works including the installation of a new ventilation system, construction of a new sunken orchestra pit, replacement of the auditorium seating, modernisation of the dressing rooms and installation of a new lighting system.

The New Theatre was listed Grade II on 19th May 1975. The stage was rebuilt and the orchestra pit was enlarged in 1976 by John Wyckham Associates Architects.

In 1986 the City Council took over direct control of the building from the Trust and undertook an extensive refurbishment in 1987/88 to plans drawn up by Renton Howard Wood Levin Architects of London that opened up the foyer area as it used to be just cramped corridors and stairs leading to the auditorium. The Theatre re-opened on April 25th 1988 with a spacious open plan foyer. The auditorium remained unchanged.

In 2006 a major refurbishment of the building exterior fabric was undertaken in advance of the building's centenary celebrations in December of that year.

In 2010 it was announced that funds had been made available by the City Council for the replacement of the audience seating on the upper balcony where leg room and audience comfort had been an issue for sometime. The Arts Team at RHWL Architects, London carried out a feasibility study that included the suggestion of creating additional circulation space in the foyers along the Park Place elevation and the installation of a new passenger lift to improve accessibility. The extra circulation space proved too expensive but the replacement seating and new lift works are planned to commence in 2012. Audience capacity will reduce by about 50 once the work is completed.

Description

The New Theatre is a well known landmark in the City centre of Cardiff. It is located close to the main retail area of Queen Street and is highly visible from Queen Street up Park Place. It stands on a corner site hemmed in by the two adjacent roads and a river on three of its sides with a large hotel/office/residential development immediately adjacent on the fourth. Opportunities for further expansion are therefore unlikely and those Architects who have developed the facilities over the life of the building deserve credit for truly optimising the available space.

The main frontage is a bold red brick curved tower framed by a pair of turrets and articulated by dressed stone features including classical columns with an ornate metal canopy over the entrance doors.

The remaining visible elevations are painted cream render. The Greyfriars Road façade is animated by plentiful windows in a two-storey block surmounted by a pitched slate roof while the Park Place façade is slightly austere and plain and the 'rear' elevation to the river is almost entirely blank apart from the stage loading bay access doors.

Entry is directly from the pavement on the level and accessibility throughout the building is very good considering the constraints imposed by the original construction.

The ground floor foyer is a transition space containing a major staircase leading down to the basement cloakroom, audience WCs and band rooms and up to the balcony level foyers above. There is a ticket desk and small crush bar and access into the stalls. The upper foyer level feels altogether more spacious but you are never in doubt that the audience spaces are simply what remained of the site after the auditorium had been located.

The auditorium is a wonderful example of its age, full of the flamboyant and elaborate details associated with other great British theatres. Boxes either side of the stage are framed with classical columns and have velvet drapes all in a lush deep burgundy. There is large stalls and two upper balconies, the Dress Circle offering unsurprisingly an excellent view of the stage from all seats. The Upper balcony is unsuitable for people of a large build due to the close row spacing (and rather uncomfortable seats) of the original design but this will be addressed during 2012 even though it will result in a slightly reduced audience capacity.

The stage has full flying capability and an adjustable orchestra pit offering flexibility and encouraging a wide range of shows to visit and perform here.

The Stage Door on Greyfriars Road is close to the stage and leads into a large suite of well equipped and furnished dressing rooms.

Loading is directly onto stage from the river side of the building and there is off-road parking capacity for two large trucks as well as other vehicles.

Despite fears expressed during the construction of the Wales Millennium Centre that the New Theatre would suffer a loss of audience (especially because of the relocation of Welsh National Opera to the WMC as its home base and principal performance location) it only suffered a temporary lull in audiences and has in fact thrived in the subsequent years, presenting a far wider range of shows more suited to its scale and original design intent. It is well supported by the Local Authority and there is little doubt that this support will continue, assuring the future of this beautiful venue in the long term.

Auditorium Capacity:

original capacity 1570

reduced to current capacity of 1144 in 1976

Stage details:

Performance space – width – 9.14m
Performance space – depth – 11.8m
Depth of apron – variable
Wing space (Right and Left) – SR – 5.87m; SL – 7.09m
Proscenium height/width – height not known, width 9.14m
Orchestra pit (maximum no of players) – variable – 3 sizes
Height from stage floor to grid – 16.15m
Rake – 1:24

Royal Welsh College of Music and Drama

Organisation: Royal Welsh College of Music and Drama

Address: Castle Grounds, Cathays Park, Cardiff CF10 3ER

Construction/Opening:

Original facilities in Cardiff Castle: construction unknown, conversion and opening 1949

Raymond Edwards Building: construction 1970-1974, opening 1974

Anthony Hopkins Building: original construction unknown; refurbishment 1998-99, opening 1999

Redevelopment project: construction 2009 – 2011, opening 2011

Architect/Builder:

Original facilities in Cardiff Castle: William Burges Architect/Builder unknown

Raymond Edwards Building: John Dryburgh, Cardiff City Architect/Builder unknown

Anthony Hopkins Building: unknown/unknown

Redevelopment project: BFLS Architects, London/Wilmott Dixon, South Wales, Builder

Current Owner: Royal Welsh College of Music and Drama

History/previous names & ownership

The origins of the College stretch back to 1948 when Dr Harold C. Hind, Director of Music to the City of Cardiff, submitted a proposal on behalf of the Cardiff Education Authority for Cardiff Castle to be used as teaching facilities for Music and Drama. The application received strong support from the Director of Education and was approved leading to the creation of the National College of Music & Drama. The College was opened on the 19th September 1949 with 250 students and 62 members of staff. Dr Harold Hind was appointed Principal.

Over the next twenty years the College grew in stature and needs and in 1967 a new site in the castle grounds was identified and allocated to accommodate the construction of a new building to meet the increasing demands of the growing college.

In 1970 the College was granted National status and was re-named the Welsh College of Music and Drama. In the same year work began on the construction of the College's brand new building to designs by John Dryburgh, Cardiff City Architect. The College relocated all of its operations to the new building, named The Raymond Edwards Building (in honour of the College Principal) in 1974. The new building contained a wide range of academic facilities and a new performance space named the Bute Theatre that was officially opened by Her Majesty Queen Elizabeth II in 1977.

After another twenty years of sustained growth, the College sought to expand again and in 1998 Oscar-winning actor and alumni Anthony Hopkins donated money to help meet the costs of converting and renovating the original Castle mews building adjacent to the main College building. In recognition of his generosity the refurbished mews was renamed the Anthony Hopkins Building and it was officially opened by College Patron HRH the Prince of Wales in 1999.

In 2002 Her Majesty the Queen visited Wales during her Golden Jubilee and announced that the College would now be known as the Royal Welsh College of Music & Drama.

The College continued to expand and build upon its success and commenced development of plans for a further capital project to increase its facilities. BFLS Architects of London were appointed to deliver the new building after an international design competition and Planning Permission was granted in 2008 for a £22.5 million development to build a new concert hall, theatre, drama rehearsal spaces and exhibition gallery to complement and enhance the existing performance facilities. Later, Willmott Dixon (South Wales) was appointed as Main Contractor. Construction of the new building commenced in September 2009 and the new building opened in June 2011.

Auditorium Capacity:

Bute Theatre: 150 - 200

Richard Burton Theatre: 160 plus 12 standing

Dora Stoutzker Concert Hall: 400

Stage details:

Bute Theatre

Information not available

Richard Burton Theatre

Performance space – width – 14.23m incl wings
Performance space – depth – 10.64m
Depth of apron – 2.4m
Wing space – SR – 2.9m; SL – 2.9m
Proscenium height/width – h 5.1m; w 8.4m
Orchestra pit (max no of players) – n/a
Height from stage floor to grid – 11.72m
Rake - None

Dora Stoutzker Concert Hall

Performance space – width – 14.1m max
Performance space – depth – 9.1m
Depth of extension – 2.2m
Wing space (Right and Left) – n/a
Proscenium height/width – n/a
Orchestra pit (max no of players) – n/a
Height from stage floor to truss – 11m
Rake - None

Description

The Royal Welsh College of Music and Drama located to the north of Cardiff Castle – one of the most recognisable and evocative buildings in the city – used to be a nondescript instantly forgettable slightly brutalist block set back off the road almost cowering in the shadow of the elegant and lavishly classical buildings across the road in the Civic Centre. No more. The new building is fabulous and speaks not only of the presence of a super-confident and extremely successful academic institution but also creates a point of entry, a monumental border post that announces arrival in the City Centre for visitors arriving from the north.

The scale of the building is perfectly in balance with its surroundings and its very length (on what was a very narrow site between the pavement and 1970s building) is exaggerated by a powerful and unifying aerofoil of a roof. There are three principal components to the building sitting sheltered beneath that roof – the bulbous (in the sense that it is like a bulb rather than fat!) timber clad concert hall, the fully transparent glazed entrance and foyer space and the crisp white block containing the Richard Burton Theatre and academic accommodation. These three elements have nestled against and incorporated the earlier building brilliantly, by the simple device of treating the earlier building's buff brick to a facelift of white make up. This now very large complex stands well back from the old Cardiff Castle stables building, now known as The Sir Anthony Hopkins Building almost deferentially and the simple treatment of the landscape between the buildings gives the feel and appearance of an Oxbridge quad without enclosing walls. This too is a major improvement on the previous arrangement where the approach to the stables was across a busy crowded car-dominated access road.

Whilst the North Road façade is rightly treated as the principal face of the College, it has another equally important aspect over the old Glamorgan Canal and into Bute Park. Given the tiny amount of space between the canal embankment and the buildings this façade too is a triumph and the timber clad concert hall and full-height glazing to the foyer space are perfect foils to the informal parkland they stand over, glimpsed as they are through mature trees and glinting in the afternoon sun.

The main entrance is through the full height glazing that separates the two performance spaces and it feels huge as it soars to the underside of the roof some three storeys above and the eye is drawn right through it into the parkland beyond.

This is clearly conceived as a meeting and resting space as well as providing useful orientation clues that minimise oppressive signage. The two performance spaces, The Richard Burton Theatre and Dora Stoutzker Concert Hall, assert their presence with charcoal grey or brilliant white curved walls softening the edge of the space and creating natural circulation routes through and across the foyer, with a third element – the stacked rehearsal studios and café similarly treated. A slender bridge at first floor level sails across the void adding a dynamic element to the otherwise calm and cool volume. A narrow and cavernous full height void lies between the new building and its predecessor leading directly towards the Anthony Hopkins building. Overlooked by offices and other rooms in the earlier building it echoes the Victorian arcades of the City Centre.

Both the Richard Burton Theatre and Dora Stoutzker Concert Hall have audience entries directly off the foyer at ground floor level and balconies at first floor reached by curving staircases wrapped against and within the curved walls that define their presence.

The Richard Burton Theatre is one of those rarely found intimate, warm and carefully detailed spaces that serve to increase enjoyment of a visit to a performance. The auditorium seems incredibly small to accommodate an audience of almost 200 whilst its stage and flytower is simply huge in proportion, driven by the need to be a teaching space for technical theatre courses as well as a generous and adaptable performance space.

The room is almost circular in form with plain painted deep purple coloured walls and seat fabric and dark grey carpet. The balcony front is an elegantly detailed stainless steel lattice extending almost to the proscenium wall before curving back into the side walls. There is no ceiling per se but a tension wire grid where a ceiling otherwise would be and the void above is painted out black so the room feels much smaller in height than it actually is. Whilst intended to be predominantly used for drama performances it is said that singers enjoy performing in this room very much too.

There are technical control rooms at the rear of both stalls and balcony audience seating and backstage there are 2 good sized dressing rooms with mirrors and clothes rails.

The very large stage is accessed directly from outside through large acoustic loading doors and is set at ground level such that the first few rows of audience seats are actually below ground. It has a fully equipped flytower with fly and loading galleries, all accommodated under the main roof of the building.

The Dora Stoutzker Concert Hall is much larger than the theatre, accommodating more than twice the audience and seemingly at least three times the volume. And it is breathtakingly beautiful.

The material and colour palette here is dominated by light coloured timber veneered plywood panelling around the concert platform and audience with tall black painted walls above the balcony and more (slightly redder) timber veneered panelling across the entire ceiling. As with the Richard Burton Theatre the materials are simply but elegantly detailed each fulfilling a role that contributes to a very good natural room acoustic but with real coherence of vision and quality of execution.

The audience is primarily accommodated on a single stepped raking stalls floor but the balcony wrapping around the entire space in an unbroken sweep provides seating to the perimeter of the room that will certainly make for an intimate feel in a performance for both audience and orchestra.

The concert platform has three integral elevators that enable orchestras to be arranged on a flat stage or stepped dais and the first two rows of audience seats are on a further elevator which can extend the platform for larger ensembles.

The ceiling cleverly integrates a profile clearly driven by acoustics considerations with the needs of lighting and rigging into an architectural wave floating above a cornice-like timber gallery that follows the continuous line of the balcony below.

Backstage there are 2 Chorus dressing rooms and 2 soloist dressing rooms with en-suite facilities.

It is difficult to be anything other than completely impressed by the wonderful new building created for the College, it is simply a triumph of intelligent and creative Architecture and will undoubtedly become a landmark building in Cardiff for many years to come.

As a professional in the construction industry it is frankly bewildering how so much high quality building and space was squeezed out of what was really quite a small budget and I am full of admiration for the work of the Architects and team that delivered it.

At the time of writing the building has only been open a few months and the new academic year only a few days old yet in that time this building has established a full programme of performances open to the general public and signs are clear that it is already growing an audience enticed and seduced by the quality of the two principal performance spaces and large and spacious foyer and café space between them at the heart of the site.

The Royal Welsh College of Music and Drama will now surely not only cement but significantly enhance its reputation as one of the leading such organisations in the UK and the future for students, performers and audiences using this building is very bright indeed.

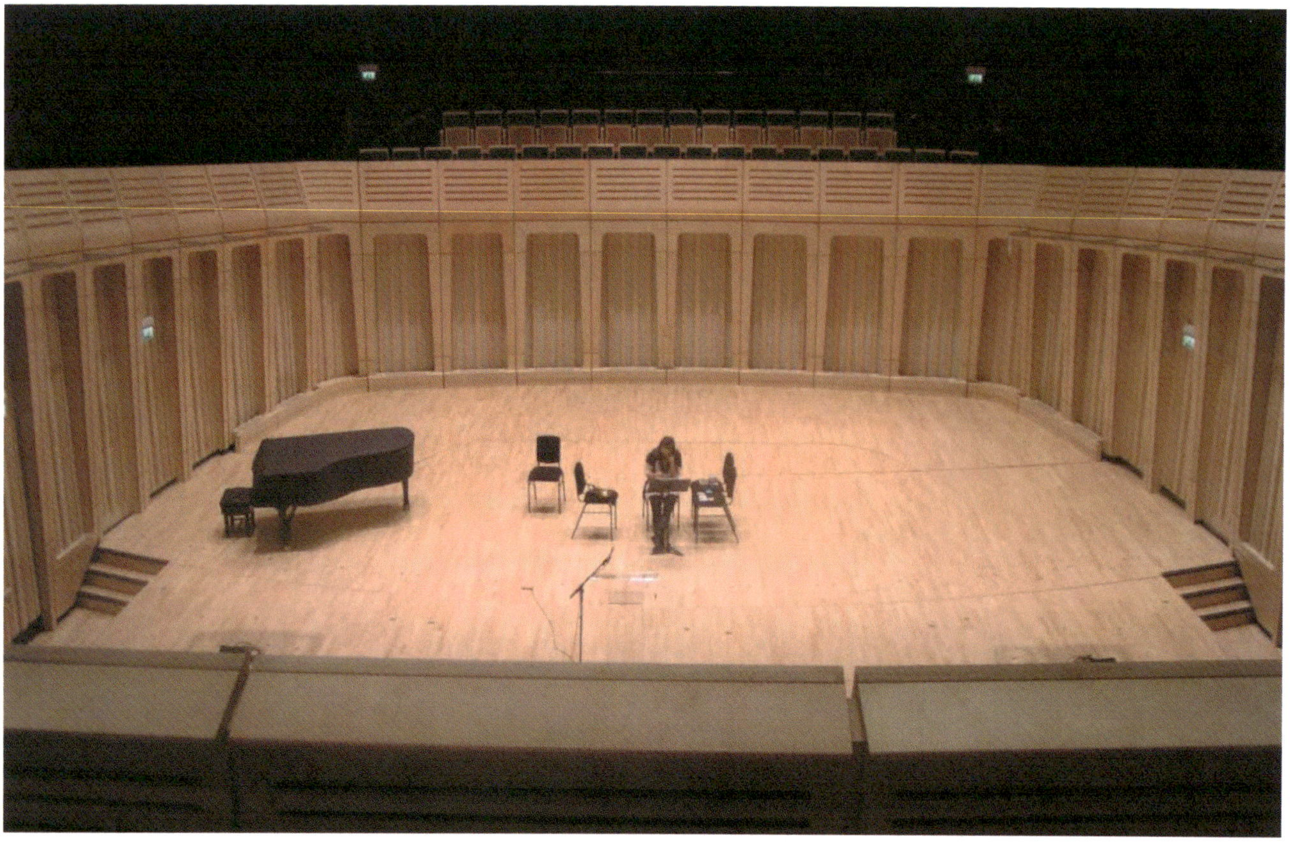

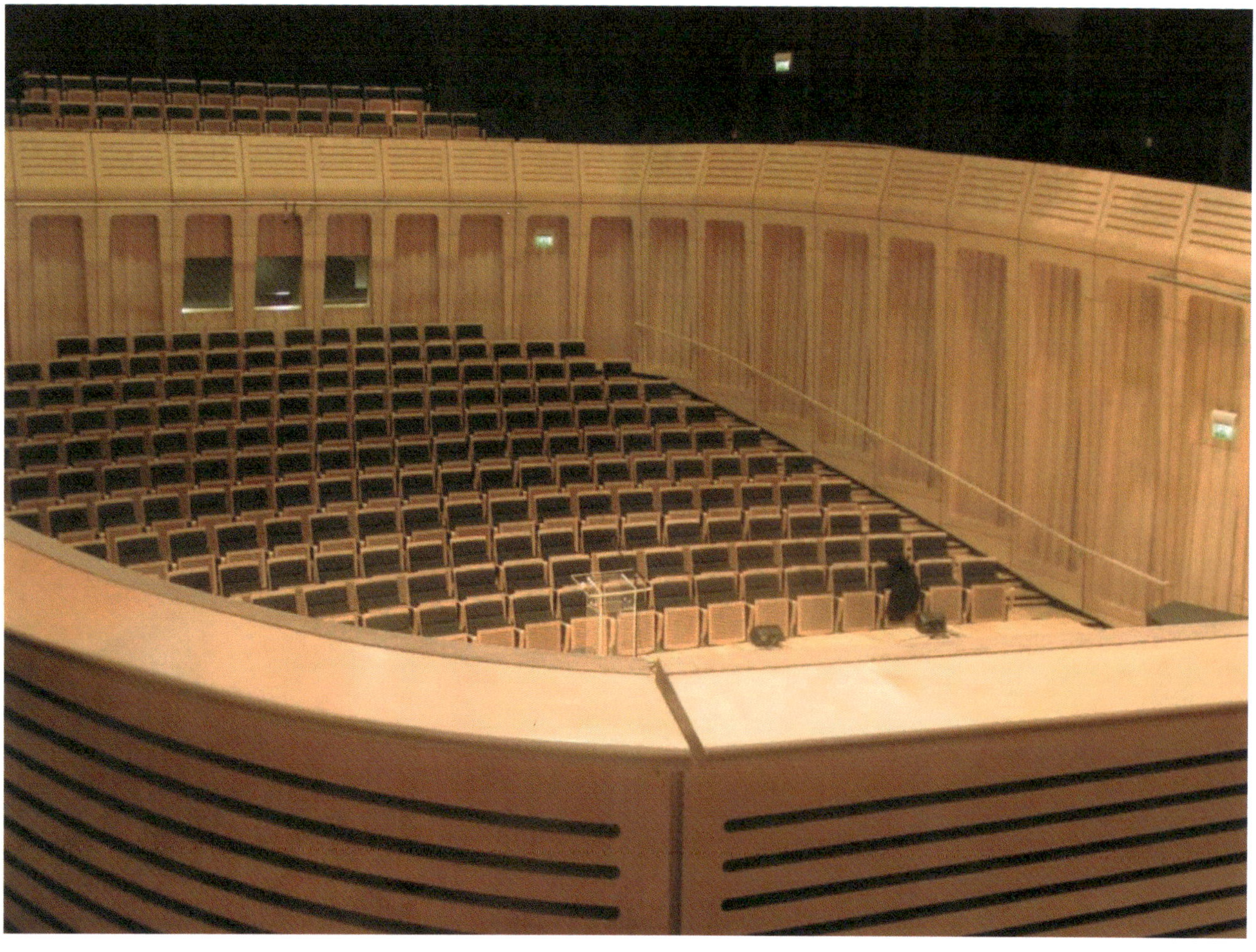

Sherman Cymru

Organisation: Sherman Cymru

Address: Senghennydd Road, Cardiff CF24 4YE

Construction/Opening: 1973

Architect: Alex Gordon & Partners, Cardiff

Builder: unknown

Current Owner: Sherman Cymru Board of Trustees

History/previous names & ownership

The original Sherman was built on the University College, Cardiff campus next to the University Students' Union building as a twin auditorium house, with substantial financial support from the University and when first opened was managed by the Drama Department of University College of South Wales and Monmouthshire.

In July 1987 University College Cardiff withdrew its financial support for the theatre and offered it for sale. The Arts Council of Wales purchased the building with a special grant from the Welsh Office and The Sherman Theatre Company was established. In 1994 the backstage areas were refurbished to plans drawn up by Architect The Lawray Partnership of Cardiff.

In the early 2000s Capita Percy Thomas Architects of Cardiff were selected to prepare design proposals for a major upgrade to the entire venue. The Sherman Theatre Company (previously the leading children's theatre company for Wales) and Sgript Cymru (previously the national agency for Welsh new writing for the theatre) merged in April 2007 to form a new company, called Sherman Cymru. The redevelopment plans were put on hold as funding difficulties delayed the project until in 2009 Sherman Cymru was awarded a total of £4.64 million from the Arts Council of Wales, the main award being a Capital Lottery Grant. Contractor Dawnus Construction of Swansea finally commenced construction operations in November 2010. The works involve the complete overhaul and major re-modelling of the foyer and front of house area including new toilets and new bar and café facilities as well as a totally new look for the exterior of the theatre building. There will also be new auditorium seating in the two performance spaces, new heating and ventilation systems as well as improvements to accessibility in all areas of the building. The backstage areas will be enhanced for staff and performers, including construction of a large new rehearsal room on the site of the current staff car park and new administrative offices for Sherman Cymru management and operational staff. Dressing room spaces will be improved.

As a result of the scale of change and redevelopment very few traces of the original building will be visible in the completed scheme. The re-opening is scheduled for 2012.

Auditorium Capacity:

Original 498; reduced to current capacity of 468 in 2002; capacity after 2010-12 alterations: 434 (Venue 1), 200 (Venue 2)

Stage details: (Prior to 2010-12 alterations)

Performance space – width – 24m
Performance space – depth – 13.5m
Depth of apron – 2.97m
Wing space (Right and Left) – (SR) 6.25m, (SL) 6.25m
Proscenium height/width – height 5.5m; width 11.5m
Orchestra pit (maximum no of players) – 30
Height from stage floor to grid – 14.63m
Rake – None

Visualisations of new designs for exterior and Venue 1 auditorium courtesy of Capita Architecture

St David's Hall

Organisation: Cardiff County Council

Address: The Hayes, Cardiff CF10 1AH

Construction: 1978 – 1982 **Opening:** 1982

Architect: The J. Seymour Harris Partnership, Cardiff

Builder: John Laing Construction Ltd

Current Owner: Cardiff County Council

History/previous names & ownership

As long ago as 1959, The Arts Council of Great Britain expressed concern that there were no proper facilities for major concerts in Cardiff and that a large, suitably designed concert hall was an amenity that should be provided in Cardiff at the earliest possible date. One idea at the time was to convert the Capitol Cinema on Queen Street into an Opera House that could also put on concerts.

However, it took until the late 1970s for a site originally earmarked for a new County Public Library on the roof of the proposed St David's Shopping Centre to become available and Cardiff City Council acquired it for a new concert hall. The decision to create a concert hall without a proscenium for theatre was taken early in the process. Taking five years from conception to completion, a 2,000-seat concert hall was built directly over the St David's Centre shopping mall in the centre of Cardiff. A special 'open day' held on 30 August 1982 attracted 21,000 people; nine days later came the first public concert, a free open rehearsal by the Polyphonic Choir. HRH Elizabeth the Queen Mother performed the official opening in February 1983.

A new sound system was installed in 2005 and has solved previous problems with performances using amplified sound.

Description

This is possibly one of the most unusual of the buildings for live entertainment in Wales insofar as it is located on top of a shopping mall and has only the minimum public face the developer would allow so as not to diminish the value of adjacent and surrounding retail spaces. As a consequence of its origins therefore the main entrance is little bigger than the neighbouring shop units and is by no means fitting for a venue of this importance and it has taken some time for the venue to establish a way of identifying itself at street level that didn't mimic the gaudy shopfronts it stands between.

The architecture of the building is also unusual insofar as the Architects also had to find a way of differentiating a nationally important building from the mall beneath it within what were probably significant constraints. Whether they succeeded in meeting this challenge or not is perhaps rather unimportant 20 years after its opening since it has over that period established for itself an instantly recognisable appearance.

Its concrete frame and oversailing terraces and upper floors have been softened over time but its huge and dominant lead clad mansard roof still looks unnecessarily heavy and monolithic.

The entrance is slightly elevated above street level and the public realm has been manipulated to accommodate steps and ramps to overcome the level difference. It's a small detail but the fact that there is this level difference does much to separate the entrance experience from the level entries of those surrounding shops and makes it feel like a more important place as a result.

Once inside the entrance hall is a curiously disjointed and oddly shaped space with escalators tucked away near the back suggesting the only way is up from here. The ticket desk is located here but really it is a transitional space and the real sense of arrival must wait until higher up the building.

Several escalator rides later the visitor arrives at the first real sense of a foyer serving such a building and it provides a clue that the spatial sequences of this building are starting to be resolved. The foyers take advantage of the fact that the shops below don't need to be particularly tall spaces and the curtilage of the concert hall spreads out over them and breaks out of the retail straitjacket below. A series of open and flowing spaces with generously wide staircases link the principal audience foyer levels and all circulation around the foyers passes the multiple entry points into the hall so it becomes much easier to navigate through the building generally.

The auditorium instills a variety of impressions depending on the point of entry – from the top tiers wrapping around the multiple tiers below it feels like a vast bowl yet from the main stalls floor everything feels rather intimate in front of the large stage. The form of the auditorium is defined as a 'vineyard' meaning rather than two or three centrally stacked tiers of audience there are many smaller tiers arranged on top and beside each other and all pointing the audience directly at the performance area. This arrangement makes such rooms very wide in relation to their overall depth but does create a large volume and a range of surfaces that combine to create a good acoustic environment for listening to unamplified music. And this room is hugely successful in this regard attaining a global reputation for its excellent acoustic. The room is visually quite plain and dominated by the bright green seat upholstery throughout. The lack of detail on the wall surfaces seems to place even greater emphasis on the conspicuously large concert organ offset to one side of the stage and located halfway up the wall. The ceiling is a perforated grid serving to mask the heavy engineering of structure and ventilation services above it but also to maximise the acoustic volume of the room.

The stage is very large (as it was designed to accommodate the largest orchestras) and is very flexible too, with multiple elevators and rostrum units enabling a wide range of arrangements of performers. There is no proscenium and when the Hall was used for ballet and other shows drapes were used to create the frame. The rear of the stage area is encircled by choir seating sometimes also used for audiences so that the performance can be completely wrapped in audience. There is a range of dressing room and other backstage accommodation grouped along the side of the building overlooking The Hayes and benefitting from windows and, in some instances, external balconies. Loading is via the adjacent multi-storey car park (recently modified as part of the enlargement of the St David's Shopping Centre) but as with the hall itself, once at the level above the mall all is well organised and works well.

St David's Hall has been acclaimed since its opening as one of Europe's finest concert halls and there is no reason to doubt it still holds such high acclaim amongst performers and critics. An orchestral hall on this scale is a vital component of any city's infrastructure, especially a capital city, and there should be no reason to suspect this venue has anything but a full and successful future.

Auditorium Capacity: 2000

Stage details:

Performance space – width – 17.3m
Performance space – depth – 16.6m
Depths of apron – variable
Wing space (Right and Left) – n/a
Proscenium height/width – n/a
Orchestra pit (maximum no of players) – 75
Height from stage floor to grid – variable
Rake – None

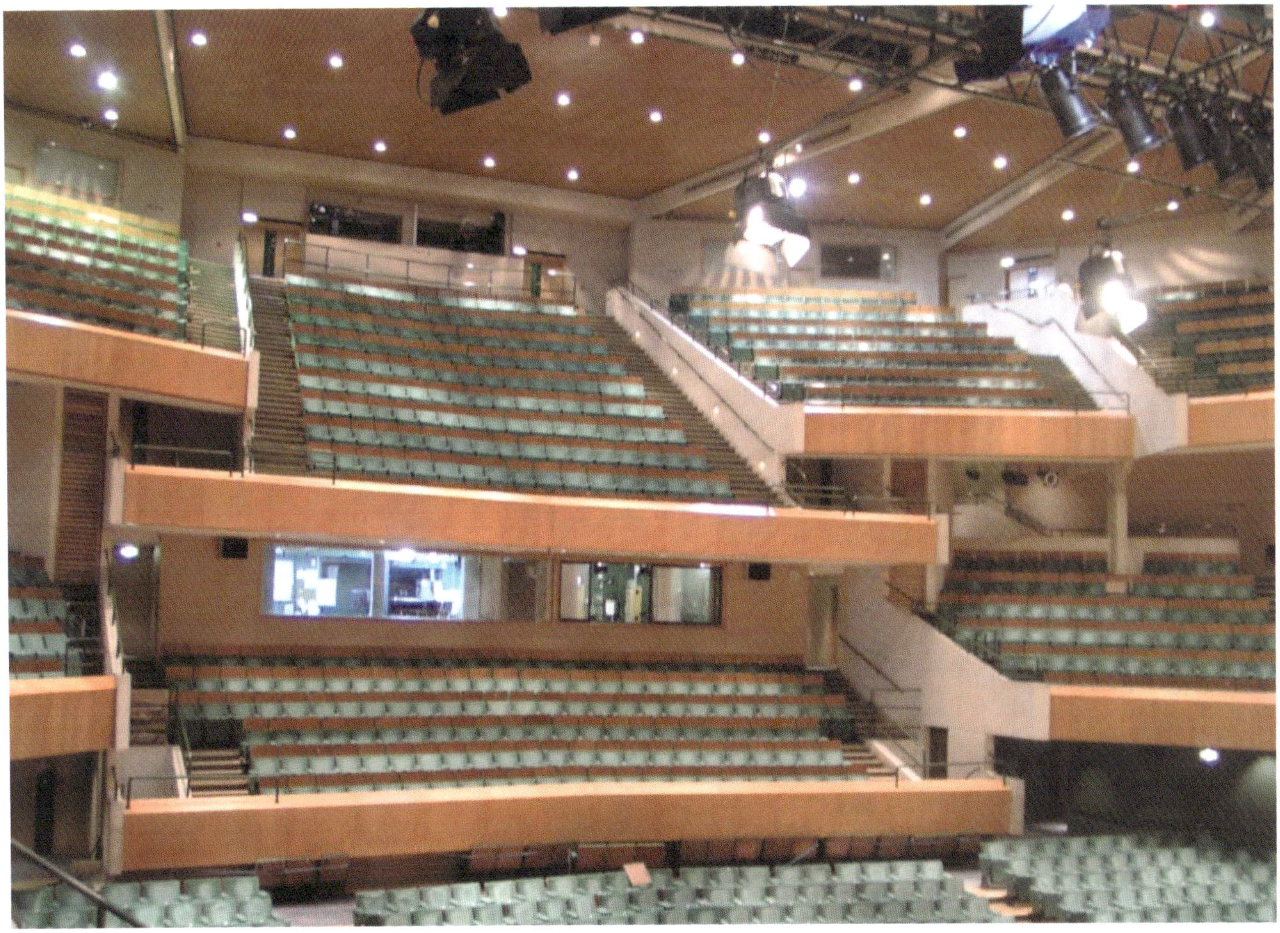

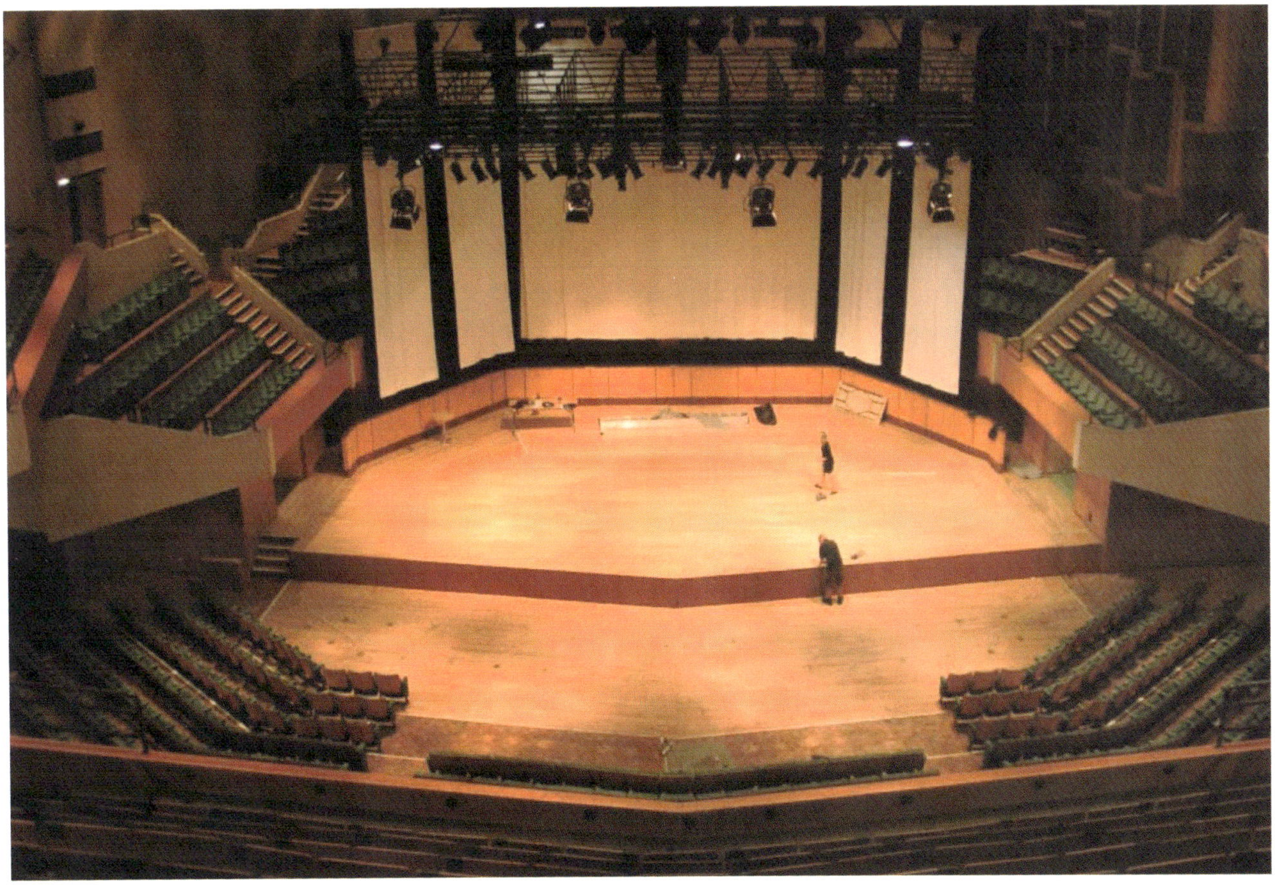

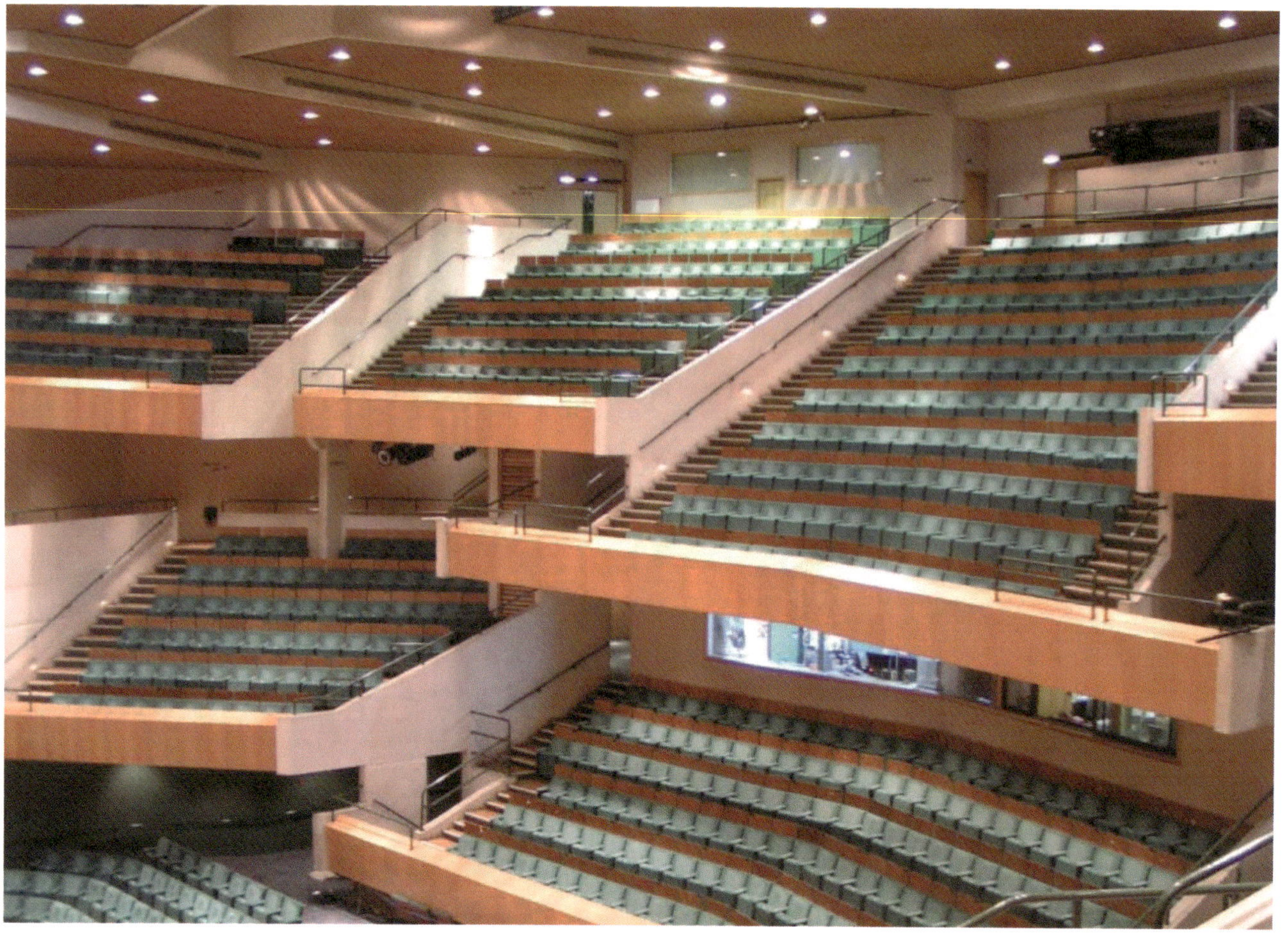

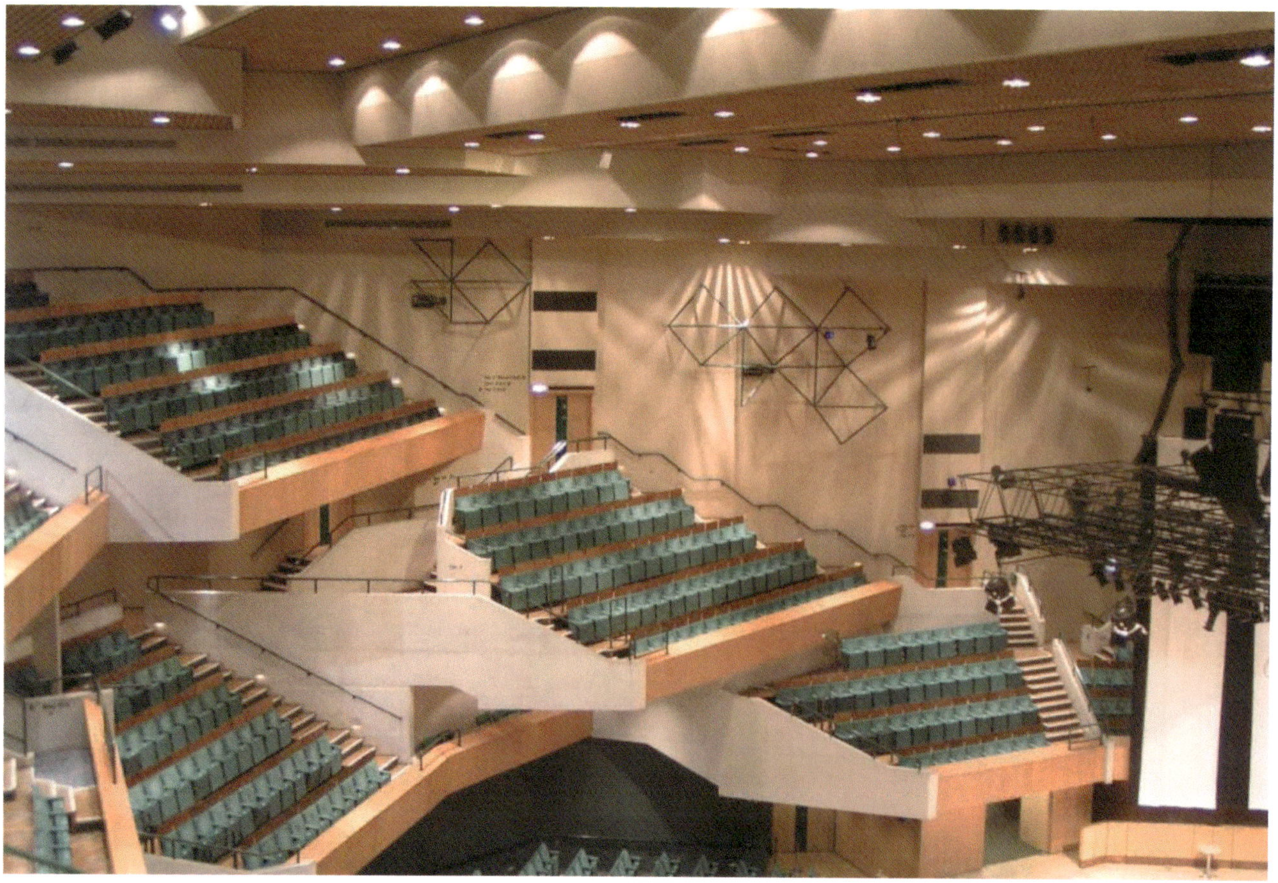

The Wales Millennium Centre

Organisation: Wales Millennium Centre Trust

Address: Bute Place, Cardiff Bay, Cardiff CF10 5AL

Construction: 2002-2004 **Opening:** 2004

Architect: Percy Thomas Partnership, Cardiff

Builder: Sir Robert McApine Ltd

Current Owner: Wales Millennium Centre Trust

History/previous names & ownership

At the end of 1995, the Millennium Commission finally brought the curtain down on plans to build an Opera House in Cardiff Bay to designs by Architect Zaha Hadid by refusing funding for the controversial project.

In the summer of 1996 the Institute of Welsh Affairs brokered a package to resurrect a project containing a large theatre for Cardiff. The Welsh think-tank drew together major public and private sector organisations and, in a report entitled Bread and Roses, made a convincing case for a Millennium Centre for the Arts. Soon afterwards a National Lottery grant to the Cardiff Bay Development Corporation was awarded to fund a feasibility study into a building on the same site as the original Hadid proposal and initial thinking was that the new building would include a 2,000-seat music theatre, an IMAX cinema, a new `People and the Sea' museum and the headquarters for Welsh National Opera. The Wales Millennium Centre constituted itself as a charity and a company to take forwards proposals for an arts venue in Cardiff Bay.

In October 1996 the architects, Percy Thomas Partnership were appointed. By October 1997 a scheme was developed that finally secured full backing of the Millennium Commission, the Arts Councils of England and Wales, Cardiff Council and The Welsh Assembly Government and with funding in place the project design commenced in earnest.

A review of the project content during the first 6 months of this period identified that the proposed Museum component would be better provided by what later became the National Waterfront Museum built in Swansea and the commercial nature of the IMAX cinema was also inappropriate for this development. Instead, attention moved to the creation of a 'cultural village' with accommodation provided around the central large theatre for several of the leading Arts Companies in Wales. As the brief developed the accommodation expanded until finally there was space designed for seven separate organisations as well as the central facilities for the Wales Millennium Centre organisation itself.

In November 1999, WMC entered into a contract with construction company AMEC to negotiate a guaranteed maximum price for construction. In late June 2000, AMEC submitted its final price which was significantly above the budget, and the WMC decided to terminate the contract. Because of the uncertainty surrounding the project, the Millennium Commission suspended its payments to the WMC. The WMC decided to embark on a process of redesigning the building with a 25 per cent reduction in size to cut costs and Planning Permission for that scheme was granted in March 2001. In December 2001 a new building contract was awarded to Sir Robert McAlpine Ltd. Construction operations commenced in February 2002 with completion achieved in just 33 months by June 2004. The Wales Millennium Centre was officially opened by Her Majesty Queen Elizabeth II on 25th November 2004.

Description

This building has become one of the most recognised in the UK if not across Europe and as such surely achieved one of the key criteria for success set out at the birth of the project, at a time when Wales was becoming increasingly self-confident as a Nation.

Of course I have to declare an interest at this point since I worked on this project from January 1998 through to its completion and opening in November 2004 during which time this was the only project I was working on. It was my magnum opus and as the Executive Architect and Project Director leading an extraordinarily talented team of colleagues and other design consultants I have nothing but pride for what we achieved. If my narrative drifts away from the generality of describing the building and into thoughts about why we made things the way we did I can only hope that this enhances the information rather than detracts from the experience of reading about it.

This is a very large building by any standards in the world of performing arts and it fully occupies a large, roughly triangular site at the heart of the Cardiff Bay regeneration area. Its scale is in part driven by the extremely complex requirements deriving from the undertaking to provide accommodation for 7 of the leading Arts Organisations of Wales on one site (along with space and facilities for the overall Centre Management) with a theatre of a capacity commensurate with its ambition to be one of the best in the world and all of the spaces and facilities audiences for such an operation would need. Of course its scale is also, in part, driven by an architectural idea to create something memorable and unique.

The orientation of the building on its site was an important factor in the development of the design too. To the west is the Oval Basin (now Roald Dahl Plass) - a remnant of the once vast commercial docks infrastructure, to the south the new Welsh Assembly Government buildings and to the north and east land ear-marked for future commercial development of an unknown character or quality. Prior to the WMC development the Oval Basin was part of the National Industrial and Maritime Museum but once the artefacts and exhibits had been cleared from that as part of the Mermaid Quay commercial development project carried out for Cardiff Bay Development Corporation it was transformed into a public plaza on a grand scale to designs by Nicholas Hare Architects of London. The new plaza became the forecourt to the WMC, allowing the building to be viewed from a distance and driving the location of the building's entrance and general organisation.

The Oval Basin and the WMC sites get very close to each other at one point and this proximity led to the asymmetrical appearance of the final design, although it enabled the main entrance to be located on the axis of James Street which is one of the main approaches to the building from Butetown and Grangetown beyond. The frontage to the Oval Basin and James Street therefore became the grand facade with the other two primary faces of the building responding to the nature of existing and anticipated developments, both in scale and material. The principal elevation is dominated by two features - the theatre clad in patinated stainless steel and the public concourse and foyer with its polychromatic welsh slate walls.

The theatre was always conceived as a distinct element within the composition perching on top of a solid base and the selection of materials was made with due cognisance to the exposed nature of the site as well as to a desire to represent something about the landscape and industrial legacy of Wales in the building. The massive inscription over the entrance was part of the original concept too, although it took a competition organised by one of the Centre's Resident Organisations, Academi, to find the final words (by Gwynneth Lewis). The inscription recognises the roman tradition of dedicating their buildings to a God, a Ceasar or patron and makes reference to the long occupation of Wales by the Romans in its font style. By making the individual letters a storey-height tall and glazing them, the theatre foyers have a unique view out from them and at night when illuminated from within, they identify the building like no other form of signage could hope to achieve.

The large cantilever of the theatre out into the plaza and over the entrance doors enables the visitor to intuitively understand where to enter and there are many doors leading into the building so there should never be a queue. On the outside, the underside of the cantilevered section is gently arched, with its high-point in the centre but as the surface passes over the entrance lobby and into the concourse area the arch reverses such that it is lower in the centre than at the edges. This compression of the volume tends to encourage vistors to move away from the potentially crowded area in front of the expansive ticket desk and cloakrooms into the much taller spaces either side and towards the entry points to the main theatre and other front-of-house facilities. Again, this is deliberate and minimises the need for extensive directional signage.

Either side of the main entrance/reception space are the concourse areas. The one to the north is smaller in footprint though no less tall than the one to the south - as a result of being close to the northern site boundary and contains a grand, wide staircase leading up to the main theatre and a suite of function rooms (and now providing access to Hoddinutt Hall added to the complex in 2009), with a coffee bar and retail unit (currently occupied by a Tourism Information Centre but in the past being occupied by an exhibition of the development of the building design, a contemporary visual art gallery and a car showroom).

In the south concourse there is a second staircase leading up to the main theatre (and also to the audience entry point for the Weston Studio), three further retail/catering outlets and a permanent stage for lunchtime performances and recitals for which audiences are not charged. The south concourse also provides access to the accommodation provided for two of the Centre's Arts Resident organisations: Ty Cerdd and Touch Trust.

Both concourse spaces are toplit by light slots formed in the construction of the roofs and around these public front-of-house areas the building has a continuous 'skirt' at ground floor level of full-height glazing allowing people outside to see the activities within. They are both visually dominated by the grand stairs and balconies, faced in indigenous Welsh hardwoods in their natural colours and echoing the coloured horizontal 'strata' of slate on the outside. The balconies are supported by randomly placed slender black columns, each with a light fitting at its head throwing artificial light up onto the white ceiling which reflects much softer, indirect light down to the floor. The columns have a textured surface which is an abstract version of prehistoric tree fossils found in the coal seams of Wales. The gentle random curves of the balcony upstands contrast with the sheer white wall behind that separates the front-of-house from Resident Organisation accommodation beyond. This white wall is approximately on the same line as the main theatre proscenium in plan and divides front-of-house from back-of-house along the entire length of the building.

Taking one of the grand stairs up from the concourses is to start a promenade through the building that provides unfolding and ever changing views of ithe spaces, culminating in arrival, effectively at second floor, in the main theatre foyer. Here is a triple height volume made to feel even larger by the outward inclination of the external wall that folds back over the audience at the highest level and is lit in such a way as to appear to have no edges or corners. The reverse view of the monumental inscription is a delight here, with each of the three levels of foyer having their own row of text 'windows' to look out over the plaza below through. Each level of foyer is carpeted in a rich brown carpet unique to the centre and is serviced with a large central bar. The organisation of audience facilities in the foyers is thought out well with toilets being close to the auditorium and the bar equidistant from the auditorium access points.

Before actually entering the main auditorium, the audience passes through one more space, known during the design period as 'Inner foyers'. These spaces deal with the level differences between regularly spaced decks of foyer and the internal tiers of the auditorium with a mixture of shallow ramps and gentle steps in an environment purposely made as soft and sound absorbing as possible. At higher levels the audience is afforded glimpses of the audience entering below as they cross bridges through a full height void against the walls of the auditorium. The idea here was to reinforce the sense of a larger community of audience within the room since once on the separate tiers the audience is arranged in smaller groups that tend to interact only with those immediately around them.

The auditorium is arranged with a stalls, stalls parterre, dress circle and upper circle balcony and a conscious decision was taken early in the design process to create an auditorium recognisably respecting traditional theatre layouts but to express that in a contemporary idiom. Above all the design development focussed on excellent sightlines from all seats and on creating a sense of intimacy between performer and audience that belied the audience capacity of 1700-1900. This was achieved by continuing the balcony fronts of the stalls parterre and the upper balconies around the side walls of the auditorium until they met two pairs of boxes immediately adjacent the proscenium wall. Between the principal balcony levels additional side-slips were introduced at intermediate levels. The brief required a programme of both unamplified performances and amplified shows and this technical contradiction led to many decisions about detail and material choices being made in conjunction with the Acoustic Consultants. The resolution of the demanding constraints of the acoustic 'science' with the architectural manifestation of the room is achieved by the use of randomly sized plaster blocks with randomly cast surfaces, some of which serving the need to reflect sound and others to disperse or fragment it. The blocks were laid individually in layers and take the idea of natural materials being laid in horizontal strata through from the exterior to the foyers and finally into the room itself. The balcony fronts complete this connection by using similar layered hardwood strips as those in the concourses. The auditorium seats are unique to the WMC and were designed by the Architects in conjunction with the manufacturer. The fabric used to upholster them was provided by a company owned by the current Marquis of Bute extending a connection between that family and Cardiff into a third century.

The stage is equipped such that it enables Wales to provide a stage for any performance by any organisation, whatever the size, and can be enlarged further from its already significant footprint by use of the 6 elevators that form orchestra pit, additional audience seating or forestage extension. There is also a rear-stage of the same overall size as the main stage performance area and access through a double layer of acoustic-barrier doors into one of Welsh National Opera's rehearsal rooms to provide a side-stage space when required.

It has a full-height flytower and extensive wing space. Indeed, the back-stage planning of this building was given as much consideration as the public areas. Dressing Room accommodation is provided for over 100 performers as well as for a full orchestra in separate band-rooms and dedicated chorus dressing spaces. There is extensive storage around and under the main stage.

The arrangement and size of the buildings around the perimeter of the site enabled a large off-road loading bay to be created and the theatre has the capacity to load/unload up to 5 articulated trucks simultaneously. Very few theatres on the UK touring circuit have such a facility. The loading bay can be split into two parts - one area serving the main theatre and the second leading into Welsh National Opera's accommodation and suite of 5 rehearsal rooms. All of these rehearsal rooms are linked by the 'scenery street', a 10 metre high, 6 metre wide corridor that enables very large pieces of equipment and scenery to be moved between truck and room and from room to main theatre stage.

Welsh National Opera is provided with 3 rehearsal rooms, each the same size as the main performance space on the main theatre stage with an additional similar sized room dedicated for use by the WNO Orchestra and a further, smaller space for rehearsals by the choir. Each of these rooms is designed with appropriate acoustics for their use. One of the 'opera' rehearsal rooms has been fitted out such that when not being used by WNO it can be used for public performances. The Weston Studio accommodates 250 people on retractable seating and with its sound/light control room and technical galleries is a successful little auditorium in its own right.

In the wing of the building on Pierhead Street and opposite the National Assembly for Wales is accommodation for four Resident Organisations - The National Dance Company of Wales (originally Diversions Dance Company), Academi, Hijinx Theatre Company and Urdd Gobaith Cymru.

The wing is a 4 storey brick-faced block but there is little ordinary about it. The bricks used are larger than normal and the wall leans away from the street allowing large windows to project through it at first and second floor levels. The parapet line follows a gentle wave curve rather than being flat.

The Dance Company has two rehearsal studios, the larger of which is equipped with retractable seating for audiences of up to 80 people and limited flying capacity. It has become an important and successful venue that many dance companies have graced.

Academi and Hijinx have accommodation focussed on administrative activities but both organisations regularly use facilities elsewhere in the building for recitals and performances.

The Urdd has accommodation thought to be unique anywhere in the world in complexes similar to the WMC insofar as it provides hostel accommodation for young people within the building as well as teaching and social spaces and their own performance space with 180 seats.

The Wales Millennium Centre has become a very successful venue, renowned globally for the quality of its facilities and presenting a range of performances by companies and individual performers of the highest quality. Subsidised by the Welsh Assembly Government as well as the Arts Council of Wales the venue should continue to enhance both its own reputation and that of the whole of Wales with which it is now inextricably associated.

Auditorium and Stage details:

Donald Gordon Theatre

Audience capacity: 1900 (maximum)

Performance space – width – 32m (including wings)
Performance space – depth – 20m
Depth of apron – variable
Wing space (Right and Left) – SR – 8m; SL – 8m
Proscenium height/width – height – 10m (adjustable); width – 13.75m – 16.0m
Orchestra pit (maximum no of players) - 95
Height from stage floor to grid – 27m
Rake – none

Weston Studio

Audience capacity: 250

Performance space – width – variable (up to 16m)
Performance space – depth – variable
Depth of apron – n/a
Wing space (Right and Left) – variable dependent on staging
Proscenium height/width – n/a
Orchestra pit (maximum no of players) – n/a
Height from stage floor to grid – 9.6m (to tension wire grid)
Rake – none

Ty Dawns

Audience capacity: 80

Performance space – width – variable (up to 12m)
Performance space – depth – variable
Depth of apron – n/a
Wing space (Right and Left) – variable (dependent on staging)
Proscenium height/width – n/a
Orchestra pit (maximum no of players) – n/a
Height from stage floor to grid – 9.6m
Rake – none

Urdd Hall

Audience capacity: 180

Performance space – width – variable (up to 10m)
Performance space – depth – variable
Depth of apron – n/a
Wing space (Right and Left) – variable (dependent on staging)
Proscenium height/width – n/a
Orchestra pit (maximum no of players) – n/a
Height from stage floor to grid – 6m
Rake – none

Vale of Glamorgan

Barry

The Memorial Hall & Theatre

The Theatre Royal

Cowbridge

The Market Theatre

Penarth

The Paget Rooms

St Donats

St Donats Arts Centre

The Memorial Hall & Theatre, Barry

Organisation: The Memorial Hall & Theatre Trust

Address: Gladstone Road, Barry CF64 8NA

Construction/Opening: 1932

Architect: E R Hinchsliff

Builder: Vickery Bros

Current Owner: The Memorial Hall & Theatre Trust

History/previous names & ownership

The building was constructed as The Memorial Hall & Theatre at a cost of £23,906 in 1932.

It was seriously damaged by fire and left derelict and open to the elements in 1943 and it wasn't until 1957 that it was reconstructed and re-opened. At this time an extension providing dressing room and stage door accommodation was added.

In 1966 the Annexe was built to designs drawn up by Alex Gordon & Partners, Architects, Cardiff as a secondary entrance and providing licensed bar facilities to the building.

In 1986 Barry Town Council and the British Chapter of the American Theatre Organ Society collaborated to install a Christie Theatre Organ (50 year old organ obtained from the Regal Cinema, Edmonton, London). With its four keyboards this is believed to be the second largest concert organ still in existence. The inaugural concert featuring the organ took place on 28th February 1987.

In 1992 a further extension was added and enveloped the earlier annex to designs by Killick McAdam Urquhart Architects and accommodating Barry Town Council Offices.

The Glamorgan Suite was refurbished in 1994 and since 2000 there have been miscellaneous internal alterations & decorations including Box Office and Administration improvements, access improvements and front-of-house upgrade.

During 2010 The Memorial Hall and Theatre Trust assumed ownership of the venue from Barry Town Council and an ongoing programme of improvement works included conversion of some dressing rooms into multi-function rooms (providing revenue generating meeting/conference facilities as well as changing facilities when required), redecoration and modernisation of Green Room and the removal of the Christie Organ allowing the sub-stage area to be cleared and converted to storage space.

Description

The Memorial Hall and Theatre was clearly conceived as a grand civic building, manifested in its stone and brick facades. The principal entrance to the building (identified by the town's cenotaph) has feature columns and significant glazing though entry is into a surprisingly small foyer space.

Between the main entrance (containing ticket desk, audience WCs and sweet shop/merchandise counter) and the main hall is a formal memorial room to the war dead of Barry from all 20th century conflicts. It is a hardwood panelled room with gold leaf inscribed names of the fallen.

The main hall is very large and has a flat floored stalls (utilising loose seating and other furniture to achieve wide variety of configurations to suit a large range of events) and a single upper balcony with fixed seating. A permanent in-room sound and light mixing desk position has been created at the rear of the upper balcony at the expense of some audience seats and the original sound/light control position separated from the auditorium volume is never used. The Hall walls and ceiling are quite plain with minimal feature mouldings and such like – they are mostly painted plaster, whilst the stalls floor is a sprung timber floor and upper balcony aisles and seatways are carpeted. The room appears to have an excellent acoustic response for unamplified music and singing. There is no orchestra pit.

The room benefits from windows at high level but these are covered with drapes and not uncovered for any performance/rehearsal/event. There are 1950's fan-coil units around the perimeter of stalls with open grilles in the ceiling at high level as the only form of heating and ventilation. No major issues of over-heating in summer/hard to heat in winter were reported during the author's visit.

The stage is raised high above the stalls level (due to an installation of a large concert blower organ underneath) and has full flying capability via a very unusual free-standing fly gallery and grid installation. Following removal of the organ installation the under-stage rooms have been upgraded and converted into storage areas.

There are 2 'star' dressing rooms accessed directly off stage right with further large dressing rooms/band rooms provided in the nearby 1950's extension which also provides the theatre with an un-manned stage door facility. The larger dressing rooms have been converted into multiple use rooms to increase building revenue streams.

Loading/Unloading onto stage is currently carried out via fire exit doors in the auditorium stalls side wall and equipment is man-handled up onto stage. The original loading bay installation is approximately 15 feet above the car park to rear of the building and is impossible to use. An alternative route to stage from the car park via the stage basement is possible but requires hoisting of incoming/outgoing equipment through a small trap against the upstage wall.

A Box Office and Bar entrance is now provided at the rear of the building with access to the general public directly from the large on-site surface car park or from the main auditorium stalls. A lift to facilitate wheelchair/buggy access has been installed adjacent some original steps to deal with the level difference. As well as the public bar that serves the main auditorium, there is a fully equipped catering kitchen which serves events such as weddings, banquets and conferences.

Above the main entrance foyer on the first floor is the 'Glamorgan Suite' – a cabaret style room with small raised stage (supported by large dressing room) and bar servery. It has veneered panelled walls with a carpeted floor and a small sprung dance floor area in front of the stage.

On the second floor is the Oriel Suite, a bright rehearsal room/dance space with mezzanine.

This venue is the only large place for live entertainment in the town of Barry and with the addition of a cinematograph licence is able to provide facilities for a wide range of audiences and users.

Under the management of an ambitious Trust further revenue streams and enhancements to the facilities in the building are being developed and its future seems assured.

Auditorium Capacity:

Original - Closely Seated 668

Theatre Seated (with orchestra/conductors pit) 554

Dancing (no furniture) 960

Dining/Dancing (cabaret style) 350

Balcony 416

Main Auditorium (incl. Balcony) 1084

Current - Main Auditorium - 387 fixed seats on balcony, 498 max loose seats on stalls (dependent on configuration)

Glamorgan Suite – 200 max (dependent on configuration)

Oriel Suite – 80 max (dependent on configuration)

Stage details:

Performance space – width - 11.85m
Performance space – depth – 7.2m
Depth of apron – 3.1m
Wing space (Right and Left) – included in overall stage width dimension above
Proscenium height/width – height 6.4m; width 10.06m
Orchestra pit (maximum no of players) – n/a
Height from stage floor to grid – 18.3m
Rake - None

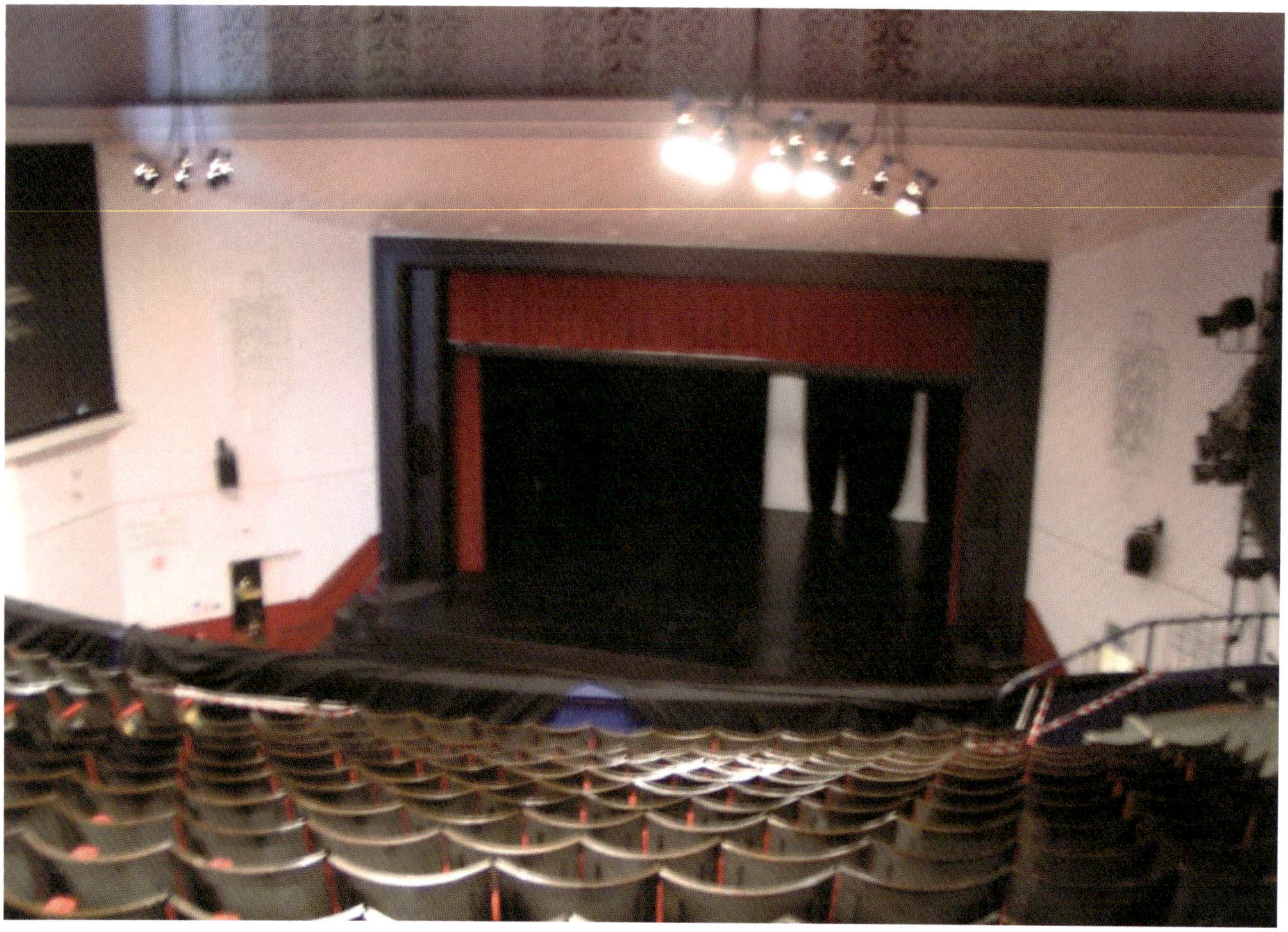

1914
1918
Mynedfa Cenotaph Entrance

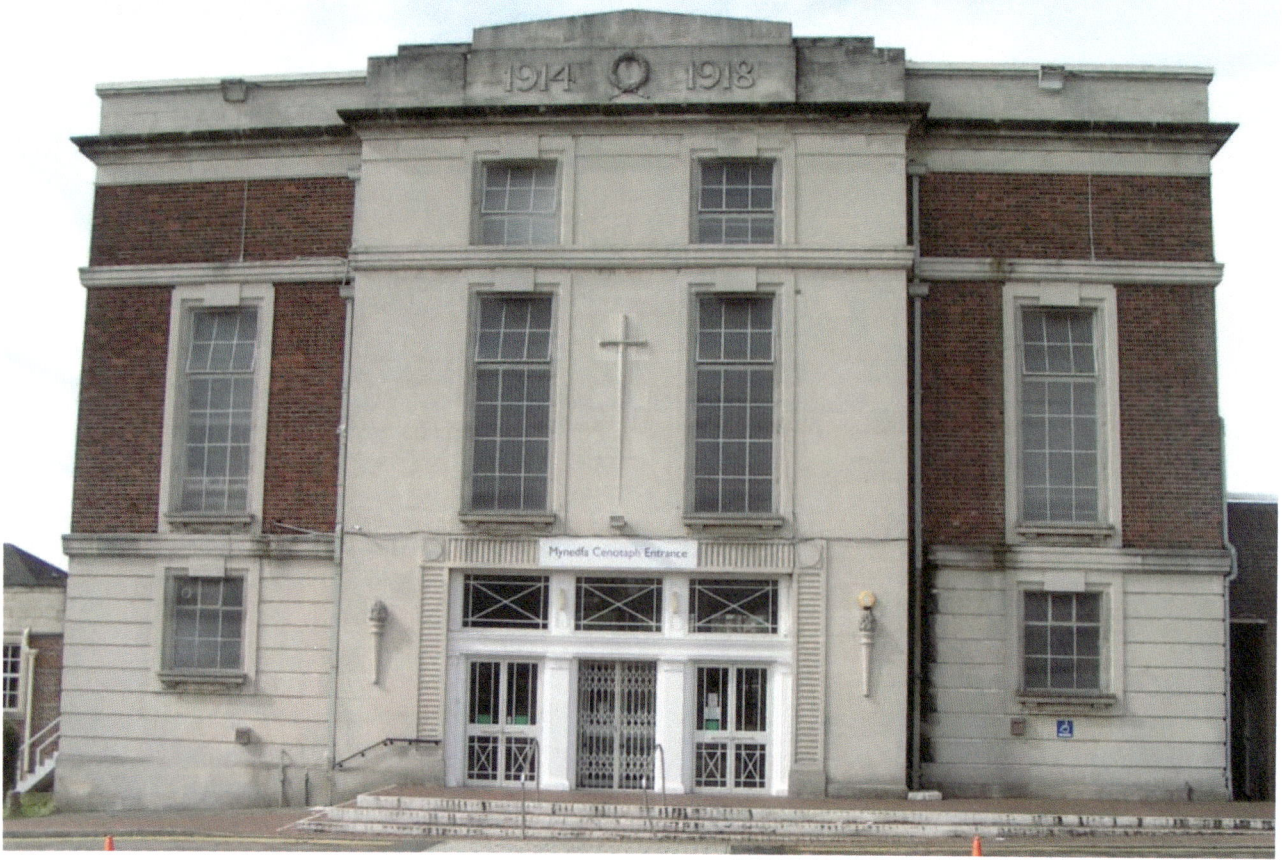

The Theatre Royal, Barry

Organisation: None

Address: Broad Street, Barry CF62 7AL

Construction/Opening: 1910

Architect: W. Ernest Knapman, Winship & Knapman, Barry Dock

Builder: Nicholds and Reynolds

Current Owner: Hafod Care

History/previous names & ownership

The original Theatre Royal and Hippodrome in Barry opened in 1907. It was constructed on the site currently occupied by the Savoy Club. It burnt down in November 1909 and the current Theatre Royal was built on the current site (across the street) to replace it. It was designed as a live theatre by local architect W.E. Knapman of Winship & Knapman and was opened on 25th July 1910 as the Theatre Royal by Messrs Tours Ltd under the management of Arthur Carlton. Remnants of wallpaper surviving from the opening have been discovered with the monogram 'AC' on it. The new theatre was equipped with an orchestral organ manufactured by Messrs Nicholson of Worcester. Famous actress Lillie Langtry appeared at the Theatre Royal in 1918 amongst many other significant performers of the era. In the pre-1930 period, stage shows were an important part of the programme, and relics of this period have been revealed in the currently closed building, early moving pictures on the "Universal Animatograph" were advertised in June 1911 and silent movies were shown as a summer season in that year.

In 1930 it was purchased by W. A. O'Connor and substantial alterations were carried out to designs by J. E. Owen, Architect and constructed by Vickery Bros which included increasing the audience capacity to 2400. The auditorium seating was re-configured into stalls and a single balcony. The proscenium was 40 feet wide, the stage was 25 feet deep and there were 12 dressing rooms. There was also a cafe for the convenience of patrons. In 1931 a sound system was installed and the theatre was effectively converted into a cinema and re-named Royal Super Cinema. In 1936 it again changed hands and was purchased by the Barton Cinema Company Ltd. On 17th May 1940 it was closed and remained so until re-opening on 3 June 1944. Renovations and alterations were carried out in this period (delayed by a shortage of labour due to the Second World War) and when it reopened as a 'Super Luxury Theatre' it had a reduced capacity of 1500 achieved by complete re-seating and increasing the row spacing with the intent of creating the most comfortable of all of the 8 cinemas in Barry at that time. It was renamed the Theatre Royal at this time.

In the period between 1944 and 1947 some more re-building occurred. A false ceiling was added and original decorative details were covered over. This included original decorations of painted scenes and trees being painted over and a new coved proscenium arch being built. Seating was now provided for 915. As was common at the time, a new "wide screen" was advertised in January 1954. An application to convert the theatre into a Bingo Hall submitted by a subsidiary of the owning company was approved in 1973 but the conversion works were never carried out. In 1980 only the circle seats were sold and the stalls area fell into disuse and neglect. The original screen remained on stage and audience capacity became 489.

Circle Cinemas purchased the building in 1985. In 1993 the original canopy over the entrance was removed as it was deemed to be structurally unsound then in 1994 the front stalls was completely closed off and left derelict and the cinema screen was brought forward to the line of the original balcony front to create 'Screen One' on the circle with a second screen created in the former rear stalls. The two screens seated 300 and 233. It is presumed that at the same time a new canopy was installed over the main entrance and mosaics installed in the pavement in front of the building.

Since April 2008 the Theatre Royal has been closed and left derelict but a local campaign to save the building as a cinema gathered pace and support in light of a proposal to demolish the building and replace with it Care Homes for the Elderly announced in summer 2010. Around the same time, the Theatres Trust included the building on its Theatre Buildings At Risk Register. In April 2011 however, full planning permission was granted by the Vale of Glamorgan Council Planning Committee allowing for the demolition of the Theatre Royal and work is expected to commence in the spring of 2012 and its loss seems certain.

Description

The Theatre Royal is located on a prominent site on a roundabout on one of the main approaches into the town centre from the recently regenerated docks area. It is the largest and tallest building for some distance around and therefore easily found and instantly recognisable. The wide four storey main frontage is constructed principally of red brick with dressed stone surrounds and features to openings and white painted rendered panels at the ground floor base and high level parapet levels. The exterior is much less elaborately detailed and decorated than original renderings of the building suggest was intended but it is not known if the Architect's intent was realised and later stripped back or if the current appearance is original.

There is a central projecting bay with a large arched window over the main entrance and stacked smaller windows above with feature stone dressing surround and surmounted by a broken pediment. The sides and rear of the building are finished almost entirely in white render, almost certainly added long after completion and the flamboyant stone pediment and balustrade around the shop units has long disappeared along with access to the garden terrace originally on the roof of the shops and accessible at intervals from the theatre auditorium.

The entrance is set back from the road and the approach forecourt features a pair of fine inlaid mosaic tiled murals of well-known film studios' logos around 'Theatre Royal, Barry' name as if to emphasise the independence of the venue. It is understood that these date from around the period in the late 1980s and early 1990s when the last significant building renovations were carried out. The entrance doors are sheltered by a clumsy and out-of-scale canopy.

The building is currently boarded up and in a state of dereliction with advanced wild vegetation growth along the small access to the side and evidence of significant graffiti and other vandalism. The shop units along its southern flank are also empty and boarded up as the building awaits its demolition.

Auditorium Capacity:

Original: 2000; 1930: 2400; 1944: 1500; 1947: 915; 1980: 489; 1994: 300 (Screen One), 233 (Screen Two)

Stage details: Not available

The Market Theatre, Cowbridge

Organisation: Cowbridge Amateur Dramatic Society

Address: The Butts, Cowbridge CF71 7AS

Construction/Opening: 1969

Architect/Builder: none

Current Owner: Cowbridge Amateur Dramatic Society

History/previous names & ownership

The Market Theatre building was constructed from two post-war prefab house units by CADS members on land owned by the County Council next to the Cattle Market in 1969.

Over the last 40 years the membership of the Society have carried out many alterations to the original building such that now the only truly original part remaining are the steel trusses supporting the roof. Modifications to the building envelope have included the replacement of the original prefab wall cladding with concrete blockwork and over-cladding of the original roof with insulated panels. They have replaced the original loose seating with fixed auditorium chairs purchased from Welsh Water Headquarters in Brecon and constructed the associated fixed stepped rake to part of auditorium along with balustrades and edge-guarding themselves. They have constructed lean-to extensions to create a bar and lounge area, additional workshop/storage space backstage, a dressing room and an entrance porch/reception and most recently installed a stair lift to connect the auditorium to the bar/lounge area for people with movement impairment (funded by grant from the Arts Council of Wales).

Description

The theatre is housed in a freestanding single storey building of a simple construction comprising exposed concrete blockwork to the walls and metal faced insulated cladding panel pitched roof. It is located just off the High Street of Cowbridge at the end of a large surface car park shared with the operators of the adjacent cattle market. The condition of the car park and approach to the theatre is evidence of extremely heavy use by large vehicles and it is seriously pot-holed and prone to forming large muddy puddles. A small grassed area separates the building from the car park and the building is signified by a small name- sign and noticeboard advertising forthcoming events. The main entrance is rather tucked away in the side of a later extension but it is sheltered from the weather and provides good access for anyone with movement impairment. The small entrance hall/reception space leads directly into the auditorium at the rear of the audience seating and it is an extremely warm and intimate space. It is a simple rectangle in plan with a raised end stage and no fixed proscenium. The room volume is open to the underside of the roof and the exposed steel trusses which are the only remnant of the original post-war prefabs that were the original building are unexpected features that add to the character of the space. The audience seating is comfortably spaced on a combination of a small area of flat floor and permanent fixed stepped straight rows and sightlines are excellent throughout. Even though the chairs are second-hand they transform the space from what could have been an ordinary small village hall to a real theatre space. The bar and lounge area opens directly off the auditorium and reinforce the sense of intimacy and direct contact with all activities in the building. There is a single quite large dressing room directly off the stage but not at the same level and this causes some difficulties from time to time. It contains much of the company's costume storage. On the opposite side of the stage is a large scenery and props store with workshop facilities. There is no stage machinery or orchestra pit and suspension of scenery is limited by the low roof structure but the stage area is well equipped with drapes, performance lighting and house sound system. This building is owned and operated by a completely self-sufficient Amateur Dramatic Society with no source of external funding. The entire operation relies on revenue from ticket sales and income generated from the wet bar. There are no employees of the company and all involved are unpaid volunteers. The Society tries to stage three main productions a year and it is the aim of the committee to present a varied programme and see that the theatre becomes a prominent part of the local community. It is a self-confident Society too as evidenced by plans to further expand the building to create additional space that could be attractive to local community groups. However, it is starting to struggle to recruit younger people into the Society and faces a constant battle to maintain reasonable access to the building for its visitors across land held under lease from the County Council by the Cattle Market Company and despite frequent approaches to the Authority for assistance there are few signs of improvement to the area outside the building.

Auditorium Capacity: 65

Stage details:

Performance space – width – 5.9m
Performance space – depth – 5.65m
Depth of apron – n/a
Wing space (Right and Left) - variable
Proscenium height/width - variable
Orchestra pit (maximum no of players) – n/a
Height from stage floor to grid – no grid
Rake - None

The Paget Rooms, Penarth

Organisation: Penarth Town Council

Address: Victoria Road, Penarth CF64 3EG

Construction/Opening: 1906

Architect: John Coates Carter, Penarth

Builder: unknown

Current Owner: Penarth Town Council

History/previous names & ownership

The Paget Rooms Theatre was built and opened as a theatre in 1906 on land leased from the Earl of Plymouth who had married Alberta Paget in 1883. Popularly known as The Paget Rooms, or "The Pag", the building was used as a cinema from its earliest days. In the 1930s, the building became the Willmore Brothers' "Regal Cinema". With the later construction of the much larger Washington Cinema and the Windsor Kinema in the town however, its use as a cinema declined. During World War II, when Penarth was a principal "Recruitment Fitting Out Centre" for the RAF, hundreds of rookie National Servicemen received their uniforms and other equipment at The Pag.

Acquired in an eleventh hour purchase deal by the former Penarth Urban Council in the 1950s, the Pag became a highly successful ballroom venue over several decades. The sprung dance floor was once widely recognised as one of the finest of its kind in South Wales.

The building is now owned and managed by Penarth Town Council and continues to be used as a theatre and concert hall, a venue for public meetings and seminars, and for a variety of community activities throughout the year.

The building was listed Grade II on 21st January 1993.

Over the last 100 years there have been various changes to the interior décor and an additional proscenium and stage extension 9 feet in front of original arched pros was inserted. A major front-of-house upgrade and re-fit was carried out in 2010 - 11.

Description

The Paget Rooms building is a single frontage Arts and Crafts building, broadly rectangular and forming part of continuous frontage to Victoria Road with small scale 'local' shops to either side. The facade is of painted roughcast render over a brown glazed brick plinth. The upper storey has a row of seven small pane casement windows with a small round window to the left. The central main entrance consists of a low round arch flanked by ionic columns with exaggerated capitals and paired glazed wooden doors with a multi-paned transom. Above the arch, there is a pair of small-pane casement windows flanked by aedicules enclosing cartouches. The foyer space is clearly not original with installations of apparently 1960's/70's origin, including suspended ceiling tiles in an exposed grid and recessed fluorescent lighting, and timber wall panelling. The foyer is small, in relation to the auditorium and has Bar and cloakroom facilities with WCs for the audience. There are no on-site Box Office facilities. Level access for audience is provided from the street directly into the foyer and main floor of the auditorium beyond.

The auditorium is rectangular, flat floored, with no fixed audience seating, and features an upper balcony with stepped seating rows (and loose seating) and 4 audience boxes with space for 4 people in each on each side of the auditorium. The boxes are set behind arched openings in otherwise flat, painted plastered walls and have banquette seating in the bays below them, used principally for dance or catering events. The auditorium appears to have a very good room acoustic for unamplified music and song and is less suitable for spoken word or amplified music. There are no facilities for modifying the room acoustic.

There is evidence of water penetration through the building envelope into the auditorium at high level, suspected due to the roof or guttering being in need of repair.

The ceiling is partly pitched and partly flat. The pitched section of ceiling incorporates significant glazed rooflights affording a high level of natural light into the space. Black-out blinds can successfully shut out all daylight penetrations when required for particular events. Both walls and ceiling feature original plaster mouldings thought to be by a significant artist/craftsman of the period.

The main auditorium floor is not original and is a comparatively recent installation suitable for use for ballroom dancing and other events requiring resilience in the floor. The main auditorium can be connected to the foyer bar by a serving hatch and upstairs the balcony features a Bar within the performance space and access to an adjacent separate fully fitted kitchen.

Backstage there are 3 separate and quite large dressing rooms, one above stage level (with access directly to the upper balcony in the auditorium) and 2 at separate lower levels below stage. Access for performers to stage is always therefore via staircases and is not ideal. The backstage layout follows a half-octagon plan apparently wilfully designed by the original Architect and having nothing to do with external site constraints or boundaries. This unusual arrangement extends into the main stage and does present some limitations to some performances. There are no wings and no access or egress for performers at all on stage right. The stage floor has a shallow rake and has been modified several times over the life of the building such that it now features a variety of gentle 'cambers'.

The original proscenium was arched but at some point (presumed post second world war) a second rectangular proscenium opening and a stage extension were constructed about 9 feet in front of the original. The later proscenium is very plain and features painted corrugated metal cladding over a timber frame construction. The original pros has been retained but is painted out black and the original plaster mouldings in the space between the 2 pros arches have been retained but also painted out black.

There is no flytower or capacity to fly any scenic effects but rigging points and lines are installed for lighting, drapes etc. There is no significant stage machinery at all and no orchestra pit. For events with orchestra the musicians are simply arranged on the main auditorium floor between the audience and stage.

Whilst the building was originally conceived as a Theatre it is now referred to as a 'Community Hall' by the owner/ operating Authority. Primary users are community groups including WRVS, Martial Arts Groups, Pensioner Groups (for regular tea dances and the like), AmDram (especially Penarth Operatic and Dramatic Society –PODS). Theatrical events are infrequent although musical events ranging from orchestral to tribute rock bands are apparently popular.

There are no permanently employed technicians or venue management and the venue relies on external promoters taking full responsibility for ticketing, catering and stewarding using the facilities provided and maintained by the Town Council.

Auditorium Capacity:

Original capacity unknown; current capacity is 300 approx (max and dependent on event) comprising approximately 200 on main floor, 70-80 on balcony and 30 in boxes

Stage details:

Performance space – width – varies from 3.35m minimum to 9.14m maximum
Performance space – depth – varies but 7.62m at deepest point
Depth of apron – variable by temporary extensions
Wing space (Right and Left) - none
Proscenium height – not known
Proscenium width – 9.14m
Orchestra pit (maximum no of players) – n/a
Height from stage floor to grid – no grid
Rake - Yes– slope gradient not known

St Donats Arts Centre, Llantwit Major

Organisation: St Donats Arts Centre

Address: St Donats Castle, Llantwit Major CF61 1WF

Construction/Opening: 1976

Architect: Chris Loyn, Loyn & Co, Penarth

Builder: Cowlin Construction, Cardiff

Current Owner: Atlantic College

History/previous names & ownership

The Tythe Barn at the centre of this venue was constructed adjacent St Donats Castle sometime in the 14th Century. William Randolph Hearst the American magazine mogul bought St Donat's Castle in 1925 and brought to it many famous visitors including Charlie Chaplin and John F. Kennedy.

The Tythe Barn that now contains the theatre auditorium was listed Grade II on 16th December 1952.

In 1962 Antonin Besse purchased the castle and donated it to the governing body of Atlantic College. St Donats Arts Centre grew out of the use of the medieval Tythe Barn at St Donat's Castle for the artistic activities of Atlantic College in the early 1970's and was established as an independent limited company and registered charity in 1976.

In 1977, work began on a major development of the Tythe Barn, converting it into a professionally equipped performance venue with additional exhibition and office space. This development won a Prince of Wales Award in 1979. By the 1980's the Arts Centre's present funding partnership had emerged involving the County Council (now Vale of Glamorgan Council), the Arts Council of Wales, Atlantic College and The Mousetrap Settlement Trust.

In 1993 work commenced on a major renovation and the Tythe barn was completely renovated including construction of a new roof, the removal and reinstatement of the audience balcony and installation of a new auditorium floor. A substantial new front-of-house extension was built to replace an earlier building and containing a reception/foyer area, catering and bar facilities, management offices and a visual arts gallery. By 1998 the capital work had been largely completed funded by The Welsh Office, The Foundation for Sport & the Arts, Vale of Glamorgan Council, The Mousetrap Charitable Trust and the Lottery Unit of The Arts Council of Wales at a cost of £1.25million.

Auditorium Capacity:

200 (comprising 143 loose seats on flat floor and 57 seats on balcony)

Stage details:

Performance space – width – 7.6m
Performance space – depth – 6.1m
Depth of apron – n/a
Wing space (Right and Left) - none
Proscenium height/width – n/a
Orchestra pit (maximum no of players) – n/a
Height from stage floor to grid – no grid
Rake - None

Description

The Arts Centre is located at the heart of a group of extremely old agricultural buildings adjacent to the spectacular medieval St Donats Castle, all of which are now part of the Atlantic College campus, and overlooking the Atlantic Ocean. The Tythe Barn that contains the auditorium of the Arts Centre is approached on foot through this group of buildings and a landscaped courtyard.

The main entrance has a distinctly temporary appearance of white painted blank timber doors with painted signage applied identifying the Centre. Apparently this is because the funds obtained for major renovation and extension works in the mid-1990's expired before the project was completed and it has not been possible for the venue to generate sufficient funds to complete the original design of a glazed porch with associated reception and storage space since.

Once inside the building however the quality of the design and construction work that was completed is immediately evident. There is a spacious reception area leading directly to the Tythe Barn performance space, the visual arts gallery (a converted agricultural building), stairs down to the management offices at the level below and the large contemporary fully glazed foyer space, known as The Glassroom. Natural timber finishes abound, on the floors, bespoke bar and refreshments counters and on the undulating curved ceiling which is the underside of the roof structure, and the contrast with the clean white lime-washed walls is very attractive. The Glassroom has wonderful views over the estate and the Atlantic Ocean in the distance from its slightly elevated position on the gently sloping hillside site.

The extension makes no gesture to mimic any of the architecture of the original agricultural buildings that surround it and is unapologetically contemporary. The timber framed curtain-wall glazing to the foyers reflects the sky and is a total foil to the introverted, solid stone lower buildings it extends. The roof sails over the glazing with a gently undulating curve, supported at its largest cantilever over the foyer within by jauntily angled coloured steel columns. The lead-clad eaves of the roof have a series of cantilevered feature steel fins that suggest there may have been an intent to install some solar shading but don't actually support anything.

The new building is attached to the 14th Century Tythe Barn that contains the performance space and entry is at the rear of the room on the longitudinal axis, under the balcony and directly opposite the stage. It is a beautifully restrained and warm space to be in with the roof structure of the barn fully exposed, white lime washed walls and hardwood floor. The original asymmetrical barn doors have been retained in the long side walls of the barn and can be used for loading and deliveries of equipment and scenic effects for visiting shows.

The room has a flat floor with loose seating offering flexibility for staging a very wide range of events, with fixed seating on a small balcony that was probably originally a dry store within the barn. A sound/lighting control room has been constructed outside the envelope of the original barn at the rear of the balcony with small windows affording views to the end stage. The fixed end stage occupies the full width of the barn and there is no fixed proscenium, orchestra pit or any stage machinery. Suspension and rigging height over the stage is limited by the exposed original timber roof trusses but there are plenty of bars spaced over the performance area for lighting and drapes. Wing space is created when needed by forming a proscenium with drapes.

There is only one dressing room for performers and it is not at stage level. Accessibility for performers is an issue but the venue has no prospect of expanding its backstage facilities due to a combination of neighbouring College facilities and sensitivity about the protection of the original Tythe Barn structure and footprint.

This is a successful venue (despite its relatively remote location from any obvious centre of population) promoting its own events ranging from theatre to live music to amateur dramatics and community events. The foyer space (known as The Glassroom) is used for meetings, tea dances, community social functions and on the first Sunday of every month for a well-supported programme of live jazz.

Bridgend

Blaengarw
The Workmen's Hall
Bridgend
The Sony Theatre
Maesteg
The Town Hall
Nantymoel
The Berwyn Centre
Porthcawl
The Grand Pavilion

The Workmen's Hall, Blaengarw

Organisation: Creation Development Trust

Address: Blaengarw Road, Blaengarw, Bridgend CF32 8AW

Construction: 1893 – 94 **Opening:** 1894

Architect: Jacob Rees, Pentre

Builder: unknown

Current Owner: Bridgend County Borough Council

History/previous names & ownership

The Workmen's Hall was built at construction cost of £3400 in 1893. Officially opened on 5th March 1894 as a community hall, it held a well stocked library and reading room as well as a cinema and theatre. The building was owned and operated by the Blaengarw Workmen's Institute.

After World War II it operated as a 450 seat cinema.

In the mid-1970's the building was closed after heating pipe failure poisoned 56 people in the cinema with carbon monoxide. This event was followed by a period of dereliction.

At some point after becoming derelict ownership passed to Bridgend County Council and then to the Unitary Authority in the mid-1990's.

In 1991 the entire building was renovated and then formally reopened as a Community Theatre in 1992. It was operated by Valley and Vale Community Arts from 1991 – 2000 when it passed to Creation Development Trust.

Description

On first impression this building appears almost domestic in scale as it nestles amongst the terraced houses of the village on a prominent corner site. However, the site falls significantly down the valley, away from the road, such that entry is at second floor level from the street with a further 2 floors both above and below the street entry level. The building envelope appears largely original although it was significantly renovated at the end of the 1980's so there may have been alterations to the fabric at that time. The Hall component of the building is symmetrical, originally having public entrances on either side of the hall each leading directly into the middle of the stalls and upstairs to the balcony. There is no foyer. Currently entry is restricted to only one of the two original entry points because it affords both level access for people with disabilities and a small space to accommodate a ticket desk.

Auditorium Capacity:
Original: unknown; 1950s: 450;
Current: Approximately 250 (dependent on arrangement of loose seats on stalls floor) and including 80 fixed seats on the single upper balcony

Stage details: Not available

The Hall is roughly square in plan and the stalls floor is flat. The stalls is split into two levels with a raised parterre area under the balcony containing a fully equipped bar. The parterre is also flat floored. There is fixed seating on the upper balcony. The decoration in the Hall is modest compared to some other venues of a similar age, with a simple moulding around the proscenium and very little else. The ceiling is a suspended lay-in tile and it isn't known if the original Victorian ceiling is retained above it. The balcony front is also relatively simple painted timber panels.

The stage is raked though the fall is quite shallow and there is some flying capacity (not used by the current management and not extensive due to constraints in the roof structure). There is not a full flytower. There is a fixed stage apron and rostra units to extend it still further when the need arises. There is a projection/control room at the rear of the balcony and the venue is used often as a cinema. A lift was installed when the building was renovated and provides good access to the entire building. Backstage is well laid out and the entire building is used well for a range of community activities.

The Dance Studio is a simple space and is heavily used both by local clubs and societies and visiting performers for rehearsals and the like. Other facilities in the building are focussed on the local community and indeed actively driven by them and appear to change fairly frequently. This is an exemplary Community facility, working extremely hard and in very good condition.

The Sony Theatre, Bridgend

Organisation: School of Creative Arts, Bridgend College

Address: Bridgend College, Cowbridge Road, Bridgend CF31 3DF

Construction: 2010-11 **Opening:** 2011

Architect: James and Nicholas, Port Talbot

Builder: unknown

Current Owner: Bridgend College of Further Education

History/previous names & ownership

Constructed within a redundant Construction Studies building with a brand new auditorium and flytower extension, the Sony Theatre was opened on 23rd June 2011 by Rhydian Roberts of 'X-Factor' fame. It was named after the the state of the art 4K screen and sound system donated and installed by the Sony Corporation and in recognition of a long relationship between the College and the major local employer.

Description

Located at the heart of the campus of Bridgend College the theatre is not visible to traffic passing by on the busy arterial route into Bridgend from Cardiff and there is no signage to announce the presence of this new facility in the town. It is however easy to locate once inside the large car park to the side of the campus and the building is clad in a crisp panelling system with large 'Sony Theatre' signage on both the side and front elevations. The front of the building was originally used for other academic purposes and has been stripped back to its frame and reclad as part of the construction works that created the new theatre. The new auditorium block side wall is distinguished from the front area by being clad in red brick and its roof parapet follows the sloping internal section of the auditorium ceiling. To the rear is a new flytower block, clad in the same panelling as the front block but with a flamboyant roof profile. The whole composition has a distinctly contemporary feel amongst the surrounding buildings of various ages, architectural styles and quality. Entry is into a generous open foyer area that can be adapted to provide front-of-house services for the audience and leads directly through a single pair of double doors into first a sound and light lobby and then directly into the rear of the stalls. Perhaps this access point was dictated by the original building into which the foyer was created but it is unfortunate that in a new-build theatre the only access point is on the centre-line of the auditorium meaning there is no audience directly in front of the stage command point and performers face a large gap between the audience seating with blank doors at the end of it.

The auditorium has a flat floor with a linoleum finish and the audience seating is fully retractable to create a very large flat-floor. The rear rows of audience seating is on tiered retractable bleacher units accessed from aisles at the sides of the room meaning quite a journey from entry point to back row that requires the audience to walk first to the front of the stage and then to the side before returning to the back again. The front rows of seats are an innovative system on the flat floor whereby each row slides along tracks in the floor towards the back wall in a concertina fashion. The front and rear blocks of seats are finished in different upholstery as they were obtained from different manufacturers but the different shades of blue work well together. There is an audience balcony of three widely spaced rows and it is quite high in relation to the stage. The balcony front has been angled steeply to facilitate audience sightlines to the front of the stage. In the centre of the balcony some seats were removed late in the design and construction process to provide a clear sightline to the stage for the film projector provided by the Sony Corporation. Above the audience balcony there is a further technical balcony providing followspot and fixed lighting and in-room sound and light control positions.

The stage is very large and is constructed from modular rostrum units that can be rearranged to provide any staging configuration required for any given production. There is no orchestra pit and this is seen as an item that may be considered in the future. At least one show presented each year will be musical theatre and the band currently has to be accommodated either to one side of the stage or even in another room completely, connected to the performance by remote camera and screens. There is a full flytower and it is extremely well equipped. Backstage accommodation is limited and there is currently only one permanent dressing room. There are plans to create a second soon and also to provide backstage toilets as well as the existing provision of showers. There is a workshop area close to the stage but the doors between it and the stage are of normal height and this has been found to limit the size of scenic effects that can be created in the workshop and then moved to the stage. There is a useful crossover corridor leading around the stage from the backstage accommodation at stage right to the usual performer entry point at stage left.

The School of Creative Arts produces up to 120 performances each academic year with a major show each academic term and a pantomime at Christmas and a wide range of musical events throughout the year. The addition of this purpose-built theatre to their accommodation is a major enhancement of facilities. Whilst the auditorium was conceived as a multi-function space suitable for lectures and important College events such as awards ceremonies it is clear that it is very much focussed on theatrical use.

There has been significant interest from local community groups in using the theatre after College hours in the evenings and a number have already established programmes of regular events and use. The School is conscious that while there is demand from local audiences for such a venue in Bridgend, care must be taken to avoid competing with Local Authority run venues elsewhere in the County and is keen to maintain the notion that the Sony space is an experimental one rather than a 'traditional' fixed format auditorium. There is obvious enthusiasm for this new addition to the theatre building estate in Wales and plans are already being implemented for further improvement of the facilities to suit the demand. It should have a long and successful future.

Auditorium Capacity:
380 (comprising 270 on stalls and 110 on balcony)

Stage details:
Performance space – width – 12.8m
Performance space – depth – 8.1m
Depth of apron – n/a
Wing space (Right and Left) – SR – 1.4m; SL – 3,25m
Proscenium height/width – Height – 5.4m; width – 12.8m
Orchestra pit (maximum no of players) – n/a
Height from stage floor to grid – 11m
Rake - None

The Town Hall, Maesteg

Organisation: Maesteg Town Hall Ltd

Address: Talbot Street, Maesteg CF34 9DA

Construction/Opening: 1881

Architect: Henry C Harris, Cardiff

Builder: unknown

Current Owner: Bridgend County Borough Council

History/previous names & ownership

Opened as a Town Hall with Theatre space in 1881 the building was renovated in 1913-1914 and re-opened on 25th November 1914. There are thought to have been at least two other major renovations since although dates are not known.

Films began to be screened here in the early 1910's but it was also used for stage performances and it is said that Richard Burton made his first stage appearance here in 1939.

The balcony was converted into a cinema with 170 seats in 1994 but this work has since been reversed and the balcony is now open to the auditorium again.

It was listed Grade II on 14th July 1997 and in 1998 Maesteg Town Hall Ltd assumed responsibility for the Hall from the County Council under a lease arrangement.

In 2005 Architect Geoffrey Cheason Associates of Penarth and Contractor Willis Construction Ltd of Cardiff carried out repairs to the external fabric including replacing damaged and missing stone details, extensive repairs to the timber clock tower, replacement of the roof ventilators and general redecoration.

Renovation of one of the dressing rooms beneath stage to overcome water penetration and dry rot problems was carried out in 2010.

Description

The Town Hall is an imposing stone building at the heart of the town of Maesteg. Significant remedial works to the fabric in 2005 have certainly enhanced its general appearance. The building comprises the Town Hall above a separately managed Market Hall and there is no level access to the auditorium from any approach route. The main entrance is tucked away around the side of the building up a steep flight of stairs and leads directly into the auditorium. There is neither on-site Box Office nor significant foyer area. Disabled visitors have to telephone in advance of arrival so that the management can arrange for the visitor to be greeted at the back-of-house lift that serves the building and be accompanied through the building to the auditorium.

Audience entry into the auditorium is at the rear only (to both stalls and balcony) and from one side only (house right). The building layout appears to be symmetrical however and there is access to the upper balcony from house left after having first passed through the auditorium to reach the staircase. There are audience toilets on the house left side of the building, with some administration offices and fire escapes into the adjacent bus station below and some storage areas behind the bar counter and under the balcony.

There is a fully equipped bar located within the auditorium against the rear stalls wall and the bar area can be partially screened off from the main auditorium by sliding wall panels hung from the front edge of the balcony. A curtain can close off the balcony from the main hall along approximately the same line effectively creating a much smaller auditorium space.

The auditorium is rectangular and flat-floored, with loose seating on stalls to achieve the required audience configuration for any particular event. There is fixed audience seating on the upper balcony. The auditorium is the full width of the building (so there is no front-of-house to back-of-house connection possible apart from through the auditorium itself or through the car park outside) and benefits from large windows on both sides. These are curtained off for most performances but for events such as conferences and weddings the curtains are opened to allow daylight into the room.

There is a projection/control room at the rear of the upper balcony but a semi-permanent in-room mixing position for both sound and light systems has been erected at the rear of the stalls just in front of the line of the balcony front.

There is heating but no forced ventilation, hot air is 'extracted' by naturally rising to the ceiling and finding its way into the roof void via a series of grilles in the (non-original) suspended ceiling. The room suffers from excessive heat build up in the summer months and is expensive to heat in the winter due to a lack of insulation in the roof-space.

The proscenium features classical decoration including pilasters and moulded cavalry and chariot mounted archers in a greek style. The auditorium walls are plain painted plaster with large paintings hung between the windows (giving a reminder of its 'town hall' status?)

The stage is flat and there is some flying capability although no full flytower and some rigging points are hampered by a major roof truss passing across the entire stage area and an access gantry installed to provide access to the auditorium ceiling void.

There are 3 large dressing rooms backstage, but none are at stage level and backstage access is impossible for performers or crew with movement disabilities due to the many steep flights of stairs that connect the various levels.

Significant damp penetration has rendered one of the dressing rooms unusable although there has been some recent renovation works carried out to address this.

The stage door is effectively 2 storeys below stage and is one of the routes into the building for loading/unloading sets and equipment (the other being through the main entrance front-of-house). There is no proper loading bay and no backstage lift.

The management company that operates this venue has ambitious plans for expansion and improvement of both facilities and range of events presented on stage but with limited access to external funding has all such plans on hold for the foreseeable future. It is obvious that with additional external support this already successful venue could really thrive.

Auditorium Capacity:

Original capacity unknown but current capacity is 650 maximum (dependent on configuration of loose seating on stalls) including 262 fixed seats on a single upper balcony

Stage details:

Performance space – width – 7.5m
Performance space – depth – 7m
Depth of apron – n/a
Wing space (Right and Left) – SR - 1m; SL - 1m
Proscenium height/width – not available
Orchestra pit (maximum no of players) –n/a
Height from stage floor to grid – 3.5m approx
Rake - None

The Berwyn Centre, Nantymoel

Organisation: Bridgend County Borough Council Arts & Culture Service

Address: Ogwy Street, Nantymoel, Bridgend CF32 7SD

Construction: 1901-1904 **Opening:** 1905

Architect/Builder: unknown/unknown

Current Owner: Bridgend County Borough Council

History/previous names & ownership

The land on which this building stands was donated by Mr. Blandy Jenkins of Llanharan in 1895 and he also gave £200 towards the cost of construction. A lease was signed for the land and for building work to commence in November 1900 and the foundation stone was laid in May 1901.

The building was opened as Nantymoel Workmen's Hall in 1905 and was known by this name until 1975. Later in this period it was also known as The Nantymoel Miners' Welfare Hall and Cinema.

Some time in the first half of the 20th Century a large extension was added behind the stage and during the 1950's the building underwent a series of major changes. It was converted to cinema use (including an extension to the front to accommodate a projection room, removal of the original audience balcony and stalls seating and replacement with single fixed rake) and then later in the same decade the extension to the front of building was replaced and enlarged, the original side windows to the main hall were blocked up and a glazed extension was added along the side of the building to connect the front entrance and foyer to the stage.

In 1975 it underwent major refurbishment and became an Arts and Community Centre. When it re-opened it was renamed The Berwyn Centre in honour of Mr Berwyn Roderick, a teacher at Ogmore Grammar School who had a passion for the Arts and had contributed much to the artistic community in the area during his life.

In 1995 the Library was moved from the Workman's Institute up to the front of the building into space under the main hall raked floor and sometime after that various alterations were made to the Workmen's Institute rooms on the ground floor.

The Main Hall has been closed to the general public on health and safety grounds since 2007 (the roof structure is considered unsafe and some of the internal concrete cornice features are severely cracked) but the rest of the Centre remains operational.

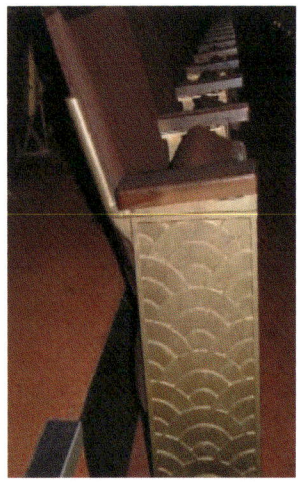

Description

c.1905. Photograph courtesy of the Berwyn Centre

A building which has been modified too many times, to the point where it has lost almost all of its original character from the outside and, by use of inappropriate materials and construction techniques, is in a state of imminent closure compounded by lack of maintenance.

Cementitious render has been applied to the entire external envelope and the majority has blown leading to significant water ingress. The roof and gutters have been badly maintained also leading to weather penetration and the discovery in 2007 of the serious and dangerous condition of ceiling joists over the main hall space. The Main Hall has been closed for public use since then and there are no signs of the local authority owner funding the necessary repairs to roof and ceiling that will enable the venue to re-open.

Over the course of several major changes to the building (not least the conversion from balconied theatre space to single rake cinema style auditorium) the original Workmen's Institute and Hall has been subsumed into a larger rather less characterful building. The extension to the front of the building that added a cinema projection room and staircase access to the rear of the seating is especially lacking in architectural quality although with the passage of time has become recognisably the face of the building. The blocking up of almost all of the original windows is also associated with the conversion to cinema use but has been done using poor quality construction techniques and has compounded the deterioration of the building envelope.

The big surprise in this building is the quality of the main hall space however. It is an elegantly proportioned rectangular hall retaining its original ceiling and (concrete) cornice and feature mouldings to the perimeter. The seats appear to be the originals from the conversion to cinema use.

The original stage was removed many years ago but the original Hall stalls sprung hardwood floor has been extended through the stage area on the flat with no stage riser. (This would be a fabulous dance venue).

The stage has flying capability and decent wing space although get-in for visiting performing companies is very difficult if not unacceptable due to very large level differences between stage and road/car park outside.

There are several large dressing rooms immediately backstage and fully accessible by performers with access difficulties (from the front of house). Backstage WCs are provided but no showers.

The original front of house is typical of similar venues elsewhere – no large audience gathering space at all – and contains the original railway station style ticket office and staircases leading directly up to the rear of the raked seating. WCs have been added in place of one of the original pair of staircases.

A glazed lean-to extension was added along the entire length of one side of the building in the 1950's and provides performer access to stage and dressing rooms beyond and audience access to the front of the raked seating. It is currently used as a cafeteria area.

There is a public library located under the rake of the auditorium seating in the location of what would ordinarily be a useful large foyer (and maybe bar area).

The Library was originally part of the Workmen's Institute located underneath the Hall but was moved 'upstairs' to front entrance level in 1995.

There is no physical internal route between the Hall and Institute beneath. The Institute contains a large licensed space (that used to be the billiards/snooker room) now used for discos, rehearsals and rock band practicing as well as a range of community group uses. A painting of a Nantymoel soldier of WW1 awarded the Victoria Cross is a feature of this space – it was painted directly onto the wall and dictates how the space has been organised and is used. This room has had a small raised stage dias built into it and plans are developing for local youth theatre groups/school drama clubs to perform shows and plays.

Other rooms in the institute are used by the local Brownies Troop, by a day care nursery, the local history society and a physiotherapist for clinics.

The auditorium is closed because the ceiling is at risk of imminent collapse due to damage caused by weather penetration into the roofspace over a period of many years. In order to re-open, significant structural repair works will be required.

If funding can be found to repair the roof/ceiling then further plans include improvement to the front of house vertical circulation by the addition of new staircase(s) and lift(s); and resolution of get-in/loading provisions (currently non-existent due to very large level difference between main stage and road /car park outside)

The building appears to be under threat of closure due to lack of both support and capital (repair) funding from its Local Authority owner. There is a possibility that the LA will divest itself of what it clearly believes to be a liability – to Creation Arts Development Trust (operators of the Blaengarw Workman's Hall) – in which case it is thought a significant funding drive will commence and a major renovation project could follow.

Auditorium Capacity:

Original capacity: unknown; capacity reduced when the building was converted to cinema use, the upper balcony was removed and single rake seating installed.

Current capacity is 296 on a single fixed rake.

Stage details: not available

The Grand Pavilion, Porthcawl

Organisation: Bridgend County Borough Council Arts & Culture Service

Address: The Esplanade, Porthcawl, CF36 3YW

Construction/Opening: 1932

Architect: E. J. E. Moore

Builder: unknown

Current Owner: Bridgend County Borough Council

History/previous names & ownership

The building was built as a Palm Court in 1932 with facilities for musical performance and theatre. It opened after a very short construction period of approximately 1 year due to the use of an innovative ferro-concrete construction method, and at a construction cost of £25,000. Throughout its life it is believed that the building has been in the ownership of the Local Authority and certainly in the period 1946 to 1962 it was owned and operated by Porthcawl Urban District Council. Sometime in the 1950's there was a fire in the auditorium although the extent of any damage caused is unknown. Over the last 60 years external walkways were encased to form internal circulation/fire escape routes, the external tennis court was removed and replaced with car parking and front of house access was upgraded including the installation of a passenger lift.

The Grand Pavilion was listed Grade II on 17th February 1998.

In 2008 there was some refurbishment works to the building envelope and interior and since then several projects have modified various internal layouts and provision, including installation of a suspended ceiling to the basement space, creation of accessible WCs, covering over of upper balcony windows in auditorium with plywood and replacement of feature lighting to the auditorium ceiling (from uplighters to 'fairy lighting'). A fire on stage in early 2010 damaged electrical systems but caused no damage to the building structure or fabric.

In advance of the 80th anniversary of the opening of the building (in 2012) there are plans in place to install new ramps to the main entrance and to relocate the Box Office to its original location immediately behind main entrance doors and to reopen the original primary building entrance.

Description

Despite the apparently ever-escalating scale of surrounding later 20th century developments, the Pavilion still dominates the esplanade by virtue of its excellent location. It is an unusual architectural blend of classical colonnade at ground floor level surmounted by an art deco clock-tower and with a massive octagonal dome over the main hall auditorium, all constructed using poured ferro-concrete and painted. Clearly the main entrance was intended to be on the central axis of the colonnade and dome into the auditorium but this route has been unused for sometime and the entrance is set now to one side where access for all has been addressed by the later installation of a (steep) ramp from pavement up to internal floor level. There are plans to reinstate the original entrance and relocate the box office desk to its original position. The foyer areas are compact and the route to the main hall space short and direct. Over the life of the building there have been many interventions into the original fabric to upgrade audience facilities and they are of a high standard.

The main hall auditorium is octagonal in plan form and has a flat floor that is a fully sprung ballroom dance floor. There is a single upper balcony with fixed seating to 7 sides of the octagon plan, the stage occupying the 8th side. There is a suggestion in the architecture that the stage area was originally planned to be contained within the octagon (presumably only intended to accommodate a band accompanying a dance event) but at some point during construction a larger stage was decided upon, complete with some capacity for flying curtains and scenery (although this is not a full flytower by any stretch of the imagination). The proscenium arch is the only brick-built element in the building which also implies that it was a later addition to the original plans. This goes someway to providing an explanation for the somewhat uncomfortable relationship between the auditorium dome and 'flytower' box in the external composition of the building. The auditorium ceiling is the underside of the concrete dome shell and on each of the 8 faces of the octagon above the balcony openings there is a (plaster?) moulded feature panel representing different performance types in a classical style. Originally the dome was painted dark blue with a representation of the night sky and was uplit from a perimeter trough that hid the light source from the audience. The uplighters were removed at some unknown point in the past and replaced with 'fairy-lights' arranged on the dome's ribs. The ceiling 'sky' has long since been over-painted.

The stage is raked and retains a footlight trough to its front. There is no orchestra pit and no stage machinery apart from the limited capacity for flying. There is ample dressing room accommodation although these are below stage level and there is no access to stage for performers with movement difficulties. There is no loading bay (the stage is a full storey height above the external ground level at the rear of the site) so equipment and scenic effects etc are brought into the hall through the front of house and main entrance. A tennis court that originally occupied part of the open space on the site around the building has been removed and is now a car park whilst on the opposite side a large area provides access for large vehicles too. This could be altered to provide a full loading bay facility subject to agreement of the planning authority and Cadw. The 'wings' to either side of the main central block are currently occupied by a cafeteria and the venue management offices.

A secondary performance space has been created underneath the main auditorium, also octagonal in plan layout. This space has a small raised stage dais and has a flat floor allowing a multitude of uses including conferences and business meetings, comedy nights, wedding banquets and cabaret shows. This space has been subjected to several upgrades including installation of a suspended tiled ceiling, new entrance doors to connect to the front-of-house and dressing room areas and the very odd addition of wall decoration to one wall surface that mimics a rock-face.

Auditorium Capacity: Original: unknown; 1946: 950; 1962: 1000

Current: Main Hall – approximately 650 maximum dependent on configuration of up to 400 loose seats on stalls floor with 250 fixed seats on upper balcony with space for further 30 or so loose seats used for certain events

'The Stage Door' flexible space - 80 seats

Stage details:

Performance space – width – 19m (including wings)Performance space – depth – 8m
Depth of apron – none
Wing space (Right and Left) – (SR) 5m max; (SL) 5m max
Proscenium height/width – height 3.74m; width 9.34m
Orchestra pit (maximum no of players) –n/a
Height from stage floor to grid – 6.4m
Rake - none

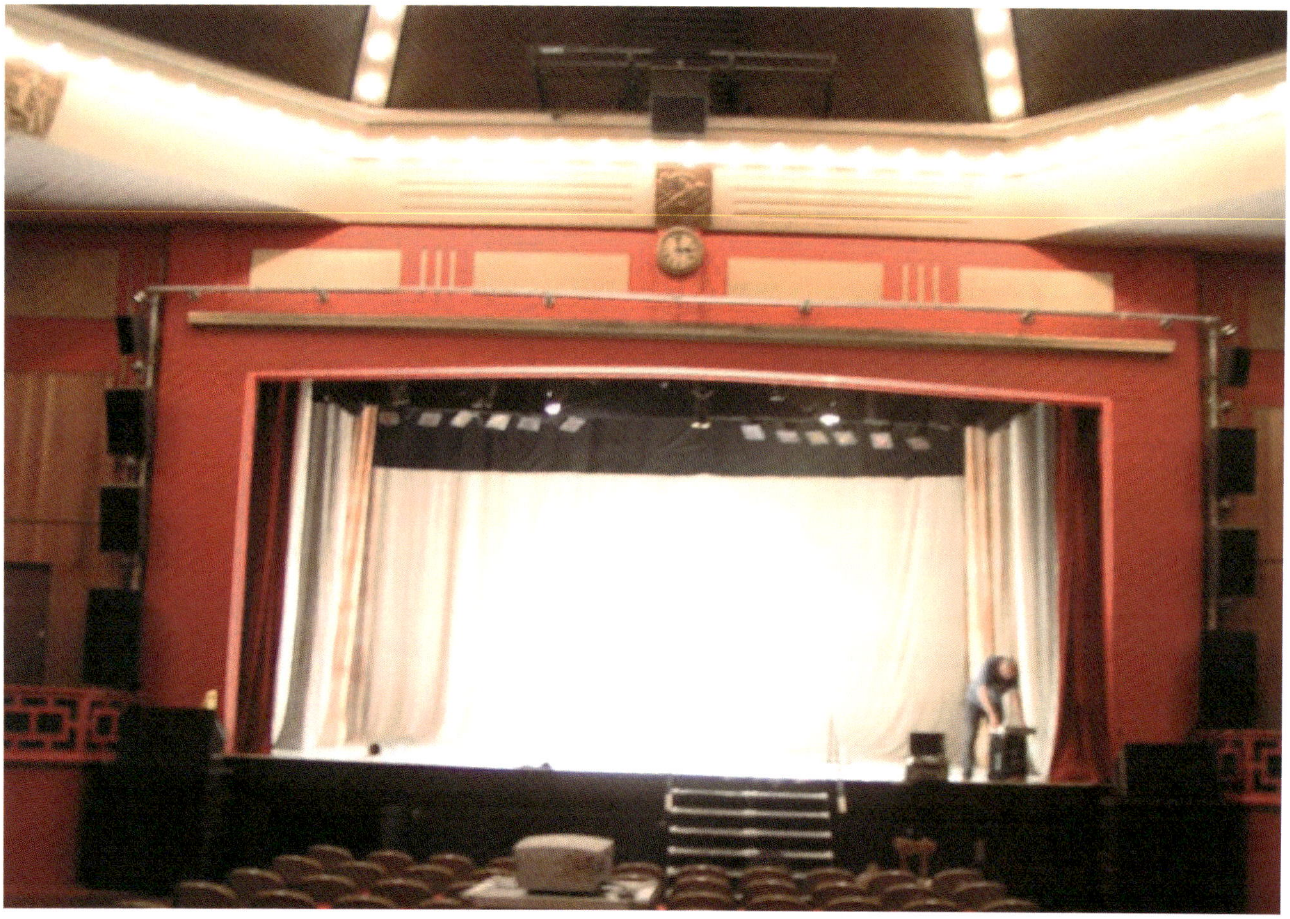

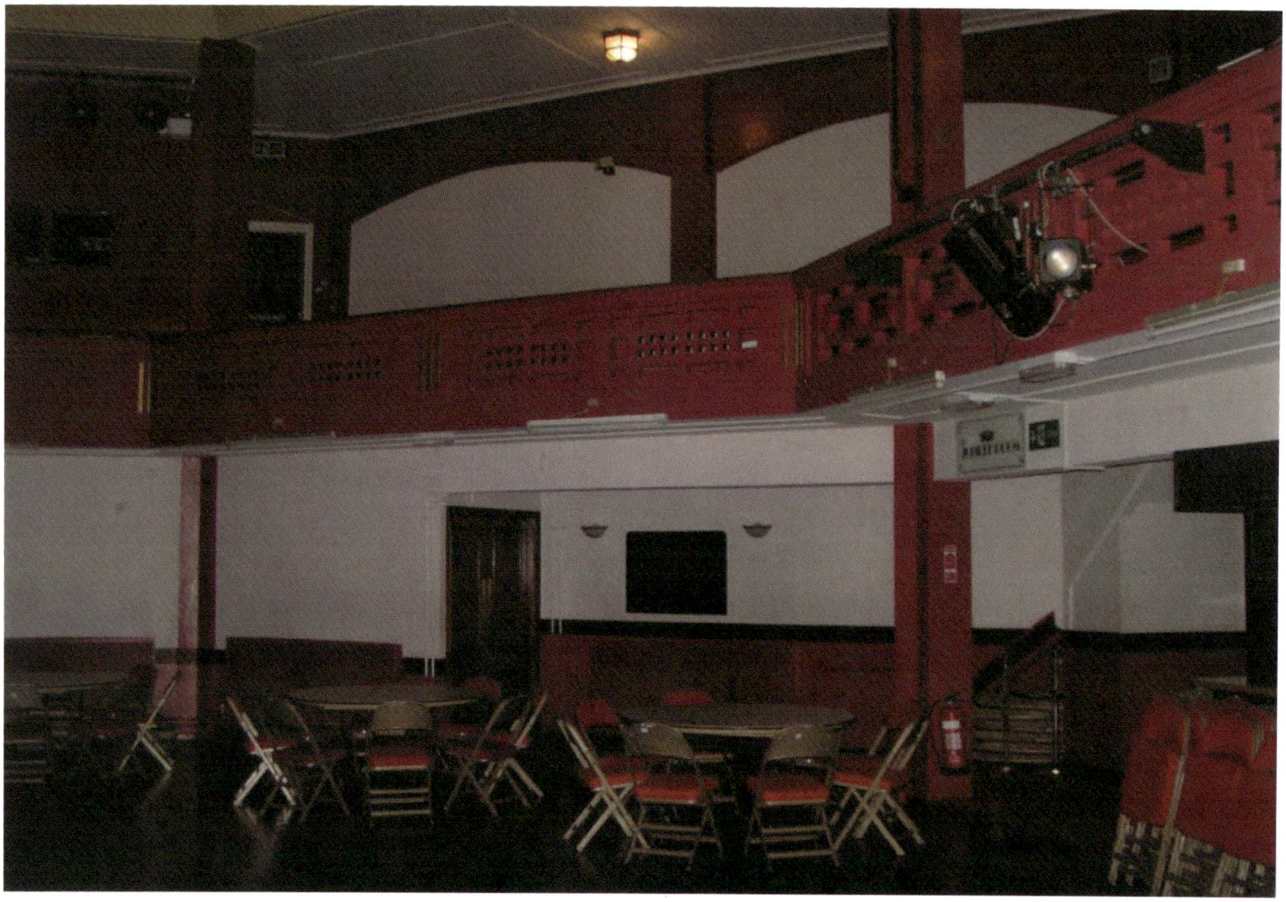

Neath Port Talbot

Glyncorrwg
    The Hall
Neath
    The Gwyn Hall
    The Little Theatre
Pontardawe
    The Arts Centre
Port Talbot
    The Princess Royal Theatre

The Hall, Glyncorrwg

Organisation: None

Address: 33-35, Cymmer Road, Glyncorrwg SA13 3AB

Construction/Opening: 1925

Architect: W. Edgar Evans & W.D Jones, Cymmer

Builder: unknown

Current Owner: Mr Leighton J.M. Davies and Mr Laurence C.M. Davies

History/previous names & ownership

Glyncorrwg Hall was originally built as a Workmen's Institute and Memorial Hall containing a tea room (dance hall), Billiard Hall, Committee Rooms and Reading Rooms with a large theatre auditorium above. 3 foundation stones were laid on 2nd May 1925 by Alderman William Jenkins JP MP, Thomas Richards JP and Ramsay MacDonald MP and the building was opened later that year by the Bishop of Llandaff and Ramsay McDonald.

It is presumed that in the 1930's projection facilities were installed and the building became primarily used as a cinema.

Some time after the Second World War the building operation was taken over from the trustees of the Workmen's Institute and Memorial Hall by the Coal Industry Social Welfare Organisation.

Extracts from the CISWO 1968 Annual Report state that work to provide licensed premises was completed at Glyncorrwg Workmen's Hall in that year. This would have been in the Billiard Room. Through the 1970's the Hall was used for Bingo for a while then fell into disuse and neglect.

The building was occupied for sometime by the local rugby club as their Clubhouse and the stage area was converted to use as a fitness gym. When the rugby club moved into a new clubhouse building closer to their pitch the Hall fell into dereliction once more. The original plaques commemorating those from the village who gave their lives in the 2 World Wars and to whom this building was built as a Memorial were removed and installed in the local Old Aged Persons' Home.

In 1990 it was purchased from Trustees and CISWO by the current owners and the restoration of the dance hall and bar commenced. At around this time, the Main Hall audience seating was deemed to be a fire risk and was removed on the advice of the Fire Service and scrapped. The Dance Hall and bar were reopened in 1996 and the building was renamed simply The Hall, Glyncorrwg. The theatre auditorium remains derelict.

The Hall was listed Grade II on 31st July 2000.

Description

The Hall is the first building seen on approaching the village of Glyncorrwg at the head of the Afan Valley and it is a large and surprisingly grand building. It is set on a very steep hillside such that it appears at first to be only single storey but it is in fact 3 storeys tall with 2 storeys below street level and the top floor accommodates the projection room and what used to be a caretaker's flat within the height of the Hall.

The building is set immediately at the back of the pavement and has an imposing stone façade. There are two sets of doors in this façade, each with a portico above and dressed stone jambs, one serving as the entrance to the Institute and Hall, the other being the exit from the Hall. It is a symmetrical elevation and the pitched slate roof of the Hall beyond rises immediately behind it. In the centre of the front elevation is a carved block on the parapet identifying the building as Glyncorrwg Workmen's Institute and Memorial Hall. The short side elevations have different treatments – the one facing the approach to the village has been rendered at some point and painted white (in an attempt to protect it from the full onslaught of the prevailing wind and rain) while the other end remains the original stone. Both ends have small punched windows into what would have been committee rooms, reading rooms and dressing rooms. The rear elevation is four storeys tall and provides a route for disabled visitors to access the building from a modest surface car park serving the building.

Entry through the main entrance from the street is up four shallow steps and into a small entrance hall containing the original ticket office (identified by its tiny window opening), entry into the rear of the Hall and a large staircase leading down to the Institute facilities. There was originally a plaque commemorating the names of the fallen from the First World War (to whom the Hall is a Memorial) mounted on the wall in the entrance either side of the doors into the auditorium but this was removed at some point and is now understood to have been installed in a local old-aged pensioner care home along with a second, smaller plaque with the names of the fallen of the Second World War that was installed in the building later.

The Hall has not been used since the late 1970's and is in an advanced state of disrepair though retains clear evidence of its original style and quality. The original theatre seats were removed in the early 1990's but the original raked floor remains and whilst some decay has occurred it appears not to be beyond repair. The auditorium is currently being used as a vast storage facility and is full of miscellaneous unwanted household furnishings. One of the cinema loudspeakers remains. The wall overlooking the valley is punctured by large windows many still having their original folding timber shutters fitted. This wall has suffered from water ingress in the past but roof repairs have been carried out and the damage has been arrested. It wouldn't be too difficult to strip the flaking paint off and redecorate and the result would be spectacular. The delicate Greco-style feature mouldings between the windows have survived well and could also be restored relatively easily.

The opposite 'long' wall of the room has evidently been over-decorated many times and there are significant signs of weather ingress to the ceiling on this side (as a result of blocked gutters above the front elevation façade?)

The stage remains although the stage floor and very large supporting timber joists have been vandalised and the two dressing rooms that occupied the sub-stage space are visible through the large gaps in the stage floor. There is no remaining sign of any theatre machinery or rigging installations for scenic effects and there is a flat ceiling over the entire stage area. Some damage has been caused to the walls around the stage by the installation of fitness equipment in a time when the building was used by the local rugby club as its clubhouse and fitness centre. The stage is set behind an elegant proscenium with more Greco-style mouldings with features in the form of flowers and a pair of lion's heads adorn the uppermost corners. A circular feature moulding is located on the centreline at the high point of the gently curved barrel vault ceiling of the room. The ceiling has an exposed timber grid with lath and plaster infill and each node of the grid has a small carved feature detail. Original moulded ventilation grilles along the centreline of the ceiling remain in place but none of the original light fittings survive.

The wall opposite the stage belies the change in use at some point after the Hall's construction from live theatre venue to cinema as there are several crudely formed holes punched through the wall at high level to allow the projection of films to a screen on stage. The projection room still contains the last projectors used in the venue and several artefacts associated with cinema machinery and operation. Sadly this part of the building has been heavily vandalised with graffiti although it wouldn't be especially difficult to remove and to repair any residual damage as the building fabric is generally sound. Adjacent to the projection room is an area that was a caretaker's flat for some period of time and it contains a rather elegant fireplace with the original range cooker. The floors in this part of the building are in need of significant repair and evidence of water ingress and/or condensation on the inside face of the external wall suggest the render applied to protect this end of the building from the weather is cementitious when it should have been lime render and the solid stone walls are struggling to breathe.

On exiting the Hall through doors adjacent to the stage there is another small hallway area off which are large rooms, presumed used as committee rooms or reading rooms in their original state. The windows in these rooms are in bad condition and there is very significant weather ingress that could only be resolved by the replacement/repair of the windows and substantial repair to the walls surrounding them. The rooms retain elegant cornices and dado mouldings. Returning to the main entrance and moving downstairs to one level below the street there is a public bar (originally the billiard room) and a large function space (originally the tea-room). These two spaces have been substantially and well restored and are well used by the local community. A small raised dais in one corner of the function room allows live music shows to be presented. It has a very good dance floor throughout and elegantly panelled walls. Windows overlooking the valley allow daylight in and it is a very pleasant room indeed.

Stabilisation of the building envelope is a high priority to prevent further decay then restoration and reopening of the Hall as a community theatre/function space, subject to grant aid and funding. This is a wonderful venue, similar in many respects to the Memo in Newbridge insofar as it has been empty and neglected for a similar period of time and was constructed at the same time. It bears many similarities to the Newbridge building in its layout and scale and if restored would be a very significant asset to the cultural provision in this area. If funds are not found to prevent further decay however the future is very bleak for this auditorium.

Auditorium Capacity:

Original not known – currently no auditorium seats

Stage details:

Performance space – width – 11m including wings
Performance space – depth – 5.8m
Depth of apron – n/a
Wing space (Right and Left) – SR - 0.95m; SL - 0.95m
Proscenium height/width – height 4.3m; width 9.1m
Orchestra pit (maximum no of players) – n/a
Height from stage floor to grid – no grid
Rake – None

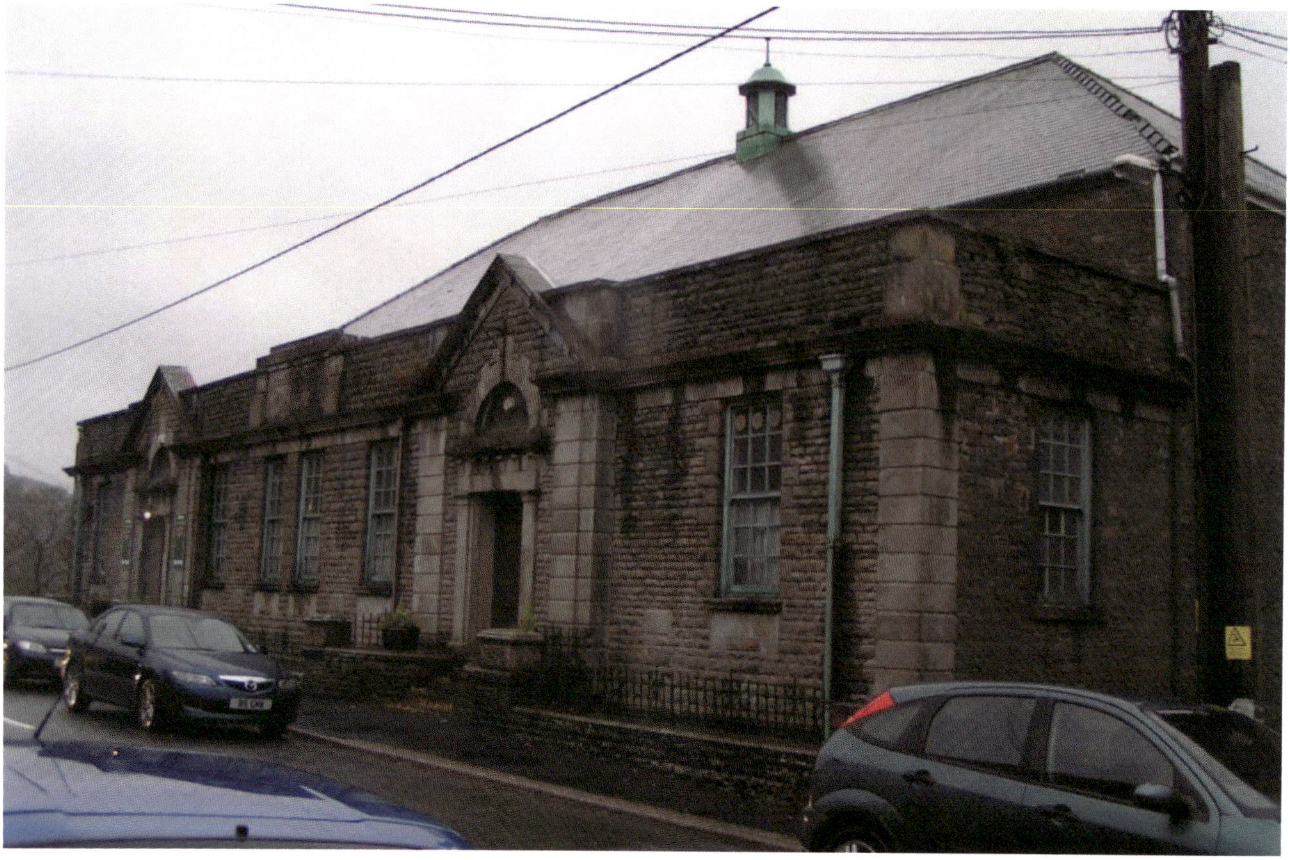

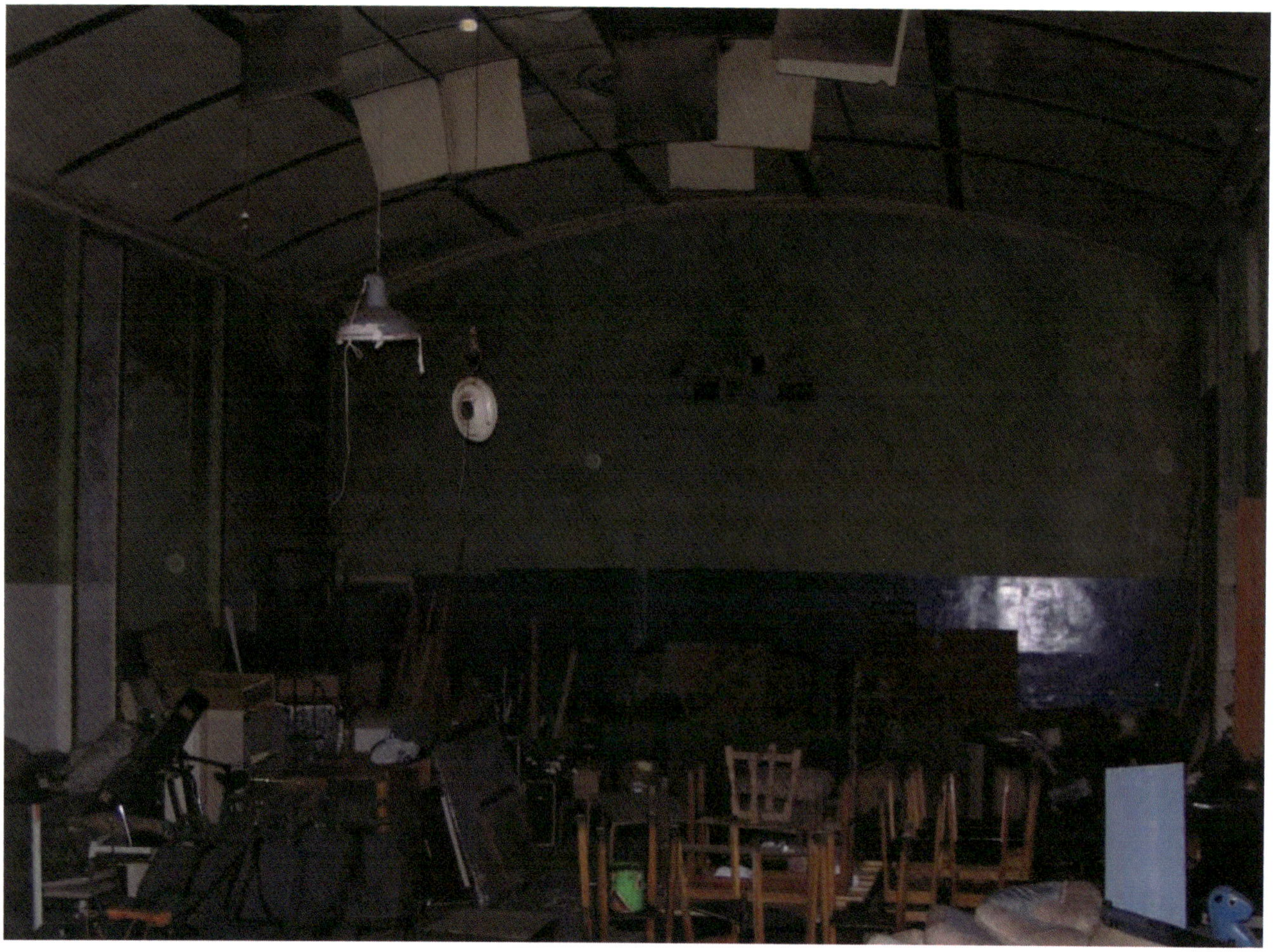

The Gwyn Hall, Neath

Organisation: Neath Port Talbot Theatres

Address: 6 Orchard Street, Neath SA11 1DU

Construction/Opening: 1887

Architect: John Norton, London

Builder: unknown

Current Owner: Neath Port Talbot County Borough Council

Image courtesy of Holder Mathias Architects

History/previous names & ownership

The Gwyn Hall was built in 1887 on land given by local businessman Howel Gwyn at a cost of £6000. The building was used for Council business as well as a music hall until the construction of the Neath Civic Centre in the 1960's. A statue of Howel Gwyn was unveiled outside the Gwyn Hall, on 26th September 1888. The siting caused controversy at the time as it was thought that it would interfere with carriages. In 1967 the statue was moved to its present position in Victoria Gardens, because of a proposed road widening scheme which never happened.

The building was listed Grade II on 1st May 1989 due to its fine architectural detailing and its value to the Neath townscape.

On 18th October 2007 fire devastated the entire building. At the time it was undergoing a £4million refurbishment. A year after the fire the local Council commissioned a feasibility study to investigate options for the remainder of the building to create a new theatre on the site of the old Hall. Work commenced on the reconstruction in 2009 to a design by Holder Mathias Architects of Cardiff with main Contractor Morgan Sindall of Gwaelod-Y-Garth, Cardiff. The scheme proposes to re-instate the original building line so that the building can take its original place as a civic landmark, make good all original external details to restore the outside of the building to its former glory, demolish the later additions to the building, retain the sense of space and volume within the shell of the original building and as many of the original details that remain on the inside. The theatre stage will be at ground level with the aim of creating space for more audience seating and a stage riser for an orchestra. The main seating will be fully retractable allowing the space to be used as a function venue.

When completed the (new) Gwyn Hall will boast a new 400 seat community theatre, a 140 capacity studio venue, a 70 seat cinema and a new cafe. At the time of writing the planned completion date is late 2011.

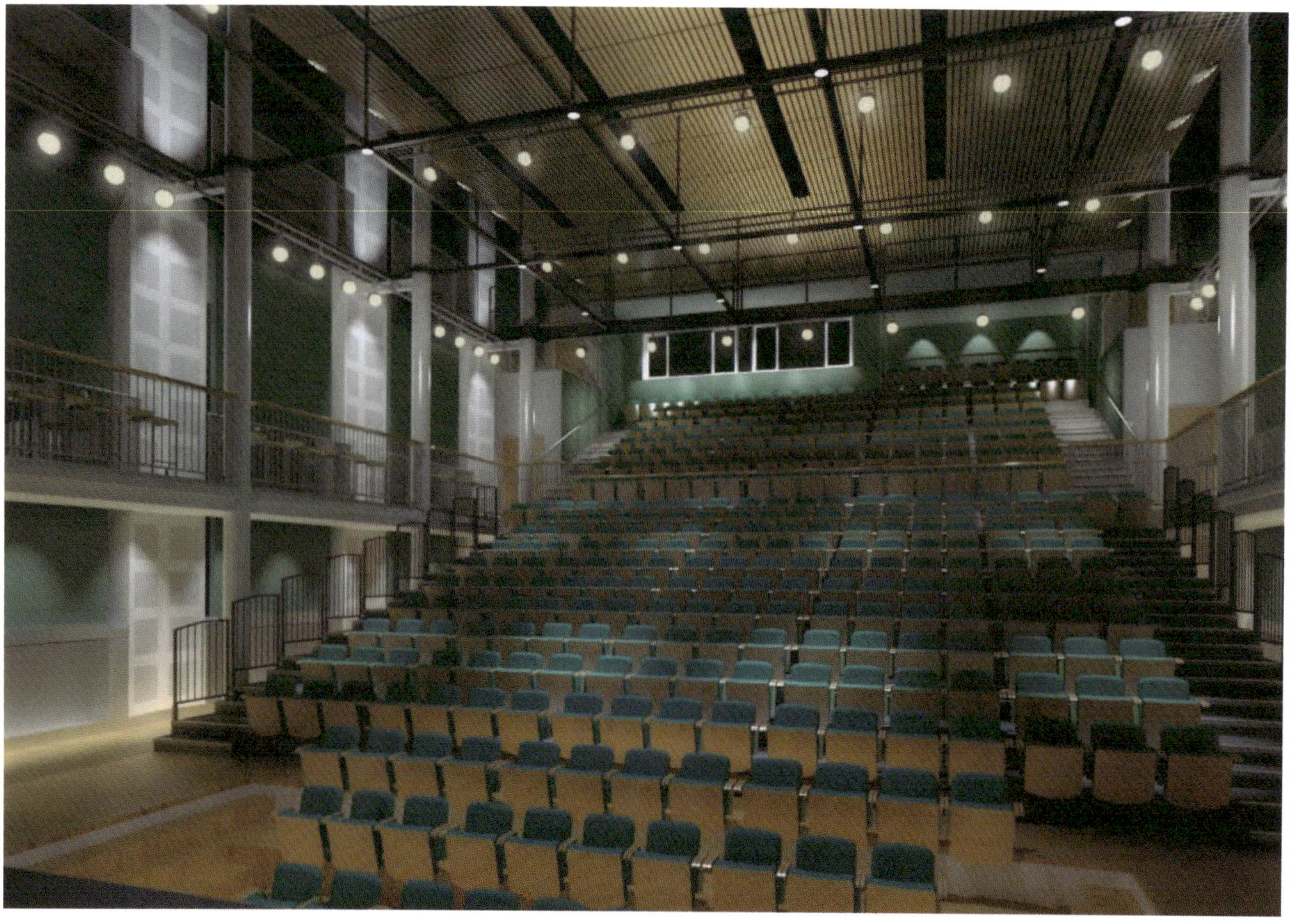

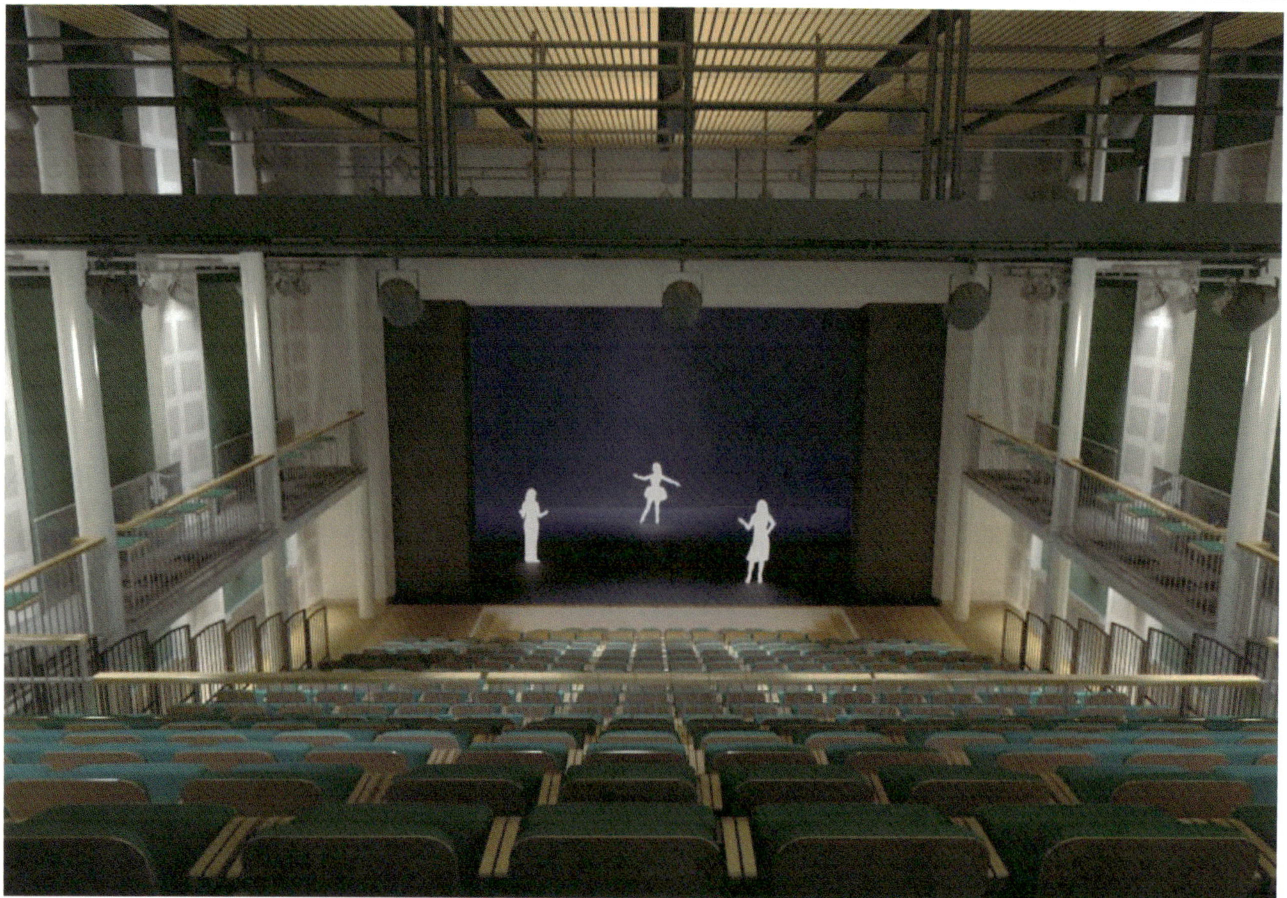

Images courtesy of Holder Mathias Architects

The Little Theatre, Neath

Organisation: Neath Little Theatre

Address: Westernmoor Road, Neath SA11 1BQ

Construction/Opening: 1955

Architect: Doug Bailey, Borough Engineer, Neath

Builder: Neath Little Theatre Company volunteers

Current Owner: Neath Little Theatre

History/previous names & ownership

Neath Little Theatre Company was formed in 1935 and moved into its bespoke headquarters theatre on 19th February 1955.

The building has been extended twice in its lifetime – first in 1960 when an extension was built to the side and rear of the auditorium, and second in 2000 when a further extension was added to the front of the building and a major front-of-house refurbishment was carried out funded by a Big Lottery grant.

Description

The Little Theatre is located in a residential area of Neath on a triangular site at the junction of two major roads and is set back from the road leaving a lawned garden area to the front and a small surface car park to one long side. The building is partially obscured from view because of a mature site perimeter hedge and tall trees.

The theatre building is a simple single storey construction with pebble dash rendered panels between exposed concrete framing members to the original building and colour matching facing brickwork to more recent single storey extensions. The main hall has a pitched concrete interlocking tile roof, the extension to the front has a flat roof.

The main entrance is axial on the building and contained in an extension built in 2000 with grant aid from the Big Lottery fund. The extension contains a modest foyer/entrance hall, audience toilets (including provision for disabled visitors) and a management office/box office. There is a ramped approach to the entrance from the adjacent road and car parking area. The foyer space walls are hung with company memorabilia and show posters and give the sense of a well established and confident company.

Entry is directly into the auditorium on the long axis. The auditorium is largely flat floored but there are 4 rows of seats at the rear set on shallow stepped units. There is a small balcony accessed from the rear of the auditorium and containing about 30 fixed seats and a small but well-equipped sound and lighting control room. The seats to the flat floored area of the auditorium are relocated in blocks of 5 giving the company the flexibility of staging shows in the round or in thrust configuration. It is a very intimate room.

The audience seats were rescued from the Gnoll Cinema in Neath at the time of construction of the Little Theatre and give a sense of heritage and create a real 'theatre' environment in a way more contemporary loose seats could never do.

The auditorium itself is a plain space with no distinguishing architectural treatment or features and the ceiling follows the pitch of the underside of the roof. The original sprung timber floor is waxed every year and is wearing extremely well.

There is a good sized raised stage with proscenium but no flytower and minimal rigging and suspension bars. Storage is at a premium in the building and the entire area under the stage is given over to this purpose along with a props store and scene dock at the side and rear of the stage area. There is a single but very large dressing room just behind stage that is split into male and female sections by a simple curtain when needed.

The Neath Little Theatre Company is approaching its Golden Jubilee and whilst attracting younger members is a constant source of concern for the sustainability of the company into the future it seems to be a robust and well supported outfit and is planning for its long term future development and expansion of its headquarters building.

Auditorium Capacity:

Original capacity: 280-300, reduced in the 2000's by the removal of 2 rows of seats to improve comfort standards
Current capacity: 250

Stage details:

Performance space – width – 9.9m
Performance space – depth – 7m
Depth of apron – n/a
Wing space (Right and Left) – SR - 1.42m; SL - 1.42m
Proscenium height/width – height - 3.08m; width - 7m
Orchestra pit (maximum no of players) – n/a
Height from stage floor to grid – 4m
Rake – None

The Arts Centre, Pontardawe

Organisation: Neath Port Talbot Theatres

Address: Herbert Street, Pontardawe, Swansea SA8 4ED

Construction/Opening: 1909

Architect: W Beddoe Rees, Cardiff

Builder: Radford & Greaves, Derby

Current Owner: Neath Port Talbot County Borough Council

History/previous names & ownership

The building was originally known as The Institute and Public Halls and was commissioned for the benefit of the workers at the W. Gilbertson Steelworks in the town. It was opened on 6th May 1909, having been paid for by funds raised in the town and with the main hall seating 1,500 in stalls and balcony levels. It was opened by famous opera singer Adelina Patti, whose home, Craig y Nos Castle is 10 miles north of Pontardawe. It was intended that the main hall be used for concerts, musical performances and recitations.

The building comprised three main elements constructed of brickwork and roughcast render with slate roofs. The three storey Institute housed meeting rooms, offices, a library and reading rooms. The single storey billiard hall was sandwiched between the Institute and Public Hall with an attractive timber trussed roof and central glazed rooflight. The Public Hall consisted of a grand auditorium with balcony. A cinema was located in another smaller hall in the building which had a seating capacity for 650 mainly on the stalls level, with a small balcony. The cinema opened in 1909 but was closed in the early 1960's.

The building remained the focal point of the town's cultural and social activities well beyond the end of the Second World War but as local heavy industry began to decline sustaining the building became increasingly difficult. The Pontardawe Snooker Club ensured that the Billiard Room continued to thrive but the fabric of the theatre building deteriorated to the point where it became unsafe and the building was closed. The Institute building was occupied for a time by the Town Council who set up offices in it and the top floor was converted to a caretaker's flat.

In 1993 Lliw Valley Borough Council sought to improve arts facilities and provision in Pontardawe and plans were set in motion to convert the Institute and Public Hall into a multi-purpose Arts Centre. In 1996 upon the forming of the Unitary Authority of Neath Port Talbot County Borough Council the building lease was purchased from the Trustees and the project commenced with funding from the Authority, the European Regional Development Fund and the Welsh Development Agency. The refurbishment was carried out to designs by Niall Phillips Architects of Bristol and the building re-opened on 16th January 1997. The main auditorium was restored to its original design although with fixed seating on the balcony only and flexible seating at stalls and now has a much reduced capacity of 450. Upon reopening the building was renamed Pontardawe Arts Centre.

Description

The three component parts of the Arts Centre stand as apparently distinct buildings on a prominent corner site in the centre of the town. The Institute building is set back from the road and the town cenotaph stands in the forecourt area. The Institute acts now as the main entrance to the complex and does not have an especially welcoming appearance about it. Constructed over three storeys with a sort of Edwardian classicism to its style, there is a brick 'pediment' and the upper storey walls are rendered and painted white. Elegant stone features surround the windows and it has a slate pitched roof. Next to the Institute is the significantly smaller and single storey Billiard/Snooker Hall building. The same brick as used on the Institute is used on the walls and it features a full-length glazed rooflight on the ridge of the roof. There is a full-height bay window at each end of this building with stone mullions.

The final component contains the theatre auditorium and it is a large building albeit its mass is somewhat disguised by its location and its length is hidden from the principal views to the site by being down a side street off the main road. The principal elevation stands very tall with a large arched entrance directly off the street and above that a double-height arched window below the gable end. A pair of towers stand on each corner of this wall containing staircases and emergency exits from the upper part of the building.

The first floor of these towers is almost entirely glazed. The towers and the ground floor of this wall are brick as the rest of the complex with white render to the first floor. Behind the gable wall the exterior of the building becomes much less elaborate and is finished with render throughout. Original windows to the auditorium inside have been blocked up (during the 1996 renovations) and are highlighted with a pink coloured render. At the stage end of the theatre, furthest from the main road, original timber doors remain and windows to dressing rooms have also been retained. This part of the building has a distinctly industrial feel to it in contrast to the rather grand civic feel of the remainder.

Entry into the complex is through the original entrance to the Institute although the original doors have been replaced with automatic sliding glass doors. On entering the building there is a compact hall area containing the reception/ticket desk and providing access to the rest of the building. Immediately opposite the ticket desk is a large room (presumably an original committee room or meeting room) that is used for various small gatherings and events and provides access to the Snooker Hall in the centre of the complex.

Originally the Snooker Hall contained 6 full sized tables but only four remain. The space occupied by the two that have been removed is now the theatre bar and foyer area, separated from the snooker area by a full height structural glass wall. The bay window in the Snooker Hall has a raised cill and there is thought being given to making this area more of a stage for events such as comedy nights. The glazed rooflight that runs the length of this block of the building provides excellent lighting conditions and the roof structure is exposed throughout. Entry to the theatre block is through the foyer/bar area created in the street end of the Snooker Hall as the entrance in the original building that leads directly into the theatre is not used.

The auditorium is quite spectacular and as with so many of the buildings across South Wales built by or for workmen represents an astounding ambition and confidence. The renovations of 1996 have substantially reduced the size and audience capacity of the theatre but the work has been carried out extremely sensitively and none of the grandeur of the space has been lost. Mechanical ventilation systems were installed during the 1996 renovations and work well. It is a tall room and the proscenium fills the entire end wall surmounted by a graceful arch and curtain over the stage. There is a single balcony on three sides presenting the management with some restricted view seating issues but the atmosphere created by the wrapping of the audience around the room is fabulous. The balcony is supported on elegant cast iron columns and the spaces under the balconies are available for additional seating. The original fixed seating on stalls has been removed and now the venue has the benefit of the flexibility offered by loose seating and a flat floor which it exploits regularly in its rich and varied programme of events. The balcony front is not original (the original having been stolen during the period of dereliction suffered by the building) but is well integrated into the architecture and unless informed that it wasn't original its unlikely anyone would notice. Above the balcony are Romanesque proportioned semi-circular arches forming a cloister effect at balcony level and making the transition between wall and gently curved ceiling work extremely well. Colourful feature mouldings abound, complimented by the use of 4 different colours of upholstery on the fixed balcony seating. The auditorium is shorter than it was originally by virtue of the construction of a sound/light control room above the balcony and of increasing the size of the stage both back towards the external wall and by the addition of a permanent apron.

There is no flytower but plenty of height above the stage and many rigging and suspension points are provided. There is no orchestra pit. The wings are reasonably generous (by the standards of this building's peers elsewhere). There are 3 good sized and well equipped dressing rooms behind the stage with windows and sanitary facilities.

Loading onto the stage is directly from the adjacent side street through a pair of large doors and the only issue with these is that the threshold is quite high in relation to the beds of trucks used in the 21st Century and loading does involve manual handling. It is difficult to imagine a way of incorporating a goods lift into this area to overcome this.

The upper floors of the Institute building contain management offices and a number of small function/meeting rooms and on the top floor there is a small but extremely popular and successful contemporary visual art gallery. The area now occupied by the gallery was once a caretaker's flat but is now an airy, light and generous space. As in the Snooker Hall the original timber roof structure is exposed and sensitively treated as part of the design of the space.

Consideration is being given to the removal of 2 of the remaining 4 snooker tables as the game's popularity wanes and to the introduction of a public café to encourage more community use through the day. Indeed, if the snooker club ceases to be supported by its membership then the existing bar may be made double sided so that it can serve the existing foyer bar area simultaneously with the new space or the new space may be used as a larger audience foyer when needed.

This is an utterly beautiful theatre that is clearly well supported by the local authority and the Arts Council of Wales. It offers a broad programme of events that are well attended and its future seems secure.

Auditorium Capacity:

Original capacity was 1500, now reduced following the refurbishment works in 1996 to current capacity of 457 comprising 261 on loose seats on stalls and 196 on fixed seats on the balcony. There are 170 restricted view seats. Following removal of the stalls seats, capacity is 150 for cabaret, 180 without dance floor.

Stage details:

Performance space – width 7.3m (excluding the wings)
Performance space – depth 6m
Depth of apron – 1.2m
Wing space (Right and Left) -SR: 1m; SL: 2m
Proscenium height/width - height 5.5m; width 6.9m
Orchestra pit (maximum no of players) – n/a
Height from stage floor to grid - 5.5m
Rake - None

The Princess Royal Theatre, Port Talbot

Organisation: Neath Port Talbot Theatres

Address: Civic Centre, Port Talbot SA13 1PJ

Construction/Opening: 1987

Architect: Conder Construction

Builder: Conder Construction

Current Owner: Neath Port Talbot County Borough Council

History/previous names & ownership

The Princess Royal Theatre was built as a part of the new Civic Centre in 1987 and it occupies one wing of the building. It was officially opened by HRH Anne The Princess Royal (after whom it is named) on 29th September 1989.

The building has remained unchanged since opening apart from some minor maintenance works including replacement of the sound system and re-upholstering of the fixed seats on the balcony.

Description

The theatre is part of the Civic Centre development in the centre of Port Talbot and is part of a larger building that contains office and administration accommodation for Neath Port Talbot County Borough Council. The Civic Centre is very close to the elevated section of the M4 motorway and Junction 41 is close by. The building turns its back on the motorway and is planned around an open square with pedestrian connection into the nearby Aberafon Shopping Centre and along the bank of the river Afan. Approaching the Centre by car is to drive past the rear of the building and into a surface car park of limited capacity.

The building is a large monolithic construction of buff brickwork with pitched slate roofs and although there is a sign identifying the theatre on the rear elevation it does not convey any sense of what lies within. This was clearly designed as Civic offices first and theatre second. The rear façade of the theatre (which is the first approached by car) is a shear face of flat and featureless brickwork punctured only by the stage loading bay door. In itself this appears unintended as it is some distance above the car park level outside and it is clearly not possible to park a truck anywhere near the flight of stairs leading up to stage level. As the visitor moves around the building from car park to entrance it opens up somewhat with windows to theatre accommodation at ground and first floor level and on the front façade a second floor of Council meeting room accommodation oversails the theatre foyers below. The front elevation is more modelled and a series of brick columns surmounted by another theatre sign indicate where the entrance is although the much grander and clearer entrance to the Civic Centre itself is distracting. The theatre entrance is fully accessible from outside but there is no internal connection to the Civic Centre Reception.

The ground floor foyer is a simple linear space along the front of the auditorium beyond and contains the box office with space for management staff, access to the upper balcony through fire doors at each end and public toilets. The upper level of foyer contains a small bar and has views over the Civic square outside. Entry into the theatre stalls is directly from the entrance foyer and on the level, into the rear of the flat-floored stalls. On either side of the broadly octagonal auditorium at the rear of stalls are two licensed bar counters. This is a multi-use venue and the flat floor, loose seating and bars within the space offer a range of uses and configurations that sets this theatre apart from others in this region. The auditorium is very wide and the architectural detailing seems to reinforce the large scale feel. The balcony front is very deep as a result it seems of incorporating ventilation ductwork into the void under the balcony and grilles into the face of the balcony. The overall effect of this is to make the ceiling under the balcony feel very low in proportion to the overall room volume. Entry into the balcony from the foyer is via a central vomitory with a very small sound/light control room set above it on the centre-line of the room.

The stage is very wide and this is now being exploited as the venue focuses on use for dance events although as a result of the proscenium having to be very wide to suit the width of the auditorium wing space off stage is virtually non-existent. There is no flytower but the stage is well-equipped with rigging and lighting points and bars. There is an orchestra pit/forestage but it is not mechanically operated and requires substantial manpower to construct either pit or stage apron. Frequently any orchestra required will simply be set on the elevator zone behind a temporary barrier at stalls floor level to avoid the need to carry out the work necessary to make the pit.

There is very little storage in the theatre and in conjunction with the difficulties imposed by the loading bay access few shows are presented that require much equipment or scenic effects. There are 6 performer dressing rooms of various sizes and all with en-suite facilities. Half of them have windows although their location in relation to the surrounding roads has led to privacy issues in the past and they are now blacked out. All of the dressing rooms are at first floor level but access is good both by stairs leading directly to the stage and a lift allowing mobility impaired performers to use the building.

This theatre is fully funded by Neath Port Talbot County Borough Council and is a thriving venue serving a broad range of events and audiences. Recently the programming of events has focussed on dance (for which the large stage is excellent), stand-up comedy and conferences and it is well used by several local amateur companies. The limitations of the stage loading have been acknowledged and touring productions are now rare and of limited scale with little or no supporting scenery.

The Council's Cultural Services Department are starting to take a strategic approach to programming in their three venues Pontardawe Arts centre, the Gwyn Hall, Neath (due to re-open in 2011) and the Princess Royal so that they each provide a distinctive programme for their audiences and don't compete with each other. This strategy ought to ensure the long-term future of this theatre is assured.

Auditorium Capacity:

798, comprising 448 loose seats on stalls and 350 fixed seats on the balcony

Stage details:

Performance space – width – 16.5m (including wings)
Performance space – depth – 6.5m (including apron)
Depth of apron – 1.5m
Wing space (Right and Left) SR – 2m, SL – 3m
Proscenium height/width – height 6.5m; width 11.5m
Orchestra pit (maximum no of players) - 30
Height from stage floor to grid – 5m
Rake -None

Swansea

Swansea
- The Brangwyn Hall
- The Dylan Thomas Theatre
- The Grand Theatre
- The Llewelyn Hall
- The Patti Pavilion
- The Penyrheol Community Theatre
- Taliesin Arts Centre
- The Townhill Theatre

The Brangwyn Hall

Organisation: Swansea City and County Council

Address: Guildhall, Swansea SA1 4PE

Construction: 1930 – 1934 **Opening:** 1934

Architect: Percy Thomas, Cardiff

Builder: E Turner & Sons Ltd, Cardiff

Current Owner: Swansea City and County Council

History/previous names & ownership

In 1907, the County Borough Council of Swansea had decided that there was a need for a larger town hall and civic complex, and began to design a scheme to provide facilities, including a public assembly hall. In 1930, the scheme went out to competition for the selection of an Architect and attracted 77 submissions, from which Percy Thomas of Cardiff was chosen. The foundation stone was laid on 4th May 1932 and in 1933, whilst the Guildhall was under construction and the foundations of the Assembly Hall were being laid, an announcement was made by Lord Iveagh's trustees that the 16 panels painted by Sir Frank Brangwyn (1867-1956), rejected by The House of Lords, would be given to a municipality or body who could house and display them. After viewing the completed series of panels at the Ideal Home Exhibition in Olympia in 1933, Swansea Councillor, Leslie W. Hefferman, insisted that Swansea must host the panels. The Council began discussions with the trustees and agreed to alter the plans for the new Assembly Hall to accommodate the panels. This included raising the ceiling by 12 inches, and making recesses in the walls to house the panel frames so the panels appeared to be painted directly onto the walls. The Assembly Hall was renamed the Brangwyn Hall when Swansea secured the British Empire Panels on 28th October 1933.

On the 23rd October 1934, the Guildhall was opened by HRH Prince George the Duke of Kent. The inaugural concert which took place in the Brangwyn Hall that evening was performed by Swansea and District Royal Male Choir. The 1935 Bronze Medal for Architecture was awarded to Percy Thomas by the Royal Institute of British Architects for the design of the Guildhall complex.

The acoustics of the hall have been praised for providing an exceptional sound for sound for recitals, orchestral pieces and chamber music alike. Many orchestras and soloists choose to record in the Hall rather than alternative venues in London or the rest of the UK. In 1936, Sir Thomas Beecham described it early on in its history as being one of the finest concert halls in Europe, when he played there with the London Philharmonic Orchestra. In more recent times, the BBC National Orchestra of Wales regularly performs and records concerts in the Hall for BBC Radio 3.

The Brangwyn Hall and Guildhall buildings were listed Grade 1 on 25th July 1994 as the most important building in Wales of its period, with a particularly fine and virtually unaltered sequence of public spaces, and as an outstanding example of the work of an architect of particular significance to Wales.

Description

The Brangwyn Concert Hall is located in the Guildhall complex consisting of the city hall, civic offices and county law courts and occupies one side of the building. It is close to Victoria Park and Swansea Bay and a straight, axial path through the park connects the central axis of the Guildhall complex and Patti Pavilion. The entire building complex is finished in white Portland stone in a "stripped" classical architectural style. The Brangwyn Hall block is a monolithic rectangle with little to identify it as a place for public entertainment – at its highest parapet there are carved roundels depicting the arts but they are difficult to read from the street. There is no external signage at all although there is very clearly an entrance into the building from the road outside. The principal entry is via a tall flight of steps up to three deep arches with coffered soffits and an outer screen of bronze with stained glass infill and panelled bronze doors below. Bronze lamps mounted on the wall to each side of the central arch alert the visitor to the main entrance.

Once inside, there is a large entrance lobby with a groined vault to the ceiling and a floor of travertine and marble. There are two polygonal bronze booths that presumably were once used for ticket sales and elaborate bronze inner doors leading to the auditorium. There is no foyer per se – original plans of the building indicate a large room adjacent to the entrance lobby was intended to be a restaurant but it is currently used for council meetings. There is a large licensed bar area on the opposite side of the Hall from the entrance however which enhances the introverted character of the building.

The concert hall is very large both in plan and volume and extremely ornate in stark contrast to the exterior. It has a deeply coffered ceiling with the original polygonal bronze and glass light fittings still in use and suspended below it. There are broad fluted pilasters either side of the stage/concert platform with a panelled frieze band above framing the view to large gilt bronze grilles covering the concert organ pipework and the choir stalls below. The side and rear walls are faced with acoustic tiles simulating Portland stone and have a walnut-panelled dado with rectangular clerestorey windows providing daylight into the auditorium. It has a flat floor and loose seating allows a range of audience capacities and configurations to be accommodated. It is understood that the floor is regarded as an excellent ballroom dance surface. The most notable feature of the walls are the Brangwyn Panels, a set of 18 paintings depicting the nations and people, flora and fauna of the British Empire. The panels gave the hall its name. They are stunningly beautiful and intensely colourful.

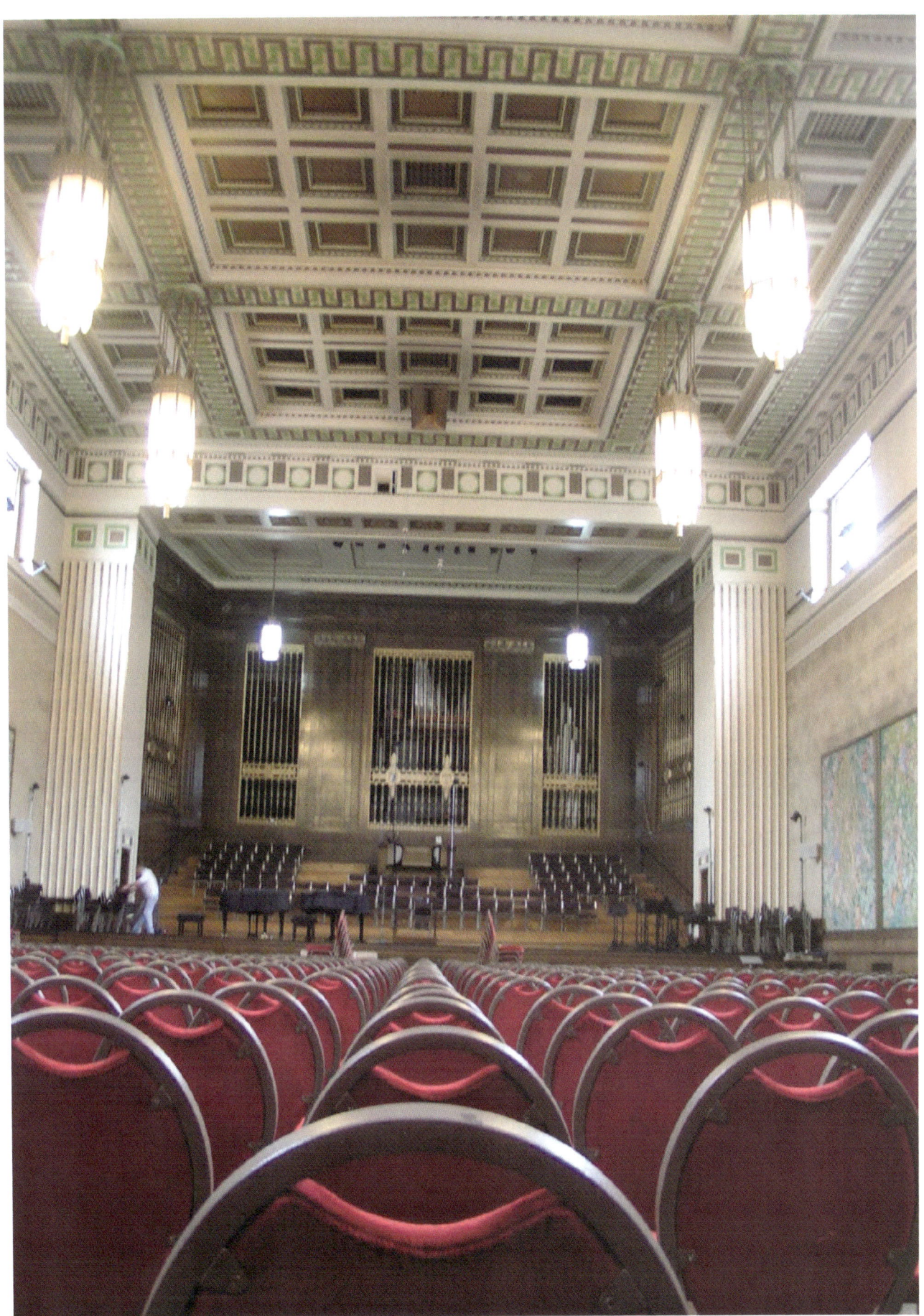

The deep stage/concert platform has ample space for the largest orchestras and risers at the rear provide space for very large choirs. Loose seating is used on the risers to allow a range of choir sizes to be accommodated. There is no fixed and permanent stage equipment and theatrical or operatic performances are understood to be quite rare although possible. Artists' rooms are provided to the rear of the stage.

This Hall is clearly regarded as a jewel in Swansea's crown and is extremely well supported by the Council and local population. It remains one of the finest orchestral concert halls in the UK and is developing a reputation as a conference and wedding venue locally. Its future appears assured.

Auditorium Capacity:

1300 maximum

Stage details:

Performance space – width – 14.63m (min); 18.79m (max)
Performance space – depth – 5.58m
Depth of apron – n/a
Wing space (Right and Left) – n/a
Stage opening height/width – height: 9.2m; width: 14.63m
Orchestra pit (maximum no of players) - no pit, Flat stage capacity for orchestra: 80; choir risers for 200 choristers
Height from stage floor to grid – n/a
Rake – None

The Dylan Thomas Theatre

Organisation: Swansea Little Theatre Company (registered charity)

Address: Gloucester Place, Maritime Quarter, Swansea, SA1 1TY

Construction/Opening: 1979

Architect/Builder: unknown/unknown

Current Owner: Swansea City Council

History/previous names & ownership

The building that is now the Dylan Thomas Theatre is presumed to have been constructed in the early 20th Century. Its original use is unknown but it was used as the Oscar Chess car showroom and repairs workshop for many years prior to falling into dereliction in the 1970's.

In 1979 Swansea City Council offered Swansea Little Theatre the derelict building in the south dock area of the city as a new venue for the company to establish its base in. Formed in 1924 in Mumbles, Swansea Little Theatre was the first Little Theatre established in Wales. Over the years the company had been based in various locations including church halls and the Palace Theatre. Major conversion works were carried out to building by members of the theatre company and other volunteers to create an auditorium and associated support spaces. The audience seats were obtained from the derelict Carlton Cinema in Swansea. Sir Harry Secombe officially opened the new theatre building on 29th September 1983 and it was named after the Company's famous former member.

In 1986 a fire caused significant damage and once again the Company carried out a major rebuild of the interior. Sometime in the 1980's the principal external facades of building were painted with a mural by students from Cardiff Art School and sometime after that the original auditorium seats were replaced with seats taken from the Brangwyn Hall in Swansea. These 'new' seats have been re-upholstered with leather on a row-by-row basis over the subsequent period.

The building underwent a major redevelopment between 2007 and 2009 to designs by Lawray Architects of Cardiff. These works improved front-of-house audience and foyer facilities (focussed on disabled toilet provision and access and reorganisation of the foyer space layout) and were funded by the award of a substantial Arts Council of Wales grant. Before the work was completed, the building was flooded in 2008 as a result of the rising water table in the Swansea Docks area. Further renovations to the interior were required to overcome the significant water damage. The theatre was finally re-opened by Dylan Thomas' grandson and actor Matthew Rhys in June 2009. A second mural entitled 'Ospreys across the Bay' was painted onto the rear façade of the building as part of Swansea City Council 'Locws' annual public art project by artist Niahm McCann. In 2010 the ever enthusiastic Company members and volunteers carried out further works in the building to create a large dressing room at first floor level, including installation of a new window, extension to the heating system, works to floor finishes and general decorations.

In 2011 the theatre won £1000 worth of paint in the Dulux 'Community in Colour' competition and set about refurbishing the front elevation of the building, in keeping with the trompe l'oeuil effect of the rest of the building, highlighting an archway over the main entrance and incorproating characters from Dylan Thomas' 'Under Milk Wood'.

Description

The Dylan Thomas Theatre is located in the docks area of Swansea but close to the central commercial district and is surrounded by an area that has undergone substantial regeneration. The immediate area contains the National Waterfront Museum, a Museum of Tramways, several old buildings converted to retail and restaurant use and residential developments.

The building is a three storey building of indeterminate age but was certainly built when the docks were still functioning and so presumably it was a warehouse or office building originally. At some point it was converted for use as a car showroom and service centre before falling derelict in the 1970's and the subsequent take over and conversion by the current occupant. It stands out at the end of a residential street and on the corner of Dylan Thomas Square not by virtue of being an outstanding building but because of the vibrant mural that adorns the full extent of the two principal facades. The mural was applied to the building after the Swansea Little Theatre took occupation and includes the painting of the ground floor part of the façade as a classical base penetrated by arched openings affording trompe l'oeuil views of Venice beyond with polychromatic geometrical abstractions over and around the upper floor windows on one side and painted arches with further trompe l'oeuil with seagulls flying over the main entrance side. The elevation facing the City Centre and National Waterfront Museum is much more restrained and simply painted render with feature stonework at low level. An interesting feature of the rear wall are two wave-form areas that have the appearance of curtains pulled away from the stage door entrance and featuring another applied mural, this one created as part of Swansea City Council's annual 'Locws' public arts project. Access to the stage door is from this side and loading is directly from a small yard area (also used for Theatre Company car parking) into a scene dock and onto stage.

The Swansea Little Theatre Company currently occupies the ground and first floor of the building and the top floor contains completely separate and unrelated accommodation for visual artists.

There are entrances into the building directly from the Street/Square but the main entrance is from Dylan Thomas Square. Significant renovations and alterations to the front-of-house facilities in the building were carried out between 2007 and 2009 including the upgrading of access and consequent improvement of the original entry. Automatic doors now lead directly into a spacious single storey public foyer with box office desk and bar counter. It is a bright and comfortable space, predominantly white and taking full advantage of the generous ceiling height. The walls are decorated with a permanent exhibition chronicling the involvement of Dylan Thomas with the Swansea Little Theatre Company. Access to the auditorium is available on both sides of the room via a short corridor leading from the foyer around the back of the theatre. The corridor contains audience toilets and access to technical areas and again the walls are liberally hung with archive material recording past performances by the Theatre Company. Some of the memorabilia dates back to the pre-Second World war era of the Company's history. The auditorium is accessed at the front of the single fixed tier, right at the junction between stage and audience seating. A further display of photographs recording the development of the theatre conversion and significant events in the recent history of the building is hung on the wall of the house left entry corridor. The seating capacity is limited both by the width of the space and its height but creates a very intimate performance space.

There is no stage riser and the front row of audience sits very close to the performance. A space at the front of the seating allows for wheelchair users. The stage is surprisingly large, especially in width, having been increased in width to create wing space required by the increasing number of dance companies that visit the venue. There is no fixed proscenium and no capacity for flying scenic effects but there is good coverage of rigging and suspension points over the entire stage and large parts of the auditorium. A pair of technical galleries run the full length of the room on each side and there are sound and lighting control positions at the back of the audience seating open to the auditorium space. The auditorium seats were obtained from the Brangwyn Hall and have been re-upholstered with leather since being fitted in this venue. The walls and ceiling of the space are painted black and the vibrant pink of the seats lends a splash of colour and is a reflection of the playful character of the building and Company. Behind the stage and at the same level there is a reasonably large fully accessible dressing room/green room/stage door area with toilets and showers for able bodied and disabled performers.. There are stairs leading up to first floor level at the rear of the building containing a recently created very large dressing room providing ample space for large dance troupes to change. There are copious areas of storage for the Company's scenery, props and wardrobe.

This is a thriving venue run by an exceptionally enthusiastic group of volunteers. Whilst the Swansea Little Theatre Company produce only 6 one week shows each year the venue is fully booked for the remaining time by touring organisations, creating a revenue stream that allows the Company to maintain a regular process of upgrade of the facilities. The ambition and proven success of this Company appears to have assured the future for the venue.

Auditorium Capacity: 144 (plus 8 wheelchair positions)

Stage details:

Performance space – width – 13.79m
Performance space – depth – 8.56m
Depth of apron – n/a
Wing space (Right and Left) – inc in performance space
Proscenium height/width – n/a
Orchestra pit (maximum no of players) – n/a
Height from stage floor to grid – 3.5m
Rake – None

The Grand Theatre

Organisation: Department of Culture, Leisure and Regeneration, City and County of Swansea

Address: Singleton Street, Swansea. SA1 3QJ

Construction/Opening: 1897

Architect: William Hope, Newcastle

Builder: D Jenkins, Swansea

Current Owner: Swansea City and County Council

History/previous names & ownership

Constructed on the site of the old Drill Hall, the Grand Theatre was constructed for proprietors Morell and Mouillet and was opened on 26th July 1897 by Dame Adelina Patti. It had an audience capacity of 2500. Very soon afterwards it was turned into one of the city's first cinemas and renamed the Swansea Cinema, though this was only for a brief time.

In 1904 the manager and lessee of the Grand, Frank Boyce died in November and the theatre closed until new management could be found. It re-opened in December under new management and lessees E. Oswald Brookes and J. W. Woodbridge. A new iron fireproof safety curtain was installed in February 1905. Around this time the theatre started showing picture-reels of major events, especially boxing title fights. In 1908 Oswald Brookes became the sole lessee of the building until May 1910. He was followed as lessee by Frederick Mouillot until his death in August 1911. Thomas Garret Byrne took over as manager and remained in post until 1939 when he retired. In 1912 the theatre was owned by David Allen & Sons Ltd. Various renovations were carried out on a more or less annual basis (during august shutdowns) and by 1928 it was being advertised as having a system of vents and electric fans that made it 'the coolest house of amusements in Swansea'.

On 26th January 1933 the theatre was closed due to the flu epidemic sweeping the nation but re-opened only a week later. It was the only theatre in Swansea to close for that reason. In May of the same year it closed again but this time due to financial difficulties and was reopened as a 'Shilling Theatre' but that idea failed and it became the Grand Cinema and Variety on 14th August. The theatre was taken over by new management and opened as the New Grand Cinema on March 26th 1934, with a seating capacity given as 1,200. It screened early Bioscope shows and from 1934 until 1947 it operated as a full time cinema.

In 1947 it reverted back to live theatre use after acquisition by Captain Billy Willis of Willis Cinemas. The Grand was the flagship theatre of the Willis Circuit and was owned and operated by that company for only 2 years until 1949. Its programme featured a mixture of films and live theatre throughout this period. Ownership passed to the Arts Council from 1949 to 1951 whereupon it was sold on again and changed hands several times in the period to 1956. From 1956 to 1969 it was owned and operated by John Chilvers.

The theatre was closed again in March 1969 until in May of that year the City Council took on a 10 year lease whilst retaining John Chilvers as Manager. It was reopened with an inauguration ceremony as a civic theatre on September 22nd 1969. The Council took on full ownership of the building in 1976 purchasing it for the sum of £100,000.

From 1983 to 1986 it was completely renovated to designs by McColl Associates Architects of London with the aid of a £600,000 grant from the Arts Council of Britain. Alterations included the raising of the auditorium roof. A complete new backstage area was built doubling the amount of dressing room accommodation and stage area designed by John Colgate of Swansea City Architects Department. The total cost of the renovations was £6.5 million.

On 4th June 1997 HRH Princess Margaret attended the theatre's centenary celebrations.

The Arts Wing was opened in 1999 comprising new main entrance to the building, box office, gallery space and studio theatre created to designs by Kim Thomson (Swansea City Architect) and constructed by Norwest Holst. Made possible with a Lottery Grant from the Arts Council of Wales, plus monies from the private and public sectors. The Arts Wing added almost 2000 square metres of extra space to the theatre. From September 1999 to 2009 the Ballet Russe was based at the Grand and regularly performed on both the main stage and in the Studio. Since that company went into administration there has been no resident company in the building.

Description

Located in the heart of Swansea City Centre adjacent to the central bus station and primary access road into the city the Grand is a major landmark on the city skyline and visible from some distance away by virtue of the expansive road network surrounding it.

The main approach by vehicle is to the rear of the building and the unmistakably late 20th Century flytower cladding and backstage block at low level. It is not an elegant architectural statement though undoubtedly is an instantly recognisable elevation. The principal elevation to the front of the building is entirely different and retains much of the character of the original building despite the architectural intervention of a two-storey extension between the two symmetrical pavilion-style blocks at each end of the main frontage. Unlike the flytower cladding and backstage block the design of the front extension sits very comfortably with the Victorian original, the ground floor replicating part of the original stone façade and the first floor a curved-roofed conservatory lean-to behind which the original external wall is retained and visible.

It is however quite difficult to read the front elevation in respect of locating the way in to the theatre. The ground floor extension has many doors to the outside, the majority of which appear to be emergency exits from the auditorium within and whilst there is a side door into the pavilion block (occupied by the 'Footlights' café/bar) the actual main entrance into foyer and box office is in the building next door to the theatre.

In 2001 the adjacent building (originally a city centre bus depot) was developed as the Grand's 'Arts Wing' and now contains the box office at ground floor, open plan exhibition spaces at first and second floor and a Studio Theatre at 3rd floor level.

Much of the original heavily engineered structure of the bus depot has been retained and a full height atrium space created behind glazing in the original façade giving a very pleasant light and airy ambience to the space. Since opening it has proven to be an extremely popular and successful addition to the Theatre with the gallery spaces regularly used for fine arts and photography exhibitions (and the atrium featuring some specially commissioned permanent installations) and the Studio has become hugely popular with a diverse range of users.

The studio seats 140 but is a very flexible space with retractable seating on 3 sides allowing its flat floor to be exploited for various audience configurations. Originally the space was open to the underside of the roof structure which was probably a very satisfactory architectural solution but since opening a suspended lay-in grid tiled ceiling has been installed complete with recessed modular fluorescent lighting and copious amounts of insulation above it to overcome serious noise ingress problems of the original design. From an architectural point of view this is not a good solution but it has worked as far as the users and management are concerned and doesn't detract from the functionality of the space under performance conditions at all.

The main auditorium is a Victorian tour de force of opulent theatre decoration and from the stage is astonishingly intimate given its audience capacity of over 1000 arranged on stalls with 2 upper balconies. The balcony fronts are extravagantly decorated and extend around the sides of the room to meet a single structure of audience boxes on each side of the proscenium. The audience balconies are supported on iron columns and these create quite a high proportion of restricted view seats but make a real contribution to the feeling of intimacy from the performers' point of view by visually fore-shortening the depth of the room, particularly at stalls level.

The stage is very large and well equipped with large wing spaces and direct access to a large loading bay and the backstage accommodation built in the mid 1980s. It has a full height flytower.

The views to the stage from the audience seating is generally good, although upward sightlines are slightly compromised from the middle balcony due to the proximity of the underside of the upper balcony above.

The ceiling of the auditorium was raised during the mid 1980s renovations to facilitate the incorporation of a technical lighting bridge within the ceiling over the upper balcony and at this point the seating capacity was increased and a control room built into the rear.

The foyers are expansive and pleasant spaces to explore and there are licensed bar areas serving each level. The conservatory at first floor level facilitates connections from one side of the theatre auditorium to the other and contains an impressive collection of show posters from the late 19th Century and the retained original façade of the building. Ornamental niches along the façade suggest the presence at some point of statues long since removed. There are signs of weather ingress into this space and re-sealing the junction between 20th Century conservatory and 19th Century building envelope is a high priority for the management.

Whilst clearly very well supported by the Local Authority and a loyal local audience there are signs that the City Council will divest itself of the theatre to a charitable trust at some point in the next few years following a precedent it has set with it's leisure centre estate. The Theatre Management expect such a change in governance to create opportunities to improve the business and obtain funding for ongoing repairs and maintenance of the building fabric.

Auditorium Capacity:

Original: 2500; 1934: 1200;

Current: Main auditorium: 1019 (comprising 429 on stalls, 290 on circle and 300 on upper balcony);

Studio: 140

Stage details:

Performance space – width – 19.8m
Performance space – depth – 14m
Depth of apron – n/a
Wing space (Right and Left) – (SR) 8m; (SL) 2.8m
Proscenium height/width – height 8m; width 8.8m
Orchestra pit (maximum no of players) – 90
Height from stage floor to grid – 21.34m
Rake – none

Llewelyn Hall

Organisation: YMCA

Address: 1, Kingsway Swansea SA1 5JQ

Construction: 1912-13 **Opening:** 1913

Architect: Glendinning Moxham, Swansea

Builder: unknown

Current Owner: YMCA

History/previous names & ownership

The Swansea Young Men's Christian Association was founded in 1868. With a huge growth in the number of members at the beginning of the 20th Century, the YMCA in Swansea outgrew its original premises in Dynevor Place and commenced the process to moving into its own bespoke building. In 1911 the Management Committee secured the freehold to Longlands Hotel situated on the corner of Page Street and St Helens Rd, with a view to demolishing and replacing it with a new building. The foundation stone laying ceremony was held on 9th July 1912 and was attended by Lord and Lady Llewelyn and other local dignitaries. It was opened on 15th October 1913 by Lord Kinnaird.

Within twelve months of its opening, the YMCA building was requisitioned for the Red Cross as an emergency Hospital for the wounded service men of the 1914 – 1918 War. The YMCA continued to function during this time but activities were limited, as most of the young men had joined the forces. In 1919 the YMCA returned to the building and inaugurated many activities. In the early thirties several rooms in the YMCA were set aside to train the unemployed in various trades and Musical Afternoons were held in the Llewelyn Hall. Some time between its opening and the outbreak of the Second World war a film projection box was constructed at the rear of the balcony and the audience seating capacity consequently reduced.

During the Second World War the Medical Board requisitioned the Llewelyn Hall as well as some other rooms in the building. In one night during the 3-day Swansea Blitz fifteen incendiary bombs were dropped on the flat roof. It is due to the fact that the building survived the Blitz that it was listed Grade 2 on 30th March 1987. The listing states that the Llewelyn Hall was added to the original building in 1920 but from plans of the building published in *The Building News* on 15th February 1915 it is clear that it was part of the original concept for the building.

The current appearance of the room suggests that the stage was enlarged at some point and a new proscenium wall constructed downstage of the original stage front too. Dylan Thomas played amateur dramatics at Llewelyn Hall and it was used by 'The Abbey Players', an amateur dramatics society who performed their first show on the stage in January 1961. The Abbey Players outgrew Llewelyn Hall by 1978 and moved to the Grand Theatre. Since then, the hall has not had any permanent company resident.

A redevelopment of the YMCA building commenced in late 2010 to designs by Architect Huw Griffiths of Swansea with a vision of creating a multi-purpose community enterprise centre when the works are completed. The initial phase involves the refurbishment and upgrade of the ground floor and it is planned to upgrade access to the Llewelyn Hall by installation of a new passenger lift in a future phase and improvement of facilities for people with movement impairment in general.

Description

The YMCA is located on a very prominent site in central Swansea, within walking distance of the Grand Theatre and Albert Hall, although the presence of the Llewelyn Hall is less obvious.

The Llewelyn Hall is at the rear of the building and announced from the outside at pavement level by a large stone-embellished door on Page Street. As Page Street rises away from St Helens Road the Llewelyn Hall is at a higher level than the YMCA and stands taller than the rest of the building at the rear of the site.

Both the original YMCA and the Llewelyn Hall have external walls of red brick with dressed stone embellishments around windows and door openings though the Llewelyn Hall detailing is much less flamboyant, restrained even, and this part of the overall building has a simple brick parapet around its roof whilst the YMCA has a carved and decorated stone parapet.

Current access arrangements are entirely through the main entrance to the YMCA and the route through the building to the theatre auditorium is slightly tortuous. The Hall is located at first floor level (which is actually first floor and a half in respect of the lower YMCA building) and access for visitors or performers with movement impairment must be extremely difficult. The building works being carried out in 2010-11 are aimed specifically at reducing the accessibility difficulties of the current layout.

The Hall is entered via a simple single door on the side, located roughly in line with the single balcony above and with the stage then to the right. It is a glorious little auditorium of elegant proportion and bathed in daylight thanks to large windows along one wall and under the balcony and ocular windows at high level on both sides disguised by decorative grilles set within the large curved cornice around the perimeter.

The stalls level has a flat parquet floor and no fixed seating whilst on the balcony the original audience seats remain in place. The walls are decorated with pilasters and mouldings of garlands and fruit but it is a restrained classicism rather than extravagant. Even the colour scheme is gentle on the eye and could well be original although that is impossible to establish. The ceiling has circular garland mouldings with light fittings at their centre and ribs between connecting the pilasters across the room. The presence of one of these circular ceiling mouldings above the stage area suggests that the stage was enlarged at some point and the current proscenium construction and location is probably not original. This supposition is reinforced by the inability to see the front half of the stage from the seats on the balcony, or the top of the proscenium from the seats under it.

The stage itself is quite small but is in proportion to the audience area. It is raised very high above the audience and has limited wing-space with no capacity for flying scenic effects (in fact it has no grid and only rudimentary suspension rigging from bars slung between crudely inserted trusses currently).

The balcony retains most of the original audience seats – some were removed a very long time ago to enable the construction of a film projection room at the rear – and they appear to be in remarkably good condition in general. The projection box has no equipment in it.

The primary uses of this beautiful little auditorium are currently small, local meetings and conferences and local fitness groups with live performance now quite a rare event. Certainly it appears that the balcony hasn't seen an audience for some considerable time.

The building management is clearly extremely proud of the auditorium and there appears to be something of a renaissance in activity in the YMCA building generally which may yet extend to the wider awareness of the existence of this space and an increase in its use.

Auditorium Capacity: 246 (comprising 150 loose seats on stalls and 96 fixed seats on balcony)

Stage details:

Performance space – width – 6.5m
Performance space – depth – 4.8m
Depth of apron – n/a
Wing space (Right and Left) – SR - 1.75m; SL - 1.8m
Proscenium height/width – not available
Orchestra pit (maximum no of players) – n/a
Height from stage floor to grid – no grid
Rake – None

The Patti Pavilion

Organisation: Raj Swansea Ltd

Address: Victoria Park, Brynmill, Swansea SA1 4PQ

Construction/Opening: 1881 (relocated to current site in 1920)

Architect: Original: Alfred Bucknall, Swansea; 2007 renovations: Powell Dobson, Swansea

Builder: Original: unknown; 2007 renovations: Mynde Management

Current Owner: Swansea City and County Council

History/previous names & ownership

Originally built as a Winter Garden at Craig-Y-Nos, the home of Dame Adelina Patti, the building was given as a gift by Madame Patti to the people of Swansea in 1918. Due to World War I there was a shortage of able-bodied men to move it from Craig-Y-Nos down to Swansea and it wasn't until 1920 that it was dismantled and rebuilt at Victoria Park. It was named the Patti Pavilion in honour of its donor who had died the previous year.

The Pavilion has been used widely for rock concerts, festivals, cultural events and a variety of other uses, but over the second half of the 20th Century fell into disrepair. The Patti Pavilion was listed Grade II on 18th August 1993 with an amendment being made to the listing on 25th July 1994. In 1994 it attracted the attention of a BBC TV make-over programme, 'Challenge Anneka', which attempted to give it a new lease of life, but again the building fell into disrepair and in 2006 it was further badly damaged by an arson attack.

Swansea City Council granted a 125 year lease to Developer Andgreen Properties at a peppercorn rent on 12th February 2004 as the building was in a serious state of disrepair and the Council was unable to fund the major costs necessary to bring the property back into economic use. The developer carried out major renovation works and extended the building at his own cost with supporting funding from the City & County of Swansea, the Welsh Assembly Government and National Lottery Good Causes. Work began on the £3million project in late 2007 to extend the Patti Pavilion with a new glass covered wing housing a 500-cover restaurant and cafe bar and a 900-person event and concert hall designed by architects Powell Dobson of Swansea. Mynde Management (Contractors) was appointed to undertake the construction works. The original sprung dance floor was overhauled and the building thermally and acoustically upgraded. On completion of the renovation works in 2008 the developer was unable to find a suitable operator/tenant for the building and it stood empty for almost a year before a consortium of local businessmen took over the lease. The Patti Pavilion reopened for business in August 2010 with an Indian Restaurant named 'The Patti Raj' in the new extension and ambitions to return the performance space to the forefront of live performance in Swansea.

Description

Located in a prime position between the St Helens Cricket Ground, Victoria Park and the seafront this is a large free-standing building visible from some distance away from the main road between Swansea City Centre and the Gower Peninsula.

It has a striking green roof with the central area over the hall comprising a shallow ogee arched profile and side areas of the hall having shallow mono-pitch lean-to sections of roof at a lower level. The two longer side elevations are fully glazed below the roof eaves to a low level pennant stone plinth. The shorter sides are original parts of the building that are rendered and painted white. The end that was the rear of the hall features elegant arched window reveals and towers and the main entrance has rectangular windows at high level (to internal toilet and office spaces) and the original front door set on the central axis of the building under a commemorative feature panel facing directly along the central axial footpath of Victoria Park to the Guildhall building.

At the end that was originally the rear of the building a contemporary fully glazed extension has been added to the original building and contains a large Restaurant. The design of the extension draws no references from the original building, for example the new building's curtain wall glazing and cantilevered blade like roof overhangs create a powerful horizontal emphasis where the original building's glazing creates a vertical emphasis, and it doesn't sit comfortably next to its older neighbour as a result. Access into the new extension is on the side rather than on the central axis, apparently because there was a desire to fully occupy the available site area with new building leaving no room on the boundary for access to be created and this too tends to unbalance the sense of the building still being a pavilion in the landscape.

The entrance to the Patti Pavilion is at the opposite end of the building from the new extension and into a small hallway containing the original ticket desk windows (now filled with opaque glazed windows and the room behind used for storage) and access to audience toilets, a small area of management offices and to the minstrels' balcony inside the hall. Access is on the level from outside and directly through the hallway into the main hall of the pavilion beyond. The auditorium is unexpectedly large, emphasised by the full height glazing along the two longer sides and the internal height to the ridge of the ogee arch shaped roof. The quality of the most recent restoration works to the auditorium space is very high and retains all of the original features of the building including the colour scheme.

The elegant steel roof structure is painted in gold which contrasts with the dark brown treatment of the timber lined roof and is supported on columns and tie beams painted turquoise blue with further gold coloured highlighting. The two solid walls of the space (the entry wall and wall against which the new extension stands) are both painted white with the entry wall containing a cantilevered minstrel balcony above the entrance doors and a small opening to a licensed bar counter and the other retaining the outline of the original stage area now blocked up to maximise space in the extension beyond.

Apart from the small Minstrels' Balcony there is no fixed location for performances to be staged although the flat floor offers flexibility in this regard. There are no fixed locations for performance lighting or sound system rigging and no suspension points at all that could facilitate their installation. Neither is there any provision of appropriate power outlets for equipment. When the stage area was blocked up the original performer dressing rooms were also removed from use.

Unsurprisingly for such a large volume of space with so much perimeter glazing it is difficult to heat in the winter months and currently uses a number of portable hot air blowers to elevate the internal temperature at occupancy level. As part of the renovation works some extract units were installed at high level on the two solid end walls with the intention that they would remove hot and used air but they were not commissioned and currently can not be used. To cool the space in the summer the many opening windows around the perimeter are opened.

The consortium of local businessmen who have taken the building on have high ambitions to re-establish the building as a major venue for live performance events but need to establish contacts with promoters to enable this to happen in a sustained manner.

The Restaurant is operating with a degree of success and business is growing but there have not been any live performance events in the hall since it reopened. In the meantime the Hall is being used for ad hoc events including Awards Ceremonies and Wedding Fayres and has a Yoga/exercise club using the hall on a weekly basis.

The absence of an obvious stage or staging area, dressing rooms for visiting performers and any rigging points for performance lighting and sound may be an issue that will need addressing at some point if the operators are to achieve their ambitions.

Auditorium Capacity: 490 (theatre style seating); 900 (standing)

Stage details: No fixed stage

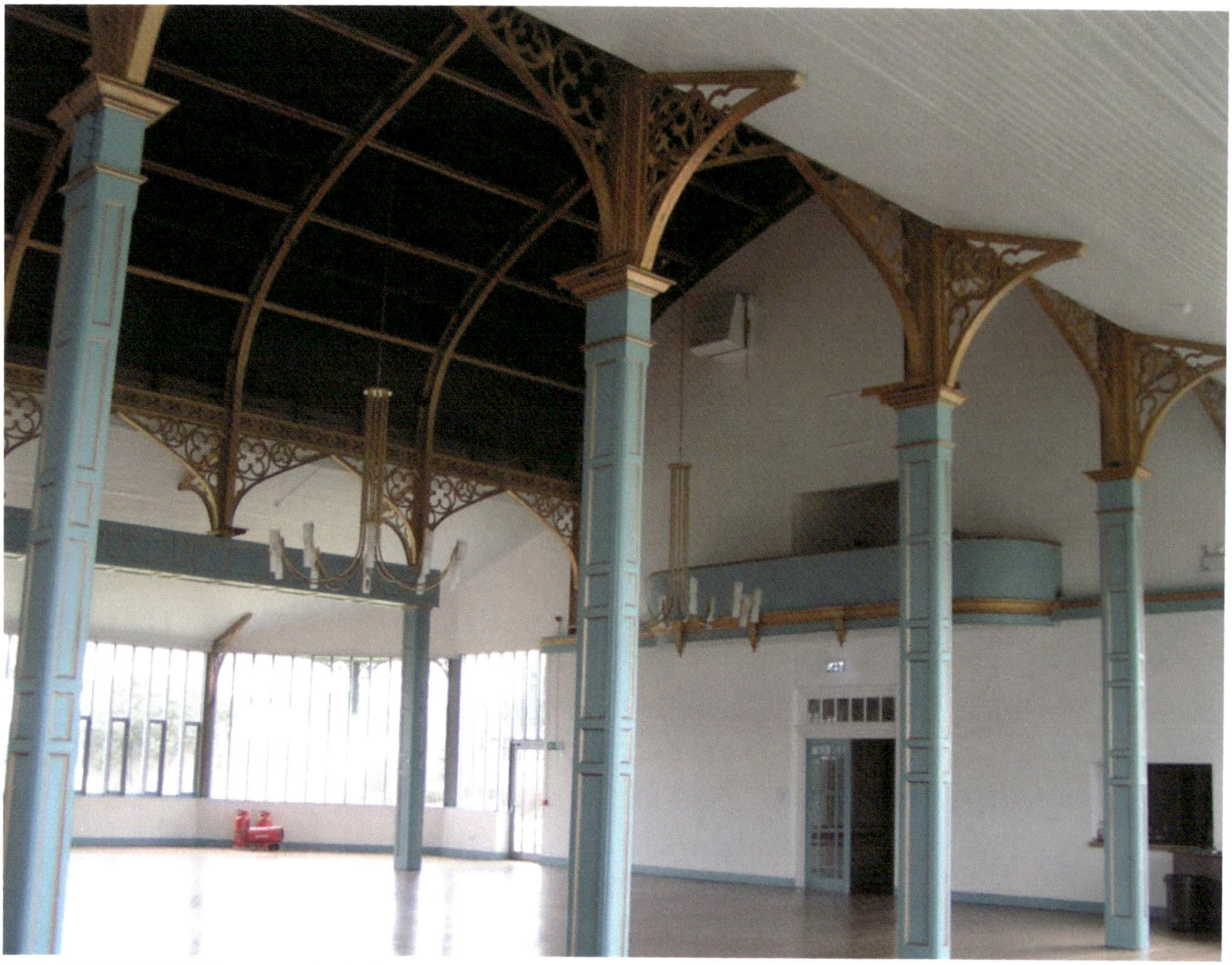

PATTI PAVILION
AVAILABLE FOR HIRE

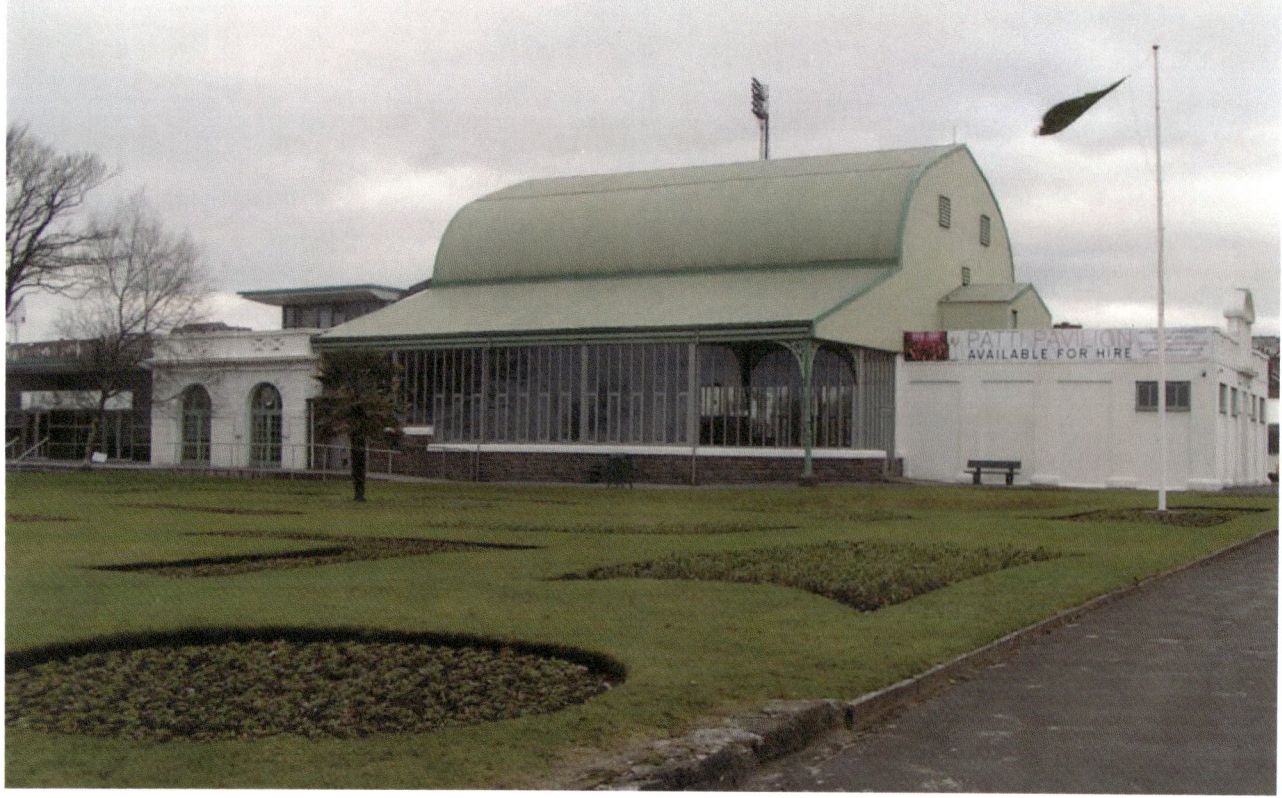

The Penyrheol Community Theatre, Gorseinon

Organisation: Swansea City and County Council

Address: Pontarddulais Road, Gorseinon, Swansea SA4 4FG

Construction/Opening: 1982

Architect: Swansea City Council Architects

Builder: unknown

Current Owner: Swansea City and County Council

History/previous names & ownership

The Theatre was built with the adjacent Leisure Centre by Lliw Valley Borough Council and opened in March 1982.

Ownership and responsibility for management and operation of the Theatre was taken over from Lliw Valley Borough Council by the new Unitary Authority of City and County of Swansea in 1996. The Theatre remains as constructed with no alterations or changes having been made to the original appearance and layout.

Description

This is a rather non-descript building that makes no signal that a theatre is within as the visitor approaches. It is located on the edge of Gorseinon and there is no signage directing visitors to it from within the town which reinforces its introverted character.

It shares a site with a swimming pool, sports hall and a large secondary school is immediately adjacent and hiding much of the theatre from view.

Indeed the only visible part of the theatre exterior is a curved red brick structure over the entrance that contains the ground floor entrance hall/reception serving both sports hall and theatre facilities and a small licensed bar area on the first floor. There is no external signage on the building pronouncing the presence of a theatre.

Entry into the building is on level access via a draught lobby with automatic doors so overall audience accessibility is excellent. The reception space is not a theatre foyer but does lead directly through double doors into the front of the flat-floored auditorium at stalls level.

The auditorium is large and roughly square on plan. On entry into the stalls, the stage is immediately to the right and it is a large stage with variable width and height proscenium formed with brightly coloured drapes. There is no fixed seating and the flexibility this encourages is highly valued by the management.

There is a balcony running along one side and the full width at the rear of the auditorium although the side balcony provides an access route only (from the first floor bar) and no seats are placed on it. An unusual feature of the Hall is the installation of motorised retractable seating on the balcony further increasing flexibility of use and audience configuration. In the house left corner of the balcony a control box is located. It is a deep balcony and the ceiling below is quite low such that sightlines to the top of the proscenium from the rear of stalls seating under the balcony are restricted.

The auditorium has a sprung timber floor throughout and the walls are also clad with timber, lacquered to retain its natural appearance. The balcony front is also clad with timber strips but is stained dark brown to contrast with the walls. There is a suspended lay-in grid ceiling with recessed modular fluorescent light fittings and no apparent other architectural house lighting.

There is no orchestra pit or capacity for flying scenic effects but the stage has an apron and is equipped with extensive rigging across the whole performance area.

Back stage consists of two green rooms - equipped with toilets, a wash area and showers- Male capacity is 27; Female capacity is 33. There is a Dance/Drama studio situated behind the stage, with access to both sides of the stage and equipped with sprung floor, wall bars and one mirrored wall. Studio Capacity is 140

The theatre is shared with the adjacent School who have access to and use of the Hall at anytime during the day. Use of the auditorium passes to the theatre management after 3.30pm each day. The school uses the Hall for assemblies and exams and stages 2 productions on stage each year.

Since operation was taken over by Swansea City Council, there has been a reduction in the number and frequency of visiting touring shows and most programming of the theatre serves local amateur dramatic, dance and musical societies. It is clearly focussed on serving its community but may be under-utilised.

Auditorium Capacity:

Main Hall: 505 seated comprising 337 seats on stalls and 168 on the balcony; 655 standing; Studio: 140

Stage details:

Performance space – width – 14.2 m
Performance space – depth – 7.0 m
Depth of apron – 1.0 m
Wing space (Right and Left) – 1.8m each side
Proscenium height/width – height variable/ width 10.6 m
Orchestra pit (maximum no of players) – n/a
Height from stage floor to grid – 6.0 m
Rake – None

Taliesin Arts Centre

Organisation: University of Wales, Swansea

Address: Swansea University, Singleton Park, Swansea SA2 8PZ

Construction: 1982-83 **Opening:** 1984

Architect: Peter Moro Partnership, London

Builder: unknown

Current Owner: University of Wales, Swansea

History/previous names & ownership

The building was constructed as a purpose built theatre and arts centre to replace the adjacent University Hall (now known as Taliesin Annexe). The foundation stone was laid by L J Drew MA Mld on 17 September 1982 and the building was completed in 1983. It was officially opened by Sir Geraint Evans CBE on 18th June 1984. Taliesin is named after the 6th century Celtic bard of the same name.

In 1997-98 the Egypt Centre was added as a purpose built museum wing extension to the original building to accommodate artefacts from the Sir Henry Wellcome Foundation collection never previously available for public view and held in Swansea since 1971. It contains the largest collection of Egyptian Antiquities in Wales. The extension was built over and around an original roof terrace and reduced the footprint of the visual art gallery adjacent and was designed by Design Partnership of Wales, Architects. The Egypt Centre was officially opened in September 1998 by Viscount St. Davids.

Description

Located close to the heart of the University campus on the primary east-west pedestrian circulation route, the building is a relatively modest two storey red brick construction notable for being the only building in the area set at 45° to the orthogonal grid on which all other surrounding buildings are organised. The building is free-standing on its own island site and is an elongated octagon in plan form with the main axis defining the internal arrangement of theatre auditorium at the centre surrounded by front and back-of-house accommodation. There are entry points in several locations and at the two principal internal floor levels by virtue of the topography of the sloping site. Access for wheelchair users is well provided at both levels.

All of the front-of-house entrances lead directly into the spacious multi-use foyer area. At the lower level there is a large bookshop and bank serving the student population. The Arts Centre box office is located inside the visual arts gallery also at this level with access to the adjacent Egypt Centre. The main theatre foyer spaces are located at the upper level and include a large café/bar space, the theatre administration reception (and access to the management offices suite) and further access to the Egypt Centre. Entry into the auditorium is directly from the upper foyer space on each side of the theatre and delivers the audience to the mid-point of the single fixed tier of seating. This arrangement has caused occasional bottlenecks at the ends of performances and limits the potential to increase spaces within the auditorium for wheelchair users.

The auditorium is a broad fan shape with minimal architectural features (limited to highlight colours on the fully exposed ceiling walkways and bridges and the seat upholstery) which gives it the feel of a technical and slightly experimental space focussed entirely on the stage and performance. There is a flexible forestage zone incorporating a mechanical elevator that can be used to create an orchestra pit or forestage extension or additional seating for 30 people in the audience. The proscenium is also flexible insofar as the side panels can rotate from their 'normal' position extending the side walls of the theatre onto stage to a position perpendicular to the stage front creating a significantly larger performance zone especially popular for dance. There is no flytower (omitted as a cost saving during construction) but plentiful height and rigging allows 'half-flying' which does not limit any of the shows presented here.

Directly off stage on each side are generously proportioned double-height spaces used for scenery and drapes storage and the like leading to the loading bay and workshop on one side and 4 stage level dressing rooms on the other that are well-equipped and all have windows. The route to the loading bay is also double height and features large acoustically rated access doors. There is no raised loading dock but access from loading bay to stage is on the level. The only difficulty experienced with the building is access to the loading bay for articulated vehicles. The original intent was for the adjacent University Hall building to be demolished following completion of the Arts Centre but that has not happened and the older building causes quite severe movement restrictions for large vehicles not envisaged by the original Arts Centre design. There are two large sound/lighting control rooms at the back of the audience seating area which are also used for projection. A large structural section of wall separates the two rooms on the centreline of the auditorium and presents some difficulties for projection of some cinemascope or similar widescreen format films.

This is clearly a very successful and thriving venue that is very well funded and supported by a loyal and growing audience. It is particularly interesting that it is not dependent on the student population with the vast majority of audience being drawn from the general population of Swansea. The venue has specialised in presenting dance events as a result of the extremely large and well designed stage area and it is worthy of comment that the operating staff could find no faults with the building at all, and were extremely complimentary about the design, particularly of the backstage spaces.

Auditorium Capacity: 360 maximum (no orchestra pit), 330 (with full orchestra pit)

Stage details:

Performance space – width – 20m (including wings)
Performance space – depth – 9.3m
Depth of apron – variable
Wing space (Right and Left) – variable
Proscenium height/width – height 6.2m; width variable
Orchestra pit (maximum no of players) – 15 max – flexible pit
Height from stage floor to grid – 9.8m
Rake – none

The Townhill Theatre

Organisation: Swansea Metropolitan University Department of Humanities, School of Performance & Literature

Address: Swansea Metropolitan University, Townhill Road, Swansea SA2 0UT

Construction: 1962 (as College of Education) **Opening:** 1997 (as theatre)

Architect/Builder: unknown/unknown

Current Owner: Swansea Metropolitan University

History/previous names & ownership

The building containing the Townhill Theatre was opened as part of Swansea College of Education by Sir Edward Boyle Bart MP, Minister for Education on 2nd November 1962. The original use of the current theatre space was as a general assembly/gymnasium space serving a teacher training course.

In 1997 the Townhill Theatre was created in the original assembly/gym space complete with a proscenium raised stage and loose seating for audiences up to 200 in a large flat floored auditorium.

Volcano Theatre Company became resident in the theatre soon afterwards and stayed until the summer of 2011 when they relocated to a new base in central Swansea.

The proscenium opening was closed and the stage area converted to use as a secondary studio/rehearsal/function room in 2009.

Description

Whilst the Townhill Campus site is easy to find and well signposted throughout the city, finding the theatre on campus is not at all easy. It is not even mentioned on the campus directory adjacent the main gates and there is no external signage on the building to identify the presence of any performance venue at all.

In large part this is because this theatre is focussed on academic training through its School of Performance and Literature and rarely invites audiences in from outside the University.

The theatre is located within an unremarkable education building of the early 1960s with an envelope of plain brickwork and green pitched roofs. Entry is on the level from a large surface car park and through revolving doors into a spacious open reception/foyer space that also serves student catering areas and contains toilets that are accessible to audiences.

The theatre auditorium entry continues the un-prepossessing nature of the place – simply two pairs of double doors with a nominal sign above extending a 'Welcome to Townhill Theatre'. The theatre floor is several steps below the external foyer area. For people with movement disabilities a stair lift has been installed to provide access down to the auditorium floor.

The auditorium has no real architectural character or identity – it is a blank canvas within which students create a wide range of staging configurations and performances. It is a single span portal frame structure with high level windows on one side that can be blacked out completely for performances.

It has a sprung timber strip floor (a legacy of its original construction as a gymnasium) and the walls and ceiling are generally white painted plain plaster. Consequently it is a pleasant space for day-time rehearsals.

The original raised stage has been blocked off as the students apparently collectively eschewed the traditional arrangements of theatre staging some time ago and prefer the flexibility of the remaining large rectangular auditorium. The original stage area has been stripped of rigging and is now predominantly used for rehearsals with occasional use for Studio Theatre productions.

The main auditorium has an extensive coverage of high level rigging bars and points but there is no other theatre equipment or machinery available. There is a high level sound and lighting control room in the corner at house-left.

There are no dedicated dressing rooms but a warm-up/rehearsal studio adjacent to the main space serves this purpose when needed. Scenery making workshops and stores are located elsewhere on campus in other academic accommodation.

The venue is focussed on providing facilities for students of the performing arts and technical theatre courses within the Department of Humanities at SMU. Students present one week of live shows each academic term and operate the box office themselves. Audiences are almost entirely drawn from within the student body although a concerted effort is being made to engage more with the local community. As a result of the focus on academic training, external/visiting company performances are rare.

The courses provided by the University are producing high quality graduates and the future of the theatre therefore seems assured.

Auditorium Capacity: Original: 200; current: 150 (maximum and dependent on staging configuration)

Stage details: No fixed stage

Powys

Brecon
　　Theatr Brycheiniog
Craig-Y-Nos (Pen-y-Cae)
　　The Adelina Patti Theatre
Ystradgynlais
　　The Welfare

Theatr Brycheiniog, Brecon

Organisation: Theatr Brycheiniog Trust

Address: Canal Wharf, Brecon, Powys LD3 7EW

Construction/Opening: 1997

Architect: Powys County Council Architects

Builder: Birse Construction

Current Owner: Powys County Council

History/previous names & ownership

This theatre was built as part of the regeneration of the canal area and received funding from the European Regional Development Fund and the Arts Council of Wales' Lottery scheme. It was opened by HRH the Prince of Wales on 27th July 1997.

In 2007 Theatr Brycheiniog became the first solar-powered theatre in Wales, generating part of its energy requirements from photo-voltaic cells on the roof.

Description

Located adjacent to a basin on the Brecon to Monmouth Canal and slightly remote from the main town centre this is a large building which it is claimed was designed to mould with the environment and traditional Brecon buildings in particular. It is constructed of red brick and the roof is covered with Welsh slate in the style of a canal wharf warehouse. It has two dark-stained timber clad projections, one to the main frontage, the other to the rear, the principal gables having stone parapets. The majority of window openings are relatively small and have arched heads although there are larger curtain-walled sections to the upper levels of the audience foyers on the main frontage. At ground floor the openings resemble glazed arcade openings, again with shallow arched heads. The main entrance is on the canal side and beneath one of the timber-clad projections. Entry is directly into a generous entrance hall containing the Box Office and reception, audience toilets and access directly to the theatre auditorium stalls and, via a large staircase up to the principal levels of audience foyer and accesses to the upper balconies in the auditorium. Lifts are provided to facilitate access to all areas of the front-of-house for visitors with movement impairment.

The foyers are generously proportioned and occupy the full length of the building, having views over the canal basin and are arranged on two principal levels associated with the two upper audience balcony levels. The foyers are extensively used for events such as conference break-out spaces and are used for visual arts exhibitions open to the general public.

The auditorium is based on traditional multi-level balconied theatres and is an intimate and warm room with the audience close to the stage at all levels. The stalls is square on plan and has a balconied parterre on three sides, with the side sections being set at stage level and providing a useful connection between the performance space and auditorium. The stalls floor is flat and has seating wagons mounted on air castors to allow a variety of arrangements with varying capacities, including cabaret-style seating and, when required, a standing audience to be accommodated. There are two upper balconies, each with seating on side slips and supported on slender columns on the balcony front line which reinforce the sense of intimacy and envelopment for the stalls audience.

The auditorium walls are plain and painted a soft pink colour which compliments the traditional red upholstery of the audience seating and carpeted floors throughout. The balcony fronts have a simple panelled timber fascia and their simplicity works well with the proportions of the room. There are three lighting bridges spanning the auditorium which effectively form the ceiling to the space. A sound and lighting control position is open to the auditorium at the rear of the stalls parterre.

The Theatr Brycheiniog describes itself as a multi-purpose community facility and with that in mind it has an adaptable end-stage with variable width proscenium. Although there is no full flytower, the stage grid is equipped with 58 counterweight lines and the performance area is large in comparison with other venues in the region of a similar capacity. It has an orchestra pit with elevator that further adds to the flexibility of the stage and forestage area. The stage has sixteen traps. Loading for visiting shows is directly from a generous yard at the rear of the building and at grade. Back-of house facilities include 2 small dressing rooms on the ground floor (stage) level, both with en-suite and facilities for disabled performers, and 2 larger company dressing rooms on the first floor with separate performer toilets and showers. There is adequate storage throughout the backstage area and a wardrobe maintenance room as well as office accommodation for the venue staff. There is also a rehearsal studio which doubles as a conference room, capable of seating 150.

This is a successful and well supported venue presenting a wide range of popular events to an audience drawn from a wide geographical area. Theatr Brycheiniog is recognised as a Regional Performing Arts Centre (RPAC) by the Arts Council of Wales. Movement into sustainable energy sources will assist in ensuring its future viability which seems secure at present.

Auditorium Capacity:

478 maximum (reducing to 426 if pit or apron is in use) comprising 280 on stalls, 92 on middle balcony and 106 on upper balcony

Stage details:

Performance space – width – 14.5m
Performance space – depth – 12.3m
Depth of apron – 0.8m
Wing space (Right and Left) – (SR) 1.9m, (SL) 2.2m
Proscenium height/width – height 9.3m; width variable
Orchestra pit (maximum no of players) – 12
Height from stage floor to grid – 11.1m
Rake - None

The Adelina Patti Theatre, Craig-Y-Nos

Organisation: Private owner

Address: Craig y Nos Castle, Brecon Road, Pen-y-Cae, Powys SA9 1GL

Construction/Opening: 1891

Architect: Bucknall and Jennings, Swansea

Builder: unknown

Current Owner: Mr Martin Gover (SelClene Ltd)

History/previous names & ownership

Madam Adelina Juana Maria Patti bought Craig-y-Nos castle and the surrounding park land for £3500 in 1878. The theatre extension to the Castle was opened on 12th July 1891. Built to be Patti's own private auditorium, it was designed with input from Sir Henry Irving. Alleged to have been briefed by Patti to be her miniature version of La Scala, Milan it is also said to incorporate features from Wagner's Bayreuth Festspielhaus opera house in Bayreuth and the Theatre Royal, Drury Lane, London although this is difficult to substantiate.

2 years after Miss Patti's death the Castle and Estate were sold to the King Edward VII Welsh National Memorial Trust for £11,000 in March 1921, and it was converted for use as a Tuberculosis Hospital. The Theatre organ, given to Patti in the United States after one of her tours was dismantled. The Castle was known as the Adelina Patti Hospital and focused on treatment of children with Tuberculosis until 1957 whereupon it was adapted for use as a Hospital for the Elderly. Throughout this period the theatre was largely mothballed and un-used.

The Hospital was closed in 1986 and the hospital equipment was removed along with domestic artefacts that were subsequently sold at public auction. The Castle continued to be maintained by the Welsh Office until 1988 when it was purchased by Mr. David Richard Cecil Jones and the Craig-y-Nos Castle Company Limited. Efforts were then made to seal the roof of the theatre and extensive repairs were carried out to much of the roof of the main building. Timber work in the theatre received treatment for dry rot.

The Theatre was listed Grade 1 on 14th March 1985 and is the only Grade 1 listed theatre in Wales.

The Castle was sold to Dr. John Trevor Jones and Mrs. Penelope Jones in 1995 and the Theatre roof was re-slated. Mr Martin Gover purchased the Castle in 2000 and its conversion to a high quality hotel commenced. Since 2000 there has been a programme of significant ongoing maintenance and repair work to the Theatre, including new gutter linings and roof parapet repairs, treatment for dry-rot and some redecoration. There remains a great deal of work to do to secure the long term integrity of the building however. Regular ongoing maintenance is in hand and the eradication of the remaining dry-rot is a high priority. Thereafter restoration of timber features affected by rot will be carried out along with other elements as and when revenue permits.

In July 2011 it was announced that the entire Castle including the theatre had been placed on the market with an asking price of £1.5m and the caveat that any prospective buyer undertook to retain the Hotel and carry on the restoration of the estate.

Description

The theatre appears rather curiously connected to the rest of the Castle building with its axial main entrance appearing offset and rather squashed against the preceding clock tower and billiard room extensions.

The envelope comprises a mixture of locally quarried red sandstone stone, carved Bath stone features and (presumably non-original) grey render. The main façade has classical features including pilasters, a balustrade frieze and pedimented panel above the main doors surmounted with a stone figure of a singing goddess. The roof is of welsh slate and there is a large rooflight lantern over the central axis of the auditorium that provides daylight and some ventilation.

Entry through the double height glazed screen and doors is into a glorious and intimate auditorium remarkable for the condition in which it survives. The hardwood floor slopes towards a magnificent and highly decorated proscenium (the audience is seated on loose chairs and the original intent was that they be removed, the floor raised to stage level and the room became a ballroom for use after dinners and/or performances) and a stage extension/movable apron can be used to cover the orchestra pit.

The ascending / descending auditorium floor is claimed to be the oldest surviving example of a moveable floor – a concept also claimed to be pioneered by Adelina Patti. Two Victorian hand-wound mechanical jacks raise and lower the floor. The floor is lowered when the room is used as a theatre, with the auditorium sloping down towards the stage. The original theatre chairs had longer legs at the front than at the back, to allow for the tilt of the floor. The hand-wound jacks are under the stage at the front of the auditorium and are accessible from the orchestra pit.

One of the original stage/house curtains has survived and is a painting of Adelina Patti riding in a chariot, dressed as Semiramide from the opera of the same name by Rossini. Ten Corinthian columns support the ceiling, and in between these are the names of composers such as Mozart, Verdi and Rossini, all gilded and surmounted by Madam Patti's monogram.

Originally there was a balcony to the rear of the auditorium above the main entrance that was used by servants and staff to witness the performances. The balcony was removed at some unknown time but the (very) small hatch in the wall through which access to the balcony was attained remains.

Much of the original stage equipment remains although is unused and the majority of the original stage cloths and scenic backgrounds were destroyed by Patti's husband after her death. All of the equipment and stage machinery was cutting-edge when it was installed and again it is remarkable that so much of it has survived. Dressing Rooms were provided on 3 levels backstage originally although all have since been converted into staff accommodation and/or bedrooms associated with the conversion of the castle buildings into a hotel.

The primary use of the space currently is, and will continue to be, for wedding ceremonies, but there is no barrier to the notion that performances can and will take place in the auditorium whenever possible.

Auditorium Capacity: 150

Stage details:

Performance space – width – 6m
Performance space – depth – 6.46m
Depth of apron - variable stage extension
Wing space (Right and Left) – (SR) 3.19m; (SL) 2.8m
Proscenium height/width – height not available; width 6m
Orchestra pit (maximum no of players) – 20
Height from stage floor to grid – 7.93m
Rake - None

The Welfare, Ystradgynlais

Organisation: Ystradgynlais Miners' Welfare & Community Hall Trust Ltd

Address: Brecon Road, Ystradgynlais, Swansea SA9 1JJ

Construction/Opening: 1934

Architect: Monod T. Seymour, Cardiff

Builder: unknown

Current Owner: Ystradgynlais Miners' Welfare & Community Hall Trust Ltd

History/previous names & ownership

The Miners Welfare Hall opened in 1934 as a theatre and cinema with 650 seats but was closed in 1937, and its cinema licence was transferred to the Capitol Cinema in Ystalyfera, with a clause that no films could be screened in the Welfare Hall for the following seven years. The Welfare Cinema did re-open later but then was closed again in the 1950's.

The building was taken over from the Coal Industry Social Welfare Organisation (CISWO) after a period of disuse and dereliction by the local Town Council in the late 1980's and refurbished as a community arts centre by Powys County Council architects re-opening on 24th November 1991. An official re-opening ceremony was held on 11th July 1992 conducted by Mr Gwilym Jones MP, Parliamentary Under-Secretary to the Welsh Office and at this time the building was renamed the Ystradgynlais Miners' Welfare and Community Hall. Some time in the early 2000's it was again renamed and is now known simply as The Welfare.

In 2010 a new auditorium floor was installed, the orchestra pit and original tilting auditorium floor mechanism removed, a new audience retractable bleacher seating unit installed, the original Hall windows blocked up and the hall completely redecorated.

Description

The building is freestanding and set back a long way from the main thoroughfare through the town, with a small surface car park to the front and road access to the rear. The accommodation is predominantly single storey with a flat roof wrapped around the main hall on all 4 sides. The main hall projects above the rest of the building and has a pitched slate roof. All elevations have a pebble-dashed rendered finish with the exception of an extension added to the building in 1991 that contains circulation and the main entrance which has white and grey coloured render treatment.

Entry is into a generous circulation space connecting back-of-house accommodation with the main hall and audience

WCs and bar at the opposite end of the building. It contains the box office and access to both the main hall and 'lesser hall'. The Lesser Hall is used as a community café facility and for the exhibition of visual arts and can accommodate other community group activities.

The main hall has two audience entry points as a result of its floor level changing across its length from stage to rear (it is higher at the rear). Entry at the front is down a shallow ramp and is at grade to the rear. The hall is much changed from its original appearance with the installation of a suspended tiled ceiling and blocking up of the original perimeter windows on the long sides of the room (carried out in 2010 to try to improve the thermal performance of the room). The windows are retained on the exterior of the building. The footprint of the hall was reduced during the 1991 renovations to create a public bar area where previously the rear of the audience seating was fixed. Much of the original art deco style wall features are retained however as has the art deco proscenium and they have been sensitively decorated to accentuate their appearance. A new auditorium floor was installed in 2010 and during those works the original orchestra pit was removed/covered over and the original hydraulically operated tilting floor mechanism that changed the rear half of the auditorium floor from raked to flat was also removed leaving the entire hall floor flat now. This adjustable floor feature is said to have been modelled on the installation at the Adelina Patti Theatre at Craig-Y-Nos further up the valley. The adjustable floor system enabled the floor to be used for dances when raised to the horizontal and flat condition. Also in 2010 a new motorised retractable bleacher unit was installed and this now connects the higher floor level to the main floor level. The automated seating unit has further enhanced the ability of the venue to stage more than one event in any day and is being exploited to the full. Behind the bleacher unit on the raised area of auditorium floor an in-room sound/light mixing position has been created. The hall has a high level projection room (with digital projection equipment) and separate sound and lighting control rooms at the rear of the room (above the bar area).

There is a large stage with demountable apron units that further increase the performance area. There is no stage machinery and no flytower but there are significant rigging and suspension bars over the entire stage area. There are 3 well furnished dressing rooms behind the stage, all with windows and loading is directly from the road to the rear of the building onto the stage. The dressing rooms tend to overheat by virtue of being above the boiler room and the heating system using exposed pipework. The pipes passing through the dressing rooms discharge large amounts of uncontrollable heat into this area of the building such that by the time the water has reached the main hall it has insufficient heat energy remaining to effectively warm the space.

There is air-conditioning equipment serving the auditorium but it is rarely used because it causes draughts as the cool air entering at high level dumps down the side walls as warm air over the audience rises. The building has a collection of artwork by Josef Herman, a polish émigré who settled in the town in 1944 and stayed for 11 years after escaping Poland during the Second World War. Herman studied working people as the subjects of his art, most notably coal miners. He became part of the community, where he was fondly nicknamed "Joe Bach". In 2004, the Josef Herman Foundation was established in Ystradgynlais, to honour the artist and his legacy, and encourage study of his work, as well as arts initiatives in South Wales.

This is clearly a successful venue and is extremely busy offering a wide range of performance types and events, often with more than one event in a day in the main hall. It clearly has a sustainable future and ambitious management who are considering future expansion to further increase the facilities they are able to offer the local community.

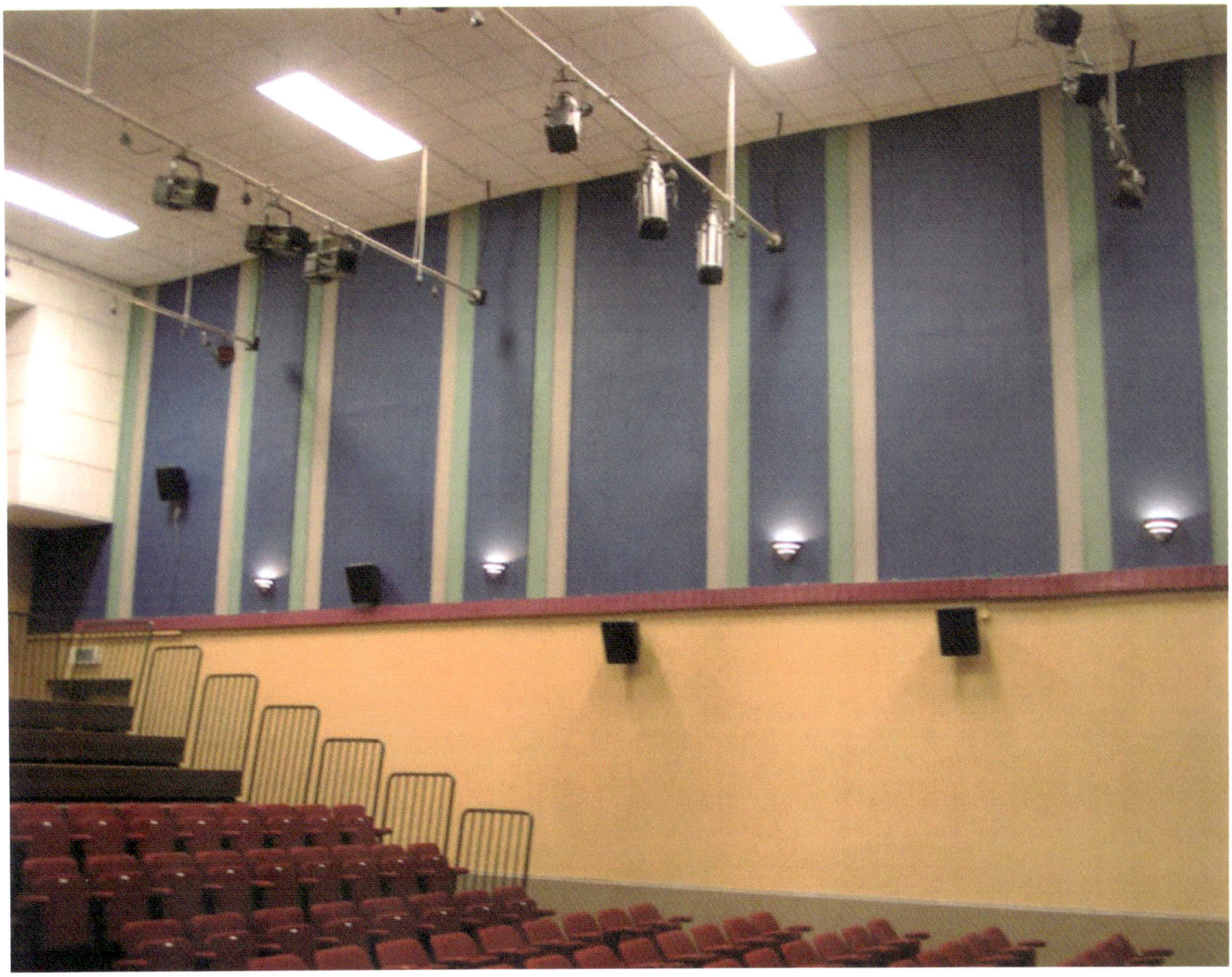

Auditorium Capacity:

Original capacity 650, reduced to 367 in 1991 and further
reduced to 300 in 2010 (comprising 147on retractable
bleacher seating and 153 loose seats)

Stage details:

Performance space – width – 12.45m
Performance space – depth – 5.8m
Depth of apron – variable by removable units
Wing space (Right and Left) – (SR)1.5m; (SL) 1.5m
Proscenium height/width – height 5m; width 9.45m
Orchestra pit (maximum no of players) – n/a
Height from stage floor to grid – 6.15m (min)
Rake – None

Carmarthenshire

Ammanford
> The Miners' Theatre

Brynamman
> The Public Hall

Carmarthen
> The Halliwell Theatre
>
> The Lyric

Cross Hands
> Public Hall & Cinema

Llandybie
> Public Memorial Hall

Llanelli
> Theatr Elli
>
> Y Ffwrnes

Pontyberem
> Memorial Hall & Institute

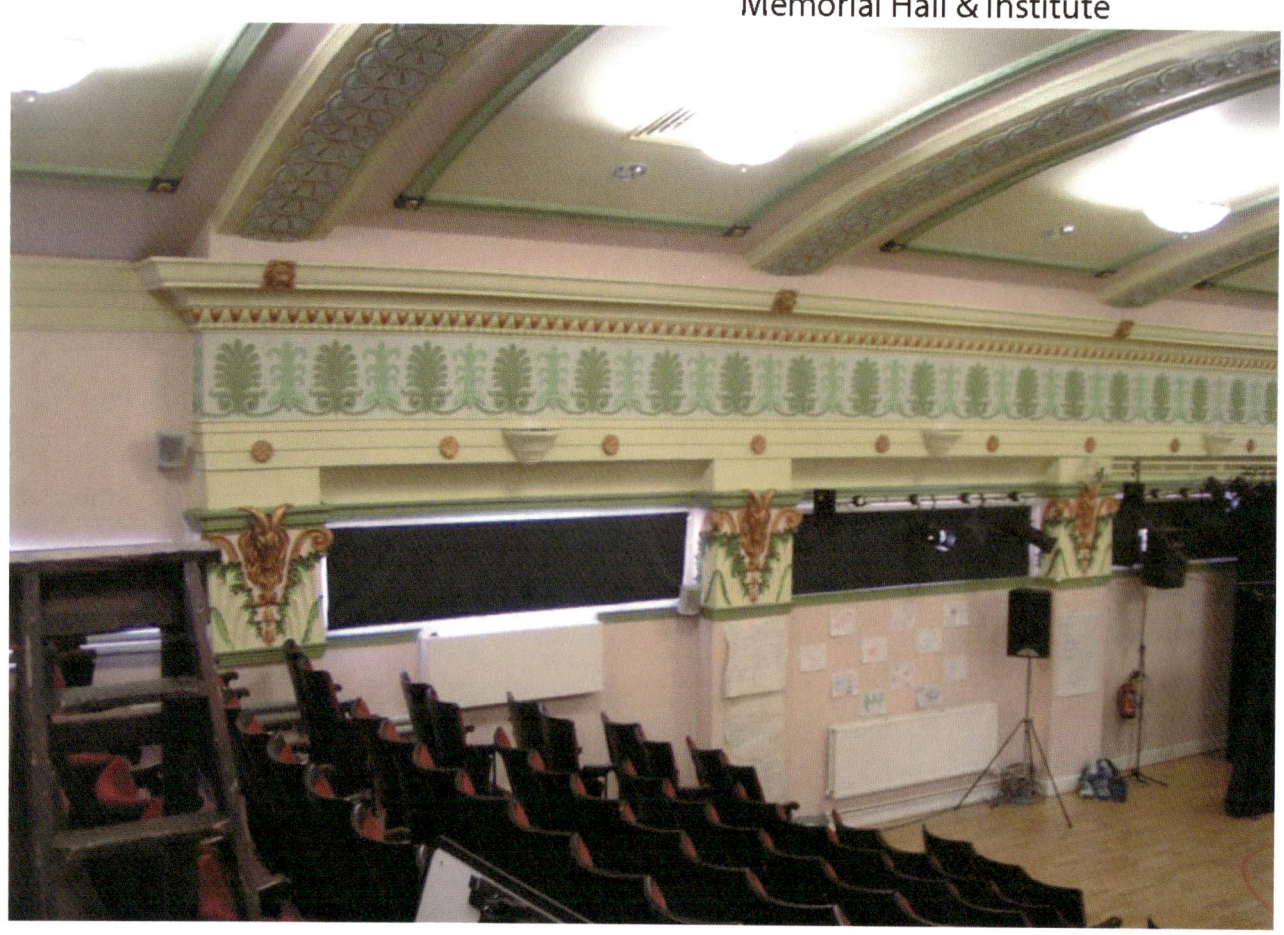

The Miners' Theatre, Ammanford

Organisation: Carmarthenshire Theatres

Address: Wind Street, Ammanford SA18 3DN

Construction/Opening: 1932

Architect: J. Owen Parry

Builder: Messrs A. H. Bond & Co. of Swansea

Current Owner: Carmarthenshire County Borough Council

History/previous names & ownership

Construction of the building was in 1931-32 at a cost of just over £5,000. The building was based on a classic design of the time with an attractive facade in facing bricks with ornate terra cotta columns, string and plinth courses, all roofed in Caernarfon slates. Inside the auditorium seating was provided for 760, with 540 in stalls and 220 in the circle. The auditorium was decorated in fibrous plaster mouldings in keeping with the fashion of the day. On Saturday, the 1st of October 1932, Mr Finlay Gibson, Secretary of the South Wales Coal Owners' Association, along with the Co-Secretary, Mr Oliver Harries, performed the official opening, supported by Mr James Griffiths (later to become the local MP). The building was known as The Welfare Hall. From 1932 to 1997 the building was owned and operated by the Ammanford District Miners Welfare Association with the Unitary Authority of Carmarthenshire County Borough Council assuming ownership in 1997.

In 1936 The Welfare Institute was constructed to the front of the original building - a substantial building, based on a more modernistic style with a less grandiose design than the Welfare Hall and providing reading rooms, a library and other recreational facilities including the 'Minor Hall', a room capable of seating 250. From 1936 to 2001 the two buildings were known as the Ammanford Institute and Welfare Hall. From 1948 to 1975 the building was primarily used as a cinema with one week in the year reserved for the notable drama week organised by Ammanford and District Arts Club. In 1965 the Institute premises were converted into a licensed club. The reading room and library became bars and the 'Minor Hall' was transformed into a concert and bingo hall. The Billiard Room was closed.

The Theatre/Cinema in the Welfare Hall closed in 1975 and the building was utilised for other forms of leisure and entertainment, all of which met with limited success and the building fell into disuse in the 1980's and was derelict until 1997 when Carmarthenshire County Council took a lease on the building. It was listed Grade II on 8th October 1994. Between 1999 and 2001 the upper floor was converted into the Ammanford Miners' Theatre by extending the floor of the former balcony forward to meet the original proscenium, the upper half of which is the only part now visible. The rear half of the original balcony has been retained and provides fixed raked seating. The barrel vaulted ceiling and plasterwork on the side-walls was renovated and a cinema projector (re)installed. It was re-opened as the Miners Theatre on 6th March 2001. In 2005 the derelict Billiard Room in the Institute building was converted into a Mining Museum.

Description

The Theatre is located in a detached building behind the Miners' Welfare building and between a surface car park and church and graveyard. It has no real street presence and is quite difficult to find if unfamiliar with the town.

The building envelope comprises red brickwork with terracotta and stone features and the building has a real civic quality to it. The envelope is in good condition (as a result of the extensive refurbishment works carried out in 1999-2001). The building is a well proportioned rectangular plan form surmounted with a slate pitched roof having two ventilation cowls equally spaced along the ridge.

Audience entry into the building is on its central axis on the main front elevation, via three steps up to the large hardwood doors set between a pair of Corinthian style columns under a stone frieze. Access for disabled visitors is afforded via one of the pairs of emergency escape doors on the car park side of the building (towards the rear) by prior arrangement with the management. The backstage lift provides disabled access to the auditorium above.

The ground floor foyer is small and typical of buildings of this age and origin but is extravagantly decorated with bright colours and applied plaster mouldings to walls and ceiling. It contains the Theatre Box Office and refreshment sales point, male audience WCs, access to the ground floor accommodation and the stairs that lead up to the auditorium. Unlike other buildings of this age the access to the auditorium is not symmetrical and a grand staircase leading up to the auditorium is on one side only.

There is a small mezzanine level foyer space even more elaborately decorated than the ground floor space and containing a collection of memorabilia relating to performances by local amateur dramatic groups in the theatre. The space is used for meetings and other events when there are no performances in the theatre.

Access to the auditorium is at the highest point and at the rear of the fixed raked seating on house right only. The original 1930's audience seats have been retained.

The auditorium walls and proscenium are heavily and ornately decorated with brightly painted applied plaster mouldings and features and is surmounted by a single span curved

Auditorium Capacity:

Original: 760 with 220 in the balcony and 540 on stalls. Current: 216 comprising 126 fixed seats and 90 loose seats

Stage details:

Performance space – width - 6m

Performance space – depth – 4.3m

Depth of apron – n/a

Wing space (Right and Left) - variable

Proscenium height/width – n/a

Orchestra pit (maximum no of players) – n/a

Height from stage floor to grid – n/a

Rake - None

ceiling containing original ventilation grilles and light fittings. The vent grilles are no longer used – a new heating and ventilation system was installed as part of the refurbishment works and apparently work very successfully with no issues of excessive heat or cold reported by the venue staff.

A flat sprung timber floor extends from the front row of fixed seating to the original proscenium wall and loose seats are used to vary audience capacity and provide a flexible staging area. There is no raised stage area or orchestra pit.

Drapes and screens are used to delineate stage areas and two alternate proscenium positions downstage of the original proscenium wall, and to create variable wing space and crossovers. There is no capacity for flying over any of the performance area. Performance sound system and lighting rigging positions have been sensitively incorporated on the walls so as not to detract from the appearance of the room.

Original windows at high level in the room have been retained and can be covered with black-out blinds for performances. They are left uncovered allowing daylight in to events on many occasions according to venue staff.

The original stage area behind the proscenium wall has been converted into a pair of dressing rooms and access to the ground floor accommodation below, The original fly gallery has been retained as a feature in the dressing rooms and there remains a large loft area above the suspended ceilings that is unused.

Loading to the stage level is via emergency exit doors to the surface car park and a backstage lift.

The ground floor (originally the theatre stalls and stage level) has been converted into a large and well-used series of spaces focussed on providing facilities for the community and primarily for youth groups. There is a resident youth theatre group that stages a new show every month on average. The facilities include a large common room/youth club-room (that is also used for rehearsals, dance classes and the like), an IT suite and staff offices.

The space is now mainly used as a theatre with various productions staged throughout the year but it is versatile enough to cater for live music and there are weekly jive dancing classes held. The building is clearly being well maintained and is a successful and sustainable venue.

The Public Hall, Brynamman

Organisation: Brynamman Public Hall Ltd

Address: Station Road, Brynamman, SA18 1SF

Construction: 1924-26 **Opening:** 1926

Architect/Builder: unknown/unknown

Current Owner: Brynamman Public Hall Ltd

History/previous names & ownership

The current building was built between 1924 and 1926 to replace the Brynamman Miners' Hall that was destroyed by fire in December 1915. It was opened in May 1926. Seating was provided for 982 in stalls and circle levels. It was furnished throughout with tip-up seats upholstered in old gold corduroy. It had a proscenium 38 feet wide and the stage was built 20ft by 60ft and had four dressing rooms below. A lounge was situated below the library and contained 12 armchairs and three settees where the miners could relax or play cards around several oak game and card tables. There was also a billiard room above the library.

It was converted and upgraded to show talking pictures in the 1930's when a projection box was added and was then known as the Brynamman Cinema. Today, as well as operating as a first run cinema, it also has children's theatre performed on its stage.

Major grant-aided renovations were carried out in the 1990's but the extent and nature of these works is unknown.

Description

The building is located on a prominent elevated site above the main road through the town. The principal elevation is a powerful but austere classical style with 6 pilasters, pediment and base. All exterior surfaces are finished in heavily textured and coloured render and appear to be in good condition and well maintained. There are five openings in the base, ordered between the pilasters, four of which may have originally been windows but now used to advertise future film showings. The central opening is a recessed door set behind ornate wrought iron gates. The main entrance to the building is to the side of the main frontage up a large flight of steps. It is not clear how access for visitors with disabilities is afforded. Windows either side of the double width entrance doors imply a foyer area within but in general the facades are not animated by windows or other openings.

Photographs of the building from the 1940's indicate that the current envelope finishes are not original and that the pediment on the main front elevation has been added at some point (in the 1940's there was a balustrade parapet with no pediment).

Interior photograph: www.ciswo-services.org.uk

Auditorium Capacity:

Original capacity was 982 but major renovations in the 1990's reduced capacity to current 800 (split between balcony and stalls)

Stage details:

Performance space – width – 18.29m
Performance space – depth - 6m
Proscenium height/width: height unknown; width 11.6m

The Halliwell Theatre, Carmarthen

Organisation: Trinity College School of Theatre and Performance

Address: School of Theatre and Performance, Trinity College, Camarthen SA31 3EP

Construction/Opening: 1963

Architect/Builder: unknown/unknown

Current Owner: Trinity College

History/previous names & ownership

In 1937 the Parry Theatre designed by H. S. Hardy, Architect was opened on Trinity College campus by HRH The Duke of Kent. Sometime over the subsequent 30 years the Parry Theatre building was converted into classroom spaces and a large studio space for Welsh Media Studies course. The original audience seating and raked floor were removed along with the original stage and original main entrance at the back of the audience seating area was abandoned. The building remains in use as an academic teaching space.

The Halliwell Theatre was built to replace the Parry and was opened in June 1963, named after an ex Dean of Trinity College. The original freestanding theatre building was extended to create the Halliwell Centre (with primary use for conferences, meetings, training events and graduation ceremonies) and was opened on 24th November 1990 by Sir Richard Lloyd Jones, Permanent Secretary at the Welsh Office.

Since 1990 the primary use of the Halliwell Centre has changed to become home for the Trinity College School of Theatre & Performance and over recent years there have been several piece-meal adaptations made to the building by the Theatre School including the creation of dressing room space in an original meeting room/classroom.

Description

The Halliwell Theatre replaced an earlier theatre on the Trinity College campus and is located in the centre of the campus within easy reach of extensive car parking and all other campus amenities. Although there is no overt signage directing visitors to the building and it has a very small identifying sign on one wall it is not difficult to find.

The original 1963 theatre building had an unusual curved roof design still visible above the surrounding 1990 extensions but the remainder of the original building has been subsumed into the later extensions such that the original external walls are very difficult to trace. The Halliwell Centre building that now encases the original is predominantly brick clad with punched windows to three walls and an extensive curtain walling glazed frontage to the main conference reception and student dining areas under the theatre. It has a mono-pitched tiled roof supported at its high end against the original theatre building envelope.

The theatre entrance is on the longitudinal centre-line of the auditorium and approached by three shallow steps on that axis or a gentle ramp perpendicular to it that affords easy access for movement impaired visitors.

Interior photographs courtesy of Steve Dennis, School of Theatre and Performance, University of Wales Trinity Saint David

The entrance doors are glazed and lead into a small lobby which then leads directly into a circulation space that is actually within the auditorium though screened from it by a half-height wall. The circulation space leads to academic spaces and audience toilets as well as directly into the rear of the audience seating on the balcony. Currently, audiences are discouraged from using this entrance and instead are directed to the entrance to the School of Theatre and Performance at the side of the building and into the auditorium at the front of stalls.

The auditorium is a double octagon in plan form with one octagon containing the stage and support spaces and the other the audience seating. Large structural columns at the junction between the two octagons define a proscenium edge but there is no fixed proscenium header. Drapes in various configurations are used to create several different proscenium locations and sizes. It is architecturally a plain room with no distinguishing features but the shape and size create an intimate and warm space. Technical equipment and lighting positions have clearly been added over the life of the building and were not conceived as part of the original design so they now look conspicuously added on to the surfaces to which they are fixed.

The stage has become much more adaptable than its original conception with much experimentation in construction of thrusts and walkways projecting into the auditorium, achieved by the removal of the front 3 or 4 rows of seats when needed. The only drawback of such experimentation is that audience sightlines from the balcony seating becomes quite restricted and for the majority of shows using staging in front of the structural proscenium, tickets for the balcony seats are not sold. Notwithstanding this, some stalls seats have restricted views due to structural columns within the space supporting the balcony construction. There is an enclosed sound/lighting control room at the rear of stalls but it is extremely small and also has a major element of structure in it that restricts headroom. There are plans to replace the dimmer racks currently housed in the control room to militate against excessive heat problems. The stage is large but there is no flytower and suspension and rigging of scenic effects and equipment is limited by the curious curved underside of the original roof structure. There is hardly any backstage accommodation – the crossover behind the upstage wall is used as much for wall-mounted storage as circulation and until fairly recently there were no dressing rooms for performers at all. The School of Theatre and Performance has converted a meeting room/classroom into a single large dressing room space that can also be used as a small rehearsal studio but if separate gender spaces are required, male performers have to get changed in a costume-making room a considerable distance from the stage. At some point openings were formed between the stage and auditorium and adjacent corridor and fitted with sliding folding shutters of no acoustic value whatsoever. Gradually these are being removed or more substantial structure built in the openings to minimise the difficulties of noise break in and break out these shutters present.

The adaptation of spaces around the theatre conceived as rooms required to support conference use is ongoing and in time it is planned for this to be a much more complete theatre entity than it is currently and for it to become much more focussed on the provision of live entertainment for the surrounding local community.

Auditorium Capacity:
332 (comprising 250 on stalls and 82 on the balcony)

Stage details:

Performance space – width – 6.1m on forestage; 9.3m on main stage   Performance space – depth – 9.9m including forestage/apron
Depth of apron – 3.65m
Wing space (Right and Left) – SR - 2.45m; SL - 2.45m
Proscenium height/width – h not known, width 9.3m
Orchestra pit (maximum no of players) – n/a
Height from stage floor to grid – not known
Rake – None

The Lyric, Carmarthen

Organisation: Carmarthenshire Theatres

Address: King Street, Carmarthen, Carmarthenshire   SA31 1BD

Construction/Opening: 1936

Architect: 1854 Assembly Rooms: James Wilson, Bath; 1934-36 Lyric Theatre: William S. Wort, Cardiff

Builder: unknown

Current Owner: Carmarthenshire County Borough Council

History/previous names & ownership

The Lyric story began in 1852 when Dr David Lloyd of the Carmarthen Literary and Scientific Institute proposed a public meeting in the town hall for the purpose of considering the best way to procure public rooms. After that meeting a capital fund of £2,000 had been raised by the sale of shares of £25.

A building was commissioned and it originally opened as The Assembly Rooms on 21st November 1854. That original building remains as part of the current Lyric buildings. The Assembly Rooms building had a frontage constructed in decorated bath stone and contained Public Rooms consisting of a large hallway, a reading room, billiard room and conveniences, and accommodation that housed Carmarthen Literary and Scientific Institute and a town museum. The Assembly Room itself was upstairs and was 71 feet long by 34 feet wide with a reported height of 31 feet. It contained a wood panelled ceiling with beams mounted on ornamental trusses. Lighting took the form of two massive gas chandeliers. The new auditorium with 600 temporary seats was available to many entertainments ranging from readings through to musical concerts including the very first performances of Carmarthen Amateur Operatic Society. The assembly room was also a venue for balls, dinners and art exhibitions.

In October 1906 programmes at the Assembly Rooms changed to include short Bioscope picture shows although it did not become a full-time cinema at this time.

In 1918 Mr Thomas Barger, proprietor of the Palace Theatre in Pembroke Dock took over the lease of both the Assembly Rooms and The Empire Cinema in Blue Street, Carmarthen and refurbished the auditorium. From 1st April 1918 the building was re-named the Lyric Cinema, with programmes of films, and concert party type shows performed on the stage. The Lyric Cinema was wired for sound and on 31st March 1920 Al Jolson in "Sonny Boy" was screened.

At the end of 1930 both the Lyric and the Empire cinemas closed and Mr William Edward Morgan became the new lessee of the Lyric. The Lyric reopened on April 4th 1931 having been completely refurbished and fitted with up to date Western Electric Sound equipment. A cafe was added and a new 20 feet wide proscenium was installed. The Lyric Cinema now had 550 seats.

In 1934, it was decided to build a new auditorium on land behind the Assembly Rooms/Lyric Cinema. Building work started to the rear of the entrance block (containing the former Public Rooms) in 1935. The existing cinema continued to operate as normal during the first nineteen weeks of building work. During the final phases of construction whereby modifications were made to the entrance block the Lyric only closed for two weeks. In a total of just twenty one weeks the new Lyric was ready to open. Seating was now provided for 900 in stalls and circle levels. There was a 36 feet wide proscenium with a fully equipped stage. Central heating and a ventilation system had been installed.

Designed in an Art Deco style, the new Lyric Super Cinema opened on Monday April 5th 1936 with Richard Tauber's new film 'Hearts Desire'. Throughout what remained of the 1930's the Lyric continued to be a huge success and it remained open throughout the Second World War.

After the War however its popularity declined and by 1980 the Lyric was subsisting on meagre income from private film shows and it was closed in late-August 1983 and then lay empty and unused.

Planning Permission for its conversion to shop use (Class I) was granted on the 28th January 1987, although it confined the conversion to retail use to the foyer area. As a condition of the permission the box office had to remain unaltered. Proposed works to the auditorium was refused. On 16th February 1987 the Carmarthen Youth Opera approached Carmarthen District Council for a Theatre licence in order to perform their farewell performance in the Lyric. In the weeks that followed the Lyric was partially re-wired, the ceiling repaired and a temporary stage constructed over the original rotten stage. The Carmarthen Youth Opera performance took place on 14th March 1987. Following the performance of Jesus Christ Superstar, the film 'Top Gun' was shown. It ran to sell out audiences between the 16th and 21st March 1987. On the 12th July 1987 a full one year Theatre Licence was granted on the Lyric and the building was effectively open for business again.

Dyfed County Council, Carmarthen District Council and Carmarthen Town Council agreed to buy the building as a joint investment. Following the purchase the building was conveyed by deed of gift to Carmarthen District Council by Dyfed County Council and Carmarthen Town Council. It was agreed that a lease be granted to a properly constituted company formed by the Carmarthen Youth Opera at a peppercorn rent of one pound a year. The Lyric Theatre Trust (Carmarthen) Limited was incorporated in November 1988.

During 1988 to plans drawn up by company member and Architect Adrian Rowlands, building work commenced on phase one of a redevelopment project. An orchestra pit had been dug out and a new stage and proscenium arch constructed. Stage facilities were still inadequate, there were no dressing rooms and a porta-loo was the backstage toilet facility.

By 1992 the new Welsh Secretary David Hunt had heard of the project and had agreed to the funding of building of a flytower and other works to ensure the Theatre was technically equipped to stage more ambitious shows. The foyers and auditorium were carpeted, follow-spot positions were constructed and a dress circle was constructed between the stalls and the circle.

A small building to the side of the theatre was acquired for potential development for use as a dressing room and very cramped rehearsal space for the Carmarthen and District Youth Opera. Interior walls were demolished in this building to open up a wider space to optimise its use. The plan was to construct a three story building at the side of the auditorium block to house dressing rooms, a green room and a multipurpose room with a projection box that could double up as a second screen and a scenic workshop. Feasibility studies were completed but the works were not implemented. The Lyric Theatre Trust responded to the loss of this development by stating their intention to surrender the lease. The Lyric was to revert to council control. The lease was surrendered in September 2004 with the council resuming business following a period of closure for hand over.

The Lyric Buildings (including the theatre) were listed Grade II on 28th November 2003.

In 2008-09 a 2-storey extension was built to designs by Lawray Architects of Cardiff and a major interior renovation was carried out. An extension was constructed to stage right in an area of the site previously occupied by various low quality outbuildings. The new extension linked front and back of house and was constructed as part of a £1.5million upgrade project. The accommodation provided includes a Studio/Community space, new performer changing room/ Green Room and additional wing storage space off stage right. Other work carried out as part of the project included the re-wiring of the theatre, installation of platform lifts to provide wheelchair access throughout the front of house areas, modification of the original listed ticket desk in the foyer and general redecorations.

Description

Evidence that there is a theatre as large as the Lyric in the centre of Carmarthen is difficult to find as it is completely surrounded by 3-storey buildings and narrow streets and alleyways and effectively has no frontage of its own. The public entrance is identified by a simple glazed canopy projecting from the surrounding shop units and buildings converted to office use into King Street and only glimpses of the rest of the theatre are possible from the surrounding streets and narrow alleyway that runs along one side. The large flytower is visible from the road at the rear (through the loading bay) and from the alleyway but there is nothing on it that identifies it as a theatre.

The audience entrance is gently ramped up from street level providing excellent accessibility for all, and penetrates the depth of the surrounding shop units before the visitor arrives in an unexpectedly large foyer area containing the ticket desk, information point, confectionary sales booth and access to the stalls and stairs leading to the upper levels.

Immediately on entering there is no doubting the age of this incarnation of the building as art deco features and detailing prevail everywhere. This is as a result of the 1935 renovations and extension works and the most recent works of 2008-09 which involved the redecoration and restoration of the foyer area.

Entry into the auditorium is at the rear of stalls and through sound and light lobbies also installed in the most recent works (at the cost of some audience seats). The auditorium is a large volume with the audience arranged on 3 levels – the large flat-floored stalls, a small mezzanine balcony and the upper circle. The seats at the front of the auditorium can now be removed for cabaret style shows. The mezzanine projects some distance along the side walls of the room and contain seats with restricted views of the stage that are apparently rarely sold. An in-room mixing desk position has recently been created in the house-left corner of the balcony which has also resulted in the loss of some audience seats. The original sound and lighting control rooms are located at the rear of the mezzanine and are quite small and conditions inside are very hot and uncomfortable. As a consequence they are only used now as the projection suite for the monthly cinema events programmed at the venue.

The balcony stops short of the proscenium wall and the gap between it and the stage is filled with technical gantries providing side lighting and loudspeaker positions. These gantries have not been designed in an art deco style and perhaps that is appropriate since they are significant recent additions. The upper balcony front is straight and simply runs across the room from side to side. It projects some considerable distance beyond the front of the mezzanine balcony giving a rather unusual proportion to the back of the room. All of the wall surfaces in the room are painted in soft pinks and greys and the balcony fronts have brightly contrasting panels of deep red, yellow and green. The ceiling is fairly plain and is also painted soft pink with highlighting colours around the original ventilation grilles. The floor is carpeted throughout. The proscenium wall is comparatively plain with grey coloured panelling to the sides and no fixed top – black drapes are used to create the top of the frame.

There is a single, large hydraulically operated forestage elevator platform that allows performance in front of the proscenium (with limited sightlines from the majority of the audience seating), audience seating at stalls level or a recessed orchestra pit capable of accommodating a maximum of 30 musicians. The stage is large although it has limited wing-space, and it has a full height flytower that was constructed in 1992. As a result of the configuration of the building and the stage right access from back-of-house, some of the flying lines are double-purchase to make space below for a set of large acoustic doors and the stage manager position is also on stage right.

The new extension built in 2008-09 is connected directly to the stage right access and provides a large space used for large company changing space and as a performer Green Room. It provides a physical link between the front and back-of-house areas that previously didn't exist and although clearly built as a back-of-house space is well used by the local community for a wide range of events.

Auditorium Capacity:

600 (1854 Assembly Hall); 550 (1930 Lyric Cinema); 900 (1936 Lyric Super Cinema); current capacity 665 max (comprising 353 on stalls, 78 on Mezzanine and 234 on balcony)

Stage details:

Performance space – width – 9.5m
Performance space – depth – 9.6m
Depth of apron – 1.03m
Wing space (Right and Left) - (SR) 3.9m; (SL) 2.44m
Proscenium height/width - height 6.8m; width 9.5m
Orchestra pit (maximum no of players) - 30
Height from stage floor to grid – 14.7m
Rake - None

On the first floor there is a large space that has been named 'The Studio' but it is not a studio theatre, rather a neutral rectangular space adaptable for social events as well as rehearsals, dance classes and the like. Glimpses of the new extension exterior envelope are possible from the adjacent narrow alleyway and it is a simple structure with cream rendered finish squeezed into the available space between the original building and the Castle Walls of Carmarthen town centre.

The extension supplements other back-of-house spaces including the original 2 performer changing rooms which can accommodate up to 8 people in each one. Neither of these original dressing rooms have en-suite facilities but there are backstage toilets and showers nearby.

Access to the stage for deliveries is quite restricted insofar as there is only off-road parking for one visiting vehicle in the narrow loading bay. Vehicles are offloaded directly into a large goods lift that connects down to the orchestra pit level and up to stage level. There is access into the backstage areas through the loading bay and a stage door although this route is not suitable for performers or visitors with mobility limitations. The new extension provides excellent access for all and is used for providing access when needed.

As with the vast majority of theatre buildings there is a distinct lack of on-site storage space in the back-of-house areas.

The most recent renovation and building extension works appear to have guaranteed the future of this theatre so nearly lost in the 1980's. The venue is now successful and is managed and operated by an enthusiastic team. It seems to be entrenched at the cultural heart of the town.

Public Hall & Cinema, Cross Hands

Organisation: Cross Hands Public Hall & Cinema Trust

Address: 10 Carmarthen Road, Cross Hands, Llanelli, SA14 6SU

Construction/Opening: 1904

Architect/Builder: unknown/unknown

Current Owner: Carmarthenshire County Council

History/previous names & ownership

A building was first opened on this site in 1904 as a Public Hall with the aim of improving the quality of life for the people of the community. The land on which the building was constructed was donated by local businessmen and the ownership of the building gifted to the local community under Trust. The upkeep of the Hall was funded by the 'National Coal Field - Miners and Dependants Welfare Fund' to which many Miners contributed a penny from their weekly wages.

In 1926 the hall was extended and was modernised into an Art Deco/Egyptian style. It is known the architect was an Italian and from Swansea, but he is not named. The seating capacity was given as 650. The 2-storey extension contained large rooms believed to have been for a library and associated reading rooms as well as committee/ meeting rooms.

In its hey-day, the Hall, regarded as one of the finest in South Wales boasted some top actors and orchestras and the Hall was the main attraction in the area with weekly shows ranging from variety and drama to oratorios and opera.

With the demise of the coal industry and the rise in popularity of television, the Hall slid into obscurity and it was closed and left derelict in 1984.

In 1991, the then Deputy Mayor, Cllr Bryn Davies began his quest of securing a grant that would restore the Public Hall to something like its former glory. Following a £640,000 restoration funded by the Welsh Office, Llanelli Borough Council and Carmarthenshire District Council, the Hall re-opened on the 26th of April 1996. The first Chief Executive of Carmarthenshire County Council opened the Hall to a concert from Cross Hands District Ladies Choir, Cor-Y-Rhyd and pupils from the nearby Maes Yr Yrfa and Gwendraeth Secondary Schools.

As part of the restoration works fixed auditorium seating was installed at stalls level for the first time in the life of the building to serve the principal planned use of the Hall as a cinema and alterations were made to the access into the auditorium to create a confectionary/ refreshment sales counter behind the ticket desk. The 1926 ornate auditorium ceiling had collapsed during the period of dereliction and was replaced with a new, plain curved vaulted ceiling. Films were initially screened on three nights a week but films have since become the mainstay of programming, although some live performances do take place.

It was designated a Grade II* Listed building on 1st December 1999.

Description

The building stands somewhat remote from the centre of Cross Hands adjacent to a school and residential properties with open countryside to one side. It is a freestanding building and quite large, on a flat site with its own surface car park along one entire side through which access to the adjacent school is gained. The front of the building sits at the back of the pavement however and is a fine example of art deco architecture. Elegantly proportioned with a 3-bay frontage, the central bay contains the hardwood entrance doors at ground level under a small cantilevered canopy with the name of the building set above with small windows at the top of a solid panel also divided into 3 panels. The elevations are rendered and painted a pinky-cream with contrasting deep red highlights on the art deco mouldings and picking out the horizontal joints in the pediment.

The original Public Hall occupies the front of the building and access is via shallow steps or a ramp to the central front doors. The entrance hall is tiny and contains the original ticket desk from the 1926 modifications immediately in front of the entrance. Symmetrical staircases are set either side leading directly up to the balcony seating in the auditorium although one has been enclosed to satisfy changes in Fire Regulations over the life of the building.

Originally access into the stalls of the auditorium was through pairs of doors either side of the ticket desk but in the 1996 restoration the foyer space such as it is was increased in size to improve access to the audience toilets and create a space for refreshments and confectionary sales in an area immediately behind the ticket desk. This caused a small reduction in seating capacity but has been carried out sympathetically and allows the front of house area to feel more open and has certainly reduced audience congestion at the new auditorium entry points.

The auditorium is smaller than expected and feels incredibly intimate. The floor under the balcony slopes quite steeply but levels out in front of the balcony overhang where originally there was a clear flat floor but now there are fixed modern audience seats. The floor is carpeted. The hall has been restored to its original condition with the major exception of the ceiling which had collapsed during the period of dereliction in the 80's and 90's and no photographic record was available that would have informed its recreation. The ceiling is now a plain single gently curved barrel vault painted dark red. The walls are plain plastered painted cream and do retain all of the original plaster mouldings and features of the 1926 make-over.

The stage riser is high but sightlines throughout the room are surprisingly good, The proscenium is arched with feature ribbed mouldings forming a recess in the proscenium wall. The stage is small and there is no capacity for flying scenery. There is no permanent infrastructure for rigging performance lighting or scenic effects (as the room is used primarily for cinema) but there is ambition to increase the use of the stage for live performances and to improve the level of house equipment available to visiting companies and performers.

Access to the stage is via steep timber steps on either side. There is no orchestra pit or performer changing rooms. Large doors on either side of the stage provide access for loading directly from outside but the threshold of the doors, driven by the internal stage level is rather high and equipment must be manually lifted into the building.

The balcony front curves gently across the room and returns to meet the side walls. Between the balcony front and proscenium wall on each side are new installations providing side lighting and loudspeaker positions. There is no facility for in-room mixing and the sound/light control positions share space with the large and well equipped projection room set at the back of the balcony seating.

The extension to the building added in 1926 contains a suite of large rooms currently being used primarily by Carmarthenshire County Council Social Services as a day-centre for the elderly. When live performances are staged in the hall some of these rooms are appropriated for use as changing rooms and green room facilities.

This is a wonderful building with huge potential to become a cultural focus of the town. It is currently struggling to open up new revenue streams and restore live performance on a regular basis to the stage – a process seen as essential if it is to survive as its future success cannot be predicated on 35mm film projection and installation of digital projection equipment is currently regarded as unaffordable. There is some confusion over what body or organisation actually now owns the freehold to the building and land. It has been claimed by Carmarthenshire County Council since they recently registered themselves as owner with the Land Registry but the Trust disputes this. This confusion is limiting the Trust's ability to seek funding for further restoration works and to push for greater use of the extension rooms to optimise and maximise use of all of the facilities on site for the local community. The management feels isolated from the wider network of performance venues and is hoping to make strategic alliances to increase appearances by local performance groups on stage in the future.

Auditorium Capacity:

Originally 650; reduced during 1996 restoration to current capacity of 310 (comprising 190 on stalls and 120 on balcony)

Stage details:

Performance space – width – 10.82m including wings
Performance space – depth – 4.9m
Depth of apron – n/a
Wing space (Right and Left) – SR - 2m; SL - 2m
Proscenium height/width – height 4.9m; width 6.55m
Orchestra pit (maximum no of players) – n/a
Height from stage floor to grid – no grid
Rake - None

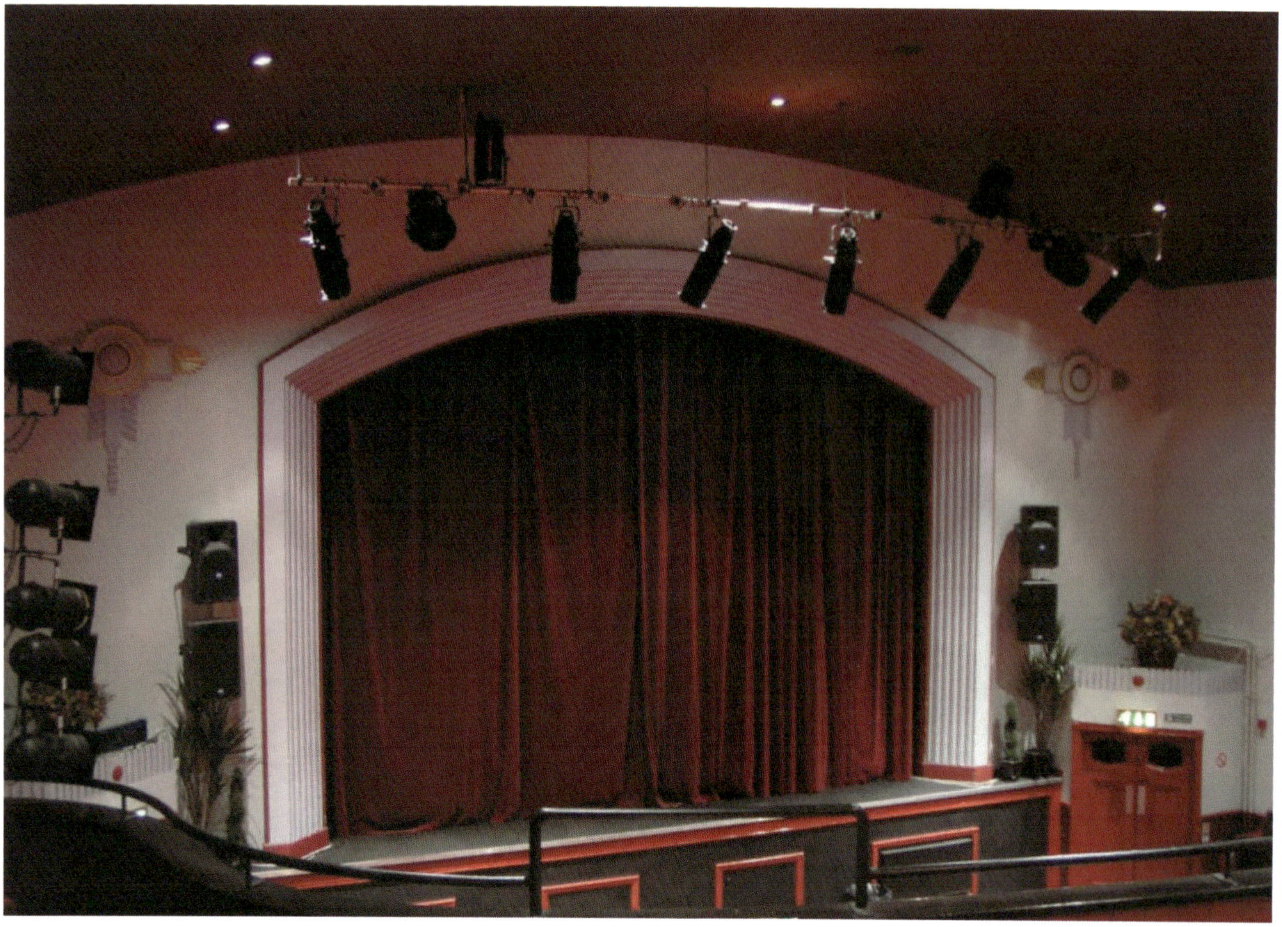

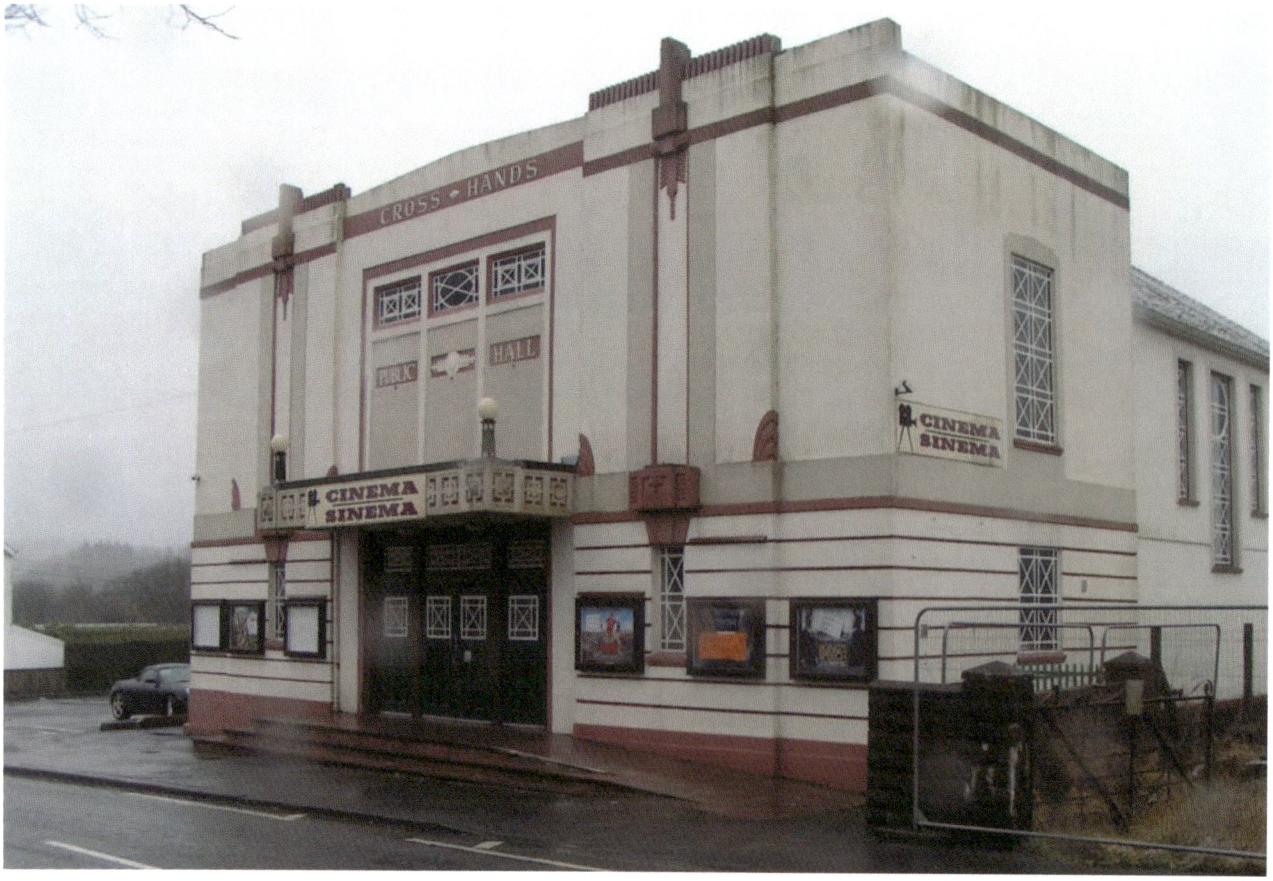
CROSS HANDS
PUBLIC
HALL
CINEMA
SINEMA
CINEMA
SINEMA

Public Memorial Hall, Llandybie

Organisation: Llandybie Memorial Hall Association

Address: Woodfield Road, Llandybie, Ammanford SA18 3UR

Construction: 1924-25 **Opening:** 1925

Architect/Builder: unknown/unknown

Current Owner: Llandybie Memorial Hall Association

History/previous names & ownership

The Hall was originally opened as a Miner's Welfare Institute and was built with the aid of a grant of £2,000 from the 1920 Miners' Welfare Fund in 1924. Foundation stones (in English and Welsh languages) were laid by Colonel D Watts Morgan, the local MP on 27th December 1924.

The hall was opened on 5th November 1925. The total cost was in the region of £4,300, the rest of the funding coming from donations, and weekly deductions from local miners' pay. It was given its name because it was dedicated as a memorial to the local men who lost their lives in the First World War. A tablet with the names of the dead from the village was erected inside the hall in 1933. A second tablet of names was added after WW2.

During the Second World War the hall was used for fund-raising events and also became the HQ of the local Evacuee Committee, an Air Raid Precaution Centre, and was used by the Home Guard for training purposes. Also during WW2 the Old Vic Theatre Company performed at the Hall. In 1944 the first five day National Eisteddfod that took place during the Second World War was held in August in the Hall with local chapels and vestries being used for preliminary rounds. Before 1946 the hall was used mainly for theatrical performances, concerts and public meetings. A cinema projector was installed in 1946 and the hall showed films until October 1960.

The Hall also owned the adjoining bowling green, tennis courts, children's playground and car park, which were eventually handed over to the Dinefwr Borough Council in 1989, allowing the committee to concentrate on running the Hall. At some point (presumed to be after 1960) the original fixed seating to the stalls area was removed and the sloping floor covered with concrete to give the Hall a flat-floor and greater flexibility of use and audience capacity.

In 2007 grants totalling over £500,000 enabled major renovations, including a side extension, to be made. The new extension provided a new main entrance, reception foyer and gallery/lounge area, along with a kitchen and toilets and a secondary hall with a moveable divider to allow multiple and flexible community use as well as a backstage facility for events.

In 2011 a new sprung floor was installed in the main auditorium in response to increased local demand for dance, fitness classes and martial arts training and rehearsal space.

Description

Located on a side street some distance from the main road passing through the village of Llandybie, this is not an easy venue to find and it immediately gives the visitor the sense that its sole purpose is to serve the community in which it stands. The main frontage to the building has an almost domestic scale and apart from the sports fields and large surface car park that surround it, it stands in an entirely residential area.

The original building is two-storeys in height and it has a single storey modern extension along the entirety of one long side and the rear. The external walls are finished with a cream coloured textured render over a rubble stone low level plinth and it has tiled roofs. The recent extension replicates these finishes. The original main entrance is on the central axis of the long rectangular building and protected by a wide projecting porch roof. Foundation stones in Welsh and English are set either side of the hardwood double entrance doors. The original entrance led into a small vestibule containing stairs leading up to the auditorium balcony and the entry into the auditorium at the rear of the stalls. This entrance is no longer used.

The current entrance is somewhat disappointing in comparison, located in a prominent position in the new extension facing the large surface car park and providing full accessibility with a gentle ramping of the external surfacing and glazed automatic opening doors. There is no signage to identify this as the 'new' main entrance however, although there is a dormer like gable above it projecting from the plane of the roof and entering here is noticeably the side door. The entrance hall contains public toilets and access to the ground floor foyer café area through a pair of solid double doors to the left and domestic style stairs leading to a small management office and the auditorium balcony. Again there is no signage and navigating this extension is not intuitive. The foyer café bar area is by contrast a pleasant, tall and light space containing a well equipped kitchen and reception/ticket office. The routes through the building make more sense from here and there is direct access to both the main auditorium and new secondary multiple-use space at the rear of the site.

The main auditorium is surprisingly large though architecturally very plain. The recently installed sprung floor has raised the floor level well above the foyer area and exterior ground level so there are ramps with metal handrails and balustrades around them penetrating into the usable floor space. These elements compromise the audience capacity and layout. A lay-in tile suspended ceiling has been installed below the original ceiling over the forestage area and balcony and has a curved bulkhead in front of the balcony which is distracting and limits sightlines from the balcony to the upper part of the proscenium. Glimpses of the original ceiling reveal a well proportioned grid of downstanding rib features and around the proscenium there remain original moulded panels and pilasters, although they are painted to match the walls and are quite difficult to see. The two memorial plaques commemorating the fallen of the two World Wars are retained in place on the auditorium side wall between balcony and stage. The balcony front has well proportioned raised and fielded panelling. The completely white decorative treatment does make the room feel very light and bright and it is well provided with daylight from a pair of roundel windows at the rear of the room at both stalls and balcony level and from 4 large windows in the side wall.

The balcony retains its original 1920's audience seating with elegant art deco styled fluted timber side panels and carved solid armrests and whilst leg room is less than would be required by today's standards the seats are comfortable and provide a good view to the stage area. The original floor boards remain on the balcony and are exposed on the rows between recently laid carpet and proprietary nosings on the off-centre stepped aisle.

The stage is small and there is limited wing space as the proscenium opening is very nearly the full width of the room. It is raised quite high above the auditorium floor and backstage areas and can only be accessed by stairs so limiting accessibility for performers with mobility difficulties and for loading equipment and scenic effects. There is no flying capacity but there are three fixed bars shrouded by inclined hardwood panels providing plentiful on stage performance lighting. The house curtains are motorised.

There are no dressing rooms, backstage storage or dedicated loading facilities but the new extension to the rear provides a large and sub-divisible space immediately adjacent the stage access which is used for changing space when the need arises. The primary use of this space is for conferences and small meetings and community activities however.

Although still capable of staging live performance, this venue is now clearly focussed on serving as a multi-use community hall supported by secondary use as a conference venue. It appears to be well funded and well supported by the community it serves.

Auditorium Capacity:

398 (comprising 302 loose seats maximum on stalls and 96 fixed seats on balcony)

Stage details:

Performance space – width – 8.7m
Performance space – depth – 6.4m
Depth of apron – n/a
Wing space (Right and Left) – not known
Proscenium height/width – not known
Orchestra pit (maximum no of players) – n/a
Height from stage floor to grid –n/a
Rake – None

Theatr Elli, Llanelli

Organisation: Carmarthenshire Theatres

Address: Station Road, Llanelli SA15 1AH

Construction/Opening: 1938

Architect: Harry Weedon, Harry W. Weedon Partnership (assistant in charge was PJ. Price)

Builder: unknown

Current Owner: Carmarthenshire County Borough Council

History/previous names & ownership

The building was constructed in 1938 and opened as Llanelly Odeon Theatre on the site of a former workmen's' club. The grand opening was on Saturday 18th June. The design was typical of the circuit style, with rounded corners and faience tiling, the main ODEON sign being placed above the five tall windows above the front canopy. The cinema was taken over by Classic on 9th December 1967 and renamed The Classic Cinema. The building was reopened on 1st October 1971 after conversion into a 3 screen cinema (as a prototype model by Classic Cinemas). The former circle became 'Classic 1' with over 500 seats and showing latest blockbusters, the front of stalls (including the original proscenium) became 'Classic 2' with approx 250 seats showing classic and repertory-style films and the rear stalls became 'Classic 3' with 121 seats used for showing adult films and horror movies. An 'american style' display marquee was installed over the original canopy and new Westrex 7000 projectors were installed to all 3 auditoria to replace the original Kalee projectors. From 1971 to 1976 the building was known as the Classic Entertainment Centre.

It was sold to Llanelli Borough Council in May 1976 and renamed Llanelli Film Centre and in the period 1977-78 Classic/Screen1 was converted into a hybrid cinema/theatre with films still being shown between live shows. A Bar area was created in the original Circle Lounge area. The new Theatre premiered in 1978 with a production of Aladdin by The Everyman Theatre Company. From 1978 to 1984 the building name was the Llanelli Entertainment Centre and in 1984 it was renamed again and became Theatr Elli. Through the 1990s a number of modifications were made. In 1991 a new lift was installed using money raised by The Everyman Theatre Group, in 1992 a new frontage was installed, returning the building appearance to that of the original Odeon building, in 1993 plans for construction of a flytower were rejected on structural grounds and Dolby Stereo was installed in Theatr Elli and Theatre 2, in 1995 a new Cinemeccanica Victoria 5 projector with platter was installed in Theatr Elli and in 1998 three stair lifts were installed in the front-of-house with Arts Council funding. Ownership of the building passed to Carmarthenshire County Borough Council in 1996. Work continued into the new century with new audience seating installed in 2003 to Theatr Elli and Theatre 2 reducing capacity slightly. Theatre 3 still retains the original 1938 cinema seats. New boilers were installed in 2008 and in 2010 the building's original 'rehearsal space' was re-launched as a Studio space for community use.

Theatr Elli was listed Grade II on 26th August 2009. In 2010, The Theatres Trust included Theatr Elli on its Theatre Buildings At Risk Register out of concern that its future had been placed in considerable doubt by the development of plans for a new purpose-built theatre venue in the town. Later that year the front of the building was shrouded in scaffolding and netting to protect pedestrians from the threat of falling pieces of the original faience tiles. It is not known if funds will be made available to enable repairs to be effected or if this is a sign of a future of decay and dereliction for the building.

Description

Located on a prominent site bounded by 3 roads, the building retains almost intact (although not in pristine condition) the original art deco frontage of 1938. There have been modifications to the entrance, including different canopies and covering of original glazed bricks and the original ODEON sign with individual letters placed within 5 square panels above the foyer windows has long gone. Behind the front façade, all elevations are finished in red brick.

The stage door access was created in 1977-78 by enclosing what was originally an external fire escape and does not provide disabled access to backstage areas (which requires use of the loading bay and stage lift). Provisions for front-of-house wheelchair access were added in the early 1990's with a distinctly un-art deco brick porch attached to a red brick enclosure constructed around original fire escape stair. Entry through the Main front doors off Station Road is directly into a small foyer area containing box office and refreshment sales point. Neither are original and have

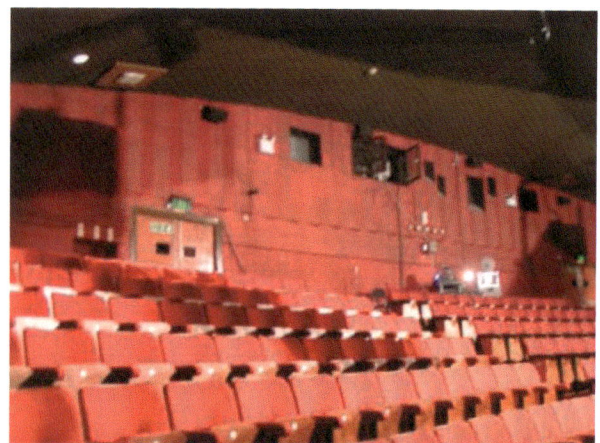

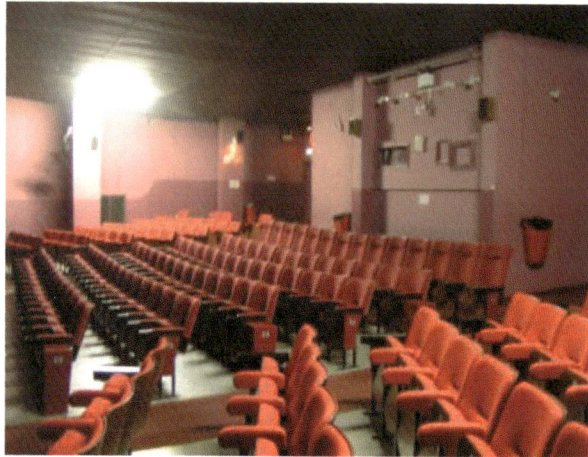

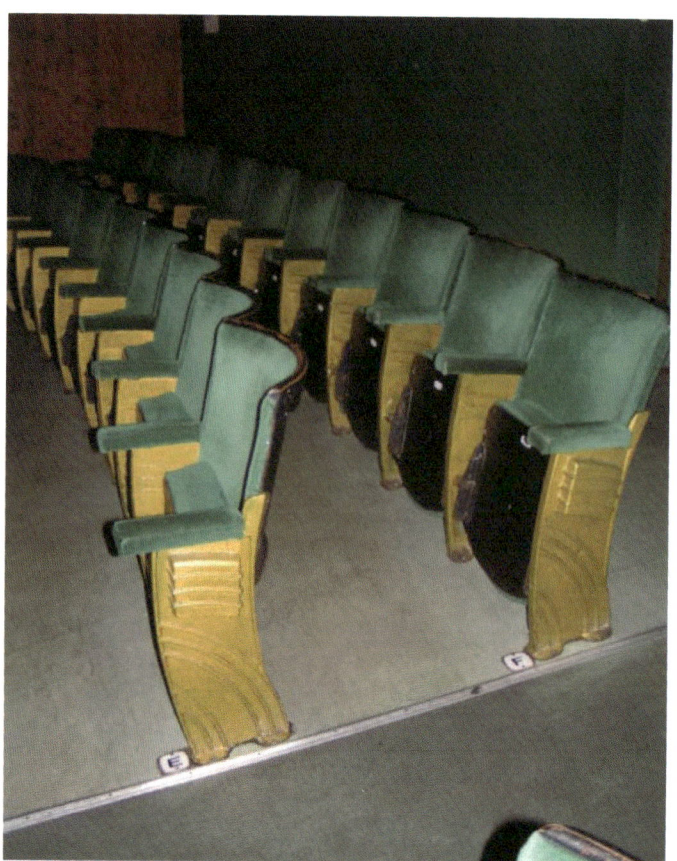

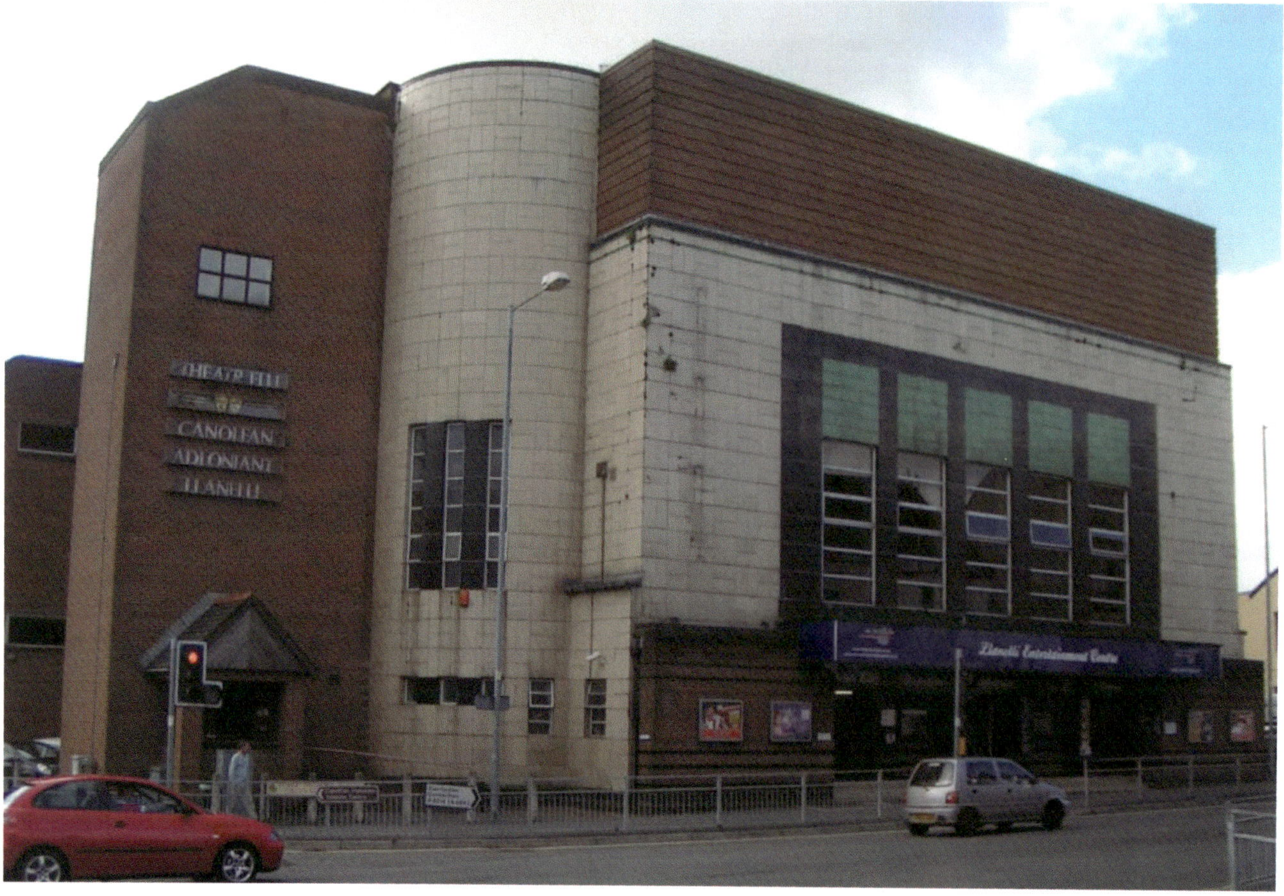
CANOLFAN
ADLONIANT
LLANELLI
Llanelli Entertainment Centre

been somewhat crudely incorporated, compromising the original interior features including lighting and clarity of circulation between the symmetrically opposed main staircases. A large and well appointed largely original foyer area is at first floor level. Access to Theatres 2 and 3 is from the ground floor foyer. Theatre 3 retains original 1930's auditorium seating (although the seats have been re-upholstered at least once in their lifetime) and art deco ventilation grilles at the rear and is an intimate cinema space with no capacity for theatrical performances. Theatre 2 is a larger space that retains only the base of the original proscenium and no other original features. When converted into a triplex cinema, a projection room was constructed at the rear and the resulting auditorium form is unusual and much less intimate than the smaller Theatre 3, with much wider seat spacing and seating extending around the sides of the projection room.

Access to Theatre 1 (Theatr Elli) is via the first floor foyer through a vomitory into the steeply raked seating (the original balcony seating of the 1938 cinema). The original cinema ceiling has been retained and some of the art deco wall features and details remain at the rear but later (presumed 1970's) wall linings in dark vertical timber strips has changed the character of the space completely. The steep rake of the seats offers very good sight lines throughout to the large stage area created over Theatre 2 below. The stage is very wide and quite deep and has a variable depth apron too. The proscenium is located approximately on the line of the original circle balcony front. There is no flytower and rigging above the stage is limited by the original roof of the cinema. Four large and well equipped dressing rooms are provided at stage level.

A new venue for Llanelli (Y Ffwrnes) is currently under development and it is not known whether the new facilities will render Theatr Elli redundant, or if they will operate in tandem. For the time being Theatr Elli is continuing to operate as a commercial film venue and offering a wide range of community-generated and professional live events.

Auditorium Capacity:

Original capacity was 1450 comprising 900 in stalls and 550 on balcony. Following the 1971 conversion to a 3 screen cinema complex the capacities of each space were: Screen 1 – 500 seats, Screen 2 – 250 seats, Screen 3 – 121 seats. Further changes were made in 1978 – Theatre 1 – 516 seats (front row of 22 seats removable), Theatre 2 – 273 seats, Theatre 3 120 seats. In 2003 new seating was installed in the 2 larger auditoria giving current capacities of each space of: Theatr Elli – 464 seats, Theatre 2 – 212 seats, Theatre 3 120 seats

Stage details (applies to Theatr Elli auditorium only):

Performance space – width – 21.31m at proscenium, 19m at cyclorama wall
Performance space – depth – 9.4m
Depth of apron – 2.42m maximum
Wing space (Right and Left) – approx 5.4m each side
Proscenium height/width – height 4.6m; width 10.44m
Orchestra pit (maximum no of players) - none
Height from stage floor to grid – 6.1m
Rake - None

Y Ffwrnes, Llanelli

Organisation: Carmarthenshire Theatres

Address: Upper Park Street, Llanelli SA15 3YN

Construction: 2010 - 2012 **Opening:** planned for summer 2012

Architect: Lawray Architects, Cardiff

Builder: unknown

Current Owner: Carmarthenshire County Council

History/previous names & ownership

This project was conceived in 2007. The initial brief for the new building was to investigate design possibilities for creating a performance space within a disused, Grade II Listed building which had been the Tin fabrication space in the old Castle Works in Llanelli. The feasibility study that ensued included a study of Carmarthenshire's Arts and Theatre provision and concluded that there was a need for a major new auditorium and associated facilities.

Originally named 'The Works', the project was submitted to the Big Lottery fund and received a £250,000 grant to develop the scheme further. Key project criteria were that the architecture was "iconic" and that the new building was "Community owned". The concept was developed by Lawray Architects of Cardiff in collaboration with ABK Architects of London. Community ownership was fostered by several public meetings and exhibitions as the design developed in order to take on board local requirements and aspirations.

The developed designs for the new centre included a 500 seat auditorium, 250 seat studio theatre, rehearsal and administrative offices for the centre, a 150 seat lecture / film studio, incubator units for starter arts businesses, Cafe and bar facilities, community arts spaces, an Art Gallery and an open piazza space for multi purpose activities. The project set a budget of £28million. In 2008, the final project was shortlisted in the last 8 for Big Lottery funding but was unsuccessful and this initial proposal for 'The Works' was abandoned.

Lawray Architects were retained and in 2008 were commissioned to design a 'Landmark' replacement for the Theatre Elli in Llanelli initially named 'The Works 2'.

This development will include an innovative new-build 512 seat Main Auditorium with associated Bars, Cafes, Dressing Rooms and administration facilities, as well as refurbishments to the neighbouring Zion Chapel that will accommodate a flexible 100-seat 'Theatre in the Round', a rehearsal space, public enterprise offices and public meeting facilities.

The ambition is to offer optimum flexibility with facilities capable of being configured to accommodate both performance and non-performance layouts that suit the requirements of a wide range of events and presentations including drama, musical theatre, opera, concerts, dance, cabaret and public meetings and social functions.

'State of the art' technical features will include power flying within the flytower, a tension wire grid throughout technical galleries, movable towers to adjust the proscenium width, a forestage elevator for stage/orchestra pit adjustments and retractable bleacher seating to enable various auditorium configurations to be created.

Image courtesy of Lawray Architects

In March 2011 it was announced that Y Ffwrnes (The Furnace) was the preferred choice of six shortlisted names for the new venue. The judging panel said the name was chosen because the image of the furnace draws on the strong metal and tinplate connections of historical Llanelli and also conjured up images of the melting pot and creating something new and exciting. The studio space on the first floor of the old Zion Sunday School is to be branded as Stiwdio Stepni, to maintain strong links with the past history of the site itself, the former Stepney Hotel, and will provide schools, colleges and community groups with a modern space for rehearsals, classes and workshops. Trinity St David University will also have a base at the complex, where it will focus on creating opportunities for students in the performing arts and creative industries.

The project is funded through £5.1 million from the European Regional Development Fund and the same from the Welsh Assembly. Carmarthenshire Council has put in £4 million and Trinity St David University £300,000. The £14.6million project is due to be completed in the summer of 2012.

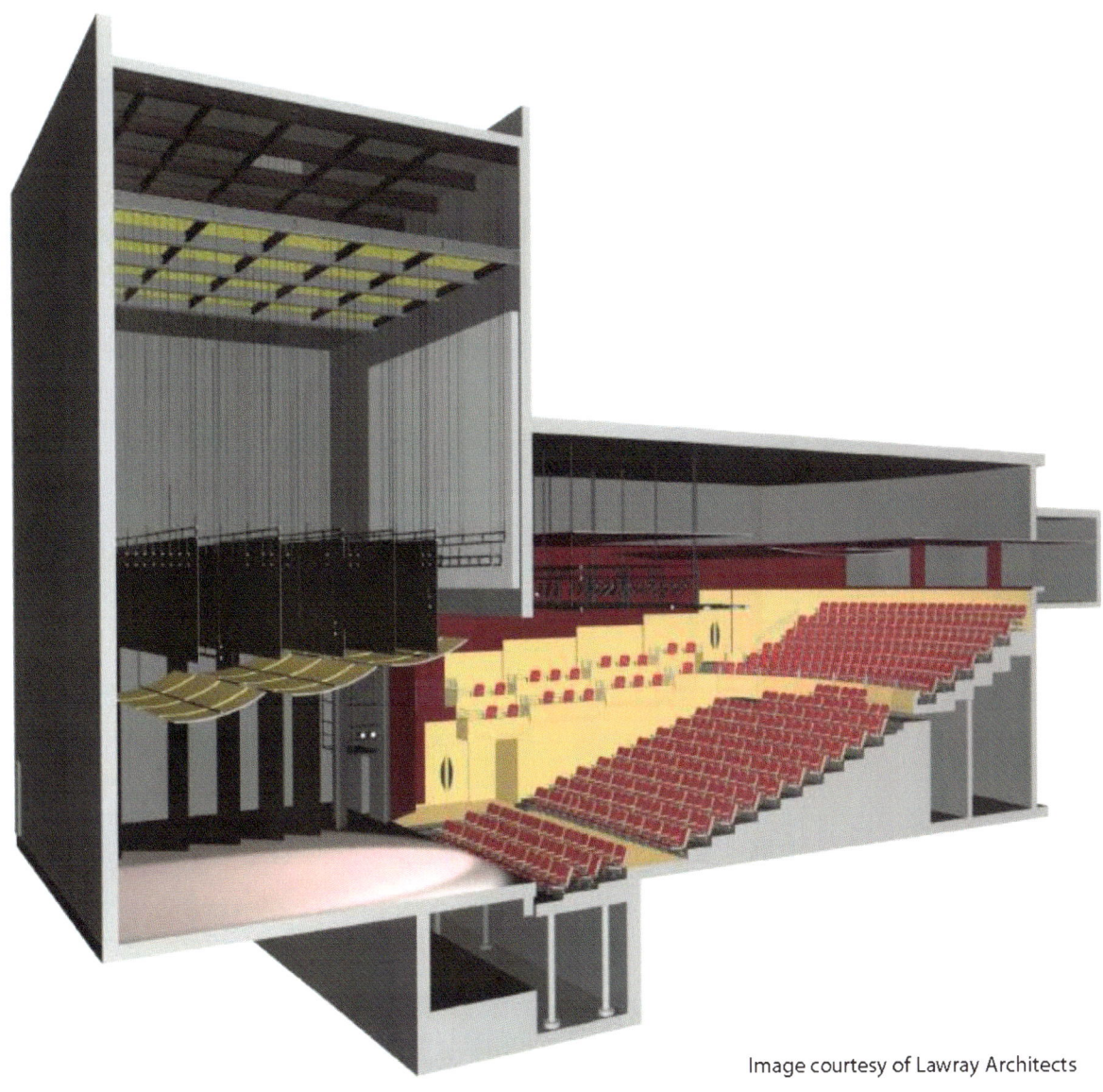

Image courtesy of Lawray Architects

Auditorium Capacity: 512

Stage details: Not available

Memorial Hall & Institute, Pontyberem

Organisation: Pontyberem Community Trust

Address: Coalbrook Road, Pontyberem, Llanelli SA15 5HU

Construction/Opening: 1926 (Institute), 1937 (Memorial Hall)

Architect: R. S. Griffiths & Partners, Tonypandy (Institute)

Builder: unknown

Current Owner: Pontyberem Community Council

History/previous names & ownership

The Pontyberem Miners' Institute was constructed in 1926. As with so many of its contemporary buildings, it was paid for by the 'Miners' Penny' deduction of a penny in the pound from the wages of the workers at the local collieries. The Institute originally contained reading rooms, committee rooms and a billiards room.

In 1937 the Memorial Hall was constructed to the rear of the Institute to commemorate the local fallen from the First World War. It is not known if the same Architect was used but the Art Deco style of the new Hall contrasts somewhat with the original building and would suggest not. Some time after 1945 a second commemorative plaque was installed to the memory of the local fallen of the Second World War.

Originally and until 1993 the buildings were operated independently and had separate entrances (the Hall being accessed from what is now a large surface car park to one side) but now there is an internal direct connection between Institute and Memorial Hall and the original billiards room was converted to use as the audience foyer for the Hall. At the same time the ground floor reading room in the Institute was converted to Library operation, managed by Carmarthenshire County Council.

From 1937 to 1975 the Hall was owned and managed by the Management Committee of the Pontyberem Memorial Hall and Institute but since 1975 it has been owned and operated by the Community Council.

Since it has been in the stewardship of the local Council, various redecorations and upgrades of the facilities and technical equipment have been made with major renovations being carried out in 2006 to improve technical installations and accessibility carried out by contractor Lloyd & Gravell of Llanelli and in the summer of 2011 the front facade underwent a major repair and redecoration.

Image courtesy of Councillor Dorothy Jones, Chair of Pontyberem Hall Committee

Description

Situated at the heart of the village of Pontyberem in what was once clearly the focus of all community activity – the Parish Church is directly across the road and although now a supermarket, the adjacent building was for many years the village cinema. The Memorial Hall is quite large and stands slightly below the original Institute in a shallow valley with a large surface car park as its approach. The Institute entrance is directly off the pavement and by using the site topography the Architect of the later building maintained the roof ridge line as a constant which serves to reduce the visual impact of the Hall somewhat. The front elevation is a relatively simple 3-bay affair with the main entrance on the central axis announced by a projecting bay of dressed stone and a small turret above the roof eaves. There is a pair of glazed doors at first floor level leading to a small balcony from which it is understood local election results were announced. The 2 bays either side have large paired windows which light the large landing inside at that level. The side elevations are finished in a light grey render which is in very good condition and the whole building has a slate roof.

Entry is into a fairly generous public lobby containing the accesses to the Memorial Hall, Library and public toilets with a staircase leading up to the Institute rooms at first floor level. A platform lift has been installed at some point providing full access to the upper floor. In the entrance lobby the 2 memorial plaques naming the local fallen from the 2 World Wars are mounted on the wall immediately facing the entrance. This level entry passes through a single pair of doors into what was the original billiards room and is now the spacious foyer serving the Memorial Hall. The difference in levels between the pavement and the auditorium is accommodated by steps and a shallow ramp ensuring full accessibility to the front of house. The original (and very beautiful) hardwood ticket box remains in its original location although is not now used. From the foyer a pair of grand staircases set on either side of the Hall lead up to the balcony and a single pair of double doors leads directly into the rear stalls of the auditorium. It is immediately apparent on entering the auditorium that it was conceived as a major statement of community pride and aspiration and it has been maintained in extremely good condition. It is a large room with the rear stalls under the balcony set on a gentle incline which levels out in front of the stage. Loose seating is used at stalls level providing a variety of staging and event configuration options. The original 1937 hardwood floor remains in place. It is also a very bright room having large windows to one side with an elegant arrangement of geometric glazing bars.

The stage is opposite the entrance and is raised quite high above the auditorium floor. The original access to the stage was provided by steps set behind doors on either side but now a series of removable and adjustable rostrum units allow access directly onto stage from within the auditorium if required. These rostrum units are also regularly used for choral concerts. The doors either side of the stage both have a decorative installation of organ pipes in an ornate niche above them but there is no organ. The auditorium has a single upper balcony which contains the original leather-upholstered audience seats from 1937, also maintained in excellent condition. To the rear of the balcony is the projection room/control room. The Hall does not offer cinema at all currently and has no plans to so the control room is used for lighting and sound control. It is very well equipped with contemporary and high quality equipment. Perhaps the most striking feature of the auditorium is the large ceiling moulding. From the central circular ventilation grille it explodes outwards with an octagonal surround and 8 ribs connected by flamboyant ripples, all decorated to accent the various surfaces. It is understood that the colours used currently may not be original but they work really well. The stage is well equipped with large wings and galleries to each side above stage level and it is well covered by rigging and suspension bars. There is no full flytower but most shows can be accommodated easily. There is a large dressing room below the stage accessed by narrow stairs from both sides of the stage and with a central movable partition that is used to create separate male and female areas when needed. There are toilets close by and a separate smaller room that can be used as a 'star' dressing room. For the majority of the time the dressing room accommodation is used as a nursery space for local pre-school children.

The Institute rooms serve a wide range of community groups and as well as the part-time opening Library there is a Chiropody Clinic and a large lounge area with adjacent kitchen and bar area. The original Committee Room appears largely unchanged and is used for Community Council Meetings, surgeries by the local MP and is available for hire for meetings. There are photographs of the building and local collieries hung around the walls, with boards recording the chairmen/persons of the Parish and Community Council since 1919. A glass fronted cabinet contains Minute books and various other records and memorabilia. All of the public rooms are equipped to a very high standard.

This is a remarkable building in many ways. It is largely self-sufficient and receives little or no external funding for its management and maintenance beyond the Community Council although grants have been obtained for major works and improvements. It is in extremely good condition with an evident ongoing programme of repair and maintenance to keep it so, and it exists with very little publicity or awareness of its presence beyond the community it serves.

The auditorium supports a range of events and productions, principally focussed on music and choral performances but it has hosted stand-up comedy and presents some shows with the auditorium set up in cabaret style. The resident theatre company present shows on stage several times a year.

Auditorium Capacity: Originally 730, reduced to 630 (comprising 370 loose seats on stalls and 260 on balcony)

Stage details:

Performance space – width – 6.5m
Performance space – depth –6.4m
Depth of apron – fixed 1.4m; variable up to 3.5m
Wing space (Right and Left) – SR - 3.4m; SL - 3.4m
Proscenium height/width – height 5m; width 7m
Orchestra pit (maximum no of players) – n/a
Height from stage floor to grid – not available
Rake - Yes, gradient not known

Pembrokeshire

Fishguard
    Theatr Gwaun
Haverfordwest
    Merlin Theatre
Milford Haven
    The Torch Theatre
Narberth
    The Queens Hall
Pembroke Dock
    Pater Hall
Tenby
    De Valence Pavilion
    The Royal Playhouse

Theatr Gwaun, Fishguard

Organisation: Theatr Gwaun Community Trust

Address: West Street, Fishguard SA65 9AD

Construction: 1878 - 80 **Opening:** 1880

Architect/Builder: unknown/unknown

Current Owner: Pembrokeshire County Council

History/previous names & ownership

The Foundation Stone of the original building was laid by Martha Philips Harries of Oefnydre in June 1878 and in 1880 the building was opened as a Temperance Hall. It was operating as a cinema by the 1920's, with 450 seats. It is presumed that the first floor extension over the entrance was added to create a film projection room around this time as it is clearly not original.

In 1980 the building was being operated by the local Council and had been re-named Studio Cinema, with a reduced seating capacity of 252. It was refurbished in 1994 and was re-named Theatr Gwaun. It screened first run films and staged live theatre performances and the audience capacity was further reduced to 180.

In the summer of 2010 Pembrokeshire County Council threatened to close the venue by the end of the year due to falling audience numbers and an organisation known as Friends of Theatr Gwaun drew up a business plan which it was hoped might ensure a sustainable future for the building. However, in March 2011, Pembrokeshire County Council finally withdrew revenue funding for the venue and it was closed.

Negotiations continued and a deal was eventually reached enabling the building to be re-opened at the beginning of June with a programme of film and live events aimed at appealing to a wide audience. The campaign to save the theatre had attracted support from Hollywood actors Beau Bridges and Sally Field. There are also plans to open a licensed bar and a coffee shop in the building. The Council has granted the new Community Trust a 3-year lease on a peppercorn rent and the building has been re-named '4U at Theatr Gwaun'.

Description

Located on a tight corner site near the town centre with roads on 3 sides and the long wall of the building parallel to the main road adjacent. The entrance is on the short axis and directly off the pavement of a small side street. It is a modest looking building, which is perhaps unsurprising given its origin as a Temperance Hall, though is clearly much changed from its original construction. There is now a bright yellow render covering almost the entire original stone envelope and windows to the auditorium have been filled in with just the recesses as evidence that there ever were any. One of the window recesses on the main road side of the building has its lower half occupied by a pair of timber doors which presumably afford access directly to the stage for loading. The building has a slate pitched roof with a single ventilator cowl on the ridge.

At some point in its history an extension has been added at first floor level above the main entrance, presumably to create a projection room for films as it is known that for a long period in its life the building was primarily used as a cinema. The extension is supported on a pair of square columns which frame and announce the simple double entrance doors in a much more elegant way than the original building entrance would have appeared although it seems that there was a large arched window in the original wall where the projection room now stands.

The entrance lobby is accessed directly off the pavement and is on the same level providing accessibility for all visitors. It is very small and contains a small ticket desk and refreshment sales counter with doors on one side leading directly into a small foyer area containing audience toilets and then to the side of the auditorium and stairs leading up to the top and rear of the audience seating on the other. The auditorium has a single stepped rake of audience seating with a central aisle and retains the 6 original window recesses along both side walls, now blocked in and painted in a dark contrasting colour to the eggshell blue plain walls throughout. The ceiling is flat but curves out of the side walls following exposed ribs painted pink. Performance lighting and loudspeakers are rigged in the window recesses and on the ceiling ribs. The stage is the full width of the building and raised above the auditorium floor.

The third visible side of the building contains some office spaces and two separate entrances in a two storey lean-to section – one door leading to the offices and the other providing access to the backstage area through a store room. Above the office are two compact dressing rooms and a reasonably sized Green Room. At the rear of the building is a boiler house with its original chimney although a much later stainless steel flue suggests a more recent heating system installation.

Auditorium Capacity:

Original capacity 450, current capacity 180

Stage details:

Performance space – width – 9m
Performance space – depth – 5m
Depth of apron – 0.6m
Wing space (Right and Left) – SR - 1.5m; SL - 1.8m
Proscenium height/width – not available
Orchestra pit (maximum no of players) - n/a
Height from stage floor to grid – not available
Rake –None

Interior Photograph courtesy of Friends of Theatr Gwaun

Merlin Theatre, Haverfordwest

Organisation: Pembrokeshire College Department of Performing Arts

Address: Pembrokeshire College, Merlin's Bridge, Haverfordwest SA61 1SZ

Construction/Opening: 1997

Architect: W. A. Spees, Haverfordwest

Builder: unknown

Current Owner: Pembrokeshire College

History/previous names & ownership

The theatre was created within the overall College building in 1997 and has not undergone any significant changes or upgrades since.

Description

Unusually for such buildings, this one is extremely well sign-posted from all major approaches and finding the College campus is easy, but once at the College it is impossible to locate the theatre. The exterior of the theatre is almost indiscernible from the rest of the College building it is part of, being constructed of buff coloured brickwork with a shallow tiled pitched roof. The only real difference is the absence of windows to the upper floors where the auditorium is located. There are no external signs announcing its presence within the College site and even once inside the main reception area there are only very small directional signs. The theatre is the central facility in the Department of Performing Arts which happens to be located about as far from the main building entrance as its possible to get and, strangely is also not clearly identified or signposted. The route to the theatre from the entrance is tortuous and along very long, low-ceilinged corridors that tend to disorientate rather than inspire.

However, imminent arrival at the theatre is identified by a collection of show-posters from past productions and, after passing through one final pair of double doors the lower level of foyer is finally reached. There used to be a small box office located in this initial space but it has been removed and it isn't clear how ticket sales are now handled for public events. The lower foyer contains toilets and access to backstage and rehearsal accommodation and is dominated by a wide gleaming white spiral stair leading up to the main foyer space. This is a much more satisfactory space, with a large bar servery, comfortable lounge seating and views out over a balcony into the college grounds.

The upper foyer space leads directly into the auditorium through a large sound and light lobby and the audience arrives in the rear corner of a roughly square room at house right. The journey is worthwhile, for this is a little gem of an auditorium. The audience seating is loose and the auditorium floor stepped around the edges in an octagonal shape with the central area flat. The stage is generally configured in end-stage format using movable rostra units but the arrangement of the auditorium floor allows theatre in the round and thrust arrangements too. A large, spacious and extremely well-equipped control room hangs at high level opposite the end-stage arrangement and is the dominant architectural feature in the room which otherwise has walls covered with a mixture of plain timber panels and soft drapes. There is no ceiling as such but instead a plane of suspension bars and house-lights with the void above painted out black. Overwhelmingly the space feels intimate and quite playful.

The stage is much wider than it is deep and with a cyclorama cloth providing stage cross-over needs the variable apron made up of rostrum units to give the performance space much needed additional depth. There is no fixed proscenium, drapes being used to create one when needed and no capacity for flying due to the restricted height under the roof structure. There are no dedicated dressing rooms but a large rehearsal/dance studio space beneath the stage (again reached by spiral stair albeit a very narrow one) and other rooms are adapted for dressing use when productions are being staged. There are also costume-making and props rooms beneath the stage along with academic teaching spaces and offices.

Use of this theatre is largely constrained by the demands of the academic programme and few visiting productions are staged. The students of the College's Performing Arts course present a pantomime and one other show each year that is open to the general public but the other primary uses are as the base for the local Film Society and for conferences and meetings. It is a very well equipped venue and popular with audiences, the course is well supported by the College and students and its future appears secure.

Auditorium Capacity: 220

Stage details:

Performance space – width – 8m
Performance space – depth – 5m
Depth of apron – variable
Wing space (Right and Left) – SR- 3m; SL – 3m
Proscenium height/width – n/a
Orchestra pit (maximum no of players) – n/a
Height from stage floor to grid – 3.7m
Rake - None

The Torch Theatre, Milford Haven

Organisation: The Torch Theatre Company

Address: St Peters Road, Milford Haven SA73 2BU

Construction/Opening: 1977

Architect: Monty Minter, Milford Haven

Builder: unknown

Current Owner: The Torch Theatre Company

History/previous names & ownership

The building was opened in 1977 as a single main theatre space with associated support facilities for the resident Torch Theatre Company.

From 2006 to 2008 it underwent major renovations to the designs of Lawray Architects of Cardiff which radically expanded the building, providing enhanced front-of-house amenities, a new Torch Studio Theatre, the Café Torch plus an art gallery. The work was largely funded by the Arts Council for Wales. It reopened in the spring of 2008.

Description

Located in a largely residential district of Milford Haven town and overlooking the haven itself this is a surprisingly large building, made to appear all the larger perhaps by its full-height flytower soaring over the surrounding buildings and by being on a fairly steep hill.

The flytower has red facing brick walls to its lower half with khaki coloured profiled metal cladding to the top half. A large 'Torch Theatre' sign is fixed near the top. This arrangement of materials on such a large box of building gives it a vaguely military appearance. The character of the building envelope changes substantially on its main approach frontage however, as a result of the refurbishment works carried out between 2006 and 2008. Here it is much more welcoming and bright with vivid red and blue rendered panels around dark curtain walling glazing to the foyer. The composition of this new frontage is literally rounded off by a playful circular tower at the point where the building is at its lowest against the street. A metal mesh screen was installed over part of the new façade with the intention of there being a public-art lighting installation included in the works but this idea has not yet been implemented.

Entry into the building is via a gentle ramp down to automatic fully glazed doors forming a draught lobby and the new space created around the original theatre auditorium is very successful. There is ample space for visitor orientation and simply milling about. Graphics are clear and routes through the building clear and obvious reducing the need for directional signage. The lobby area contains a ticket desk, a small lounge space, sweet shop and accesses to the theatre, studio, café and gallery. It is all very crisp and comfortable.

The original part of the building contains the main house which was left more or less untouched by the refurbishment and extension of the building (apart from the installation of new audience seats). Entry is at the rear of a steep single raked auditorium with gently curved rows of seats. Audience sightlines to stage are excellent throughout. The room has no real distinguishing architectural features – instead a virtue has been made of the engineering and theatre lighting bridge installations with all such things left exposed and painted black at high level in the space. The walls are exposed concrete blockwork painted a deep purple colour and provide a plain backdrop to the bright red upholstery and rich timber of the new audience seats. There is a sound/light control room at the back of the room which also serves as a projection room when the room is used for cinema presentations. The stage is large in both width and depth and there is a forestage elevator providing a reasonably large orchestra pit or forestage extension.

There are 4 small and 1 large dressing rooms close to the stage and a performers' Green Room adjacent. The dressing rooms all have en-suite facilities and are fully accessible to wheelchairs.

The Studio Theatre created as part of the 2006-08 works is an excellent example of the type both technically and architecturally. Flat-floored with retractable bleacher seating and a section of floor nicknamed 'the moat' that contains additional seats. It is a 'black-box' but has character in the clever use of different materials and detailing at junctions. It is a tall space and is understandably popular with performers for both shows and rehearsals and with audiences for its intimacy. The only slightly odd feature of the room is the tortuous route around it to get to the one and only audience entrance and exit. In addition to being extremely well equipped it has loading doors opening directly to the street outside and has 2 dressing rooms associated directly with the Studio rather than shared with the main house.

The café/foyer bar is light and airy, located between the two auditoria and with large windows and access to an external terrace/balcony overlooking the harbour below. The gallery is perhaps the least confident space in the building but is of a size that offers the opportunity to convert it into a meeting room or secondary rehearsal space if its use for the display of contemporary visual arts proves unsuccessful in the long term.

This is a successful producing house with facilities at its disposable following the most recent extension and alteration works that are enabling it to diversify and increase the range of performance types presented and increase its audience.

Auditorium Capacity: 295 (Main House); 102 (Studio)

Stage details:

Performance space – width – 9.7m
Performance space – depth – 9.65m
Depth of apron – 2m
Wing space (Right and Left) – SR - 3m (downstage), 0m (upstage); SL - 0m (downstage), 3m (upstage)
Proscenium height/width – height 5.8m; width 10m
Orchestra pit (maximum no of players) – 20 max
Height from stage floor to grid – 14m
Rake - None

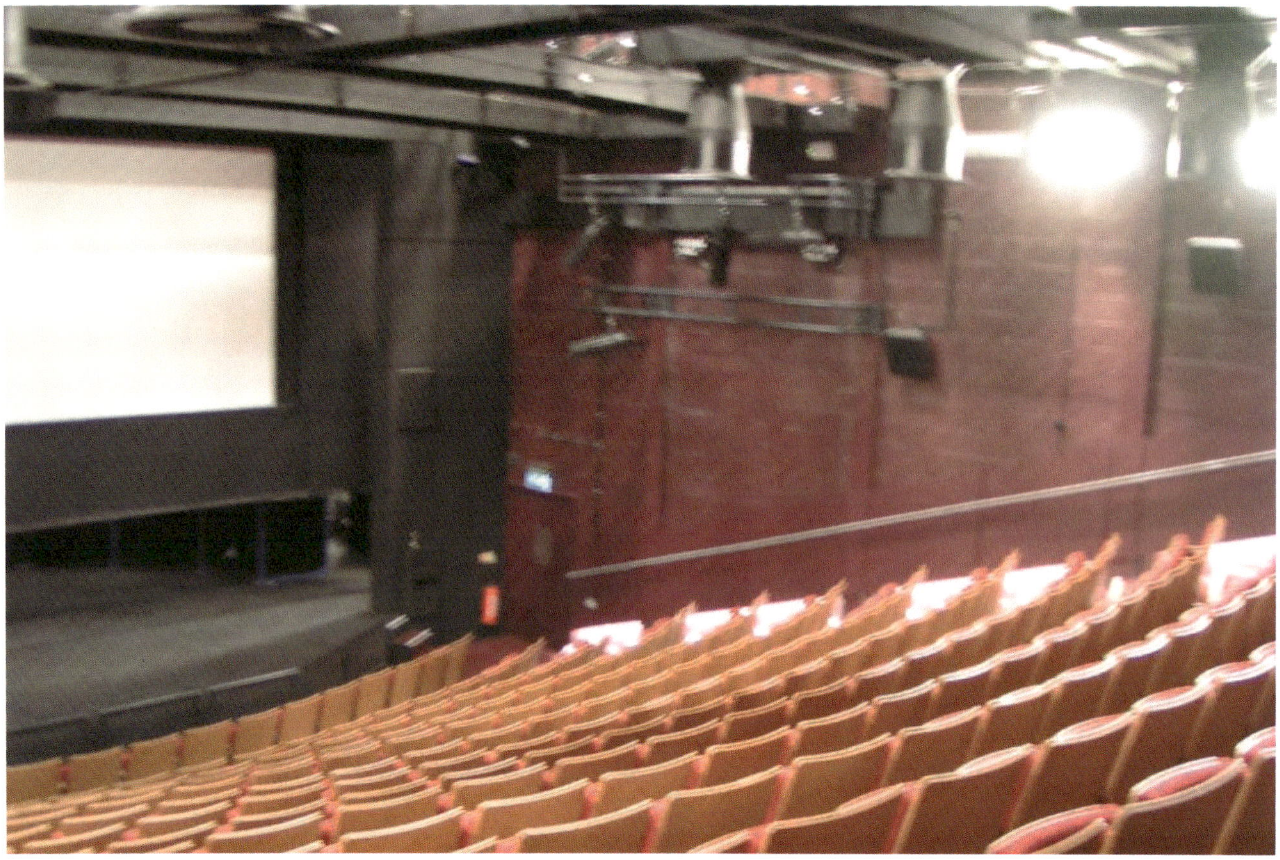

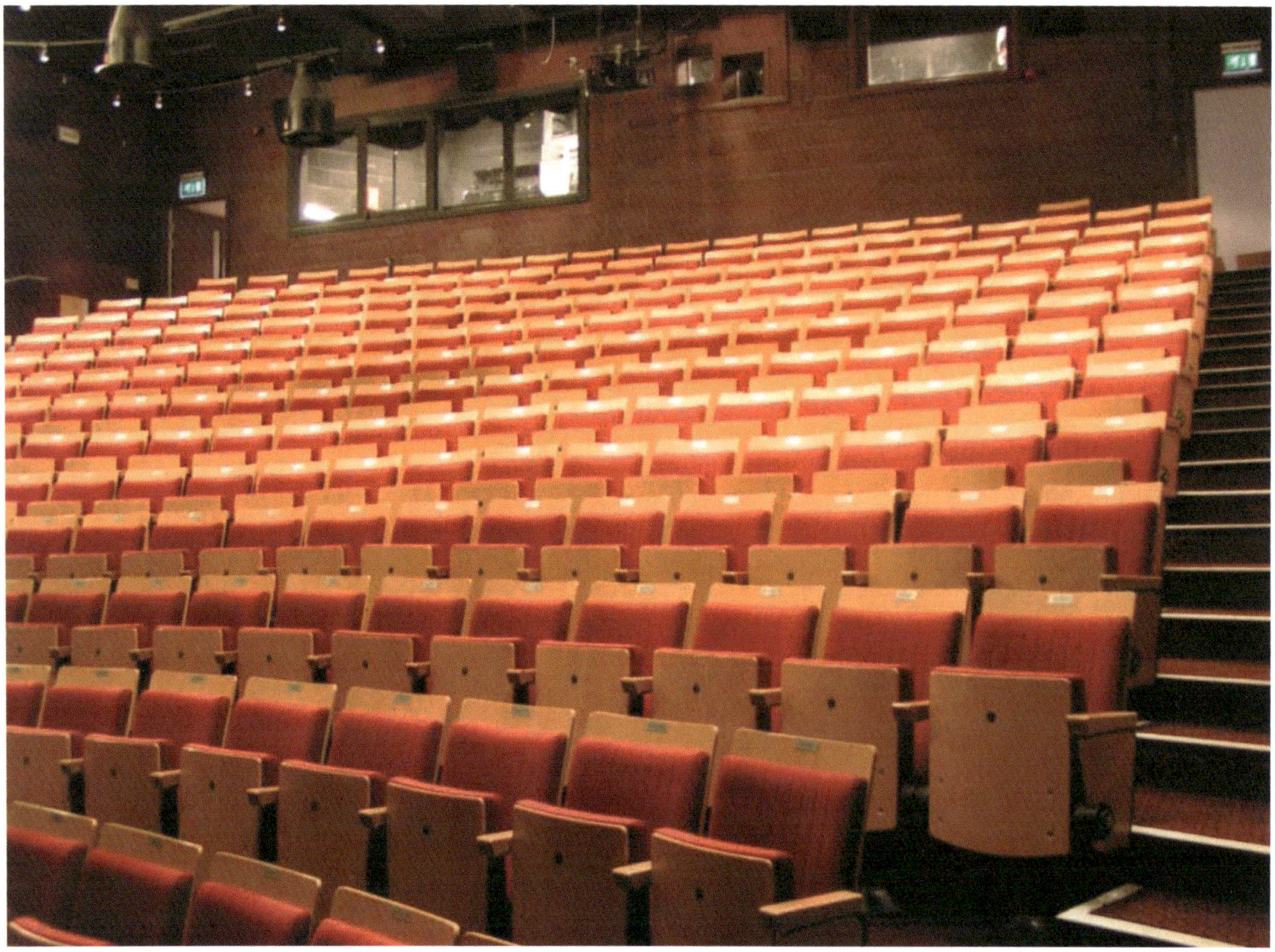

Queen's Hall, Narberth

Organisation: The Queens Hall Trust Ltd

Address: High Street, Narbeth SA67 7AS

Construction/Opening: 1958, partially demolished 1993, current building opened 1994

Architect: Ken Morgan, Narberth

Builder: TPT Construction, Narberth

Current Owner: The people of Narberth

History/previous names & ownership

Originally opened as The Victoria Town Hall Cinema, a small hall located in the main street of Narbeth its elaborate facade suggested that the hall dated from the early days of cinema. The cinema closed circa 1947 and the building was unused for some years.

The Victoria Town Hall was purchased by a group of local business people and individuals in 1953 with the aim of providing a community hall and function centre and five years later the original Queen's Hall was opened on 1st February by the High Sheriff of Pembrokeshire, Mr J. Edward Gibby. Over the next 30 years it became an established live music venue with sell out crowds of up to 1100 regularly hearing artists including Elton John, Deep Purple, The Move and other major acts of the 1960's and 70's.

Due to its ongoing success as a venue, the original Queen's Hall entrance building fronting onto High Street was demolished in September 1993 and the current Queen's Hall entrance building was opened on 6th May 1994 by David Rowe-Beddoe, chairman of the Welsh Development Agency at a cost of £350,000. Funding of the new building was obtained from the Welsh Strategic Office with additional support from the Lottery Fund, South Pembrokeshire District Council, the Welsh Development Agency, Dyfed County Council, The European Community and the Wales Tourist Board with donations from Narberth Town Council and many local organisations and individuals. Since 1994, the management have carried out various upgrades and refurbishments including the relocation of the bar and kitchen, upgrading of the toilets, dressing rooms and redecoration of the foyer, balcony room and staircases.

Description

Set back from the pavement with a small hard landscaped forecourt the building is apparently intentionally designed to have the appearance of a much older building than it actually is. The front elevation has something of a Victorian 3-bay frontage town-house appearance with a busy café dominating the ground floor and a balcony at first floor level. The gable on the central bay has an ornate verge board and small dormers in the two side bays emphasise the impression that the building is a converted old house. The hall to the rear of the site is simply rendered and has a profiled metal roof covering. The envelope to the rear of the building is showing signs of ageing and a lack of regular maintenance but there are no reports of any difficulties with weather penetration, apart from the backstage spaces being difficult to heat and keep warm.

Auditorium Capacity:

Original capacity > 1100 (standing),

Current capacity 300 (theatre); 500 (standing)

Stage details:

Performance space – width – 8m
Performance space – depth – 5m
Depth of apron – n/a
Wing space (Right and Left) - variable
Proscenium height/width - variable
Orchestra pit (maximum no of players) – n/a
Height from stage floor to grid – 3.6m
Rake – None

The entrance to the Queen's Hall is not in the central bay, under the balcony where one would expect the front door to a civic building to be but instead the doors in that location provide access to the café. The Queen's Hall entrance is off to the side making it seem very much secondary in importance. Once inside there is a large entrance hall leading directly to the Hall at the rear of the site past the box office, a secondary means of access into the café, audience WCs and a staircase leading up to the management offices, lettable function/meeting rooms on the first floor and a visual arts gallery on the second floor. Access for movement impaired visitors is easy and a lift provides access to all floors and facilities.

The Hall is a deceptively large space attached to the back of the entrance building and completely different in character. Audience entry is at a rear corner of the hall, opposite the stage. It is a flat-floored rectangular room with no distinguishing architectural features – it is a very basic space with hardwood strip floor, painted walls and a suspended tiled ceiling. A 10m long tapestry created by the Narberth Women's Institute is hung on the rear wall of the hall. There are large windows along one side and smaller, high level ones on the opposite side. Access to the venue bar is directly off the hall through large retractable doors. During recent renovations to relocate the venue bar and kitchen, the contractor removed the 1994 air-conditioning system air-handling unit serving the hall so now there are two temporary units in it which are unsightly and not efficient. The gas-fired high level heating units are similarly inefficient with one not actually working at all, but despite these issues there are no reports of major problems in maintaining comfortable conditions for audiences.

Various suspension bars and lighting installations hang from the ceiling and roughly in the centre of the room a cinema screen can be unfurled to reduce the size of the room volume for cinema presentations to an audience of 120. The projection room for cinema is actually an annexe to the management office at first floor level and there is no permanent sound/lighting control position – all mixing is done within the room using portable desks. Around the same point in the room is a suspended curtain track and drapes are used to split the room into smaller sections for events requiring a slightly more intimate space. The ability to split the room along its length in this way affords many different opportunities for staging of events.

The main stage comprises modular units so theoretically the entire footprint of the room could be cleared and made flat (although this doesn't happen). Various stage configurations can be created using these modular units. There is no fixed proscenium so drapes are used to create sides and header panels when performances or events require a proscenium. There is no orchestra pit and no stage machinery, no flytower but a good coverage of suspension bars over the stage area.

Loading to the stage is directly from the car park at the rear of the site onto stage. There are two dressing rooms behind the stage but neither is at stage level. Only one has en-suite facilities.

This is a thriving venue serving the local community with a very wide range of regular events and touring music and theatre. Its ownership is vested in all residents of the town in perpetuity and it is operated under trust by a small group of employees supported by part-time workers and volunteers.

Pater Hall, Pembroke Dock

Organisation: The Pater Hall Community Trust

Address: Lewis Street, Pembroke Dock SA72 6DD

Construction: 1955-57 **Opening:** 1957

Architect/Builder: unknown/unknown

Current Owner: Pembroke Dock Town Council

History/previous names & ownership

A Temperance Hall was constructed on the site of current building in 1868 by William Griffiths of Pembroke Dock at his own expense and for the use of the Total Abstinence Society. It was the only public hall in town in the nineteenth century and soon became a centre for more general entertainment and events.

The Temperance Hall was destroyed by a Luftwaffe bomb on 2nd September 1940 and soon afterwards the Trustees of the Total Abstinence Society dedicated the damaged hall to Pembroke and Pembroke Dock Borough Council.

Construction of the Pater Hall on the site of the bombed Temperance Hall commenced in 1955, commissioned by the Borough Council as a Community Theatre and it was officially opened on 11th December 1957 by the Mayor of Pembroke Dock, Alderman W Nevin. In 1965 an extension was built at the rear of the Hall to create a bar area and overcome a restrictive covenant imposed on the original site by the Total Abstinence Society that it never be used for the sale and consumption of alcohol.

Changes to the structure of local authorities in Wales leads to ownership passing from Pembroke & Pembroke Dock Borough Council to the newly formed South Pembrokeshire District Council in 1973 and then in 1994 to Pembroke Dock Town Council. The Pater Hall Community Trust was established in 2006 and assumed responsibility for the management and operation of the Hall under lease from the Town Council.

Auditorium Capacity: 200 (theatre style); 300 (standing)

Stage details: Not available

Description

Pater Hall is a simple and elegantly proportioned two-storey brick and stone building on a corner site in the heart of the commercial district of the town centre. It has a symmetrical front elevation with a large central entrance, large sash windows and a modest full width projecting balcony at first floor level. The side elevations are relatively plain and dominated by a series of high level sash windows into the Hall, emergency exit doors and the loading doors that provide access directly from the street onto the stage inside. The upper section of the exterior brickwork has been replaced within the last four years as the original bricks were weathering badly and their surface was delaminating. Entry into the building through the main doors in the front elevation is up 3 shallow steps and into a modest entrance hall/foyer area containing a cloakroom area on each side and a staircase leading to the first floor Council Chamber room above. The entrance hall has a terrazzo floor with inset feature star patterns, plain painted plastered walls and a flat ceiling. The original 1950's fixtures and fittings remain, including original light fittings. The auditorium is entered directly off the entrance space through a single pair of double doors into the rear of the audience seating area. It is a surprisingly large room, fully occupying the footprint of the building and having a flat, sprung dance floor throughout. The perimeter walls have panelling treated with horizontal recessed 'joints' to have the appearance of a stone base and with the cream painted walls above there is a distinctly civic atmosphere to the space. There are good sized windows on both long side walls of the room above the 'panelling' with velvet curtains that are pulled over the windows for performances and evening events. On the end wall opposite the stage there is a large hardwood commemorative panel recording the names of the men of the town who gave their lives in the two World Wars. A large feature cornice wraps around the room under a suspended tiled ceiling which retains the original light fittings. The stage is at the opposite end of the room from the audience entrance and has a moulded plaster proscenium. There is no apron, orchestra pit or any stage machinery. There is no flytower either and stage equipment is extremely limited. There are plans in place to completely re-equip the stage area. There are no dressing rooms but immediately behind the stage is a large room (built as an extension to the original Hall in 1965) that is given over to this use when needed. This large room has a fully equipped wet bar and is frequently used for meetings and training sessions by local companies and groups providing an additional income stream to the venue.

This is an example of an extremely successful operation under the management of an enthusiastic and very capable Trust. Events are held most weeknights and the plans for future alterations and improvements are intended to open up opportunities for greater use of the Hall at weekends.

A high level of commitment from Trustees and support from the local community seems to ensure a secure future for this well-maintained and ambitious venue.

De Valence Pavilion, Tenby

Organisation: Tenby Town Council

Address: Upper Frog Street, Tenby SA70 7JD

Construction: 1972-74 **Opening:** 1974

Architect: Allan Colley, Pembroke Dock

Builder: unknown

Current Owner: Tenby Town Council

History/previous names & ownership

In 1904 the site now occupied by the building was laid out as De Valence Gardens and opened on July 18th by the Town Mayor, Alderman George Chiles. A Dance Hall was constructed on the gardens site during the 1930's and survived until the late 1960's when it was completely demolished to make way for the current Pavilion building.

The De Valence Pavilion was built by Tenby Borough Council between 1972 and 1974 and was named after the 12th Century De Valence Earl of Pembroke, creator of Tenby town walls. Immediately after the building opened its ownership passed to the newly constituted District Council of South Pembrokeshire.

In 1986 as preparations were in hand for the abolition of District Councils and the creation of new Unitary Authorities across Wales the building was purchased from South Pembrokeshire District Council by Tenby Town Council for the nominal price of £15,000. The Town Council operated it for the next 17 years. By 2003 concern was growing about the condition of the building fabric and the extent of maintenance required and in an attempt to open up new avenues of grant funding for such works the De Valence Trust Ltd was established by Tenby Town Council and the Trust took over management and operation of the venue under lease. Soon after taking over the operation a Feasibility Study carried out with Pembrokeshire County Borough Council and Welsh Development Agency funding for demolition of the existing building and its replacement with a smaller venue was completed for the Trust by Pembroke Design Studio Architects. These proposals never materialised due to Trust's inability to generate revenue and secure external capital funding.

In early 2010 De Valence Trust Ltd ceased trading and entered liquidation. The building was closed and the auditorium mothballed in July and the Town Council put the venue on the open market in August. Local press coverage since has reported that several potential operators have expressed interest but at the time of writing its future is uncertain and the Theatres Trust included the De Valence on their TBAR 2011.

Description

This is a curiously named building insofar it is most definitely not a Pavilion. By definition such buildings are usually a light, often open building used for shelter, concerts, exhibits and the like in a park or fair or are a small, ornamental building in a garden.

This building is really quite large and impermeable and although it stands on the site of an Edwardian urban town garden it is constructed hard against the medieval town walls in a narrow street with no open space around it at all. It presents a largely blank façade to that narrow street with an entrance offset into one corner and glazing at street level that has the appearance of a shop front and contains a café area only used when events were held in the Hall inside. Some attempt to liven the otherwise blank façade has been made by the addition of sail-like structures and canopies and the building name is cast or carved into the wall at high level but it gives no outward messages that it is a place for live performances. The building is shared with Town Council Offices on the opposite side of a dull corridor that serves as the building entrance and this entry point provides the only access into the entire building, either for visitors, audience or equipment and scenic effects for shows. There is a covenant that restricts the number of times the front entrance can be used for late night loading/unloading of shows and associated equipment which restricts the venue's ability to attract companies or bands engaged on a tour of the area and only playing for one night.

The auditorium is large and really quite wide and entered through two pairs of double doors off that corridor. It has a flat floor which gives opportunities for many functions and events to be presented with a large stage at one end and a small balcony at first floor at the opposite with a wet bar underneath it. The balcony is only accessible via a pair of

steep staircases against the side walls within the room and it also has a flat floor and separate bar area. Sightlines to the stage from the balcony are consequently quite restricted, both by virtue of the height above the main floor, the flat floor of the balcony itself and its distance from the stage. The walls of the auditorium are plain painted plaster with no notable architectural features and the ceiling is a quintessentially 1970's affair of individually fixed small silver foil 'blades' about 100mm square. Apparently this ceiling makes access to the light fittings above it in the ceiling void extremely arduous. An attempt to make parts of the auditorium more 'intimate' for people on the main floor has been made by the suspension of brightly coloured drapes below the suspended ceiling. Whilst these drapes can be pushed to the sides of the room they further diminish the quality of view from the balcony down to the main floor and stage. The auditorium is heated and ventilated by the original forced-air system and it doesn't function well, is almost impossible to obtain spare parts for and is highest priority for replacement should funds become available. The stage itself is a long way above the main floor level and this has been mitigated to an extent by the addition of a substantial apron set about 300mm below the main stage level. The stage has a very shallow rake from back down to the front. The apron is constructed from movable elements that can be adapted to create a thrust stage or catwalk for certain shows and events as appropriate. The proscenium is not original and was constructed to reduce the size of the original structural opening and improve the presentation of theatre shows. There is no stage machinery and no flytower (which is seen as a particular problem and limits the venue's ability to attract touring shows). There are few rigging and lighting bars on stage and only one bar front-of-house. A large dressing room is located above the stage level but immediately behind it and can be separated into two sections by a sliding/folding wall. The dressing room(s) have toilets and washing facilities but no showers. These rooms are effectively at first floor level and the rooms underneath are used for storage of loose furniture and equipment.

Prior to its closure in July 2010 the venue had been used for live music, amateur dramatics, touring theatre and dinner dances and the last event held was a wedding banquet. The prospects for this venue appear bleak. It requires the appointment of an operator (either commercial or charitable trust) capable of raising capital to carry out essential repair or replacement to the heating and ventilation system and capable of programming events that will generate revenue despite the limitations of the existing building. Whilst not of any architectural significance and not a dedicated theatre it would be a tragedy to lose this performance space as its loss would deprive local groups of a platform for performing and would require audiences to travel to Pembroke Dock or Milford Haven to see live performances.

Auditorium Capacity: 500 (theatre style), 700 (standing)

Stage details:

Performance space – width – 10.85m (including wings)
Performance space – depth – 4.27m
Depth of apron – variable
Wing space (Right and Left) – (SR) 1.42m; (SL) 2.1m
Proscenium height/width – height 3.3m; width 7.3m
Orchestra pit (maximum no of players) – n/a
Height from stage floor to grid – 5.1m
Rake – Yes (shallow)

Royal Playhouse, Tenby

Organisation: Fry Enterprises

Address: White Lion Street, Tenby SA70 7ET

Construction/Opening: 1857

Architect: original - unknown; 1865 re-modelling – H Maule-ffinch; 1880 re-build - unknown

Builder: unknown

Current Owner: Fry Enterprises (Mr Graham Fry)

History/previous names & ownership

Built in 1857 as the New Assembly Rooms and located close to the Gate House Hotel. It was then remodelled in 1865 by H Maule-ffinch with a new front portico of eight Tuscan columns. In 1880 it was burnt down and then reconstructed with the present simpler facade. In 1909 touring theatrical companies were appearing here and it was known as the Royal Gate House Assembly Rooms and owned by the Gate House Hotel Company. At this time it had an audience capacity of 700. From around May 1911 it was screening films and the gallery was extended in 1914, increasing capacity to 865.

The Royal Assembly Rooms were partially re-built in 1928 and re-opened as the Royal Playhouse on 15th July 1928. Seating was now provided for 800 in stalls and circle levels and there was a ballroom attached. It was independently operated and this has continued to-date.

In 1953 the building was owned by Gatehouse Estates, a company that incorporated the adjacent Royal Gatehouse Hotel, the old De Valence Pavilion and the Gatehouse Garage and car park and long-serving projectionist/manager Mr John Hill commenced working in the Playhouse.

Cinemascope was installed in 1954 yet this was the era when pantomimes were staged in the building as well as bingo, wrestling and scout and guide gang shows. During the early 1970's further technical upgrades to the projection and sound systems were made but longer films were shown with an intermission to facilitate reel changes right up to the 1990's. Until the late 1970's gas was still being used to light the emergency exits.

The Royal Playhouse was listed Grade II on 26th April 1977 for its street facade and as the remains of a C19 assembly room

The current owners bought the building in 1978. In September 2000 the building was closed for almost a year while alterations were made to comply with changes to fire regulations

In 2004 following the retirement of the Manager who had served the building for 50 years, plans were mooted to restore the building including the conversion of the disused snooker room and leisure complex at the rear of the site into a 200 seat second cinema auditorium and the creation of 50 seat 'film-club' in former squash courts on the site but they failed to materialise. Around this time however, the front elevation was painted yellow over the then pink render.

The adjacent Gatehouse Hotel building was destroyed by fire in 2008 and the owner developed a scheme to demolish the cinema auditorium behind the listed façade and replace it with an arcade containing bars, restaurants and a 160 seat cinema (plans drawn up by Cardiff Architects Chichester Nunn Partnership/C2J Architects) but this scheme too has failed to be realised. Around the same time the building was again closed but it reopened and operated until December 2010 when it again closed for business. It remains disused.

Auditorium Capacity: Original capacity unknown; 1908: 700; 1914: 865; 1928: 800; current capacity 438

Stage details:

Performance space – width – 10.36m (including wings)
Performance space – depth – 4.27m
Wing space (Right and Left) – 2.44m both sides
Proscenium height/width – height not known/width 5.5m

Description

Located close to the seafront and commercial centre of Tenby, the prominent bright yellow painted stucco front elevation makes this building easy to find.

The front elevation is a well proportioned, symmetrical and classically inspired arrangement of pilasters and arched recessed panels surmounted by a pediment. The 'Royal Playhouse Cinema' signage is not in keeping with the architecture and looks out of place and proportion.

The arched recesses may well have contained windows in the original configuration of the building and have been blocked up when it was converted to full-time cinema use.

The main entrance is on the central axis of the front elevation directly off a small forecourt between the building and the road and entry is directly into a small foyer/ticket desk area containing refreshment sales point and access directly into the auditorium beyond.

There is buddleia growing behind the parapet and the sides of the building show further evidence of lack of maintenance with damaged rainwater goods allowing rain to run over the dark grey plain roughcast rendered surfaces and the majority of original doors and windows are boarded up. Overall the impression of the building is that it is in a poor state of repair.

Whilst no access to the interior was possible on the date of visit, comments on local websites suggest it too is in a poor state of repair and cleanliness. Negative comments include that the seating is uncomfortable with very restricted leg room and the heating system doesn't work very well. It has earned the sobriquet of 'flea-pit' amongst some who have commented. Positive comments made include that it provides a 'retro cinema experience', is a fantastic old-fashioned cinema and that the décor is 'classic' and 'original'. A gently pitched curved fronted balcony is said to survive with Art Deco type motifs on the front. It is unclear how much longer this building will survive.

Monmouthshire

Monmouth
Monk Street Theatre
Rolls Hall
St Mary Street Theatre

Monk Street Theatre, Monmouth

Address: Monk Street, Monmouth NP25 3NZ

Construction/Opening: 1797

Architect/Builder: unknown/unknown

Current Owner: The Ancient Fraternity of Free and Accepted Masons in the Province of Monmouthshire

Current Use: Masonic Lodge

History/previous names & ownership

Built as a theatre in 1797 but converted to a Masonic Hall in 1837 by Architect George Vaughan Maddox of Monmouth at the request of the Rolls family. A new façade was installed in 1846, to further designs by Maddox and similar in appearance to that designed by the same Architect for the Monmouth Methodist Church in St James Street. The foyer and gallery have been retained.

The building was listed Grade II on 15th August 1974.

Description

The building is set back a long way from the street and has the appearance of a rather grand residential property with its applied classical portico and timber front doors. The front elevation is finished in white painted render and appears very well maintained. The side elevations similarly do not suggest the presence of an auditorium inside although are largely blank and finished in a yellow render.

It is widely reported that some features of the original theatre remain inside as part of the Masonic Hall.

Auditorium Capacity: Not available

Stage details: Not available

Rolls Hall, Monmouth

Address: Whitecross Street, Monmouth, Monmouthshire NP25 3BY

Construction: 1887-88 **Opening:** 1888

Architect: F. A. Powell, Monmouth

Builder: David Roberts

Current Owner: Monmouthshire County Council Library Service

Current Use: Library

History/previous names & ownership

The building was given to the people of Monmouth for use as a lecture hall and theatre by John Alan Rolls of the Rolls Family, later Lord Llangattock, F.S.A., of The Hendre to commemorate Queen Victoria's Golden Jubilee in 1887 and was presented to the town on the Queen's birthday in 1888. It was built at a cost of £8,000.

It was substantially built of local red sandstone with dressings of Forest of Dean stone, and comprised a spacious hall, entered from a vestibule and wide corridor, with at one end a gallery and at the other a proscenium, the stage being available for suppers on the occasion of balls. It possessed a fine organ, also the gift of the donor of the hall, and numerous valuable paintings presented by him and others.

It was converted to Library use in 1992 and it is understood that further works were carried out to the Library to improve accessibility in 2010. The building was listed Grade II on 8th October 2005.

Description

This is a rather grandiose stone fronted building with a curious mix of architectural detailing and features. It has a rough red asymmetrical stone base and front elevation with dressed stone features in a classical style to the main entrance with string courses. The original form of the auditorium is evident in the side elevations of red brick with high level roundel windows presumably used when the room was used for lectures.

Conversion to a library in 1992 removed the stage area but retained the large volume of the auditorium which has more classical detailing and proportion than the exterior including pilaster mouldings and surrounds to the roundel windows. There is an elegant curved junction between walls and ceiling.

Auditorium Capacity: not available

Stage details: Not available

Interior photograph Monmouthshire Library Service

St Mary Street Theatre, Monmouth

Address: 14, St Mary Street, Monmouth NP25 3DB

Construction/Opening: 1775

Architect/Builder: unknown/unknown

Current Owner: unknown

Current Use: Restaurant

History/previous names & ownership

According to the Theatres Trust database, Roger Kemble brought his company here in 1775. It is not known when it ceased operation as a theatre.

As part of its recent history it has been a furniture warehouse and part of it an antique shop and the building is currently occupied by a Thai restaurant on the ground floor.

Description

There are no outward signs that this building was ever a place of live entertainment and it is an unassuming building standing in the middle of a terrace of similar size (and presumably age) residential buildings within easy walking distance of the main commercial centre of Monmouth.

The visible and principal elevation is finished with stucco, lined out as stonework and is three storeys tall. The right hand section is domestic in appearance, one window wide with the restaurant shopfront on the ground floor. The left hand bay is higher with a carriage entrance and two storeys of loading doors above topped by a flat-topped parapet unique on the street.

It is not known if any of the original theatre internal structure remains but it would seem extremely unlikely given the many changes of use of the building over the last 200 years.

Auditorium Capacity: unknown

Stage details: not available

Newport

Newport
The Albert Hall
Tredegar Hall

The Albert Hall, Newport

Address: 3 Powell's Place, Lower Dock Street, Newport NP20 1EL

Construction/Opening: 1875

Architect/Builder: unknown/unknown

Current Owner: unknown

Current Use: Drop-In Centre/Cafe

History/previous names & ownership

The Albert Hall (also known as the Royal Albert Hall and the Drill Hall) was opened in 1875 and was capable of seating 1,100 persons. It had numerous anterooms and was used for lectures, concerts and other entertainments.

It was listed Grade II on 26th January 1999.

The building is currently used as a drop-in centre and cafe widely used by local unemployed people.

Description

The Albert Hall is located at the end of a small cul-de-sac off Lower Dock Street, originally one of the most important commercial streets in Newport as it developed as a centre of commerce around the docks. Today, the area has a down-at-heel feel about it and there remains nothing on the building that alludes to its past as a major entertainment and function venue in the town, apart perhaps from its scale.

It is a conspicuously large building surrounded by small scale terraced housing and light industrial operations and has some quite flamboyant architectural detailing. It is constructed predominantly in red brick with feature panles and details in a buff brick and, around doors and windows, elegant carved stonework.

The scale of windows at first floor level suggests that the Hall was (or perhaps still is) located at that level with the anterooms and other smaller scale spaces underneath. It appears as though these rooms are currently functioning as the 'drop-in' centre and a cafe occupies much of the ground floor.

Insofar as it continues to provide a social function it remains a public building as it was originally intended but it seems a shame that it is all but invisible to the majority of the people of the City.

Auditorium Capacity: 1100

Stage details: not available

Tredegar Hall, Newport

Address: 12 – 26 Stow Hill, Newport NP20 1JD

Construction/Opening: 1895

Architect/Builder: unknown/unknown

Current Owner: unknown

Current Use: Retail

History/previous names & ownership

Tredegar Hall was built in 1895 as a general purpose hall although films were screened from 1906. It staged Boxing matches every week in the period 1916 – 1917. Following a change of ownership it was re-opened in 1922 as a public hall and was then converted to full-time cinema use in 1929. Its name was changed to the Tredegar Hall Cinema. By 1930, it was operated by London & Southern Super Cinemas and they were taken over by Odeon Theatres in July 1937. Seating was provided for 1,019 with 600 in the stalls and 419 in the circle.

It was closed by CMA (Rank Organisation) on 29th March 1958 and in April 1958 a new, £30,000 ballroom, The Majestic was opened in the building. Later the building was taken over by the Star Cinemas Group, it became a bingo club, and was operating in this use in 1989, then a nightclub known as Metro and then the Jesper Bar & Nightclub. By 2010 it was an Argos store.

Description

No evidence remains of any previous use of this building as a place for live entertainment or even cinema and it blends into the general streetscape with its ground floor retail frontages just like any other inner city Victorian building in the area.

It has a curiously asymmetrical front elevation above the shop frontages surmounted by a 4 sided turret which, presumably originally served to announce the location of the main entrance to the Hall.

The original main entrance remains but access to the interior is very different from what can be imagined of the original building layout. Now, immediately on passing under the large arched opening that is the entrance the retailer turns the visitor left off the axis of the building and directly into the shop unit.

The ground floor of the building is almost entirely occupied by the large open-plan retail showroom typical of all Argos stores on one side of the entrance with 2 smaller shop units to the other side. The upper floors appear to be used for office accommodation.

The building fabric appears to be in very good condition.

Auditorium Capacity: 1019 in 1937 comprising 600 at stalls and 419 in the circle.

Stage details: Not available

Tredegar Hall c 1950; Photograph www.newportpast.com

Caerphilly

Abertridwr
Workmen's Hall

Workmen's Hall, Abertridwr

Address: The Square, Abertridwr, Caerphilly CF83 4DH

Construction/Opening: 1910

Architect: Illtyd Thomas

Builder: unknown

Current Owner: unknown

Current Use: Bingo Hall (derelict)

History/previous names & ownership

Opened in 1910 as a Workmen's Hall and Institute, a Library was added in 1911. It was also known as the Windsor Colliery Workmen's Institute, Library and Hall. Originally the main auditorium had an audience capacity of 700 but this had increased slightly to 712 by 1951.

It had a 25 feet wide proscenium and was operated as a cinema between 1937 and 1966. By 1966 bingo had been introduced and ran in parallel with film shows. Occasional variety shows sometimes replaced film. The cinema finally closed in 1969. It was left derelict until conversion to full-time bingo use and operation as the Aber Bingo Club sometime after 1980. The Aber Valley Sports Gymnasium business occupied the ground floor for some time before the building was closed. It has been closed for several years and left boarded up and derelict.

Description

Located on a highly visible elevated site in the centre of this small linear village, the Workmen's Hall is immediately striking for both the scale of the building in this setting and the state of disrepair and neglect it stands in forlornly. It appears as though some attempts have been made over time to protect the envelope against the ravages of natural decline, particularly on the two long sides where monolithic finishes have been installed over the original brick and all openings into the building have been blocked up, not simply boarded over. despite these attempts it is a building in an advanced state of decay. The topography of the site on which it stands is far from unusual insofar as there is a very steep level difference across the land but the orientation of the building, presumably dictated by an existing road layout is unusual. Ordinarily such buildings stand with their entrance at the high point providing level access to the front but in this case the main frontage is conspicuously elevated above the pavement which falls steeply in front of the building and an innovative wide plinth of dark rubble stone has been constructed across the front with access at the 'level' end leading to the main entrance in its typical central axis position. The central door is flanked by a pair of single leaf doors and small windows and the lower storey and flanking massive brick buttresses at the corners have been painted over the rubble stone. Above the central entrance is a faded sign proclaiming the last use of the building as the Aber Bingo Club (presumably mounted over an original sign identifying the building as a Workmen's Hall) and an unusual semi-circular window and curved feature to the apex of this gable wall. In its original condition this would have been a fine looking building. The sides and rear of the building are a mixture of painted render and untreated metal sheeting and generally in a worse condition than the front. It seems unlikely that in this location this building has any future prospect for renovation and is surely lost to the estate of theatre buildings in Wales all bar the actual act of demolition.

Auditorium Capacity: Original: 750; increased to 712 by 1951
Stage details: not available

Blaenau Gwent

Ebbw Vale
Workmen's Hall
Tredegar
Palace of Varieties Theatre

Workmen's Hall, Ebbw Vale

Address: West End Terrace, Ebbw Vale NP23 6HS

Construction/Opening: 1907

Architect/Builder: unknown/unknown

Current Owner: Top Ten Holdings

Current Use: Bingo Hall (derelict)

History/previous names & ownership

The Workmen's Hall was built in 1907 and was equipped for a variety of uses including live performance, bingo and cinema. Following the closure of the rival nearby Astoria Cinema the venue switched to showing films. The interior featured original gas lighting as house lights on the side walls during the 1970's.

Following a pattern seen elsewhere, the original club and theatre became a cinema and then a bingo hall before closing down. It operated as a bingo hall until around March 2010 and is now boarded up and for sale.

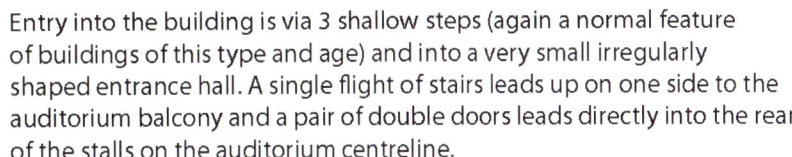

Description

The Workmen's Hall is located at the end of a street running parallel to the main commercial street in Ebbw Vale town centre and is slightly elevated above that main street. As such this is an odd location for such a building – others of its era were located in much more prominent sites at the heart of their towns. It has a curious, probably unique main frontage insofar as it is curved to follow the line of the road and this has manifested itself in some unusual detailing on the building envelope. The main entrance is proudly announced with flamboyant stone feature detailing and a decorated frieze in a triangular pediment panel over with the building name and date of construction prominent.

The sides and rear of the building have been covered with pebble-dash render at some point in the building's history such that there are no visible signs of any original features other than on the main frontage remaining. It is likely that behind the pebble-dash are original openings for windows originally built into the envelope as was common for such buildings. The windows were probably blocked up when the building was predominantly used for cinema productions. There is vehicular access to the rear of the building but no openings into the building (serving the original stage) remain. The roof is finished with slate and a ridge ventilator remains but has surely not been functional for many years.

Entry into the building is via 3 shallow steps (again a normal feature of buildings of this type and age) and into a very small irregularly shaped entrance hall. A single flight of stairs leads up on one side to the auditorium balcony and a pair of double doors leads directly into the rear of the stalls on the auditorium centreline.

The Hall is flat-floored and retains an original balcony on 3 sides but little else appears to be original. Indeed the only sign of any original finishes is in the meter cupboard under the entrance hall stairs where a small area of original floor tiles is exposed. The original stage (proscenium) opening remains but the stage itself has been removed to create maximum usable floor space for Bingo tables.

A mezzanine balcony has been introduced about halfway up the stage opening to accommodate even more players and this added floor extends into the original side-stage area where presumably there would have been performer dressing rooms. Bingo tables have been fitted everywhere, including along the 2 side balconies and over the entire main balcony area, where any original tiered seating has been removed and the balcony floor is now largely flat with one area of raised floor either side. The balcony front is of elegant metalwork and extends around the 3 sides of balcony right up to the proscenium wall. The balconies are supported on elegantly proportioned and slender iron columns with ornate brackets. The original ceiling has been covered with a lower level suspended lay-in grid tile ceiling typical of similar conversions to Bingo use and lighting is provided by a regular arrangement of surface mounted fluorescent strip lights.

So, apart from that wonderful balcony front the original character of this auditorium has been completely lost.

The building is currently being used as a warehouse for un-used fruit machines, and although it has been on the open market for over a year there are no signs of sale and potential regeneration. It is difficult to imagine what use the building could be put to in the future apart perhaps from a publicly funded re-fit as a theatre for community use.

Even this use is unlikely however given the proximity of the Beaufort Theatre (owned and operated by the County Council) and the potential for a new 500 seat theatre to be built on the old steelworks site elsewhere in Ebbw Vale. The site location does not appear conducive to any other development as it is remote from residential areas and not close enough to the main shopping street to attract income from retail use. Consequently the prospects for this building appear bleak.

Auditorium Capacity: Not available

Stage details: Not available

Palace of Varieties Theatre, Tredegar

Address: Park Place, Tredegar NP22 4LD

Construction/Opening: before 1920

Architect/Builder: unknown/unknown

Current Owner: Two-time world snooker champion Mark Williams

Current Use: Snooker Club

History/previous names & ownership

Presumed built before the First World War this theatre was initially used as a vaudeville hall but was not successful and, while operating as the Palace Cinema, the business failed in the early 1920s.

The Tredegar Medical Aid Society (widely acknowledged to be the fore-runner of the National Health Service introduced by local MP Aneurin Bevan) purchased the building in 1925 and converted it to include consulting rooms, a treatment room and waiting area. The dispensary occupied the old projector room at the back of the building, slightly raised from the auditorium. The entrance was still through a foyer (minus ticket booth) at one side, with an exit through a one-way turnstile at the other side. Throughout this period the name "Palace of Varieties" was visible on the building wall.

At some point after the Second World War the building was converted into a snooker club and it continues in that use to date. Two-time world snooker champion Mark Williams took over Tredegar Snooker Hall on 7th January 2010.

Description

Located some distance from the main town centre but in a group of small retail and commercial buildings, it is immediately obvious that the building was built for live entertainment. It is a large building and its high roof line distinguishes it from its immediate neighbours but it is the principal front elevation that speaks of the building's origins and history most of all. The 3-bay main frontage is gloriously flamboyant in its decoration and applied mouldings around windows and its quirky stepped roof parapet. The larger central bay has a large semi-circular window at high level with a coat-of-arms style feature at its head. Old photographs suggest the rendered surfaces of the external walls of the building were painted bright yellow for sometime with the feature mouldings highlighted in browns and reds. Presumably the original entrance to the building was via two sets of double doors in this front elevation although now there are windows in those positions set at a level where a view to the inside is not possible. Entry into the building is now via a door in the side and is elevated several steps above the surrounding ground level. It is not clear if access for people with movement limitations is possible. It is understood that none of the original auditorium is retained.

In early summer 2011 the front elevation was completely renovated and redecorated suggesting that the current owner is serious about preserving the building in the long term for the works have been carried out to a very high standard and the building looks to have a secure future.

Auditorium Capacity: Not available

Stage details: Not available

Merthyr Tydfil

Merthyr Tydfil
 The Miners' Hall
 The Theatre Royal

The Miners' Hall, Merthyr Tydfil

Organisation: None

Address: Church Street, Merthyr Tydfil CF487 0BA

Construction: 1853 (original Chapel) **Opening:** 1921 (conversion to Miners' Hall)

Architect/Builder: Isambard Kingdom Brunel

Current Owner: unknown

Current Use: Night Club (derelict)

History/previous names & ownership

Originally built as Shiloh Welsh Wesleyan Chapel in 1853 and commonly believed to have been designed by Isambard Kingdom Brunel, engineer of the Vale of Neath Railway Company who erected the new chapel when the railway station was built on the earlier site. A prominent corner tower was cut down and the building lengthened in 1921 when it was converted to the Miners' Hall. The building was a popular venue for live music and other events for over 40 years until it closed in 1962. It is presumed that its use as a place of public entertainment continued but no evidence has been found of this for the next 25 years.

In 1987 the building was converted to club use as "Charbonniers" Night Club. The building was listed Grade II on 13th January 1988.

The main hall was gutted by fire in 1992 and the building has been left derelict and un-used since. The annex was restored and re-opened as a pub shortly afterwards and still operates as 'The Miners Arms'. The site was identified for possible residential or nursing home development in the Merthyr Tydfil Borough Council Local Plan published in 1999 but no development has yet taken place.

The derelict Hall was again extensively damaged by fire (believed to have been caused by an arson attack) on August 6th 2004 and later that year Minutes of a Cabinet Meeting of Merthyr Council record that the council was making bids for funding under the European Union Objective 1 programme encompassing a range of town centre initiatives, including the potential refurbishment of the Miners Hall building, with potential links to the Old Town Hall and proposed streetscape improvements to Lower High Street, as part of the creation of a café quarter.

In 2011 the building remains derelict and un-used.

Description

Located near to the town centre and the derelict Victorian Town Hall building (currently undergoing restoration and conversion to an Arts Centre to designs by Austin-Smith:Lord Architects of Cardiff) and the site of the recently demolished Castle Cinema this building is a sad reflection of the decline of Merthyr in the post-industrial era.

It has stood derelict for almost 20 years, protected from outright demolition perhaps by its listed status but gradually succumbing to the forces of decay. It is a testament to how well it was originally constructed that so much of it remains standing.

Since two fires ravaged the building, first in 1992 and then again in 2004 the walls of the building have stood without a roof to support and what is visible of the interior is thoroughly covered with plant growth, some of which now quite large trees.

The Romanesque style rubble stone main frontage remains with its dressed stone window and door surround details but any glazing that remains has been subjected to sustained attempts by vandals to break it. The tower of the original chapel that was cut down when the building was converted into the Miners Hall also remains.

The original main entrance is approached across a small terraced forecourt and steep steps with a wrought iron fence along the boundary. There are (or were) three doors entering the building but the architectural detailing suggests that the central door was the main entry point, probably leading directly into a small vestibule with stairs up to the original chapel/auditorium balcony and doors leading straight into the hall.

To one side a small single storey annexe is used as a public house whilst on the other, bounded by a narrow alleyway all low level openings have been blocked up and rendered over while the high level pointed arch clerestorey is open to the elements with none of the original glazing remaining.

At the rear of the site is a two-storey block, clearly not part of the original construction and curiously apparently unaffected by the two fires that destroyed much of the main hall. It doesn't appear to be currently occupied however despite retaining all window glazing and its slate roof intact.

Auditorium Capacity: Not available

Stage details: Not available

The Theatre Royal, Merthyr Tydfil

Organisation: None

Address: Penydarren Road, Merthyr Tydfil CV47 0LJ

Construction/Opening: 1891

Architect: T C Wakeling, Merthyr

Builder: unknown

Current Owner: Private Individual

Current Use: Bingo Hall (derelict)

History/previous names & ownership

Built as a theatre 1891, little is known about the history of the building despite it being by some distance the largest theatre in Merthyr and the surrounding area.

In 1910 J.W. Wilkinson was Manager and South Wales Entertainments Ltd was lessee and in the period 1920 - 1929 the auditorium was rebuilt, a balcony inserted and the building effectively converted to full-time cinema use. In its 1920s heyday the theatre had two different entrances, dependent on which class of ticket had been purchased.

The building was listed Grade II on 22nd August 1975 (along with the adjacent building known as Thespian House)

The Theatre Royal was converted to use as a Bingo Hall in 1982 but retained the Theatre Royal name.

It has stood derelict and un-used for an unknown period of time now although a number of original features are believed to remain, including parts of the organ and the pulley mechanism for scenery.

Expectations are for its demolition and redevelopment of the site in the future but given that the interior is understood to be in reasonably good condition perhaps it could be resurrected.

Auditorium Capacity: Original: unknown; 1951: 1217; current: unknown

Stage details: not available

Description

Located at the slightly unfashionable end of the High Street and on one of the major arterial routes into Merthyr this building is vast in scale compared to its neighbours and it is remarkable that it survives at all.

The building is currently boarded up and derelict and the external envelope appears to be in a poor state of repair. What little open space there is on the site around the building (particularly at the rear) is overgrown with vegetation and clearly hasn't been accessed for a considerable period of time. The security fencing seems extremely robust.

The main building frontage to Penydarren Road is in a grand and imposing Victorian Classical style, finished with red coloured render and featuring dressed stone details around openings and to the ground floor annex building. The sides and rear of the building are of a much simpler and functional masonry construction with the upper part of the flytower clad in timber boarding and the whole building has a slate roof which appears to be relatively intact.

The interior is understood to be relatively unchanged over time and since closure has remained untouched.

The Theatre Royal has been described as one of Merthyr's hidden gems and the envy of the valleys but the future for such a huge building in this location must give serious cause for concern, compounded by the current focus on the regeneration of the town centre and initiatives such as the conversion of the Old Town Hall into an Arts Centre.

Perhaps a case could be made for a theatre of this scale serving the Heads of the Valleys region but it is difficult to imagine how issues such as accessibility, audience parking and raising the necessary funding would be addressed and resolved.

Rhondda Cynon Taff

Abercwmboi
Workmen's Hall
Aberdare
Constitutional Club
The Little Theatre
The Palladium
Beddau
Cwm & Llantwit Welfare Hall
Tonypandy
The Judge's Hall
The Theatre Royal
Tonyrefail
Picture Theatre

Workmen's Hall, Abercwmboi

Address: Bronallt Terrace, Abercwmboi, Aberaman CF44 6BW

Construction/Opening: 1913

Architect/Builder: unknown/unknown

Current Owner: Abercwmboi Christian Centre

Current Use: Christian Centre

History/previous names & ownership

Abercwmboi Workmen's Hall was paid for by contributions out of the local miners' wages and was built in 1913. It has also been known as Abercwmboi Miners' Institute and Abercwmboi Welfare Hall. In 1914 permission was granted for a hall and library to be erected. The hall later became a cinema and bingo operation whilst the institute building housed the library, reading rooms and a billiard room. In 1968 the trustees of the building decided to operate the building as a licensed bar in order to boost revenue for the upkeep of the buildings. Two years later a fire damaged parts of the hall. The building was listed Grade II on 29 November 2002. It was taken over by a Christian Society in early in the 2000s and currently operates as a Christian Centre.

Description

Located in the centre of the small community of Abercwmboi between Aberaman and Mountain Ash and with its main frontage against the back of the pavement, this building has a slightly austere and rugged appearance in comparison to similar buildings of a similar age. It is constructed with few windows and has walls predominantly of dark rubble stone with small areas of contrasting dressed stone feature detailing around the doors and windows with a roof of welsh slate. The most striking feature of the building is a projecting balcony at first floor level with solid door into the building between a pair of small windows with stone surrounds of a light classical nature. It is not clear what the purpose of the balcony may have been and it is an unusual element on this otherwise quite introverted building. The side of the building that is exposed to the prevailing wind and weather moving through the valley has had an applied render finish added over the original rubble stone that is retained on the opposite, more sheltered side. The main hall appears to be accessed directly from the street level with the slightly earlier Institute building set down the steeply sloping site some distance from the road behind a metal perimeter fence and gate and a steep flight of steps. The Institute building has a quite different architectural appearance – more akin to arts and crafts styling with many more windows of generous size and proportion set within rendered stone walls.

Auditorium Capacity: Not available

Stage details: Not available

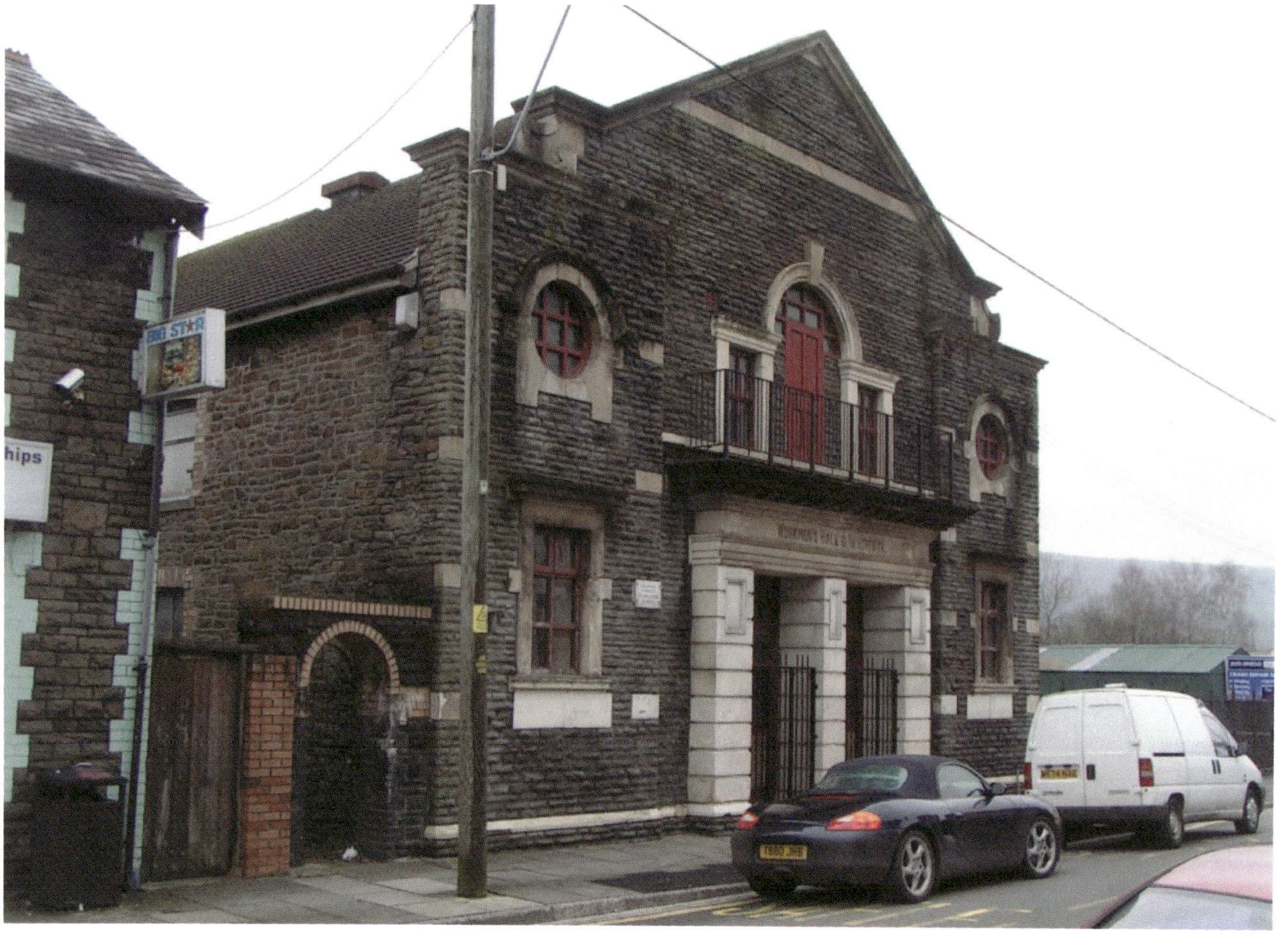

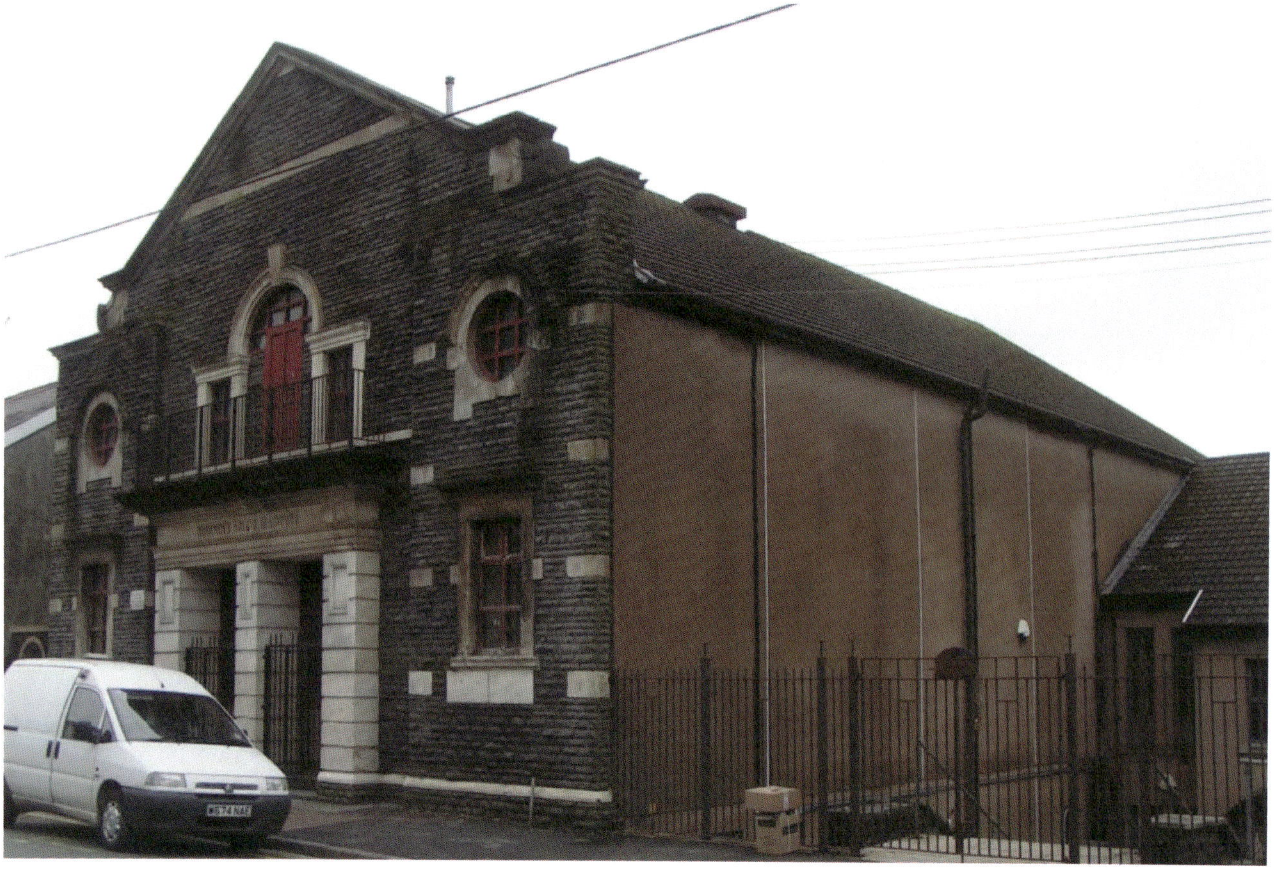

Constitutional Club, Aberdare

Address: Constitutional Buildings, Canon Street, Aberdare CF44 7AW

Construction: 1890-93 **Opening:** 1894

Architect: T. C. Wakeling, Merthyr Tydfil

Builder: unknown

Current Owner: Aberdare Constitutional Club

Current Use: Social Club

History/previous names & ownership

The first Aberdare Constitutional Club was founded at premises in Commercial Place (Victoria Square) in 1884. In 1885 the Club moved to larger premises at 28 Canon Street, but as the club continued to prosper attempts were made to secure a new site for development.

In 1888 Lord Merthyr purchased the land on which the Aberdare Constitutional Club was to be erected. The plans of the building were approved and work had been completed by July 1893. The Constitutional Club contained 3 shops, a bar and the Constitutional Hall on the first floor; on the second floor a billiards room, card room, reading room, library and committee room; and the third floor contained the kitchens with a lift to the ground floor.

The Club was officially opened on 15th March 1894, when the opening ceremony was performed by J M Maclean, the Conservative candidate for Member of Parliament for Cardiff.

When originally constructed the architecture of the Constitutional Club was more ornate than it is now. It had a balustrade that ran along the roof, a clock tower and a rather imposing ornamental porch.

The Constitutional Hall became an important place of entertainment for the population of Aberdare, being used in a number of different ways as the tastes of the inhabitants changed. In 1905 the Hall became the 'Palace Theatre of Varieties', and in 1909 reopened as the 'New Empire Theatre'. After the Theatre closed down the 'Empire Hall' became a ballroom and concert hall.

In the 1960's the Hall was converted into the 'Go-Go Bar' and its last incarnation was as the 'Decker's Nightclub' before conversion into a social club and re-naming as The Constitutional Club again. The building was listed Grade II on 1st October 1991.

Description

This building stands in a very prominent position in the town, on a corner site at the head of Canon Street and its vibrant colour and very large corner roof tower with ornate metalwork makes it impossible to miss. There is no doubt that when this building was opened it was an extremely bold statement and the architectural detailing, especially around the many large windows is particularly ornate. The principal façade is ruthlessly symmetrical and a large facet addresses the road junction and corner site by containing the central main entrance door (not currently used) with a small projecting balcony over it at first floor level and that large rooftop tower. At first floor the importance of the original Constitutional Hall is emphasised by very tall windows each dressed with white stone carved jamb mouldings and classical style pediments and scrolls.

It is clearly not such an important centre for entertainment in the town as it once was though and appears somewhat neglected and a bit scruffy. The ground floor is given over entirely to use as a pub, complete with the typical big screen TVs so normal for pubs these days. It isn't clear how often the function room is used but occasional live music events are promoted.

Auditorium Capacity: unknown

Stage details: Not available

The Little Theatre, Aberdare

Address: Lambert Tee, Aberdare CF44 08AT

Construction/Opening: 1931

Architect/Builder: unknown/unknown

Current Owner: unknown

Current Use: undergoing conversion to Double-Glazing showroom and warehouse

History/previous names & ownership

The Aberdare Little Theatre opened on 19th February 1931 in a converted railway engine shed. The conversion to a bespoke theatre was originally commissioned by the Trecynon Amateur Dramatic Society which changed its name to the Aberdare Little Theatre Company on moving into the new building. In 1942 it was requisitioned as a food depot by the Ministry of Food and the theatre company didn't move back in until 1958. Refurbishment works were carried out at this time and it operated unchanged for a further 20 years until being largely destroyed by a fire in 1978. It was re-opened in 1979 after further renovations and again operated largely unchanged until its closure in the late 2000's. At some point in time the Aberdare Little Theatre Company became The Little Theatre Trust and they were the last owners of the building in its life as a theatre venue. The building was placed on the open market and sold in early 2010 for redevelopment as a Double-Glazing warehouse and showroom.

Description

The Little Theatre is a small scale building in a site set well below the adjacent roads and footpath level but with ramped access to its entrance through a garden approach, now significantly overgrown as the building has not been occupied for some time. The site has a high hoarding to its entire perimeter indicating redevelopment is imminent.

The building envelope features off-white rendered walls surmounted with a metal clad pitched roof believed to have been added after the 1978 fire. It is a rectangular building retaining much of the original form of the engine shed it occupies but bearing no resemblance to it as a result of many changes over its life. The entrance is on the side of the building near to the front and the auditorium occupies the majority of the available space inside with the stage at the rear and having separate access from the large surface car park on the site. There is no evidence of the auditorium form in the external appearance of the building.

Auditorium Capacity:

Original capacity 318

Stage details:

Performance space – width – not known
Performance space – depth – 5.65m
Depth of apron – not known
Wing space (Right and Left) – not known
Proscenium height/width – height not known/ width 7.5m
Orchestra pit - none
Height from stage floor to grid – 4.35m
Rake – None

Photograph: www.archive.rhondda-cynon-taf.gov.uk

The Theatre on opening in 1931

The Palladium, Aberdare

Address: Canon Street, Aberdare CF44 7AT

Construction/Opening: 1858

Architect/Builder: unknown/unknown

Current Owner: Top Ten Holdings

Current Use: Bingo Hall

History/previous names & ownership

The Palladium was originally built as a Temperance Hall at a cost of £3,000 by the Total Abstinence Society. The Hall consisted of an auditorium, which could seat 1,500 people, a temperance hotel with 11 rooms, committee, rooms, a library and temperance coffee house. At the time of its construction the Hall was the largest space available in Aberdare to hold public gatherings and was used extensively for public meetings, lectures and entertainment.

In 1895 it was converted into the New Theatre and Hippodrome when alterations were made to the interior and façade and a portico was added. In 1918 it was renamed the Palladium and began showing films. From the 1920's onwards it was primarily used as a cinema. In the late-1920's, the building was given a new look, with rebuilding being undertaken internally. The proscenium was 35 feet wide, the stage 25 feet deep and there were three dressing rooms.

During the 1930's significant Auditorium remodelling was undertaken (presumably as a result of the advent of 'talking pictures') and over the next 30 years the portico was removed and an extension constructed to the Canon Street elevation to accommodate a larger film projection room and staircases and then later the portico was re-instated and the extension removed. The Palladium Cinema was closed in the early 1970's and converted into an independent bingo club and remains in that use. Since then, in 1988 and in 1994-95 there have been two significant modifications and upgrades to the Bingo audience seating and equipment and catering facilities.

Description

The Palladium is one of the largest buildings in Aberdare Town Centre and dominates the town skyline. It has an imposing classical style front elevation and coloured rendered facades all round. The building envelope and fabric are in very good condition although perhaps in need of a significant clean since the smoking ban and some internal areas could be redecorated.

Most features of the original Temperance Hall have disappeared although there is evidence of fairly elaborate moulding around the proscenium that could be the original. The Main Hall has been changed many times over its life with the biggest influences appearing to have been the introduction of talking pictures when the building was used as a cinema and most notably when the building was converted to Bingo Hall use in the late 1960's.

The interior of the auditorium is surprisingly plain but art deco detailing towards the front of the room hints at the great age of 'talkies' and a major redecoration around the 1930's period. The upper balcony is still predominantly furnished with the last cinema seats that were installed (age unknown but including rather lovely examples of 'love-seats' in the back rows). The original Victorian ceiling (presumed to still be in-situ) has been covered with a lay-in grid suspended tile ceiling to increase sound and thermal insulation.

The main floor and front part of the upper balcony are both fully occupied by Bingo booths comprising ranks of banquette seating either side of central tables, capable of seating up to 6 'players' in each booth.

A bar servery and food counter have been installed within the room at the rear of the stalls floor and the bingo caller has a permanent position on the stage. The stage area remains intact but has long been stripped of any theatre equipment and flying installations and has been left as an undecorated volume, open from stage to underside of roof.

The front-of-house spaces are compact and are dominated by the symmetrical staircases leading up to the balcony from the ground floor. The main entrance is on the central axis and several steps above pavement level. A hardwood ticket desk of unknown age remains directly in front of the entrance although is used only for storage in the current operation. Access for people with disabilities is afforded by use of a side door to the main auditorium. There is no access for people with disabilities to the upper balcony.

The auditorium is pleasantly cool in the summer (as a result of its considerable thermal mass from its heavy construction and multi-layered ceiling) but is difficult to keep warm in the winter months. Ventilation is minimal.

Auditorium Capacity:

Original seating capacity was 1500 but it is clear that there have been reductions in this capacity over time as the various internal modifications have been carried out.

Current capacity (for Bingo) is approximately 700 but there are approximately 400 un-used cinema seats on the upper part of the balcony believed to have been installed in the 1930's.

Stage details:

Performance space – width – 10.7m
Performance space – depth – 7.62m
Depth of apron – n/a
Wing space (Right and Left) – n/a
Proscenium height/width – height not known/ width 10.7m
Orchestra pit - none
Height from stage floor to grid – no grid (removed)
Rake – None

Cwm & Llantwit Welfare Hall, Beddau

Address: Gaiety Cinema, Parish Road, Beddau, Pontypridd, CF38 2BT

Construction/Opening: 1933

Architect/Builder: unknown/unknown

Current Owner: Cwm & Llantwit Welfare Hall & Institute Trustees

Current Use: Social Club

History/previous names & ownership

In 1932 a lease was granted to local men working in the mining industry for the purpose of erecting a welfare hall and institute. At the time there were restrictive covenants put in place in respect of the sale of intoxicants although during the 1950's these restrictions were removed.

Originally constructed as the Cwm & Llantwit Welfare Hall & Institute the building was opened in October 1933. Concerts, dances and even boxing matches took place there but in 1935 it became the Gaiety Cinema. The building had a 22 feet wide proscenium, an 11 feet deep stage and two dressing rooms. Seating was reduced to 416 seats by 1951. In 1960 the lease was surrendered and after a negotiation process between the National Coal Board, the Ministry for Education and the Miners' District Welfare Committee the freehold for the property was entrusted to the Welfare Hall and Institute trustees. Seating was further reduced by 1966, possibly to cater for the new lines of sight when Cinemascope was installed in the fifties when the proscenium was noted as being 30 feet wide containing a 26 feet by 11 feet 6 inches screen. The building had three dressing rooms by that time so it is possible that occasional variety shows had been introduced. The cinema ceased showing films around 1970 and today the building is a social club. Extracts from the 1968 Annual Report of the Coal Industry Social Welfare Organisation record that in that year work was carried out to adapt and improve the existing kitchen facilities.

Description

Located on the main road through the centre of Beddau there is little about the external appearance of the building that suggests it might contain an auditorium with a capacity of over 400. It is not quite of a domestic scale but neither is it grand or expressive of either its original function or its 25 years as a cinema. It has a simple layout and construction being rectangular with a pitched slate roof that wraps around the front elevation at the edges with a small hipped section of roof to frame the central bay and gable. The external walls are treated with a greying white textured render and all original window openings have been blocked up. The only features are the unusual exposed timbers to the top of the gable at the front and dressed quoins to the external corners. There is a simple cantilevered canopy over the main entrance supported on carved stone brackets. The building is approached through a small forecourt setting it back off the road slightly but on the building line of adjacent properties. The centrally located main entrance is several shallow steps above the forecourt level and it is not clear if disabled access is provided elsewhere to the building (although there is an obviously later addition of accommodation to one side providing the principal social club facilities). This building looks very tired indeed and presents itself more as already being closed than as being valued by its owners and the local community. The original hall is understood to remain relatively intact but it hasn't been used for many years and would probably require a major injection of both funding and enthusiasm to resurrect it for beneficial use.

Auditorium Capacity: Original: 420; 1951: 416:

Current unknown

Stage details: not available

The Judge's Hall, Tonypandy

Address: Bridge Street, Tonypandy CF40 2TU

Construction/Opening: 1909

Architect/Builder: unknown/unknown

Current Owner: Top Ten Holdings

Current Use: Bingo Hall

History/previous names & ownership

The Judges Hall was built in 1909 by Lieutenant Colonel Sir Rhys Williams at a cost of £6,000. It was opened on 23rd July 1909 by Queen Victoria's daughter, Princess Louise and the Duke of Argyll under the original name of The Judge Williams Memorial Hall. It was commemorated to Sir Rhys Williams' father, the late Judge Gwilym Williams.

The building was a gift to the residents of the area and boasted a 1,500 capacity concert hall with removable seating on stalls to enable major dance events to be held, as well as a library and billiard room. There were 2 large spaces below the concert hall – a meeting room and Lesser Hall. 4 orchestra and performer dressing rooms were provided below the stage. Over its history the hall has held dances, concerts and around 300 boxing events.

In 1961 the building was converted to a Bingo Hall and operated full-time Bingo use on two levels in the main auditorium with additional capacity in Lesser Hall in the basement. Some live events continued to be staged in the main hall up until the 1980's. The auditorium capacity was reduced to around 1000 as a result of the initial conversion. It has remained a bingo hall to this day.

As part of the conversion to bingo use some significant changes were made to the main hall auditorium. The original highly decorative 'night sky effect' ceiling was covered by a lay-in grid tiled suspended ceiling (although remains intact above the 'modern' ceiling), catering facilities were constructed in place of the original fixed tables and booth seating under the upper side balconies and the main hall stalls floor was re-fitted with purpose-built fixed bingo booths and tables.

Through the 1990's, the large basement rooms operated as an extremely successful drinking club with popular karaoke evenings. Around this time the original orchestra and performer dressing rooms below the stage were removed and replaced with cellars supporting the basement bar operation. The stage and original proscenium mouldings were also removed around this time.

In 1998 major works were carried out in several areas of the building including the closure of the original entrance door below the external name feature on the north west façade of the building (with construction of a management office in the area previously occupied by covered entrance steps), construction of a new extension to provide full wheelchair accessibility and draught protection to a new entrance providing access directly into the main hall from Trealaw Road, installation of a disabled WC, installation of new booths and fixed furniture on the main hall stalls floor, the removal of the original fixed wooden 'pew-style' bench seating from the upper balcony and their replacement with individual cinema style upholstered seats on the main part of the balcony and fixed bingo booths along both side balconies on two levels and significant redecoration of the whole venue. Around the same time the basement drinking club operation ceased trading and the rooms were left unused and derelict and remain unused.

The building has changed ownership several times in its life but records are not complete. Most recently it was purchased by Anstruther Properties Ltd and operated under lease by Planned Amusements until Top Ten Holdings acquired the freehold for Judges Hall and took over operation of the building from Planned Amusements in February 2005.

Major renovations to the building external walls were carried out in 2006 including repainting and replacement of the high level windows in the main hall and there is an ongoing process of maintaining the building in place.

Description

A large freestanding building adjacent the main road bypassing Tonypandy town centre and immediately adjacent the town's railway station, Judge's Hall is a landmark on the route up or down the Rhondda valley. The building is 3 storeys tall, with each storey height quite large so that the elevation facing the town is very tall, reaching from the platform of the railway station below in the cutting to the top of the balconied auditorium inside. The exterior is finished in rendered brickwork painted pinky-beige and the building has a complex pitched slate roof to accommodate the unusual footprint of the building below. There are high level windows to the two side elevations but the main front and rear elevations are blank. The main front elevation has a moulded inscription of the building's name and date of opening over the original location of the front doors painted a contrasting deep red.

The main entrance to the building is now located along Trealaw Street on the long side elevation and was created in the late 1990's to overcome accessibility issues and improve the weather resistance of the original fire exit doors in that location. Entry is straight into the stalls floor of the auditorium on the level and there is no foyer space of any kind.

A small circulation space remains where the original front entrance was, leading to audience toilets and stairs up to the auditorium balcony and down to the basement public rooms. The basement rooms have been mothballed and left un-used for over 10 years.

The auditorium retains many of its original features despite undergoing many changes over the last 100 years. It is a large rectangular room with one upper audience balcony and a high ceiling. The decorative wrought iron balcony front with its colourful floral pattern stands out as a wonderful evocation of the grand statement the original hall must have been. The auditorium was opened as a flat-floored space with removable seating such that dances and other events could be presented as well as concerts and it retains the flat floor now albeit with many fixed booths and tables serving the current Bingo operation covering it. The original stage has been removed along with the proscenium moulding features around and above the stage and the orchestra/performer dressing rooms below, but the stage recess remains and it would be relatively easy to assemble temporary staging in the recess and stage a live event. The original banquette seating and booths that filled the side spaces under the upper balconies have also been removed with the space now generally occupied by refreshment outlets.

The single balcony upstairs is split into two distinct sections both on the main body of the balcony and along both sides. Originally the seating on the balcony was on long wooden 'pew-style' benches but they too have been removed. Modern individual cinema style seats now occupy the main part of the balcony with booths and fixed bingo-playing tables on two levels down the side balconies. The doors at the front and rear of the balcony retain large parts of original moulded plaster architrave features. There are three large hardwood framed semi-circular windows to each side of the auditorium above the side balconies providing an excellent quality of light to the auditorium. The walls are painted in bright yellows and pinks over plastered very thick solid masonry and pink is the dominant colour in all of the upholstery and fixed furnishings. The original flamboyantly decorated ceiling is understood to still be in place but it was covered by a suspended lay-in grid tiled ceiling at some point to try to improve the thermal performance of the space. The original ceiling is said to be decorated to appear like the night sky and to have feature mouldings decorated to reflect light and sparkle. The floors are carpeted throughout the auditorium, presumably over original more robust finishes (in the circulation corridors and staircases around the auditorium original terrazzo floors have been retained). The building presents the operators with no heating or cooling issues and although there is no mechanical ventilation it is an extremely comfortable place to be in.

The building appears in general to be in extremely good condition and is clearly being well maintained. There are some signs of the ageing process accelerating (cracks in some floors and walls) but these are being addressed as and when the need arises. The future of this building appears secure based on a loyal local customer base showing signs of growth and extremely dedicated on-site management team giving appropriate priority to building maintenance issues. There may be a possibility to reinstate occasional live performances on temporary staging should demand from the audience be identified.

Auditorium Capacity:

Original capacity was around 1500 (comprising approximately 1000 at stalls level in a combination of loose seats and fixed banquette seating in booths under the side balconies and approximately 500 on continuous wooden pew-style benches on the upper balcony)

Current capacity is around 500 for Bingo.

Stage details: Not available (stage removed)

Theatre Royal, Tonypandy

Address: De Winton Street, Tonypandy CF40 2QU

Construction/Opening: 1892

Architect/Builder: unknown/unknown

Current Owner: unknown

Current Use: Retail/Leisure

History/previous names & ownership

The Theatre Royal was one of two variety theatres in Tonypandy, the other was the Empire Theatre. The Theatre Royal opened in 1892 in the Town Hall building and it is claimed that Charlie Chaplin once appeared there. It had an incredibly vibrant and highly decorated auditorium complete with two levels of audience boxes along the sides and an orchestra pit. Re-modelled in 1912, it was operated by Sam Duckworth & W.E. Willis and became the Royal Cinema. The Royal Cinema closed at the end of World War I in 1918 but it re-opened in 1922 under new owners. The Royal Cinema closed for the second time and permanently in 1959. At some point afterwards the building became known as the Town Hall once again (its original purpose?) and it is possible that it was used for local administration during the next 30 years although little is recorded about this period.

The Town Hall is still in existence but not in its former guise as a centre for live entertainment. The building was converted around 1990 into shop units on the ground floor (and presumably office accommodation on the upper floors) and is now only partially occupied by a snooker club and amusement arcade. It is not known if any of the original auditorium remains within the building.

Description

The Town Hall building is located at what appears to be the rather unfashionable end of the main commercial street running through the town but remains one of the most striking and dominant buildings in the town centre. It is an imposing chapel-like building with a grand frontage influenced by Classical architectural proportions. The main frontage is constructed of dark grey rubble stone with red brick used to create contrasting colour feature detailing around windows and at corners.

The main entrance is on the central axis of a high ground floor storey set deep into the wall under a shallow arch with 3 two-storey high arched windows above and a pediment with an ocular window at attic level now containing a contemporary metal louvre. The original split dedication of the building as The Town Hall dated 1892 remains.

The sides of the building have recessed panels with a grey render finish set between rubble stone 'pilasters' and containing regularly spaced small windows. At the rear (presumably where the stage was located) there are pairs of doors set on the central axis and reached from external steps. A metal gantry runs around the perimeter at third floor level, presumably to provide a means of escape from the upper levels of the auditorium within.

Although there is a small sign on the building identifying the occupier as a snooker and amusements club the building currently appears un-used and derelict.

Auditorium Capacity: unknown

Stage details: not available

Theatre Royal interior c 1905

Photograph: www.archive.rhondda-cynon-taf.gov.uk

Picture Theatre, Tonyrefail

Address: Collenna Road, Tonyrefail, Porth CF39 8EL

Construction/Opening: 1914

Architect/Builder: unknown/unknown

Current Owner: Mr Denis Lloyd – Triple Crown Bingo

Current Use: Bingo Hall (derelict)

History/previous names & ownership

The Picture Theatre opened in 1914 as a cinema/variety house. By 1937 it had become known as the New Cinema, with a seating capacity of 560 and it was operated under lease by W.R. Thomas of the Empire Theatre, Llanbradach. The proscenium was 18 feet wide.

By 1944 it had been re-named the Savoy Cinema and with seating given as 500, it continued under the management of Mr. Thomas. The Savoy also hosted a number of good concerts involving the Gentleman Songsters. Some very famous performers took part and one favourite was Max Java a world renowned violinist.

By 1947 it was managed by T. Williams who continued to operate it into at least 1954. The Savoy Cinema closed in 1969.

In 1983 the building was converted to a bingo hall and it operated as the independent Savoy Bingo Club until 2006-7. At that time the building was closed for major interior renovations but by the time the works were completed the customer base had disappeared and it has never re-opened.

In September 2010 the local authority planning department recommended approval of a Listed Building consent application for the conversion of the building from Bingo Hall to 8 (2 bed) residential units arranged over two floors, within the fabric of the existing building with associated parking for 6 vehicles. Part of the development proposals was the restoration and repair of the front façade of the existing building. In 2011 it was standing derelict and unused and subject to vandalism.

The former Picture Theatre was listed Grade II on 19th October 2000 due to its 'architectural and historical interest as an exceptionally rare example of an early cinema with a strong and prominent façade'.

Description

The hall is a prominent building, which occupies a plot on the junction of Collenna Road and School Street. Its front elevation is designed in a free classical style. The 3-bay facade is set at an angle to the auditorium, respecting the road layout, and slopes down from north to south, following the topography of the site. Large square pilasters divide and flank the bays. The facade is built upon a plinth of rusticated dressed stone.

The central bay is the widest and has a moulded round arched head and a moulded stringcourse at first floor level. The upper storey has a central flat-headed window with moulded sill, flanked by smaller narrower windows. The recessed entrance to the front elevation is located to the left hand side of the façade.

The side and rear elevations have a painted render finish, with 3 access doors and an escape stair being located to the southern elevation. At present there are currently no openings to the northern elevation, however it is known that in the 1970's there were a number of openings to this elevation, and it is understood that window reveals are visible inside the building.

Auditorium Capacity: 560 (1937), 500 (1944), current capacity unknown

Stage details: not available

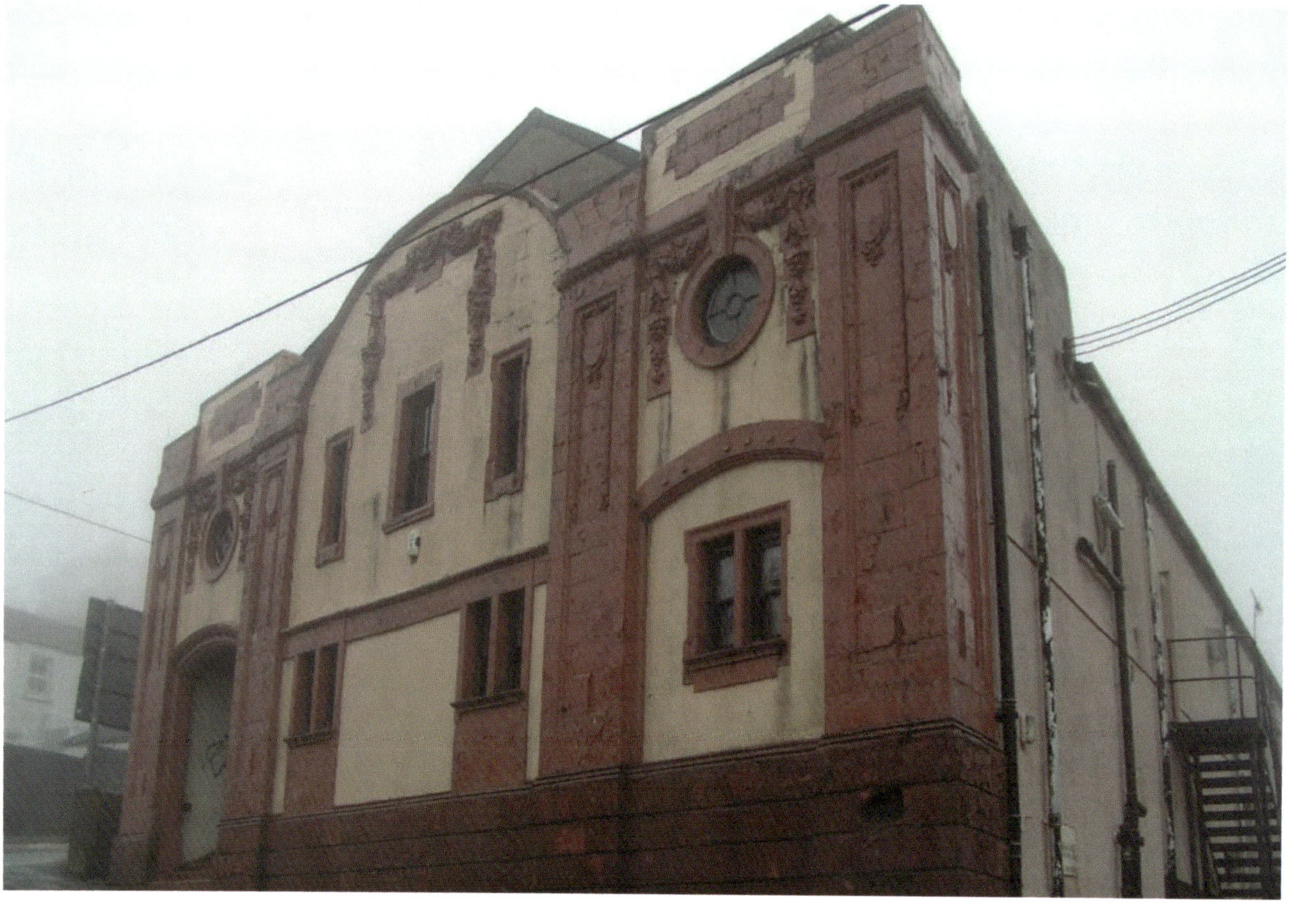

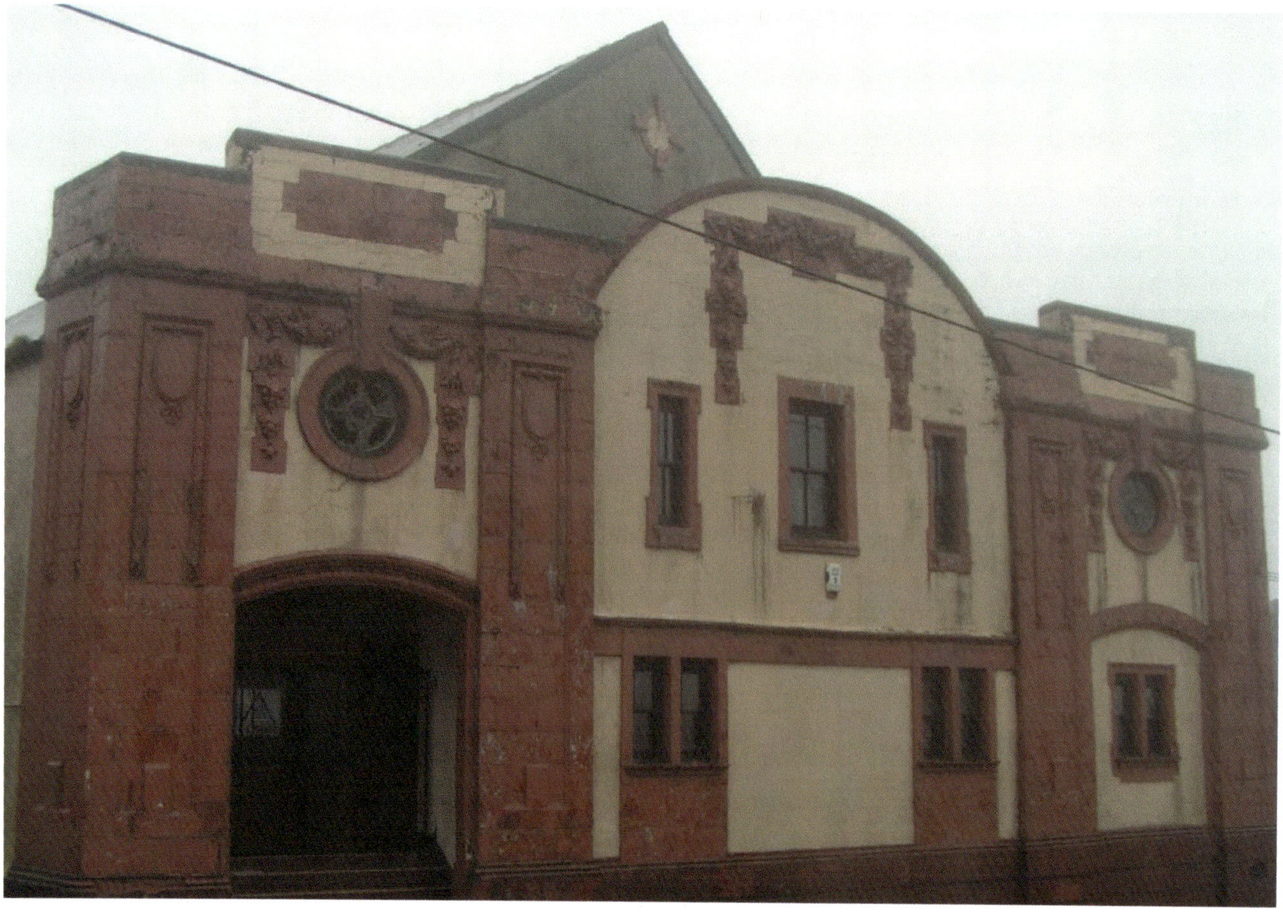

Cardiff

Cardiff
　　The Grand Theatre
　　Park Hall
　　The Philharmonic Hall
　　The Prince of Wales

The Grand Theatre, Cardiff

Address: 9 Westgate Street, Cardiff CF10 1DD

Construction/Opening: 1887

Architect: J P Jones and Waring & Son

Builder: unknown

Current Owner: J D Wetherspoon (Pub Company)

Current Use: Public House – The Gate Keeper

History/previous names & ownership

Originally planned as Day's New Grand Theatre of Varieties, the building opened as the Grand Theatre in 1887 although later had periods as a silent cinema. Adverts from the period show the top music hall stars of the time appeared there. In its early years it changed hands and operator frequently. From 1887 it was leased and managed by Harry Day until it was sold on to Clarence Sounes in 1895. It was sold on again to Edward Quigley in 1899. When the Empire was rebuilt in Queen Street by Frank Matcham in 1900 the Grand must have struggled as in 1904 it was advertised as the King's Theatre offering drama and was leased by a Mr Bateman. The name Palace next appeared then Palace and Hippodrome (together) as the Bioscope became a regular feature. In 1907 it was re-named Hippodrome Cinema by new owner Frank MacNaughton showing silent movies and from 1912, operated under lease by B H Ward with Douglas Watson as Manager, it was the Palace Cinema and then in 1913 became the Hippodrome Picture Palace. In March 1927 it became part of the Biocolour cinema circuit.

In the early 1930's when every available building in the city was showing films, including the New Theatre and Empire Theatre, short-lived attempts to resurrect the building used the Hippodrome name and there was also an attempt to revive "Variety" and another period as the "Kings". From press advertisements and comments it appears that some redecoration was undertaken but the venture did not prove successful particularly when several nearby cinemas were rebuilt with modern standards of comfort. The Grand closed as a theatre in 1932.

A plan was submitted by March 1939 to convert the site into a garage (bearing the names of the proprietors of the former Castle Cinema almost adjacent) and contained a copy of the original theatre design. The war intervened and the Ordnance Survey map of the time shows the site as derelict.

After the Second World War the building was substantially altered for use as a warehouse and very little of the theatre structure was incorporated into the warehouse building. After that it was used as an auction house. When the auctioneers relocated to a site with better access the building was acquired by the Wetherspoon pub chain in 2001. In this case there was very little, other than the frontage onto Westgate Street, to restore, so the "Gate Keeper" is a new-build pub, but retains external features from much earlier.

Description

It is quite difficult to imagine that this popular pub just across the road from the Millennium Stadium was ever a theatre as there remains no evidence whatsoever of that former use on the interior and the exterior bears no remnants of any theatre signage or other similar identification. Indeed perhaps it is remarkable that the façade survives given the number of opportunities there have been over the last 80 years or so for it to have been demolished.

The frontage is 4 storeys tall matching its neighbours with the lower two storeys probably most changed over the years. The upper two storeys has a rather elegant bowed central bay containing 3 large windows with stone pilasters and pediments, all supported on a large projecting cornice. The symmetrical pair of outer bays are less flamboyant but styled in a similar fashion with the pilaster capitals supporting nothing but a small and very plan horizontal solid balustrade parapet.

Auditorium Capacity: Original:1300

Stage details: Not available

Park Hall, Cardiff

Address: Park Place, Cardiff CF10 3AL

Construction/Opening: 1884

Architect: Habershon & Fawckner, London

Builder: unknown

Current Owner: Guoman Hotel Management (UK) Ltd

Current Use: Hotel

History/previous names & ownership

In the 1880's local businessmen built a large hotel and concert hall on the site of the Theatre Royal (destroyed by fire in 1877) for the then enormous cost of £40,000. The Hall could accommodate an audience of 2,000, and was used for concerts, meetings, religious services, exhibitions etc. It held a Cinematograph Licence from 1910 but regular use as a cinema did not begin until World War One, and then the hall was still in use for other purposes. It was equipped with a Willis concert organ which accompanied the film programmes, together with an orchestra.

In 1936 Architects I Jones and Percy Thomas of Cardiff were employed to redesign the hall and convert it to full-time cinema use. The flat floor was retained but the Victorian balcony was replaced and a new proscenium replaced the concert stage. The Willis organ was re-built and the console was placed on a lift. The new Park Hall Cinema had a grand opening by organist Edgar Lewis.

In 1954 the Park Hall Cinema became the first-run cinema for 20th Century Fox's CinemaScope features having installed a 37' screen and full stereo sound system as part of alterations again drawn up by Architect Percy Thomas. As it remained independent of the circuits, in later years the Park Hall Cinema struggled to book the best of the new releases and in 1964 took the bold step of rebuilding, internally, for Cinerama. Opening in late 1964 with the three-projector system and "How the West was Won", the Park Hall Cinerama showed almost all of the early Cinerama productions while other Cinerama Theatres were converting to "Single Lens Cinerama" (70mm).

The Park Hall closed as a cinema in 1971. After lying derelict and then being used as storage, the rear portion of the hall was demolished and the hotel car park was extended onto the site. The remainder of the building had windows introduced and bedrooms were added, with the main entrance foyer becoming commercial (retail) use. The Parc Hotel was listed Grade 2 on 25th June 1974. The site is now fully occupied by the Parc Hotel.

Description

The Parc Hotel is a landmark building on Queen Street. There are no signs anywhere in the building that until only 40 years ago it contained a very large auditorium.

The building is probably best described as typically Victorian in appearance, manifested in a French 'Hotel de Ville' style quite popular at the time yet it was (and is) incredibly ornate (and so records suggest, expensive). The modern shopfronts at ground floor level are much changed to suit developing tastes and fashions in retail design of course though retain the subdividing stone columns of the original building and the upper three storeys appear to be as original save perhaps for replacement windows and the corporate signage of the Hotel within.

The principal elevations are subdivided into 4 horizontal bands, largest at the base, with 2 roughly equal bands in the centre and a smaller band at the top. There are many windows, all with dressed stone features and two projecting curved bays on each side, at the centre of the composition and either side of the corner. The roof line is punctuated by myriad chimneys and rectangular roof turrets with a large 4 sided dome at the centre of the Queen Street frontage. Each of the roof turrets has dormer windows surrounded by classically inspired 'porticos' and pediments.

Auditorium Capacity:

Originally 2000, reduced to 1850 following conversion to full-time cinema

Stage details: Not available

The Concert Hall c 1920; Photograph: Cardiff Central Library

The Philharmonic Hall, Cardiff

Address: 76-77, St Mary Street, Cardiff CF10 1FA

Construction/Opening: 1877

Architect/Builder: Jackson & Son

Current Owner: Greenalls Brewery

Current Use: Night Club/Pub (derelict)

History/previous names & ownership

Originally opened as The Philharmonic Hall in 1877 over the years the building has housed various entertainments. The Hall was re-modelled in 1887 by James & Morgan Architects. In 1892 it was known as Stoll's "Panopticon" and it is known that from 1912 it was in the ownership of Moss Empires until 1916 when it was taken over and renamed The Panopticon by The Biocolour Picture Company Ltd. Alterations were made to the interior at this time and canopies added to the exterior to plans drawn up by Architect S Williams. In 1918 it reopened after the First World War as a full-time cinema called the Pavilion Picture Theatre, still owned and operated by the Biocolour Picture Company Ltd who carried out only minor alterations in 1919 drawn up by Architect J A Lawrence. In common with other cinemas the Pavilion also offered a soda-fountain, restaurant, and ballroom at various times.

Alteration work was carried out by new lessee ABC to plans by W. R. Glen dated December 1934 and mostly involved rearrangement of the upstairs seating, in particular in the front part of the balcony where stepping was improved as was the seat pitch. The best of the existing seating was moved downstairs where spacing was marginally improved. In a letter to the planning authority W. R. Glen gave details showing that the overall effect would be, Stalls 765 to 752, Balcony 326 to 308 "chairs", providing "greater comfort to patrons" and improved access to balcony stairways. Associated British Cinemas took over the operation around 1929 and for some years operated in conjunction with the Queens Cinema on Queen Street, moving the manager and orchestra to the Pavilion while sound was installed for the first Talkie (Singing Fool). The Queens and Pavilion became ABC's second string cinemas when the Olympia (also on Queen Street) was reconstructed and frequently showed the same programme. After being given up by ABC the management passed to Emery Cinemas in 1952 and advertisements reveal that most films were re-runs and occasional 75 minute cartoon shows. The interior retained many old features and no attempt was made to accommodate Cinemascope. When necessary the screen masking was lowered and the edges of the image were blanked off. At this time the audience capacity was 1100.

The Gala Company took over in 1962 and renamed the cinema and after some redecoration closed off the balcony and offered stalls seats at four prices for Continental films, art-house and many sword and sandal products from Italy. Capacity around this time was 1040. Closing as a cinema in 1968, inevitably Bingo eventually took over (in this case under the Coral Bingo brand) and it is thought that around this time the side balconies supported on steel columns were lost. The building was listed Grade II on 11th November 1980. It was being used as a Bingo Hall in 1989. After use as a Bingo Hall came to an end a major refurbishment took place restoring many of the features of the old building into which modern video screens were added within a "Music Hall" environment. For a time photographs were displayed in the foyer showing the building "before and after" refurbishment. Acoustic panelling and a reopened balcony were revealed. The building was purchased by the Greenalls Brewery in 1997 and converted to a Public House to designs by Inside Out Design Partnership. The building underwent external repair in 2008 but since April 2009 the building has not been in use and is available for lease.

Description

Of the four Victorian Theatres in Cardiff that have been converted to other uses over their lifetime, this is perhaps the saddest example, appearing today to be uncared for and ripe for redevelopment or loss. Apart from the ground floor the building appears to be little changed in appearance with the upper two storeys subdivided into large bays by stone pilasters, each containing a large window with an arched head and keystone. The proportions are slightly heavy and the detailing in brickwork rather plain. The ground floor has suffered from multiple changes of use and tastes but retains Doric style columns between the garish club entrances. The interior is understood to have been significantly altered throughout but the current entrance area and foyer was reconstructed during the last modifications to resemble the old building.

Perhaps the fact that the building is located in the heart of Cardiff's social district, surrounded by clubs, pubs and restaurants suggests that an operator will take advantage of its heritage and redevelop it once again in the near future but in the current economic climate its prospects look bleak and the envelope is already suffering the onslaught of natural deterioration.

Auditorium interior as Bingo Hall;

Photograph from Stagedoor's photostream; www.flickr.com

Auditorium Capacity:

Original capacity: unknown; 1933: 1091; 1934: 1060; 1952: 1100; 1962 1040; later capacities unknown

Stage details: Not available

The Prince of Wales, Cardiff

Address: 81-83 St Mary Street, Cardiff CF10 1FA

Construction/Opening: 1878

Architect: T Waring & Sons and W D Blessay

Builder: unknown

Current Owner: J D Wetherspoon (Pub Company)

Current Use: Public House – The Prince of Wales

History/previous names & ownership

The current building was built on the corner of St Mary Street and Wood Street for Edward Fletcher of The Cardiff Theatre Company in 1878 and opened as The New Theatre Royal. Ownership passed to Robert Redford in 1898 (who later went on to manage the New Theatre in Park Place) and when it was gutted by fire in 1899 it was completely rebuilt. It passed to R Redford Jnr in 1908 under lease from his father. The lease passed to Southern Theatres Ltd in 1912 and alterations to designs by Architect B Crewe changed the audience capacity to 2800.

In 1920 the auditorium was rebuilt and a new elevation to St Mary Street was created to designs by Wilmott & Smith Architects. The audience capacity was reduced to 1036 and it was renamed the Playhouse Theatre. The first incarnation of the Playhouse Theatre closed in 1925 but it reopened in 1927 still known as The Playhouse. In 1935 it was renamed the Prince of Wales Theatre and offered live theatre until 1957. The first performance by Welsh National Opera took place in the Prince of Wales Theatre on 15th April 1946 – a production of 'Cavalleria Rusticana'. Further alterations were carried out to plans drawn up by Architect E M Lawson in 1949 coinciding with a further change in ownership from The Prince of Wales Theatre to Theatre Properties (Cardiff) Ltd.

After closure as a Theatre in 1957 it operated as a cinema until 30th June 1984 when it closed after a period of renown as a cinema showing 'X-rated' films. The building was listed Grade II on 11th August 1960.

During the 1980s it underwent many changes of use and ownership. First it was converted to use as a Bingo Hall, then converted again to Caesar's Nightclub. In 1988 internal alterations were carried out to facilitate multiple uses including as a bargain store and laser game venue.

In 1999 it was purchased by the current owner, partially restored and converted to use as a Public House to designs by Laurence Tring, Architect. It opened as a pub (reputedly at the time the largest pub in the whole of Wales) on 21st July 1999 and continues in this use to date.

Description

The Prince of Wales stands in stark contrast to its neighbour The Philharmonic Hall as an excellent example of how conversion from theatre use to other activities can be achieved whilst retaining the character of the original and credit is due to the owner and Architect of the latest incarnation of the building for achieving this. The building is now firmly established as a landmark once again and the retention of so much of the original building appears to have enhanced its popularity.

The exterior retains the decorative features that survived all of the previous adaptations and the installation of extremely large feature windows into a pair of pointed-arch openings on Wood Street has opened up the building in a way the original architects could only dream of. Only the rendered solid panels at street level on this elevation are disappointing, however practical and robust.

The main entrance to the building is now firmly located under these two arches within the 'Victorian Gothic' styling but the building retains the smaller entrance off St Mary Street under a contrasting classical temple-like façade of cream stone with its recessed central bay containing a statue of a muse in a 'doorway' framed by fluted Doric columns surmounted by a shallow pediment.

Inside, many of the original features of the auditorium have been retained, including the balcony front and it truly is a 'theatrical' place to go for a drink.

Original auditorium interior

Photograph www.peoplescollectionwales.co.uk

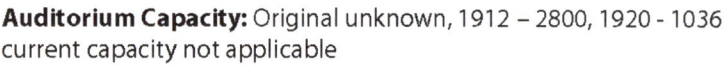

Auditorium Capacity: Original unknown, 1912 – 2800, 1920 - 1036 current capacity not applicable

Stage details:

Performance space – depth – 14.6m
Proscenium height/width – height unknown; width 7.92m
Orchestra pit (maximum no of players) - 16

Neath Port Talbot

Neath
The Empire

The Empire, Neath

Address: Ropewalk, Neath SA11 1AS

Construction/Opening: 1926

Architect/Builder: unknown/unknown

Current Owner: Top Ten Holdings Ltd

Current Use: Bingo Hall (derelict)

History/previous names & ownership

The building opened in October 1926 as The Empire with an audience capacity of 1300 on a large raked stalls floor and single upper balcony. Initially it had a programme policy of films and variety, although the stage was not large, it had a 25 feet wide proscenium opening. The building also contained a cafe and a dance hall. A Christie 2Manual/6Ranks theatre organ was installed in October 1931 and the console was on a lift. It was opened by organist Jack (Coutney) Taylor. The building underwent some refurbishment in the summer of 1935 and it was closed until November of that year. After the end of the Second World War the building was taken over and operated by South Wales Cinemas Ltd. of Swansea (Jackson Withers circuit) and was officially renamed The Empire Cinema.

In the early 1960s the building was sold and was converted into a bingo club, owned and operated by independent organisation and renamed The Empire Bingo Club. It continued to operate as an independent Club until 2005.

The original auditorium was destroyed by a major fire in the first half of the 1970s, with only the perimeter walls remaining standing. The building was rebuilt within the original shell, the raked stalls floor covered over with a suspended flat timber floor, the stage area significantly reduced to increase seating capacity at stalls for bingo and 2 balcony platforms constructed where the original balcony stood. The projection room remained but was concealed above a suspended tile ceiling. A large extension was constructed to contain emergency exits from the auditorium. Audience capacity (for bingo only) had now increased to 1500. Live music performances continued in the dance hall.

Major refurbishments were carried out in the building in both the 1980s and 1990s and the original dance hall was closed and converted into a Snooker Club finally bringing to an end the use of the building for live entertainment.

In 2005 the independent operator sold the building to Top Ten Holdings Ltd who continued to operate it as a Bingo Club until the impact of rising overheads and the reduction in attendances blamed on the ban on smoking in public buildings threatened the building with closure in September 2009. It continued operating however, until finally holding the last bingo session on February 14th 2010. The building was closed and placed on the open market for sale.

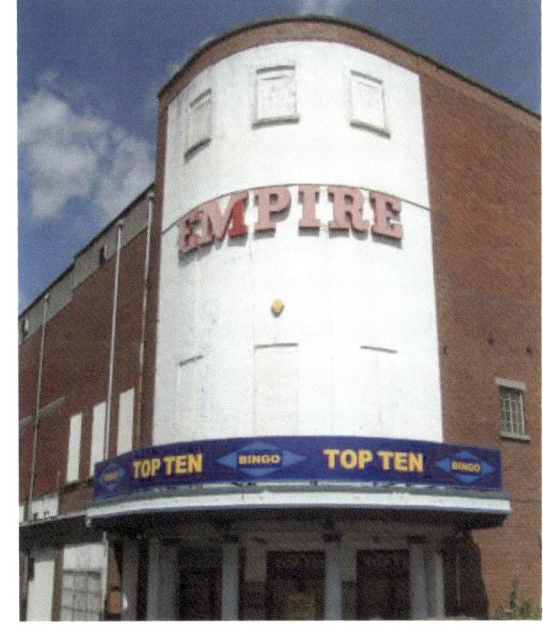

Description

This is an extremely large building located close to the commercial centre of the town but surrounded by residential streets (and its main entrance is constrained by the presence of 2 small cottages, the owners of which allegedly refused to sell their plots to the original developer of the Empire and thereby denying the building a much more prominent corner plot and entry).

The main front entrance strives to achieve a presence on the nearby main road as a towering 4 storey high curved form with the curve highlighted in white render and a large 'Empire' sign at high level. This form suggests that it may not be original and it may have been added in the mid 1930s upgrade works given its art deco influence.

The majority of the exterior is red brick with vestigial signs of storey height painted 'Empire' on both the rear and short end of the building (which face towards the town centre). The original separate entrance to the dance hall remains although is boarded up and hasn't been used for many years. It has highlighting features and mouldings to the sides and above that could have been quite grand in the building's heyday. To the rear of the building is a monstrous profiled metal sheet clad extension constructed after a serious fire destroyed the interior of the building in the early 1970s and providing emergency exit routes from the upper balcony and main floor of the auditorium within.

Entry is under the large curved wall through a bank of doors and into the foyer on the level. This must have been quite an impressive space in its original form and decoration but is now simply a space to pass through without pausing en route to the bingo hall. There is now a central ticket desk where surely there would have been open space originally and the whole experience of approaching the theatre is now fragmented. A grand stair with two separate flights rises to a single half landing and a large final flight up to the first floor and the stalls level of the auditorium. Disabled access is provided by the original pair of lifts, still retaining their inner metal folding grille leaf doors behind much later (fire safety induced) solid metal outer doors.

On the half landing of the stairs is one of the few surviving features from before the fire - a beautiful art deco inspired stained glass window of a maiden in a ballet tutu holding a theatrical mask which clearly confirms that this was a place of live entertainment as well as a cinema for most of its life. On the main foyer landing there are two other, smaller art deco stained glass windows though not so evocative in their content.

A ramp leads from pairs of doors on either side of the main axis of the auditorium up to the main floor of the room and the first impression it gives is of the sheer size and volume of the place. It is simply enormous inside and in its original form must have been even taller and more breathtaking.

The main floor is understood to have originally been gently sloping down towards the stage but is now flat throughout and bingo playing booths and tables are crammed in everywhere. There are refreshment sales points constructed within the volume along one side and access to toilets directly from the space. The original balcony disappeared in the fire and has been replaced by a pair of tiered or stepped plateaus with flat floors and again rammed full of bingo playing booths and tables.

The original roof and ceiling were lost in the fire too and now there is a horizontal, featureless suspended tiled ceiling throughout at a level below the floor of the projection room (which does still remain but is inaccessible).

The floors are carpeted throughout and the walls plain apart from a cornice frieze around the perimeter with a repeating stylised representation of the word Empire above festoons and some panels highlighted with perimeter mouldings.

There is a vestigial stage but purely there to provide a platform for bingo callers and understood to be much reduced from the original. The stage is curiously off-centre within the room as the 1970s addition of emergency exit stairs encroaches into the original room volume on house right. There are no dressing rooms remaining.

The building has been left empty and disused since February 2010 and is showing signs of distress with significant water ingress and mould growth over the seat upholstery and carpets throughout.

The building is currently on the market and expectations are that if sold it will be demolished and the site redeveloped, most likely for housing. The prospects for this building are very bleak indeed.

Auditorium Capacity: Original: 1300; current: unknown

Stage details: not available (stage removed)

Swansea

Swansea
The Albert Hall
Elysium Theatre
The Palace Theatre

The Albert Hall

Address: Cradock Street, Swansea SA1 3EP

Construction/Opening: 1864

Architect: Richard Richards, Swansea

Builder: unknown

Current Owner: Top Rank/Mecca Bingo

Current Use: Bingo Hall (derelict)

History/previous names & ownership

The Albert Hall opened on 19th May 1864 and was built as a concert hall and reading rooms at a cost of £4650 with an audience capacity said to be 2000. It had an orchestra and fine organ, which cost £600. The Albert Minor Hall, erected in 1881, cost £1500.

In 1914 it was screening C.W. Poole's great 'Myriorama' show. The frontage was re-furbished in 1920, including the relocating of the main entrance from its original location into the new foyer block. In 1922 it underwent an internal rebuilding and conversion to cinema use to the design of architect Charles Tamlin Ruthin of Swansea. From August 1922 it had re-opened as a full time cinema and was operated by South Wales Cinemas Ltd. A new foyer extension, façade and new canopy were added to the building in 1935. It was leased to Union Cinema from March 1937 and fully taken over by them in October 1937 (managed by Associated British Cinemas-ABC). From 1st October 1939 it was taken back by South Wales Cinemas Ltd. The Cardiff based firm of Jackson Withers took control from 1955 and they operated it until 1st November 1976 when they were taken over by the Rank Organisation. The Albert Hall was closed as a cinema on 3rd December 1977 with 'The Exorcist' as its last ever film presentation and it reopened in April 1978 as The Top Rank Bingo Club although had changed to the Mecca Bingo name before closing.

It was listed Grade II on 30th March 1987. In 1989 the main frontage of the building had been painted in red, brown and cream highlighting and emphasising the features on the elevation but some time during the subsequent 20 years the entire elevation was painted a single cream/off-white colour with minimal areas of a beige/light brown colour on the cornice and cill course.

The building closed its doors for the last time as a bingo hall on Saturday 31st March 2007 and it remains unused, derelict and for sale. Rumours about its future include conversion into apartments, retail units or reopening as a casino.

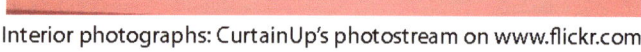
Interior photographs: CurtainUp's photostream on www.flickr.com

Description

Prominently sited on the corner with De La Beeche Street and just off the Kingsway in Swansea city centre, this is a very imposing building on Cradock Street. It has a wide and asymmetrical three storey rendered and painted frontage with an open pedimented bay to the right hand side over what was the main entrance into the building. The location of the original main entrance can be seen on the left hand side of the main front elevation blocked over and displaying evidence that poster boards occupied that space at some time. The upper storeys of the front elevation feature elegantly proportioned sash windows at first floor and blank panels at second floor between groups of pilasters. The long side elevation of the building along Cradock Street is not rendered and contrasts strongly with the classically influenced front. This wall is constructed from roughly finished stone set between dressed feature cornice course and window surrounds. There is a regular rhythm of windows at all three storeys on this side of the building and the classical cornice of the front elevation extends at eaves level along its entire length.

The original auditorium interior was apparently much like an old music hall with a very deep and steep circle with two 'arms' reaching towards the screen / stage. Photographs found on the internet of the interior prior to the closure of the building show how ornate the interior décor was and how the various alterations made to it over its life have affected it. Most noticeable of the changes are the removal of the original stepped raked stalls audience seating, installation of a balcony into the stage area and creation of a film projection booth within the depth of the circle balcony construction. There was also some extremely garish over-painting of the original feature mouldings and details on the walls and the ubiquitous bingo hall installation of a lay-in grid suspended ceiling with requisite recessed fluorescent light fittings under the circle. The original heavily moulded ceiling did however remain in place and exposed even after conversion to bingo use.

Auditorium Capacity:

Originally >2000, presume reduced on conversion to cinema in 1922 and to bingo use in 1978, current capacity unknown.

Stage details: not available

Elysium Theatre

Address: 204 High Street, Swansea SA1 1LG

Construction/Opening: 1914

Architect: Ward & Ward, London

Builder: unknown

Current Owner: unknown

Current Use: Bingo Hall (derelict)

History/previous names & ownership

The Elysium Theatre opened on 11th April 1914 in a building which was part used as the Dock Workers Hall. The Swansea docks were a major employer in the town during the early part of the twentieth century. Eventually the Dock Workers Hall became home to the Labour Party in Swansea and the party's local headquarters were located in the upper floors of the building. Also sharing the ground floor along High Street was a small shop which was occupied by a branch of W H Smith. There was a small stage for variety and the auditorium was capable of seating 900 in stalls and its circle gallery. The auditorium was equipped by Kalee one of the leading manufacturers of projection equipment at the time and they also supplied the cast iron seats. Although the building was designed from the outset as a moving picture house the auditorium also featured a medium sized stage and a full fly tower capable of handling backdrops and scenery. It became known as The Elysium Cinema from early in its life. The cinema remained open for the duration of the Second World War, during which Swansea was the target of heavy bombing by the Luftwaffe. Following the heaviest period of bombing known as 'the three day blitz' the Elysium was one of only two buildings left standing on High Street. After the war the town centre was redeveloped and audiences declined through the 1950's. It closed as a cinema in 1960. A few years later the Elysium was reopened as a Bingo club. The entrance lobby contained an amusements arcade with one armed bandits and other amusements machines and its ceiling was decorated with strips of coloured lighting. Behind this a small reception area led to the former stalls area in the auditorium where a two tier bingo hall was laid out complete with bar and fast food kitchen in the space below the stage. A suspended ceiling along the forward part of the auditorium cut the auditorium volume in half leaving the upper circle above the ceiling and disused. The shop on High Street had also been vacated by W H Smith and it reopened under new ownership as the Bingo Boutique. By the 1990's the bingo business was also declining, despite the installation of a modern electronic bingo system in the early 1980's and the Elysium closed its doors for the last time in 1994. The Dock Workers Hall declined too as working men's clubs became less popular and in its last few years it traded as a private members club called the Elysium until it also closed in 1998. Since then the whole of the building has been disused and boarded up. The City Council has attempted to intervene and find a new use for the building despite its private ownership and in 2006 they commissioned a consultants survey of the building and report on possible reuse, This survey caused some controversy when the council refused to release the findings while the building still sat empty. More recently the Swansea Housing Association/Coastal Housing Group announced a major project to develop an Urban Village on the upper part of High Street to regenerate the area where the Elysium stands. It is not known if the building is to be included in the plans or will be simply demolished to make way for the development.

Description

The Elysium is located in a high fronted Edwardian building 5 storeys tall at the top end of High Street just seconds away from the main railway station. The elevation is constructed of red brick with stone feature detailing and has a pair of faceted projecting bays either side of a central flat bay all with elegantly proportioned sash windows. The fifth storey is within the roof mansard and set back behind a stone balustrade. The sides of the building that are visible from the street are finished with untreated render. The theatre/cinema was entered from High Street through a large entrance on one side of the building with a shop to the other side. The original W H Smith & Son sign is retained above a far less elegant one for the 'Bingo Boutique' – the last occupant of this part of the building and next to one for the 'Labour Hall' which occupied the space underneath the Elysium. The auditorium volume is set back some distance from the entrance and is rotated slightly against the entrance axis to optimise the topography of the site in the building layout and construction (the site slopes steeply away from High Street to The Strand behind and below the building). The ground floor doors and windows are now boarded up and in a poor state but the upper floor windows appear to have survived over 10 years of dereliction without being subjected to vandalism.

Auditorium Capacity:

Originally 900, reduced on conversion to Bingo use in the early 1960's, current capacity unknown.

Stage details: Not available

Photograph: www.urbexforum.co.uk showing view to stage from balcony above ceiling installed over bingo operation in stalls

The Palace Theatre

Address: 156 High Street, Swansea SA1 1NE

Construction/Opening: 1888

Architect: Alfred Bucknall, Bucknall & Jennings, Swansea

Builder: unknown

Current Owner: messrs Paul and Christopher James

Current Use: Night Club (derelict)

History/previous names & ownership

Opened as The Pavilion Theatre on Christmas Eve 1888 the building was commissioned by the Swansea Improvements and Tramway Company and cost £10,000. It is probably the only music hall to have been built by a tramway company. When the company was formed in 1874 to construct tramways in the streets of Swansea, it was felt that building plots would have to be sold by the tramways company to defray the building of new roads housing the tramways. The economic climate of the time resulted in sales being too slow and an offer was made to the company by a Mr Almond to build a music hall in return for shares in the company. Such a prestigious development would raise land values in the area and prove a fitting addition to the new road now named Prince of Wales Road.

The quite early and extensive use of concrete in the floors and staircases at all levels led to the building being described as "absolutely fireproof", and safety from fire was one of the primary advertising claims when the building was first opened.

From 1890 to 1892 it was managed by Mr and Mrs Lafargue. The building was re-named New Empire Theatre in 1892 having been leased to Adelaide Stoll and her son Oswald, and hosted the city's first cinema show in 1896. It then became the Palace Theatre of Varieties in 1901 when Stoll relinquished the lease having opened the Empire in Oxford Street. At this time stars such as Charlie Chaplin, Lilly Langtry, Marie Lloyd and Dan Leno appeared on stage. For 2 years from 1902 it was managed by Lady Mansell and W L Hunt and from 1904 the lease was taken over by T W Graham.

In 1906 William Coutts became manager of the Palace and 'The Star' in Wind Street (later the Rialto Cinema) and The Palace re-opened as a house of 'legitimate' drama and films and was re-named 'Palace Bioscope'. By 1908, films were being screened as part of the variety bill and by 1912 it was a full-time cinema and was known as the Swansea Popular Picture Hall and Peoples Palace owned once again by Swansea Improvements and Tramways Ltd with William Coutts retained as Manager. In 1916 it was leased by South West Electric Theatres Ltd and managed by W G Christian.

By 1923 it had reverted back to live theatre again and took the name Palace Theatre of Varieties for a second time.

In 1932 it was wired for sound and gradually went back to full time cinema use. Renamed the New Palace Cinema by 1937, it became the Palace Cinema until around 1954 when it went back to live shows as the Palace Theatre. It managed to avoid the World War II "Swansea Blitz" which flattened much of the city's central district but In March 1949 it caught fire and the stage, dressing rooms and the stage end of the auditorium were destroyed when part of the roof fell in.

In 1952 it was restored, re-equipped and reopened by Maudie Edwards who intended to run repertory theatre in the building (transferred from the Swansea Grand) but that failed and it became the home of Swansea Little Theatre in 1954, operating the building under lease from its owners. At this time the projection room was used for the ice cream fridge but still had two sets of steel pipes set in the floor with bolts at the top to take the 3 legs of the projectors. There was a manager's flat at the back of the gallery, used for wardrobe. An original gas sun burner was still in the roof space to ventilate the hall. A very large motor generator set was in a room at ground floor level at the rear which must have powered the projector arcs. The basement under the building was used to store flats and props. The ground floor was a pub. Sir Anthony Hopkins made his first professional stage appearance here in 1960 when he starred in Have a Cigarette. Swansea Little Theatre moved out in 1961 when their lease expired and the building first became a bingo club from 1967, then by the 1970's a 'private' club.

The Palace Theatre was listed Grade II on 11th March 1980, amended on the 30th March 1987. It is thought to be one of just two Grade II listed purpose-built former music halls left standing in Britain. Closed again in 1991 it then became a nightclub from 1992, changing hands again during that year. The building was finally closed once more and placed on the open market in July 2007 and remains derelict.

Description

The building occupies a triangular island site bounded by High Street, Bethesda Street and Prince of Wales Road and follows the site footprint in its internal layout with the stage end being at the apex.

The building is a tall three-storey Baroque block with elevations of red Ebbw Vale brick and Bath stone dressings, slate roofs, a very prominent four-storey circular tower at the apex facing down High Street towards the City Centre (now without the original dome), and square towers with curved pavilion roofs to the five storey Bethesda Street elevation.

The building is in an advanced state of dereliction and there is protective fencing securing the building and preventing pedestrians from walking on the pavements around it. Large plants are growing behind the roof parapets and on ledges and openings and all of the windows are boarded or blocked up.

The auditorium stalls is at first floor level, leaving the ground floor to house shop units and offices. The concrete floor of the auditorium is supported by cast iron columns and steel cantilever beams. The stage is small and wedge shaped, suited for variety. Inside the auditorium there are two steeply raked upper balconies curving round close to proscenium without stage boxes, which have open iron balustrades, the upper balcony still retains its original bench seating. The main orchestra floor is now levelled for use as a dance-floor.

The orchestra pit and band room beneath the stage accommodated 30 musicians. Behind the stage was the green room. Also at this end the dressing rooms were situated at three levels in the round tower, which overlooks High street. The star dressing room was closest to the stage with the other acts occupying the others in order of prominence. At the corner of each dressing room was a triangular trap door under which a ladder went down to the next dressing room, providing a means of escape for artists in the event of a fire.

Auditorium Capacity: originally 893; 1889: 901; 1912: 1200; last known capacity approx 500

Stage details: Proscenium height/width – height 7.92m; width 8.53m

Interior photographs courtesy of Adam Slater

367

Powys

Abercrave

Miners' Welfare Hall

Miners' Welfare Hall, Abercrave

Address: Henneuadd Road, Abercrave SA9 1XA

Construction/Opening: 1937

Architect: Edward R. Griffiths, Swansea

Builder: unknown

Current Owner: unknown

Current Use: Working Men's Club and Community Hall

History/previous names & ownership

Originally a Miners' Institute, the front part of the building contained extensive institute offices, a billiards hall and reading room and opened on 27th October 1927. In 1937, the Welfare Hall and cinema was added at the rear, designed by architect Edward R. Griffiths of Swansea. Seating was provided for 430 in the stalls and 110 in the balcony. The proscenium was 34 feet wide, and it was used for cinema from the outset of its life. It was the first cinema in the area to install Cinemascope & stereophonic sound in 1953. The mid-positioned projection box had a side entrance as an emergency escape route. The Miners' Welfare Hall was closed as a cinema on 30th August 1962. Alterations were made to the building in 1963 and illuminated signs added to the exterior in 1964 to plans drawn up by Architects Jonah Arnold and Smith of Neath. The main alteration to the hall has been the levelling of the stalls area to provide a general purpose hall that can be used for a variety of purposes including formal dinners. The balcony is still as it was in the hall's cinema days. It was converted into a working men's club, and is little altered.

Description

This is an unusual Miners' Institute building insofar as it was built relatively late in the period when communities were creating such facilities and consequently has an appearance quite different from the vast majority of other, similar venues. The principal frontage has a kind of civic grandeur about it with its stripped-down classical influences and plain surfaces and it is certainly unique in this regard compared to the architecture elsewhere in the town. The main entrance is reached via a small elevated forecourt containing an old coal-truck and some exterior furniture and is announced in the architecture by paired plain pilasters either side, a large window at first floor level and '1937' inscribed on the panel between doors and window above. Two large curved bays project to either side containing more large windows with more pilasters at the corners of the building. The 'civic' appearance wraps around to both sides with more windows presumably serving the Institute rooms within and, on the northern side what appears to have been a separate entrance to the Hall. About halfway along the flanks (where the auditorium is located) the wall and general elevational treatment changes to a much more basic and more 'traditional' treatment of grey render and blank facades where the Hall was a later addition to the Institute at the front. The whole building has a pitched slate roof.

The main entrance leads into a small hall which in turn leads into the large rooms on either side now given over to licensed premises operation. The hall is at the rear and seems a bit incongruous in the context of a 'club' as it is so little changed and could easily return to use as a live entertainment venue. It seems a shame that its potential is not being realised. It retains a fixed stage with proscenium (although there is no stage equipment and the space is now simply an elevated 'annex' to the larger room) and the upper balcony (though this is not used). In many ways the hall is typical of its type (and therefore contradicts the appearance of the building exterior) insofar as it features a single curved vaulted ceiling, some ornate feature panelling on the walls and windows to one side allowing daylight in but with drapes to darken the room for evening events.

There is little to suggest that the building is not well supported by the community although some areas of the building fabric appear in need of some attention, and there is perhaps an opportunity to exploit these facilities more in the way that the Welfare at nearby Ystradgynlais has achieved, and particularly because the only other nearby venue is perhaps the Patti Theatre at Pen-y-Cae which does not regularly promote live entertainment.

Auditorium Capacity: Original: 540; current capacity: unknown

Stage details: not available

Interior photograph: www.ciswo-services.org.uk

Carmarthenshire

Garnant

Cwmmamman Workmen's Hall

Cwmamman Workmen's Hall, Garnant

Organisation: None

Address: Cwmamman Road, Garnant SA18 1NH

Construction/Opening: 1927

Architect: Gilbert H. Davies, Garnant

Builder: Mr. D. J. Thomas (Main Contractor), David Evans and Son, Brynamman and Mr. T. Bartholomew, Gwaun Cae Gurwen (Decorating subcontractors), Mr. James Fuller, Glanamman (Plumbing subcontractor), Birchgrove Steel Structural Co. (Steelwork subcontractor), Mr. Harry M. Fuller, Glanamman and Mr. Henson, Ammanford (auditorium furnishings supplier/subcontractors)

Current Owner: London-based Property Company (identity unknown)

Current Use: Leisure Centre/'Fun Factory' (derelict)

History/previous names & ownership

Cwmamman Institute was built as a Workmen's Hall with a large theatre auditorium in 1927. The Architect carried out the work free of charge except for payment of office and out of pocket expenses. On receiving payment for his work, the Main Contractor immediately donated £50 to the Workmen's Hall. It was opened on 19th February 1927 on land owned by the Amalgamated Anthracite Collieries Ltd, who agreed the leasehold on very favourable terms. This company was the owner of the Gellyceidrim Colliery at Glanamman.

The two commemorative stones built into the front wall are the best Sicilian Blue Marble with lead letters and cost £3 each. The main bulk of the money came from contributions made by the workmen of the community; mostly miners and tin plate workers who each donated 6d per month from their wages. A considerable contribution was also received from the Miners Welfare Committee; a body made up from an equal representation of colliery owners and workmen, who made a grant of £3,000 towards the building of the hall. The total cost of the project amounted to £11,607 7s 7d.

The stage, capable of holding a large choir or hosting any play likely to tour the area, measured 55 feet by 30 feet (Approximately 18m by 10m). Underneath were 6 dressing rooms and an instrument room. The orchestral stalls contained tip-up plush seats which could be removed to enable the space to be used as a dance floor.

The ground floor consisted of an entrance hall with pay box, whilst the 1st floor housed a mezzanine floor with refreshments room, manager's room, 2 large store rooms and a lounge which gave access to a balcony overlooking the main road at the front of the building. Above, there was a 2nd floor and a gallery. The building also contained heating apparatus, a ventilation system and electric lighting.

From its opening in 1927 to 1972 the building was commonly known locally as Hall Y Cwm although its official name was Cwmamman Workmen's Hall.

The Workmen's Hall closed in February 1972 and was left derelict and unused until it was purchased by Mr T. Wyn Jones, a local businessman, in 1982 who initially used it as a builders' merchant outlet. After carrying out renovation work to the building, Mr Jones opened the hall as a private leisure centre on 14th December 1985. The building was renamed Canolfan Hamdden Dyffryn Aman/ Amman Valley Leisure Centre.

Sometime later it became a "Fun Factory", where children had use of a soft play area with slides and climbing frames. It was closed and left derelict again sometime in the 1990's.

In 2007 it passed into the ownership of a London-based property company, was boarded up and left derelict.

In January 2009 the police discovered that the empty and boarded-up hall was being used as a drugs factory, when 5,000 marijuana plants were discovered in the building. A Notice was issued to the owners by Carmarthenshire County Council to make the building safe or demolish it. It is unclear whether there has been any response to this.

Description

Located on a very prominent site at a gentle curve in the main road through Garnant, the building has an imposing red brick frontage with first floor balcony extending over the full width of the pavement and providing shelter to the main entrance.

The central bay of the main front elevation is surmounted by a classical style pediment/gable and features an unusual semi-circular window with doors accessing the balcony at first floor level. Windows on the main front elevation suggest the many rooms supporting the original Workmens Hall (and Institute) functions were located here while the side elevations are clad in white boarding and contain few windows.

The building appears to follow the contours of the hillside with the auditorium stage presumed to be located at the lowest level and furthest from the road.

After so many interior alterations and use-changes and an unknown period of neglect and dereliction the prospects for the future of this large building appear bleak.

Auditorium Capacity:

Original seating capacity was 915, current capacity is unknown

Stage details: Not known (stage presumed removed)

Monmouthshire

Chepstow

The Palace Theatre

The Palace Theatre, Chepstow

Address: Bridge Street, Chepstow

Construction/Opening: 1914

Architect/Builder: unknown/unknown

Demolished: 1938

History/previous names & ownership

The Palace Theatre was opened around 1914, and was a small cine-variety theatre, which had an 18 feet wide proscenium. Audience capacity was 424. It was operated by Albany Ward, as one of the cinemas in his small chain.

The Albany Ward Circuit was taken over by Provincial Cinematograph Theatres (PCT) chain in the early 1920s. PCT were taken over by the Gaumont British Theatres chain in February 1929.

Gaumont British Theatres decided to build a new Gaumont Theatre in the town, using part of the Beaufort Hotel and Assembly Rooms site, and this was opened on 16th May 1938. The Palace Theatre was closed that same week, and was subsequently demolished.

Auditorium Capacity: 424

Stage details: not available

Newport

Newport

The Empire Theatre
Evans Concert Hall of Varieties
The Gaiety Theatre
The Little Theatre
The Lyceum Theatre
The New Theatre
The Prince of Wales
The Victoria Hall

Lyceum Theatre,
Newport, Mon.

The Empire Theatre, Newport

Address: Charles Street, Newport

Construction/Opening: 1899

Architect: Frank Matcham

Builder: John Linton, Newport

Demolished: 1942

History/previous names & ownership

The Empire Theatre on Charles Street and Talbot Lane, Newport, was built for Oswald Stoll and was managed by J. T. Tetlow on its opening on the 3rd of July 1899. The Theatre was built on the site of the former New Theatre also managed in its later years by Tetlow.

The ERA (a weekly newspaper about theatre, actors, music hall, and all related matters) reported on the opening of the Empire in their 8th of July 1899 issue saying:

'The long-looked-for reopening of this palatial palace of varieties came off amid much enthusiasm on Monday evening, and, judging by the interest taken in the affair, the new Empire bids fair to even outstrip the popularity of the old house, which was in many ways a most inconvenient structure. The new one is in all respects one of the finest places of amusement to be seen in the provinces.

The Empire Theatre. Painting by Victor Morgan, Newport
from www.website.lineone.net/~victor-morgan

The site of the former building has, of course, been utilised, but it has been greatly extended by the acquisition of six shops in Charles-street, so that the new hall extends from the Talbot Hotel to Talbot-lane. It has a frontage of 120ft. to Charles-street, with a return frontage of 80ft. to Talbot-lane. The façade is of St. Julian bricks with Bath stone dressings. It is ornamented with busts and designs representing Comedy and Drama, and niches with handsome vases, the central portion running up to a height of 70ft. For illuminating at night there are four arc electric lamps in front. Over the main entrance is an iron and stained glass shelter of pretty design, which lends attractiveness to the front by the large number of electric lamps fitted thereto.

The main vestibule has a handsome mosaic floor and walls, and the mahogany entrance doors have cut-glass panels. The grand staircase - a very wide one - gives easy access to the grand circle. In the foyer is a fine glass screen, and a striking architectural feature is the shape of a column supporting two arches. Immediately to the right is the grand circle waiting-room, 22ft. by 15ft., which is fitted with velvet lounges. Another short flight of stairs leads to a landing in which are more lounges. The crush-room has a beautiful fibrous plaster ceiling, and is covered with a Wilton carpet.

The circle itself has a fine broad sweep, and it might here be remarked that the hall, being built on the cantilever principle - there being only two columns (in the pit) in the whole house - a full and uninterrupted view of the stage is obtained from all parts. In the circle, which is carpeted in the finest Brussels, there are six rows of tip-up chairs, upholstered in terra-cotta velvet. The boxes are six in number, and over each is an electric lamp, and the fronts are richly draped. Brackets of electric lamps hang here and there along the front, the walls are of peacock green, and the circle has entrances and exits distinct from other parts of the house.

The entrance to the stalls is over the main approach. It has a waiting-room fitted with lounges, and richly carpeted, and, like the grand circle, has separate exits. The seating consists of tip-up chairs upholstered in velvet. The pit has a fine rake.

The orchestra is divided from the stalls by a mahogany railing of pretty design, having brass mountings and being prettily draped. Divided from the stalls by a stout barrier is the pit, to which access is gained through a separate door. It likewise possesses a waiting-room and three separate exits. The pit seats are also upholstered, and at the back is a commodious lounge. The entrance to the balcony and gallery is separate from those leading to other parts. The balcony has six rows of upholstered seats, and the floor is carpeted. Behind this is the gallery, which is as comfortable as one would desire.

The stage has an opening of 29ft., height of 29ft, and depth of 35ft., the height to grid being ,50ft., and any scene can he lifted bodily to the top and not rolled. Above the flies, at a height of another 20ft., is a glass dome on the roof. A fine asbestos fireproof curtain comes down flush with the proscenium uprights, and it has the advantage of a water-sprinkler at the top. All electric and gas lights have been protected so as to make an accident well-nigh impossible. Seven new sets of scenery have been specially painted by Messrs Fox and Barry, and the front of the fire-proof curtain is embellished with a fine representation of the rising sun. The heavy tableau curtains are of terra-cotta embroidered velvet, with hangings to match.

In the roof, immediately over the stalls, is a glass dome which gives ample light in the day time, and attached to this is a sliding roof to give additional ventilation at night. Another dome (a third in the building) surmounts the gallery. The ceiling surrounding the central dome is also dome-shaped, and is very handsomely decorated in gold of Oriental design with Oriental symbols of Music and the Arts. The cornices are in the same style, and the side walls are in harmony with the whole. On either side of the proscenium is a panel upon which are painted artistic figures.

Hydrants are provided in every part with complete appliances and automatic couplings. The electroliers are of handsome design, and in all parts of the hall the fittings are not only arranged with taste, but in such a way as to give added beauty to the decorations. The seating accommodation is for 2,500. '

The building was completely destroyed by fire in January 1942 – an electrical fault on stage suspected as the cause - and it was demolished soon afterwards.

Auditorium Capacity: 2500

Stage details: 29 feet wide by 35 feet deep

Evans Concert Hall of Varieties, Newport

Address: unknown

Construction/Opening: 1876

Architect/Builder: Mr Thomas, Newport

Demolished: unknown

History/previous names & ownership

Evans Concert Hall of Varieties was a Music Hall in business in Newport in the 1870s and run by Edward Evans. The Hall was destroyed by fire on the 11th of January 1876 but was rebuilt in the space of three months and then reopened on the 17th of April the same year. The ERA (a weekly newspaper about theatre, actors, music hall and all related matters that was published in London between 1837 and 1939) reported on the opening in their 23rd of April edition saying:

'On Monday last this new Concert hall was opened to the public, and an audience assembled that packed the building from floor to ceiling. When a few months ago the Hall which formerly occupied this site was gutted by a devastating fire, the Proprietor determined that the new Hall should be a building worthy the pretensions of a place of public amusement, and right well has he carried out such determination.

The Hall as it now stands is indeed a perfect little palace. The whole of the ground floor is filled with chairs, and is adapted to accomodate about 400 persons. On the next storey are the balconies and promenades, designed in horse-shoe shape, and fitted up with everything calculated to add to the ease and enjoyment of its patrons. Above this again is the large gallery, specially adapted for the "gods," and built to seat between 500 and 600. The sitting room afforded in the whole building is thus for about 1,400 persons.

The Hall is capitally lighted, the fittings are in blue and gold, and the tout ensemble is pleasing in the extreme. The painting and decorations (under the personal supervision of Mr W. H. Brown, of Hull) are of an elaborate nature, and reflect great credit upon his skill and judgment. The stage arrangements are very complete, and leave nothing to be desired. The Hall has been built by Mr Thomas, a Newport tradesman, and the cost has exceeded £2,000.'

Auditorium Capacity: 1400

Stage details: not available

The Gaiety Theatre, Newport

Address: Charles Street, Newport

Construction/Opening: 1870s

Architect/Builder: unknown/unknown

Demolished: 1887

History/previous names & ownership

The first theatre constructed on a site that subsequently became the New Theatre and then the Empire Palace.

Auditorium Capacity: unknown

Stage details: not available

The Little Theatre, Newport

Address: Dock Street, Newport

Construction as St James's Church 1814; **Opening** as Newport Little Theatre: 1937

Architect/Builder: unknown/unknown

Demolished: 1966

History/previous names & ownership

Newport Playgoers Society was founded in 1925 and from the origins of the Society there was a desire to create a theatre of their own. In 1933 a resolution was passed at the annual meeting of the Society calling on the Playgoers' Council to make investigations into securing a suitable site for a building. In 1936 the disused St James's Church on Dock Street was identified as a potential new home for the Company and with sufficient funds raised the building was purchased in that year.

In a report published in the Wales Argus of 7th January 1937 a description of the theatre stated:

'Some details of the theatre are surely exciting and interesting. There will be comfortable seating for about 450 people, which is considered the maximum audience desirable for such a theatre. The sightlines are excellent from every part of the interior. The players will have the joy of playing on a stage of ample proportions of 45 feet wide by 26 feet deep. An entirely new lighting and heating system has been installed, and an elaborate and thoroughly up-to-date system of stage lighting will afford ample scope for those experiments in lighting which are such an essential feature of modern theatrical productions. Refreshments will be available in the intervals in the Green Room, and there is full provision for the other necessary accommodation, such as dressing and rehearsal rooms. New settings can be comfortably constructed in a large room that has been alotted to the Stage Director. The Society, in fact, fully realise, the fundamental conditions for a succesful little theatre, which are, scope for players and producers and comfort for the audience.'

The conversion works carried out retained only the outer walls and windows of the original church building, transforming the interior completely by the installation of a large stage and an audience gallery. The plush red audience seats were purchased from the Savoy Theatre in London. The cost of the works was around £5-6,000. The Little Theatre was officially opened on January 11th 1937 with a performance of a costume comedy 'And So To Bed' and the Mayor of Newport officiating. In 1959 the Little Theatre was closed for during the summer and an ambitious programme of alterations and redecoration carried out. At the time, the President of the Playgoers, Alderman A.F. Dolman was quoted as saying 'By the time we have finished we shall have the best Little Theatre in England and Wales'. The works included the replacement of the original audience seats with 337 'modern ones in full bucket style' and upholstered in blue velvet. The new seats were also second hand but their origin is not recorded. They were said to be in very good condition. The reduction in seat number was intended to improve audience comfort and every seat was more than 6 inches wider than the original ones and the rows were more widely spaced improving legroom. The back rows of the stalls were raised on rostra and acoustic linings were introduced upstairs (including over one of the original windows) to reduce traffic noise ingress. The proscenium arch was redecorated in brown over what was reported to be a previous bright colour that some thought distracted from the plays on stage. The auditorium walls were painted cream and gargoyle figures surrounding the tops of the walls were highlighted in arctic blue (matching the ceiling). Beyond the auditorium, many other changes were also made. The Playgoers had by this time purchased 3 or 4 buildings between the church and Emlyn Street and whilst some parts were let out, they retained a three-storey building immediately next to the theatre which was converted to contain two rehearsal rooms each the same size as the main theatre stage. The Green Room was extended and redecorated and dressing rooms, workshops and wardrobe accommodation was renovated. kitchen facilities were improved so that catering could be done on a larger scale than before and additions were made to the stage equipment. The Little Theatre re-opened after these renovations on 13th October 1959 with a performance of Ben Levy's comedy 'The Rape of the Belt' and it continued to operate as a successful theatre until it was demolished in1966 as part of the wholesale re-development of Newport Town Centre. The Little Theatre Company (Newport Playgoers Society) moved to the newly constructed Dolman Theatre (named after the President of the Playgoers Society).

Auditorium Capacity: Original: 450, reduced to 337 in 1959

Stage details: 45' wide x 26' deep

Photographs courtesy of Newport Playgoers Society

The Lyceum Theatre, Newport

Address: 66, Bridge Street, Newport

Construction/Opening: 1897

Architect: W.G.R. Sprague, London

Builder: John Linton, Newport

Demolished: 1967

History/previous names & ownership

After fire destroyed the Victoria Hall a new theatre was built on the same site in 1897 by W.G.R. Sprague at a cost of £20,000 and named The Lyceum. The Lyceum Theatre was built by Mr. Councillor Linton for the Manager, Clarence Sounes, within the exterior walls of the former Victoria Theatre. The Lyceum was an elegant structure of Bath stone, in the Classic style with a pediment supported by 6 lofty columns. It was 150 feet long, 60 feet wide and 70 feet high. It was licensed as a theatre and boasted first-class companies appearing weekly throughout the season. The Theatre opened on Monday the 4th of October 1897 with a production of 'The Geisha'. The Lyceum's auditorium was designed in the Renaissance style in cream and gold, with draperies of peacock blue, and consisted of stalls and pit, dress circle, balcony, gallery, and boxes, and could accommodate some 1,250 people.

The ERA (a weekly newspaper about theatre, actors, music hall and all related matters that was published in London between 1837 and 1939) printed a report on the new Theatre in their 9th of October 1897 edition saying:

'Twelve months ago last May the old Victoria Theatre was completely gutted by a fire which broke out late at night, only the exterior walls and massive columns being left standing. For a considerable time negotiations for the erection of a new building proceeded, but ultimately the site and ruins of the old building were acquired by Mr Clarence Sounes, lessee and manager of the Grand Theatre, Cardiff; Queen's Theatre, Birmingham; and Theatre Royal, Aldershot. Mr Sounes determined from the outset that the new theatre should hold a place amongst the best in the kingdom, and he commissioned Mr W. R. Sprague, the well known theatrical architect, to prepare plans for a new building.

Upon examination, it was found that the walls and columns of the old building had not been weakened by the fire, and that they might therefore be used in the construction of the new building so that the handsome exterior of the old Victoria Theatre might be preserved. When the plans came before the Works Committee of the Newport Corporation, they were submitted to the borough engineer, who, after a thorough inspection of them and the ruins, recommended their adoption, subject to certain modifications, the chief of which was the erection of a retaining wall inside the walls then standing, with cross-stays, to prevent any danger of the old walls giving away. The plans were amended to meet the requirements of the borough engineer in this and other respects, and, finally, the contract for the new building was given to Mr John Linton, of Newport. The contractor took the building in hand only five months ago, and has now practically completed it. After removing the old ruins he had to excavate and underpin the walls, erect the retaining walls of sufficient strength to meet the Corporation's requirements, and then proceed with the construction of the theatre proper. From the day the work was commenced it has been continued without interruption, without difficulty, and without any accident of any sort.

The new theatre is a vast improvement upon the old one. The whole of the auditorium is constructed of iron and concrete, the only woodwork that could possibly burn being the doors, the fittings, and the seating, while the wood floors are laid upon solid coke breeze concrete. The stage has been so constructed that the chances of fire reaching the flies, scenery, &c., are very remote indeed, while, as an additional guard against the very improbable outbreak, a fireproof curtain, constructed of asbestos and iron, has been provided, which can be lowered in four seconds. In addition to this, the doors communicating with the auditorium and the stage are of solid iron, while the roof is of asphalt on concrete. The management has provided exceptionally ample means of egress. There are six exit doors from the stalls and pit alone, and special exits from the dress-circle, balcony, and gallery, while the stage itself has three separate exits. It is estimated that in case of a panic the building could be emptied in three or four minutes. The provision of fire hydrants has not been omitted, the building having been fitted throughout with this useful apparatus by Messrs Merryweather, of London.

The pit floor is some 2ft. below the level of the roadway, and the fall of the pit to the stage is about another 4ft., so that occupants of seats on the ground floor, on leaving the building, will ascend a few steps to the street, instead of descending a long flight as in the case of the old theatre. The arrangement of entrances, as in the case of everything else, differs from the old Victoria.

The entrances to the stalls, dress-circle, and balcony saloon are from Station-street, and to the pit and gallery from Bridge-street. There are three separate entrances from Station-street, over the chief of which is to be placed a graceful portico of iron and glass. From the ground level a flight of broad steps leads to the entrance vestibule, from which is entered the grand crush-room, the ceiling of which is panelled out and the whole decorated in most elaborate style. The dress circle is reached by two corridors from a marble staircase leading from the centre of this room, whilst the entrance to the stalls is on the right-hand side, and that to the balcony on the left. The dress circle and balcony saloon open out on to a large balcony over the portico, to be used as a smoking lounge. In addition to this, there is an outside promenade for smokers on the balcony overlooking Station-street, a balcony which existed in the case of the former theatre, but was never used.

The seating in the dress circle consists of tip-up chairs of mahogany and rich peacock blue cushions. At the back of the circle are six boxes with separate entrances from the promenade, at the rear of which is the refreshment bar. This bar is for the exclusive use of occupants of the boxes and circle, but the other parts of the house will have no cause for complaint, seeing that there is a separate bar on every floor for stalls, pit, and gallery. In addition to these, there are elaborately-fitted ladies' and gentlemen's lavatories on every floor.

From the level of the circle, a stairway leads to the floor on which are Mr Sounes's private office and other rooms. In addition to the six boxes at the rear of the dress-circle, there are two larger ones on either side of the proscenium. The orchestra stalls will be fitted in the same style as the dress-circle, and will have separate entrance and exit from the pit. The latter is most comfortably and conveniently arranged, and pittites in particular will be glad to learn that one of the most striking features of the auditorium is that it is built mainly on the cantilever principle, there being only two small iron columns in the whole of the interior. The top balcony, commonly called the gallery, will be found most accommodating and comfortable, and from every part commands a view of the stage. The decorations and fittings are on a handsome scale. The Renaissance style of decoration has been adopted throughout, the prevailing tints being cream and gold, while the large dome, which is 65ft. above the level of the pit, and has seven sunlight gas burners for emergency purposes, has been beautifully painted with Cupids representing the arts. The proscenium and balconies have also been finished with open scroll work and figures. All the draperies are of peacock blue, and the saloons and lounge are handsomely treated in a style similar to that of the crush-room, with rich ornamental and decorated ceilings, and the walls panelled out with silk tapestries and mirrors.

Although gas burners have been provided throughout the building, the theatre will be lighted by electricity. The chandeliers are of handsome design, and add to the attractive appearance of the interior. The building will be heated on the hot-water system. In the daytime ample light is supplied through large lanterns over the gallery and stage, and by means of lead light windows over the doors and in the walls, of decorative design. The old flight of iron steps, which formerly led to the stage, has been abolished, and in its place is a stone stairway, which will be used only as an exit from the dress-circle and balcony when necessary. The actors will reach the stage by means of a covered way running alongside, and on a level with, the pit floor. The stage itself is of great size, and will give ample room for extensive scenery and effects. It is no less than 72ft. in height. There are ten dressing-rooms for the use of the performers. Under the stage is the band-room, with accommodation for the players' instruments. The orchestra will be seated in a gap of considerable width between the footlights and the orchestra stalls, and will be on a level much lower than that on which the occupants of the stalls will be seated'.

Newport Operatic Society staged their operatic shows there once a year performing mainly Gilbert & Sullivan from 12th December 1921 to until 1936 They had a 2 year break when performances were presented at the Empire then returned to the Lyceum in 1948 continuing in an unbroken run until their final show in 1960. It was used as a cinema from the 1930's as well as staging live theatre. The Theatre was demolished in 1967 and an ABC cinema was built on the site to the designs of Architect C. J. Foster. The new cinema opened on 28th November 1968 and was originally a one screen cinema which could seat 1,320 people in a "stadium" auditorium. The screen was large even for the standards of the day; it was 58 feet wide by 27.6 feet high. The auditorium was converted to 3 screens in the 1970s utilizing the two outer projectors for the two smaller auditoria. It was closed as the ABC in 1999 and taken over by an independent operator and re-named City Cinema. The cinema was finally closed on 3rd April 2008 and work began immediately to convert the building into a hotel thereby ending the use of this site as a place of public entertainment after 142 years.

Auditorium Capacity: 1250

Stage details: Not available

The New Theatre, Newport

Address: Charles Street, Newport

Construction/Opening: 1888

Architect: W. Gardner

Builder: W. Blackburn, Newport

Demolished: 1898

History/previous names & ownership

The New Theatre, on Charles Street and Talbot Lane, Newport was built for David Humphreys, who had previously been running the Prince of Wales Theatre in 1881. The Theatre was opened on Monday the 27th of February 1888 with a production of the play 'Follies of the Day'. The Theatre's exterior was designed in the Renaissance style and the building was constructed on the site of the former Gaiety Theatre. The Newport Western Mail reported on the imminent opening of the New Theatre in their 20th of February 1888 edition saying:

'There is now rapidly approaching completion and the opening will take piece on February 27, a new theatre for the playgoers of Newport. The new structure has been built for Mr. D. E. Humphreys on the site of the old Gaiety Theatre in Charles-street and, when finished, will have a very imposing facade in the Renaissance style of architecture. The principal entrance, 22ft. in width, is situate in the centre of the block of buildings, facing the street. It has two fine door-ways opening into lofty and spacious vestibules that afford entrance for the audience to the stalls, pit, balcony, and gallery. There is a separate exit to the pit and an extra entrance to the gallery by means of two flights of stone steps, starting in the adjoining lane at a distance of 35ft. from the building. The stage entrance adjoins the Talbot Hotel, together with a passage 5ft. wide communicating with the stage and dressing-rooms. The entrances to the auditorium are exceptionally wide and spacious, giving 42ft. lineal of door opening. Adjoining the vestibules are the lobbies, forming entrances to the pit and stalls, and containing the stairs to the balcony and gallery, which are constructed with solid stone steps, 4ft. 10in. wide, in easy flights. It is hardly possible with such wide and well-balanced stairs and passages that the audience can ever be stopped for any length of time when leaving the house. There are, of course, the usual crush room, retiring-rooms, and lobby for balcony, office and ticket-box.

The theatre comprises four rows of stalls and a spacious pit on the street level; three rows of seats in the balcony, and ten rows in the gallery. The lines of these are arranged to give a clear and distinct view of the stage. A wide passage is constructed round the auditorium on each tier, giving access to both sides of the seats. The proscenium wail is built of masonry to the height of 3ft. 6in. above the stage roof. The opening is finished with pilasters and caps in two tiers, surmounted by a cornice and an enriched sofit in fibrous plaster, which is coated with asbestos fire-proof paint, and decorated in blue, white, and gold, on a pink ground. The fibrous plaster is virtually fire-proof, and is specified by the Metropolitan Board of Works as the covering for all iron and wood work in the public buildings under their control. It has also received the approval of the best architects of the day.

The ceiling over the stalls is domed in the centre, and finished with cornices and cartonpierre enrichments. A large gas sunlight is fixed under the crown of the dome for occasional use. Arrangements are made on a large scale for ventilation,, and places for retiring are provided for each tier. The stage has a more than usual width, and the cellar beneath is very lofty. The dressing-rooms are fitted up in the latest style and built entirely outside of the main walls of the theatre, adjoining the passage from the stage entrance. Wrought iron fire-proof doors are fixed in the openings from the auditorium to the stage and from the stage to the entrance passage.

The general tone of decoration is pink, white, blue, and gold. Rich colour will be derived from the curtain and coverings of the seats, which will be of crimson plush. A complete system of fire hydrants, supplied with water from the main, is fitted on the stage, and there is ample precaution its the other parts of the house. The electric light will be used for lighting the theatre throughout. Magnificent forest scenes and Landscapes are being painted for the opening by Mr. Wyatt, scenic artist of the Grand Theatre, Birmingham, who is generally admired for the truth and beauty of his colouring and that gradation of tone which so closely resembles Nature.'

Auditorium Capacity: unknown

Stage details: not available

Image www. arthurlloyd.co.uk/Newport

The Prince of Wales Theatre, Newport

Address: Charles Street, Newport

Construction/Opening: 1870s

Architect/Builder: unknown/unknown

Demolished: 1898

History/previous names & ownership

The Prince of Wales Theatre was run by Edward Evans in the late 1870s, Evans had previously been running his own music hall in Newport; Evans Concert Hall. It seems the Prince of Wales Theatre was sometimes run as a drama house and sometimes a Music Hall.

The Prince of Wales Theatre was later run by David Humphreys who spent a 'large sum of money' on improving and renovating the Theatre in June 1881. When Humphreys applied for the transfer of the licence from Edward Evans there was a lot of local opposition from the religious fraternity but the licence was nonetheless granted. The Theatre reopened under Humphreys management on Monday the 6th of June 1881 with the National Grand Opera Company's production of Donizetti's opera 'Lucrezia Borgia' and Dibdin's operetta 'The Waterman', both of which were well received.

David Humphreys would go on to run the New Theatre, Newport in 1888.

The Prince of Wales Theatre was demolished in 1898 to make way for the New Empire Palace.

Auditorium Capacity: unknown

Stage details: not available

The Victoria Hall, Newport

Address: Bridge Street, Newport

Construction/Opening: 1862

Architect: Habershon and Pite, London

Builder: H. P. Bolt

Demolished: 1896

History/previous names & ownership

In the early 1860's it was decided to build a public hall suitable to Newport's increased size and growing importance and Henry Pearce Bolt was engaged to do the job. He had lived in the town for a number of years having arrived from Devonshire as a working carpenter and had by his thrift and industry become a builder of some renown. By 1862 he had built the Victoria Hall at a cost of £12,000, a magnificent structure which was featured in the Illustrated London News of February 1st 1868.

The hall became the venue of all the great actors of the day and also served the town for large assemblies and official banquets. It was said to have a capacity of 3000.

The basement consisted of massive arched brick cellars; and on the ground floor was a large room used for the County Court and other purposes, a number of offices, well - arranged Turkish, Warm, and swimming baths, a gymnasium, and also a reading-room for the use of visitors to the baths. Above these was the Assembly Room, which was described as having 'noble proportions'. A gallery, constructed to hold a large number of people, ran round three sides of the hall, having four rows of seats on each side and twelve at the semicircular end. The gallery front was of a very elegant design; its ironwork, together with the columns supporting it, was cast at the Emlyn foundry. The ceiling, which was 42 ft. from the floor, was cored and enriched with cornices and trusses, and so designed as to render the acoustic properties perfect. The stage opened to the hall with a proscenium formed by an elliptical cornice and enriched frieze, supported on each side by handsome composite pilasters. At the other end of the hall was a commodious, lofty refreshment-room, and on one side were several small retiring-rooms.

In 1876, the manager of the time oversaw a 'complete metamorphosis' of the building. The stage was rebuilt and the wings repainted. The walls and ceilings were regilt and decorated. A pit, capable of holding 1,000, was created with 'magnificent' stalls covered with rich crimson velvet and fitted with spring seats. The floor was covered with a rich Brussels carpet. The building was re-named The Victoria Theatre when it re-opened.

A fire gutted the building on the night of May 27, 1896 and The Victoria Hall/Theatre was demolished to be replaced by The Lyceum.

Auditorium Capacity: 3000

Stage details: 43 feet by 30 feet

c:1874; www.newportpast.com/gallery

Torfaen

Pontypool
The Pavilion

The Pavilion, Pontypool

Address: Pontnewynydd, Pontypool

Construction/Opening: 1914

Architect/Builder: unknown/unknown

Demolished: 1990s

History/previous names & ownership

The Pavilion was opened on 27th April 1914 just before the outbreak of World War I. It featured musical comedies, dramas and pantomimes. During the 1920s when silent movies were introduced, an organ was housed on the left hand side of the circle for musical accompaniment.

In its heyday, the Pavilion played host to more than just movies, it was also a well equipped and impressive theatre, witnessing a series of high class concerts, especially during the Second World War.

The Pavilion continued to thrive after the war, and later formed part of the Pontypool Cinemas chain Ltd. The Pavilion ran its last film in 1968.

Within a month of closure as a cinema on the 10th October 1968, the Pavilion was reopened as a bingo hall under the operation of Top Rank Bingo. The circle area retained all its original cinema seating. Bingo finally ceased in 1989 when Top Rank moved out, leaving the building closed but intact with seating, bingo tables, carpets and drapes all inside.

An attempt was made to reopen the cinema by a local cinema operator in the early 90s, but the necessary funding for such a large undertaking did not become available, and the building become neglected and was finally demolished and the site redeveloped.

Auditorium Capacity: not known

Stage details: Not available

Caerphilly

Blackwood
 The Capitol
Llanbradach
 Workmen's Institute

The Capitol, Blackwood

Address: 8 Hall Street, Blackwood NP12 1NY

Construction/Opening: 1914

Architect/Builder: unknown/unknown

Demolished: 1980s

History/previous names & ownership

The Capitol started life as a theatre in 1914 although sometime afterwards it became an indoor market before conversion to a cinema in 1939. Originally the venue seated 900 with a vast auditorium comprising of stalls and balcony. There was a huge stage with dressing rooms and flytower. During conversion to a cinema the Capitol then seated 1200. The configuration of the venue had been changed considerably since its days as a theatre and market. Changes to the building for cinema use seemed awkward, in particular within the foyer areas. The screen was originally erected in front of the Proscenium arch with black masking top and no tabs. Evidence suggests that a change took place later where the screen was erected on the stage and tabs introduced. The balcony/circle was stadium style while the stalls were raked with long curved rows featuring aisles either side but no central aisle.

Above the main entrance to the cinema was a neon sign name in yellow and almost all other cinemas of the Jackson Withers circuit boasted yellow neon signage during the 1960's. The Jackson Withers circuit operated the Capitol Cinema in Blackwood during the sixties through to the seventies. It screened first run movies. This continued through to the summer of 1969 when it closed as a cinema and re-opened as a bingo hall.

Bingo wasn't a success and the venue closed again in July 1970, the cinema remained unused and derelict with all fixtures intact from its days as a cinema and bingo. During 1977 the local authority considered plans for conversion to a sports and leisure centre, this never took off and the building was demolished in the 1980s to make room for a small KwikSave store and car park, this has also since been demolished and the site is now home to the new law courts.

Photograph from v b brighton's photostream; www.flickr.com

Auditorium Capacity: original capacity 900; increased to 1200 on conversion to cinema in 1939

Stage details: not available

Workmen's Welfare Hall & Institute, Llanbradach

Address: High Street, Llanbradach

Construction/Opening: 1913

Architect: E. M. Bruce Vaughan, Cardiff

Builder: unknown

Demolished: 2000

History/previous names & ownership

The first Llanbradach Workmen's Institute in the 1900's was a timber and corrugated iron structure which had previously served as a village hall, school and religious meeting house. In 1910 a committee was set up to replace the structure with a new, purpose-built, stone building.

The new building was officially opened in 1913. Among the amenities available to the members were a billiards and snooker room, Hall, reading room and lending library. Before the Second World War the Hall was converted to full-time cinema use which was in operation by 1937. At this time the auditorium had 650 seats.

It remained active into the 1960's but it ceased functioning as a cinema around 1970. The hall continued in use for other purposes until about 2000. The site is now a car park.

Auditorium Capacity: original 900,

reduced to 650 on conversion to cinema 1937

Stage details: Not available

The Hall around time of opening. Photograph: www.localinfohistory.moonfruit.

Blaenau Gwent

Ebbw Vale
Central Hall
Tredegar
Workmen's Hall

Central Hall, Ebbw Vale

Address: Church Street, Ebbw Vale

Construction/Opening: not known (late 19th Century presumed)

Architect/Builder: unknown/unknown

Demolished: late 1980s

History/previous names & ownership

The Central Hall was built as a general assembly hall and also served as a venue for live entertainment.

In July 1903 the famous American showman Buffalo Bill brought his Wild West Show to South Wales and played various venues in the valleys, including the Central Hall. Charlie Chaplin also performed here and mentions the venue in his autobiography.

The building changed ownership some time afterwards and was re-opened as the Palace Cinema in 1912 during the cinema boom in the South Wales Valleys. It operated as a cinema for 40 years but closed during the late-1950's and remained derelict but standing for another 30 years. Local people would use the doorway to shelter from the rain while waiting for the bus.

The cinema featured posters for films showing at other cinemas in Ebbw Vale and Tredegar while it remained unused. Falling into disrepair the Palace Cinema was eventually demolished during the late-1980's and the area it stood on is now a landscaped grass area leading up to an housing estate that stood behind the cinema.

Photograph from v b brighton's photostream on www.flickr.com

Auditorium Capacity: unknown

Stage details: Not available

Workmen's Hall, Tredegar

Address: Morgan Street, Tredegar NP22 3ND

Construction/Opening: 1861

Architect: unknown

Builder: Mr David Roberts

Demolished: 1995

History/previous names & ownership

Originally constructed as a Temperance Hall, the building was built in 1860- 61. The Hall soon became popular as a centre for instruction and entertainment and in 1862 a large and very important eisteddfod was held there. 1866 saw the first performance of any Amateur Operatic Society formed in the town when it staged 'Harvest Storm' and in 1867 the first Dramatic Society in the town played 'The Maid of Genoa'.

In 1865 the Temperance Hall put on Poole's Myriorama, an early type of slide show. This consisted of full stage size paintings of various capitals of the world and other interesting sights on a roll. The roll, on rollers, was unwound slowly with differing lighting to create different effects. After about a dozen slides were shown, a variety artist would take the stage whilst another roll was set up. The hall was granted a full Cinematograph License by the local authority in 1909.

In 1911 the Tredegar Workmen's Institute was formed and they bought the Temperance Hall for £2000. In November 1916 the freehold of the building was purchased.

Within the Workmen's Hall was the spacious Lesser Hall, a public auditorium that was used for music concerts, amateur theatre productions and community shows as well as political speeches by many Worldwide Socialist politicians including the local MP, Aneurin Bevan. Much later, using the facilities offered World Snooker Champions Ray Reardon and Cliff Wilson crafted their skills here.

As cinema became a popular and affordable pastime in Britain and Wales the Lesser Hall exhibited films and was leased to a local exhibitor and showed silent movies.

In 1931 an extension was built to the Billiard Room providing seven tables instead of the original two and In 1936 extensive and costly alterations were made to the venue remodelling it into a modern cinema seating 800 people. At the side of the Hall a new extension was built to cater for the reading room and library. The Lesser Hall, to seat 200 people was constructed above the snooker hall. A dedicated lobby/foyer area was constructed while allowing a separate entrance to the remaining facilities of the hall. With exotic staircases in an Art Deco style lobby decorated in steel, glass and marble the lobby was a showpiece unlike any other Workmen's or Miners Institute Cinema.

The remodelled hall seated 800 with 300 in the newly constructed balcony and 500 in the newly designed stalls; plush, comfortable cinema seating was installed. Professional 35mm projection equipment was purchased through a grant as well as the best sound system that money could buy, later Cinemascope was also introduced.

The facade of the cinema dominated the street and either side of the modernistic entrance doors were large poster displays advertising the current or forthcoming attractions with stills from the films in display cases either side of the entrance. Above these entrance doors was a canopy lighting the stairs to the doorway while along the canopy was coloured neon lighting. Additional neon lighting decorated the facade that also featured a large neon sign spelling out 'WORKMEN'S HALL'.

In the 1960's a licensed bar with a large ballroom was opened above the library.

The last film was shown in The Workmen's Hall in 1981 and the Institute closed in 1982.

The Club was kept open by some local business people until during the 1990's, the venue roof was blown away in a storm following a number of years of neglect. In 1995 it was decided to demolish the Workmen's Hall and the site is now a car park.

Auditorium Capacity: Original: unknown; 1936 : 800

Stage details: Not available

Tredegar Temperance Hall c 1900. Photograph www.tredegar.co.uk

Tredegar Workmen's Hall auditorium interior; Photograph from v b brighton's photostream on www.flickr.com

Tredegar Workmen's Hall c1980; Photograph www.tredegar.co.uk/starlight

Merthyr Tydfil

Treharris
Workmen's Hall

Workmen's Hall, Treharris

Address: The Square, Treharris, Merthyr Tydfil CF46 5HE

Construction: 1891 - 93 **Opening:** 1893

Architect: F. R. Bates, Newport

Builder: Morgan & Roberts, Newport

Demolished: 2000

History/previous names & ownership

Treharris Workmen's Hall also known as Treharris Public Hall was built in 1891-93 and opened on Whit Monday May 22nd 1893. The funding of the building being paid by subscriptions from the miners employed at the nearby Deep Navigation and Ocean Collieries. Following the opening the Merthyr Express reported that the directors of the public hall company should be congratulated on having secured an handsome and commodious building, in return for their outlay. The final cost of the Public hall was around £3,300, and it included a Library, committee rooms and reading rooms. The library had over 1400 books, some in Welsh.

The building was a typical Workmen's' Hall design with two shops at its base, either side of the entrance and facing the square. In 1920 one shop unit was a grocery store and the other housed a branch of Barclays Bank. It was a community building and was used for great events, with huge crowds attending. Gaumont acquired the building and renamed it The Palace Cinema when they took over Provincial Cinematograph Theatres (PCT) in 1927. They quickly sold the venue and it was taken over and re-opened by an independent company in 1930. By 1937 it was known as the Palace Theatre, and had a 28 feet wide proscenium and a 20 feet deep stage. There were three dressing rooms. At that time the Palace Theatre was equipped with a cinema sound system and by 1954, an upgraded sound system had been fitted. By 1963, Cinemascope had been installed, with a screen within the original 28 feet wide proscenium. There were now four dressing rooms and an audience capacity of 750 seats and it had been renamed The Palace Cinema again. The building was closed by 1980 and it fell into disrepair with various operations sustaining it including as a Bingo hall, snooker club and even as an indoor market (for one week). During 1996, there were plans to try to save the building, by then under private ownership but demolition commenced on the 25th of January 2000.

The site is now a simple grassed over open space but it is understood that it has been acquired by the Merthyr Tydfil Housing Association who are proposing to construct flats on the site.

Photographs: www.treharrisdistrict.tech-hosts.co.uk

Auditorium Capacity:

originally >1000, last known 750 in 1963

Stage details: 13.1m wide x 5.79m deep

407

Rhondda Cynon Taff

Aberaman

The Grand Theatre

Abercynon

Workmen's Hall & Institute

Cilfynydd

Workmen's Hall

Ferndale

Workingmen's Hall and Institute

Maerdy

Workmen's Hall and Institute

Mountain Ash

Nixon's Workingmen's Institute Library and Public Hall

Pentre

The Lyceum Theatre

Tonypandy

The Empire Theatre

The Hippodrome

Ynyshir

Workmen's Hall and Institute

The Grand Theatre, Aberaman

Address: 171 Cardiff Road, Aberaman CF44 6RB

Construction: 1907 – 1909 **Opening:** 1909

Architect: Thomas Roderick & Son, Aberdare

Builder: John Morgan and Son

Demolished: 1994

History/previous names & ownership

Built as a Miner's Public Hall and Institute this building was more of a landmark than most. The movement to build a Public Hall and Institute in Aberaman began with a public meeting at Saron Chapel in 1892. However, following a number of setbacks, it was fully fifteen years later on 2nd October 1907 that the ceremony to lay the foundation stone took place. And it was not until 14th June 1909 that the hall was officially opened by Keir Hardie MP built for a cost of £7,500.

The hall was built on a site previously occupied by the Aberaman Reading Institute, chosen for its proximity to the commercial centre of Aberaman at Lewis Street.

When opened the hall could boast of an impressive list of facilities. The Institute was on the ground floor and contained a first-class library which almost all locals used. It had one of the best snooker halls in the whole of the valley comprising 2 Billiards Rooms, a first class reading room which contained all the daily newspapers and other magazines. It also provided 2 Games Rooms, Baths and a Swimming Pool in the basement; a Committee Room and a Reference Room and Lecture Hall on the Ground Floor.

On the first floor it had the main auditorium with seating for 1,800 people plus gallery on three sides of the room. The auditorium had a fully equipped stage - 6.4m (21ft) proscenium, 8.5m (28ft) depth and 11.9m (39ft) grid.

The theatre was altered on conversion to cinema use in 1930 - 1939 and at some point was named Poole's Palace. It later became a Bingo Hall. It suffered a major fire in 1972 and was completely destroyed by another fire on 30th October 1994. The site is now an open park.

Photograph: www.archive.rhondda-cynon-taf.gov.uk

Auditorium Capacity: 1800

Stage details:

Performance space – width – not known
Performance space – depth – 8.54m
Proscenium height/width – height not known; width 6.4m
Height from stage floor to grid – 12m

Workmen's Hall & Institute, Abercynon

Address: Mountain Ash Road, Abercynon CF45 4

Construction/Opening: 1904

Architect/Builder: unknown/unknown

Demolished: 1994

History/previous names & ownership

Built in 1904, the building contained a lending library, reading room, billiards hall and theatre which was also used as a cinema. It was the second largest hall in the South Wales coal field after the Parc & Dare in Treorchy.

In 1906 there was a miners' meeting addressed by Keir Hardie. The theatre was operating with cinema use prior to 1914. By 1929, it was the first cinema in the town to fit sound equipment and it became the Workmen's Hall Cinema. It had a 25 feet wide proscenium.

The Workmen's Hall went over to part time bingo and films in the early 1960's and later became a full time bingo club. It was demolished in 1994 and the site is now open parkland.

Auditorium Capacity: 1203

Stage details: not available

Photograph: Larry Stoter's photostream; www.flickr.com

Workmen's Hall, Cilfynydd

Address: Howell Street, Cilfynydd, Pontypridd CF37 4NR

Construction/Opening: 1890s

Architect/Builder: unknown/unknown

Demolished: 1988

History/previous names & ownership

The Workmen's Hall was paid for by subscription from miners at the Albion Colliery and throughout its life it served as an important meeting place and social centre within the community. The building was maintained by the miners themselves.

The building contained reading rooms and a library on the ground floor in addition to the Hall and dramas were performed on the stage every week during the 1950s. Cilfynydd & District Amateur Dramatic Society produced stage plays of the highest calibre, winning massive acclaim in the local press.

An annual subscription was also made by the council that meant that all of Cilfynydd's residents had access to the reading rooms.

When use for live entertainment reduced the building became a popular bingo hall until closing.

The prominent corner site in the centre of the village is now occupied by a Community Centre that was constructed in 1989.

Auditorium Capacity: not known

Photograph: www.archive.rhondda-cynon-taf.gov.uk

Stage details: Not available

Workingmen's Hall and Institute, Ferndale

Address: High Street, Ferndale CF43 4XX

Construction/Opening: 1907

Architect/Builder: T Richards, Pontypridd

Demolished: 1995

History/previous names & ownership

Built in a flamboyant Baroque style Ferndale Workmen's' Hall was completed at a cost of £12,000. It had seating for 1,000 and was one of the most expensive buildings of this type ever built in South Wales.

Around 1956 the building underwent significant reconstruction and conversion to full-time cinema use and its appearance was radically changed.

The building was demolished in 1995 and a doctor's surgery now stands on the site.

c.1956; Photographs: www.archive.rhondda-cynon-taf.gov.uk

Auditorium Capacity: originally 1000

Stage details: Not available

Workmen's Hall and Institute, Maerdy

Address: Ceridwen Street, Maerdy CF43 4DA

Construction/Opening: 1905

Architect: Edmund Williams

Builder: unknown

Demolished: 2009

History/previous names & ownership

The original hall was built in 1905 on the site of an old coffee tavern and reading room. The land was a gift from the landlords of the Maerdy estate to the workmen of the local collieries. The institute cost £9,000 to build and furnish. Accommodation was provided on three floors and included a lesser hall, billiards room and offices in the basement, with a women's reading room, men's reading room, library and refreshment room. The third floor had a large hall capable of holding 1,000 people.

In 1922 the building burnt down, killing its then treasurer, John Jones, whose body was found in the caretakers' cottage next door. A little more than two years later, in 1925, the institute was reopened, the miners having raised £20,000 for its rebuilding.

In 1934 the Miners' Welfare Fund gave a £900 grant to install a complete sound system for films and it was operated as a cinema throughout the inter-war years. It had closed for film presentations by 1980.

The building was finally closed in September 2001 and remained unused and derelict until in late October 2009 the last standing walls of the building were demolished. The site has been grassed over and remains undeveloped.

Photograph: Aberdare Blog's photostream; www.flickr.com

Auditorium Capacity: original capacity: 1000, capacity after 1925: 837

Stage details: Not available

Nixon's Workingmen's Institute Library and Public Hall, Mountain Ash

Address: Oxford Street, Mountain Ash CF45 3HD

Construction/Opening: 1898

Architect: Dan Lloyd, Aberbeeg

Builder: unknown

Demolished: 1995

History/previous names & ownership

In 1897 the trustees of Nixon's Workmen's Institute and Library signed a 998 year lease with the desire to erect an Institute building on the site. The theatre, opened as Nixon's Public Hall in 1898 was part of a very large and flamboyant Miners' Institute. It was erected at a cost of £8,000 funded by subscriptions paid by the miners who worked at the nearby Nixon's Navigation Colliery in Mountain Ash. It was the largest of all the Miner's Institutes built in South Wales with a theatre seating capacity of over 1,500 in its early years. It also accommodated a library with reading and lecture rooms also used for meetings, billiards and other games rooms and a gymnasium with a basement swimming pool 16.45 metres long (54ft).

The Institute rooms occupied the ground floor whilst the theatre (on two levels) was at 1st & 2nd floor level. The balcony front was notable for two reasons - firstly it was not returned to the stage wall but had a flight of steps down to stalls level culminating at the stage and secondly for its elaborate cast iron balcony front. The building was constructed in the typical Welsh welfare hall style of the 1890's using local stone and boasting some very attractive arched, gothic style windows. In the 1920's the trustees were also assigned recreational land, commonly known as Bryn Ifor Park, but this land was later transferred over to the local authority with restrictions upon use so that it could only be used for recreational purposes and not for site development. The bowling green and pavilion still bear the name of 'Nixons' to this day.

By 1937, the building had become known as the New Theatre and had been fitted with a British Acoustic sound system. Just after World War II, in around 1946, it was re-named the Workmen's Hall. In the mid-1950's, it was fitted with a more up to date sound system. The proscenium was 30 feet wide for Cinemascope, and the building was listed as having a cafe & dancehall attached. It closed as a cinema sometime after 1966 and then became a bingo hall. Around 1984 it was known as Rowes New Theatre. Common with a lot of these large buildings in the South Wales coalfield the costs to maintain and run this building grew too large and the parcel of land on which it stood was sold off in 1987. It was demolished in 1995 after a fire.

Photograph: www.archive.
rhondda-cynon-taf.gov.uk

Auditorium Capacity:

Original capacity 1500.

Stage details:

not available

The Lyceum Theatre, Pentre

Address: Llewellyn Street/Bridgend Square, Pentre CF41 7XW

Construction/Opening: 1902

Architect/Builder: unknown/unknown

Demolished: after 1977

History/previous names & ownership

The Lyceum Theatre opened in 1902 as a theatre but by 1910 was known as the Grand Theatre/Cinema.

The theatre closed in 1970 and was demolished after 1977. The site has been redeveloped and now accommodates a large block of flats.

Auditorium Capacity: Original unknown

Photograph c. 1977: www.archive.rhondda-cynon-taf.gov.uk

Stage details: not available

The Empire Theatre, Tonypandy

Address: 106/108 Dunraven Street, Tonypandy CF40 1AR

Construction/Opening: 1909

Architect/Builder: unknown/unknown

Demolished: mid-1970's

History/previous names & ownership

The Empire Theatre of Varieties was opened in 1909 and was originally built as a theatre. Up to the late 1950s it ran a mix of film and live theatre and indeed from the early days it was screening films as part of the variety programme on the 'Empirescope'. The Empire Theatre was the first in the town to fit sound equipment to screen talkies in 1929.

It was a Willis circuit cinema from at least 1937 and was operated as a flagship hall. It hosted the likes of George Formby, Robb Wilton, Harry Secombe, Gracie Fields, and also played a pivotal role in the early career of Ferndale film star Sir Stanley Baker.

It had closed as a cinema in 1963, and was used for bingo until the time of it closing. After demolition in the mid-1970's a new Woolworths store was constructed on the site and that has since been replaced by an Iceland supermarket.

Auditorium Capacity: not available

Photograph: www.peoplescollectionwales.co.uk

Stage details: not available

The Hippodrome, Tonypandy

Address: Dunraven Street, Tonypandy

Construction/Opening: 1895

Architect/Builder: unknown/unknown

Demolished: 1986

History/previous names & ownership

Opened in 1895 as Alexander's Circus on Pandy Field, the original building had an arena, boxes, stalls and a promenade. It was owned and operated by Ada Alexander in 1902 who leased it on to Jesse Burton in 1903 who employed Lily Marney as manager. It became The Hippodrome Cinema by 1909. The auditorium was at the rear of a terrace of shops, with flats above.

It was remodelled in 1912, to become a music hall and cinema (or cineariety theatre) and was operated under lease by Will Stone with Edgar Harper as Manager. The decoration in the auditorium was rather plain and it had one balcony. It had a 20 feet deep stage and a fully equipped, but rather low fly tower.

It was re-named New Hippodrome Cinema in the 1930's and around 1939 it was re-named the Plaza Cinema. It was closed by 1960 when it was operating as a second run cinema but after the town's Picturedrome Cinema closed in 1969, the Plaza Cinema was re-opened as a cinema under the ownership of the Willis circuit. It now had a seating capacity of 644, It was converted into a bingo club around 1976 but continued to show films.

The Plaza Cinema was closed on 28th July 1982, then was re-opened on 18th February 1983 for a 'trial period' after concern that the town would be without a cinema. This didn't work, and the Plaza Cinema finally closed in June 1983. It was then reconverted into a full time bingo club which continued through to 1986 when the building was demolished.

Photograph: www.archive.rhondda-cynon-taf.gov.uk

Auditorium Capacity: Original capacity 900, reduced to 644 in 1969, later capacities unknown

Stage details: Not available

Workmen's Hall and Institute, Ynyshir

Address: Ynyshir Road, Ynyshir CF39 0EN

Construction/Opening: 1905

Architect: E Williams, Cardiff

Builder: unknown

Demolished: 2006

History/previous names & ownership

The Ynyshir Standard Colliery Workmen's Hall and Institute was opened in 1905 and was built at a cost of £8,000. The Institute comprised a hall capable of holding 1,500 persons, a library and reading room, a reading committee, two billiard tables and a gymnasium

The auditorium was remodelled around 1930 (presumably to convert it to cinema use). In 1959 in the Ynyshir Cinema a film was showing that proved to have an ironic title in view of the fact that the building would catch fire during the screening. The film was about Zorro, and was titled 'The Flaming Arrow'.

In 2006 the Ynyshir Hall and Institute was demolished to make way for a new medical centre.

Auditorium Capacity: originally 1500   c.1910 Photograph: www.archive.rhondda-cynon-taf.gov.uk

Stage details: not available

Cardiff

Cardiff
Andrews Hall
The Empire Theatre
The Theatre Royal

Andrews Hall, Cardiff

Address: 67 Queen Street Cardiff CF10 4AT

Construction/Opening: 1898

Architect: E Webb

Builder: unknown

Demolished: 1999

History/previous names & ownership

A Planning Application for a new Public Hall on Queen Street was submitted by Architect E Webb on behalf of S Andrews and Son in 1896 followed by further applications in 1899 for balconies and approaches to the Hall and again in 1900 (by Teather & Wilson Architects) for a wrought iron and glass roof over the entrance. The Solomon Andrews Concert Hall opened in 1898 as a 2047 seat public hall. By March 1911, it had become known as the Olympia Picture Theatre. By the time talking pictures arrived in the early-1930's, it was known as the Olympia Cinema.

At this time the cinema was still run by the Andrews family of Cardiff (as Olympia Cardiff Ltd) until 1935 when it was leased to the Associated British Cinemas (ABC) chain. The cinema was substantially altered to plans drawn up by Architect Howard Williams, but still retaining its huge capacity in stalls and balcony of around 2,000. It remained known as the Olympia Cinema until at least 1956.

In 1955 the cinema was refitted to plans drawn up for ABC Ltd by Architect C J Foster and it was made-over for 70mm films on its huge 58 foot Cinemascope screen. Its name was formally changed to the ABC Cinema at this time. The prime location in the centre of the main shopping area in Cardiff made this a very busy cinema and long runs of films often played here.

The final film to show in the cinema was "Jaws", and after a three-month run of the film, the cinema closed in 1976 for conversion to a three-screen complex. After completion, Screen 1 in the original circle area seated 617, Screens 2 and 3 in the former stalls area seating 318 and 150, new projection rooms were also fitted to serve Screen 1 and a combined projection room was fitted to serve Screen 2 and 3, all equipped with Phillips projectors. The cinema was now known as the ABC Queen Street Cardiff.

In 1986 the cinema was re-named Cannon, and in 1991 re-named MGM, converting back to its original name of ABC in 1996. With the opening of the five-screen Capitol Odeon and the UCI multiplex in Cardiff Bay, and with plans for two further multiplexes in the city, ABC finally made the decision to close the cinema in 1999, the prime location making it more viable for other retail purposes.

The site on the North side of Queen Street, which included the former Odeon as well as the Olympia (ABC) was totally cleared, with the exception of the frontage of the former Andrews Buildings, which included the entrance to the Olympia, and the former office of architect H. Teather. A totally new retail development was built on the site, but where new frontages were included they are similar in size and slightly resemble the old buildings. The site is now occupied by a River Island clothing store which has incorporated the original Andrews Buildings entrance into its shop display.

Auditorium Capacity: originally 2047, reduced after conversion to 3-screen complex comprising 617 seat Screen 1, 318 Screen 2 and 150 seat Screen 3

Stage details: not known

Andrews Hall as The Olympia Cinema, 1956 Photograph v b brighton's photostream, www.flickr.com

The Empire Theatre, Cardiff

Address: 43-45 Queen Street, Cardiff CF10 2NG

Construction/Opening: 1887

Architect: T Waring

Builder: unknown

Demolished: 1962

History/previous names & ownership

The site in Queen Street had been a music hall since 1877, known as Levino's Hall. The poster for the Grand Opening of "Levino's Museum of Varieties" on November 7th 1887 reveals that the building had been "thoroughly remodelled and decorated" and describes many paintings and decorations and refers to Balcony, Gallery and Boxes. Drawings by architect T Waring dated October 1886 show the building to be let to "Professor Levino". Dolph and Henri Levino were "Crayon and Musical Artists" and "mesmerists". The Hall had theatre seating only in the first six rows and the balcony. Benches are shown on most of the ground floor (Pit) and on the entire large gallery.

In 1889 it became the first theatre to be operated by Oswald Stoll and it re-opened as the Empire Theatre on 30th September 1889. The first public exhibition of films in Cardiff took place in the Empire Theatre in 1895. Oswald Stoll employed the celebrated theatre architect Frank Matcham to re-build the theatre and it reopened in August 1896 as The Empire Palace of Varieties. During the rebuild in 1895/6 the "Empire" relocated to the Philharmonic Hall on St Mary Street. Fire destroyed most of this building on 30th October 1899 and again Frank Matcham was employed to re-build a new Empire Theatre. After the fire the recently completed Andrews Hall, a few yards away, was home to the Empire during the reconstruction. The theatre re-opened on 29th September 1900 as the Empire Palace Theatre and had a seating capacity of 1,726. The press preview report of the 1900 re-opening reveals that lessons had been learnt from the disastrous fire the previous year as steel and concrete were used as the principal building materials with safety curtains and shutters to isolate the stage from the auditorium. Cherry red was the main internal colour instead of peacock blue.

In 1915 more rebuilding work was carried out, this time by noted theatre architects W. & T.R. Milburn and seating capacity was increased to 2,820. It operated as a major theatre on the Moss Empires theatre circuit for all its early life. By 1918 The Empire was being used, in part at least, for film exhibition. The Empire Theatre was purchased by Gaumont British Theatres Corporation and they equipped it and made alterations to convert into a cinema to plans prepared again by Architects W & TR Milburn, with provision being retained for live shows. It re-opened on 7th September 1931. Live shows ran exclusively during September and October 1932. It closed in June 1933 for extensive alterations to be carried out (to plans by Architects W E Trent with W & T R Milburn) which involved the remodelling of the foyer and circle, and new audience seating by Turners of Birmingham was also fitted. It re-opened in August 1933 as a Cine-Variety Theatre. A Compton 3Manual/10Ranks theatre organ was installed and it was opened by Fredric Bayco.

A neon sign installation was carried out in 1950 by messrs Ionlite Ltd and in 1953 further alterations were made to plans drawn up by Architects I Jones & J Bishop. The Gaumont name was adopted in 1954 when the theatre/cinema was programmed by the Rank Organisation a new widescreen installation was completed. At this time the cinema was usually receiving the second release of films behind the larger Capitol Cinema located further along Queen Street. Much of the internal decoration survived from earlier times and to cope with the very high projection box the screen had to be designed to slope backwards to reduce "keystoning". As audiences dwindled Rank debated which of their three cinemas to close and eventually selected the Gaumont, closing it on 30th December 1961. Live shows which had been ideally suited to the Gaumont's large stage and backstage facilities were relocated to the Capitol where there were some stage facilities but larger seating capacity. The Empire was finally demolished in 1962 and a new building for the now-defunct C&A clothing business was built with a large ballroom in the basement initially bearing the "Top Rank" name. This has now been demolished and replaced by a new building for the clothing chain Primark.

Auditorium Capacity: original capacity unknown; 1726 in 1900; 2820 in 1915; capacity following alterations in 1931, 1933 and 1953 not known

Stage details: not available

c 1901; Photograph Cardiff County Library

Photograph www. arthurlloyd.co.uk

The Theatre Royal, Cardiff

Address: Park Place, Cardiff CF10 3AL

Construction/Opening: 1826

Architect/Builder: unknown/unknown

Demolished: 1877

History/previous names & ownership

The first purpose built theatre in Cardiff, the Theatre Royal, opened in 1826, on the site of what is now the Parc Hotel. The Theatre Royal was destroyed by fire in 1877 and replaced by Park Hall around 10 years later.

Auditorium Capacity: Original: unknown

Stage details: Not available

Bridgend

Bridgend
   The Drill Hall
Maesteg
   New Theatre
Ogmore Vale
   Workmen's Hall & Institute

Drill Hall, Bridgend

Address: Derwen Road, Bridgend CF31 1LH

Construction/Opening: 1890's

Architect/Builder: unknown/unknown

Demolished: 1975

History/previous names & ownership

Located in Bridgend Town Centre this building began its life as a Drill Hall and at the turn of the 20th century was operated as the Eberley Olympic Theatre & Skating Rink. In November 1910 it re-opened as the Electric Picture Palace with 800 seats. By 1914 it was re-named Palace Cinema.

The Palace Cinema was enlarged in around 1936 and the seating capacity increased to 850. In 1938 it was enlarged again, this time to accommodate 1,324 seats. Cinemascope was fitted in 1956 and the proscenium was 33 feet wide.

There are records of exhibitions in the 1950s, '60s and '70s in 1969 at the Old Drill Hall in Derwen Road as part of the Bridgend Festival and again as part of the town's own festivals.

The Palace Cinema was closed by Bridgend Cinemas Ltd. in 1960, and was converted into a bingo club. By 1975, the bingo club had moved to newly built premises and the former Palace Cinema was shuttered. It was later demolished and the Tabernacle Church was built on the site.

c 1977; Photograph: www.bridgend.gov.uk/english/library/localphotos

Auditorium Capacity: 800 in 1910, 850 in 1936, 1324 in 1938

Stage details: Not available

New Theatre, Maesteg

Address: 7 Commercial Street, Maesteg, CF34 9DF

Construction/Opening: 1914

Architect/Builder: unknown/unknown

Demolished: 2010/11

History/previous names & ownership

The New Theatre was built in 1914, and converted to full-time cinema use in the early 1920's, continuing to operate as an independent cinema into the 1950's. After closing as a cinema it was converted to a Bingo Hall operated by Dunraven Leisure Ltd and at some point New Theatre Family Leisure. Most recently the building was operating as a furniture shop under names including Simply Home Furnishings and Happy Furnishings.

Planning permission was granted in September 2008 for the conversion of the building from furniture store to a Wetherspoons pub but those plans were abandoned early in 2009 due to the excessive cost of the restoration works required as conditions of the planning approval and of conversion to a viable public house.

The theatre was destroyed by fire on Monday, 13th December 2010 and it is anticipated that what remains will be demolished and the site cleared for redevelopment.

The New Theatre entrance. Photograph www.ejhales.co.uk

View to stage from balcony after fire December 2010. Photograph courtesy of The Theatres Trust

Auditorium Capacity: unknown

Stage details: Not available

Workmen's Hall & Institute, Ogmore Vale

Address: Commercial Street, Ogmore Vale CF32 7BL

Construction: 1908-1910 **Opening:** 1910

Architect/Builder: unknown/unknown

Demolished: 1983

History/previous names & ownership

The land on which this building stood was donated by Mr. Blandy Jenkins of Llanharan in 1895 and he also gave £100 towards the cost of construction, a sum then matched by the Ocean Colliery Company.

The Hall and Institute was built in 1908 - 09 and was financed by subscription from the pay of the working men, mainly colliers, though it is known that the Nantymoel Industrial Co-operative Society workers also contributed to the fund, as did King Edward VII. There was a foundation laying ceremony on 22nd September 1908 and one of the three foundation stones was laid by Charles Burt, the oldest workman in the Aber colliery. It opened for business in 1910 though it wasn't officially opened until 1912 and it immediately laid claim to being one of the finest workingmens' halls in South Wales.

In the 1950's film shows were presented in this building and there is a suggestion that local people referred to it as "The Lymp", that being an abbreviation for Olympic (or Olympia) Cinema. It may have been used as a cinema from soon after opening. For some time before its collapse it was used as a bingo hall.

On the 11th March 1981 the main hall collapsed into the River Ogmore which had eroded its foundations. The tower was left standing but had to be demolished soon afterwards because it was unsafe. The demolition work was completed in October 1983 and the site was redeveloped. Since November 1987 the site has been occupied by a doctors' surgery.

Photograph of demolition; Dylan Roberts, www.peoplescollectionwales.co.uk

Auditorium Capacity: unknown

Stage details: Not available

Photograph c.1955: www.images.francisfrith.com

Photograph c.1964: www.images.francisfrith.com

Neath Port Talbot

Aberavon
Vint's Palace Theatre
Briton Ferry
Public Hall Cinema & Institute
Cwmllynfell
Miners' Welfare Hall
Glynneath
New Theatre
Pontardulais
Tivoli Theatre
Port Talbot
Empire Theatre
Grand Theatre
Seven Sisters
Welfare Hall

Vint's Palace Theatre, Aberavon

Address: Water Street, Aberavon

Construction/Opening: 1910/11

Architect/Builder: unknown/unknown

Demolished: 1972

History/previous names & ownership

The Palace Theatre was opened as a live theatre by Leon Vint in around 1910-11, and from opening it was equipped to screen films and was the local cinema in Aberavon. By 1922, it was operated by Max Corne and renamed The Palace Cinema until it closed in 1944.

The building was converted to a David Evans furniture store to plans by Architect Jonah Arnold and Smith of Neath in 1949 and it continued in that use for many years.

The former Palace Theatre and Cinema was demolished in 1972.

Auditorium Capacity: unknown

Photograph : www.stephenquick.co.uk

Stage details: Not available

Public Hall Cinema & Institute, Briton Ferry

Address: Neath Road, Briton Ferry, Neath SA11 2AX

Construction/Opening: 1911

Architect/Builder: unknown/unknown

Demolished: 1962

History/previous names & ownership

The Public Hall opened in 1911. Some films were screened in the early days, but it didn't begin operating as a full time cinema until 1931 when it was known as "The People's Own Picture Palace". It was closed as a cinema in 1937.

The building continued as a Public Hall and often presented amateur productions on its stage. The Briton Ferry Musical Theatre Company first performed in this theatre in January 1949 and continued to make it their home until just before it was demolished in 1962. A car dealership/garage was built on the site.

Photographs : www.swanseasgrand.co.uk

Auditorium Capacity: unknown

Stage details: Not available

Miners' Welfare Hall, Cwmllynfell

Address: Gwilym Road, Cwmllynfell SA9 2GH

Construction/Opening: 1934

Architect: E.D. Jones, Pontardawe

Builder: unknown

Demolished: 2001

History/previous names & ownership

The Miners' Welfare Hall opened 4th September 1934 and it was constructed at a cost of £9,404. The Welfare Institute building was financed by a deduction of 6d a week from the pay packets of the miners at the local collieries.

It was a large four story building, with an auditorium and balcony capable of seating over 600 people, a minor hall, four committee rooms, snooker room, a kitchen and three smaller rooms, it hosted every type of village activity over a period of 66 years supported by a series of volunteer management committees.

The auditorium had seating installed in stalls and circle levels. Cinema projection equipment and a screen and RCA sound system were installed in November 1935. The projection box was located at the very top of the hall with the projectors being steeply angled. Typical of the silent and inflammable film era, the box had an exit door that opened onto a balcony to facilitate rapid escapes in the case of fire. At the right hand side of the balcony was an iron ladder that could be used to reach ground level in an emergency.

Live shows were also staged. It lasted as a full-time cinema until 1967, when part time bingo was introduced, and dances were held on Wednesday evenings. This mixed use policy lasted until 1970, when the building was closed.

By the late 1990's, it became apparent that the reinforced concrete building, although structurally sound, could not be cured of damp; its heating and plumbing systems could no longer cope and the hall could not meet the demands of modern fire regulations. Eventually, at a public meeting held on11th November 1997 it was agreed by an overwhelming consensus that on economic, community and environmental grounds the old hall should be demolished.

It was demolished in May 2001, and a new community hall was built on the site opening on 7th May 2002.

Auditorium Capacity: 629

Stage details: Not available

New Theatre, Glynneath

Address: Park Avenue, Glynneath

Construction/Opening: unknown

Architect/Builder: unknown/unknown

Demolished: 1970/>1993??

History/previous names & ownership

Originally built as a Miner's Welfare Hall, the money that paid for the building was contributed from the miners wages towards a fund to build the hall and later to maintain it. The hall had a snooker room & library on the ground floor and an auditorium on the upper floor.

By 1937 it was operating as the New Theatre, it had a 22 feet wide proscenium, a 20 feet deep stage and three dressing rooms. Then by 1944, it had been re-named Glynn-neath Theatre and this name continued to be used until around 1954, when it became the New Theatre again.

It was a second run and independently operated hall and cinema, and it was largely destroyed by fire on Friday night 1st May 1970. It was demolished sometime after 1993.

Auditorium Capacity: 600 seats

c. 1993. Photograph: bigal1940's photostream; www.flickr.com

Stage details: Not available

Vint's Palace Theatre, Aberavon

Address: Water Street, Aberavon

Construction/Opening: 1910/11

Architect/Builder: unknown/unknown

Demolished: 1972

History/previous names & ownership

The Palace Theatre was opened as a live theatre by Leon Vint in around 1910-11, and from opening it was equipped to screen films and was the local cinema in Aberavon. By 1922, it was operated by Max Corne and renamed The Palace Cinema until it closed in 1944.

The building was converted to a David Evans furniture store to plans by Architect Jonah Arnold and Smith of Neath in 1949 and it continued in that use for many years.

The former Palace Theatre and Cinema was demolished in 1972.

Auditorium Capacity: unknown

Photograph : www.stephenquick.co.uk

Stage details: Not available

Empire Theatre, Port Talbot

Address: Royal Buildings, Talbot Road, Port Talbot SA13 1DN

Construction/Opening: 1887

Architect/Builder: unknown/unknown

Demolished: main auditorium demolished after fire 1936

History/previous names & ownership

The theatre was part of the Royal Buildings, a complex unlike any of the buildings of old Port Talbot in its architecture. The Royal Buildings are currently used for retail and commercial operations but are largely empty. The imposing Italianate restrained neoclassical style, with its three massive stone pediments and highest quality brickwork, is highly distinctive and typifies late Victorian tastes in commercial and public buildings.

In any event, the structure is very rare, as the only remaining vestige of a Victorian music hall, the Empire Theatre, once located at the rear, which was reached through the central arcade entrance of Royal Buildings - the original walls of the theatre form part of the adjacent Empire Buildings.

The main auditorium disappeared after a major fire in 1936 when it was being used for cinema under the name 'New Empire Theatre' but it is understood that the original stage and backstage areas survive within the complex of buildings remaining on the site.

A Planning Application was submitted in late 2009 by Coastal Housing to demolish the Royal and Empire Buildings and replace them with a mixed use residential and commercial development to plans drawn by Architect W Griffiths of Swansea. The plans were approved in February 2010 but no works have been carried out yet as there has been growing demand from the local community to preserve the Victorian buildings.

Photograph : www.smphoto.co.uk

Auditorium Capacity: Not known

Stage details: Not available

Grand Theatre, Port Talbot

Address: High Street, Port Talbot

Construction/Opening: 1908

Architect/Builder: unknown/unknown

Demolished: after 1972

History/previous names & ownership

Located on the corner of High Street and Forge Road, The Grand Theatre (also known as the Grand Cinema) was built in 1908, and was constructed at the rear of an existing building, with the entrance through a former shop front. It was enlarged in the 1920's when it had an audience capacity of 1100 seats.

The Grand was used as a cinema until at least 1944, but by 1947 it was known only as the Grand Theatre and was operated by Woodward Cinemas. Its last operators were the Portavon Cinema Co. Ltd., from around 1954. It never fitted Cinemascope, and was closed in the mid-1950's.

The Grand Theatre was converted into a bingo club in 1963 but this operation closed in 1972, and the building was demolished in a redevelopment of the area making way for a shopping centre.

Auditorium Capacity: 1100

Stage details: Not available

Welfare Hall, Seven Sisters

Address: Martyns Avenue, Seven Sisters, Neath

Construction/Opening: 1914

Architect/Builder: unknown/unknown

Demolished: 2001

History/previous names & ownership

The hall was built in 1914 by Evan Evans Bevan, a local coal mine proprietor. The building consisted of a brick built auditorium with a rendered front and a small metal canopy over the entrance. It had a 20 feet wide proscenium and a 14 feet deep stage, with two dressing rooms and became known as the "Palace."

It was used for community gatherings and for travelling drama shows and from 1916 it showed films. It was purchased by the local Miner's Welfare Association in 1926 which became the Seven Sisters Miners' Welfare Society. Soon after this it was officially renamed the Palace Cinema and then by 1937 it was re-named again and was known as the Welfare Hall Cinema. The Society later established a children's playing field, a football field and in 1935 the construction of an outdoor swimming pool. The Society was taken over by the National Coal Board on nationalisation in 1947.

Cinemascope was fitted in the 1950's and extracts from the 1968 Annual Report of the Coal Industry Social Welfare Organisation state that Work to provide licensed premises was completed at Seven SIsters Welfare Association in that year.

The Welfare Hall Cinema was closed in the early 1970's and by 1978 it had fallen into a state of disrepair. It was demolished in 2001.

Auditorium Capacity: unknown

Photograph : www.oldukphotos.com/wales

Stage details: Not available

Swansea

Swansea
    The Empire Theatre
    The Star Theatre
    The Theatre Royal

The Empire Theatre, Swansea

Address: Oxford Street, Swansea

Construction/Opening: 1899

Architect/Builder: unknown/unknown

Demolished: 1960

History/previous names & ownership

Built for Oswald Stoll as a replacement for his Empire Theatre in High Street (later renamed the Palace), The Empire Theatre in Oxford Street opened on December 10th 1899 and was a large building dominating the middle of Oxford Street. It was the second Empire Theatre to be opened by Oswald Stoll, the first being the Empire Theatre, Cardiff. It has been described as being very beautiful inside and was the first public building in Swansea to be lit by electricity from the Corporation Power Station in the Strand.

It screened films just after the war and The Empire was widely considered the premier entertainment venue in Swansea until it closed in 1957 when Moss Empires Ltd. decided to down size their operation on the huge variety circuit around the UK. The Empire Theatre was demolished in 1960 and a Primark store now stands on the site.

Photograph c1899: www.swanseaheritage.net

Auditorium Capacity: 1200

Stage details: Not available

The Star Theatre, Swansea

Address: 40-41 Wind Street, Swansea

Construction/Opening: 1873

Architect/Builder: unknown/unknown

Demolished: 1968

History/previous names & ownership

Before construction of the Star Theatre (also known as The Theatre and Star Opera House) a circus and Music Hall and prior to that a public house stood on the site.

Andrew Melville Robbins (1853-1896) father of The Melville brothers, theatre impresarios, was born in Swansea, where he became proprietor of The Star Theatre in Wind Street. Andrew moved to Birmingham in 1894, by which time he owned the building and renamed it The New Theatre. On his father's death in 1896 Andrew Jnr looked after the Theatre. He was aged just fifteen. Andrew Jnr later returned to his studies, and a full time manager was appointed. His two older brothers eventually sold the Swansea Star Theatre and it became a silent movie cinema house.

Rather than simply having a face-lift in the 1930's, the building was totally demolished and rebuilt - opening in 1932 as the Rialto Cinema and it operated as a full-time cinema until its closure in 1958 and demolition ten years later.

Photograph c. 1905:

www.swanseasgrand.co.uk

Auditorium Capacity: 3000

Stage details: not available

The Theatre Royal, Swansea

Address: Bank Street (later renamed Temple Street), Swansea

Construction/Opening: 1806

Architect: C. J. Phipps

Builder: unknown

Demolished: 1898

History/previous names & ownership

George Haynes (1745-1830), entrepreneur, pottery manufacturer, banker, and newspaper proprietor was involved in the construction of this theatre. The Swansea bank Haynes, Day, Haynes & Lawrence acted as Treasurer to the Swansea Tontine which was formed in 1805 to build the Theatre Royal, with Haynes as one of its promoters and its Secretary. The Theatre Royal opened in 1807 on the corner of Bank Street (later renamed Temple Street).

The first pantomime staged in Swansea was presented at the Theatre Royal in 1809 – a production of 'Mother Goose'. Andrew Cherry (1769 – 1812) was the first manager of the theatre and a well-known London theatre star. After his death the theatre spent a lot of time dark save for the occasional visiting touring group or private hire. In 1858 John Chute managed the theatre

Following the demolition of the theatre the site was redeveloped as the new David Evans department store. It remained in use as the store until it was again demolished in April 2007. The site is now an up market apartment block with retail use on the ground floor.

Auditorium Capacity: 800

Photograph: www.swanseasgrand.co.uk

Stage details: not available

Carmarthenshire

Ammanford
   White's Palace
Gwaun Cae Gurwen
   Workmen's Hall
Llanelli
   The Royalty Theatre

White's Palace, Ammanford

Address: The Arcade, Ammanford

Construction/Opening: 1914

Architect: possibly Henry Herbert

Builder: unknown

Demolished: 1978

History/previous names & ownership

Opened in 1914, just prior to the commencement of World War I. White's Palace, also known as The Palace Cinema was a silent movie house, which also had music hall acts and occasional theatre use. The theatre was originally owned by Evan Evans, leased by Sidney White with S J Parell as General Manager. It is thought that it wasn't used for live performances after the nearby Miners' Theatre had opened in 1932. The Theatres Trust website states that the architect for the Palace was possibly Henry Herbert.

The auditorium was set back behind a three storey building, and there was a glass roof arcade on the left, which led to the entrance and exits of the building. Originally opening with 847 seats, it was enlarged in the 1920's when it was taken over by the Swansea based South Wales Cinemas chain. Seating was increased to 895, with alterations to the balcony. Taken over by the Union Cinemas chain in March 1937, they were the also taken over by Associated British Cinemas (ABC) in October 1937. In the 1950's, it was equipped for Cinemascope and a new 35 feet wide proscenium was installed. ABC gave up on the Palace Cinema on 30th September 1956, and it was taken over by an independent operator until it was closed in 1973, to become a bingo club.

It was badly damaged by a fire on 4th June 1977 and was demolished in 1978 along with the adjacent Primary School and Central Bus Garage to be replaced with an open-air bus concourse and Co-operative retail store.

The Palace at bottom right; Photograph: www.terrynorm.ic24.net

Auditorium Capacity: Original capacity 847, increased to 895 in the 1920's, later capacity changes not known

Stage details: Not available

Workmen's Hall, Gwaun Cae Gurwen

Address: Gwaun Cae Gurwen,

Construction/Opening: 1932

Architect/Builder: unknown/unknown

Demolished: 1995

History/previous names & ownership

On March 31st 1928 Gwaun Cae Gurwen's old hall burnt down, but this proved a blessing in disguise because the local Welfare Committee were now able to apply for a grant from the Welfare Fund and build the largest—and most expensive—hall in the Amman Valley. The original tin-shed hall had been built in 1898 when a disused Swansea church, purchased for £8, was transported to the village where its wooden frame and tin-sheets were quickly redeployed for rather a different purpose than worship.

The Welfare Committee were nothing if not determined in their task: from the 1928 fire to the opening of the new hall in 1932 they held 63 meetings with an average attendance of 25 committee members. (Source: Amman Valley Chronicle 1st October 1932.) When the hall—and its gardens—opened for business on October 1st 1932 it had cost £14,888.

For some time it operated as the "New Cinema" under the proprietorship of the Gwaun Cae Gurwen Committee with a British Thomson Howell sound system and 750 seats. By 1951 its name had changed to "Workmen's Hall" under the same ownership and now held 642 seats. The proscenium was 20 feet wide and the stage was 14 feet deep. There were two dressing rooms to cater for when variety was held.

The Gwaun Cae Gurwen Workmen's Hall was demolished in February 1995 to make way for a clubhouse for the local rugby club.

Photograph: www.terrynorm.ic24.net

Auditorium Capacity: Original: 750; 1951: reduced to 642

Stage details: 6m wide x 3.6m deep

The Royalty Theatre, Llanelli

Address: Market Street/Water Street, Llanelli

Construction/Opening: 1892

Architect: T. P. Martin, Swansea

Builder: Tom Hughes, Llanelli

Demolished: 1977

History/previous names & ownership

The Royalty Theatre was built by Victorian theatre impresario John E Noakes. Construction was completed by Boxing Night December 1892, ready for the opening performance of Alfred Cox's comedy drama 'A Detective' which was performed by C.H. Ross's Comedy Company. Local press reports on the 'first night' performance stated that the theatre could accommodate over a thousand people. According to the newspapers, the proprietor, Mr J.E. Noakes and the manager Mr Sidney Beltram were to be congratulated on the enterprise.

The theatre was illuminated by gaslight which was installed by the Llanelli plumber and gas fitter Messrs. Vivian & Co.

The Royalty is said to have been a venue for performances by many Victorian and Edwardian actors, performers, singers and speakers including Charlie Chaplin, Mari Lloyd and Gracie Fields. Keir Hardie, one of the founding members of the early Labour Party, addressed the people of Llanelli there in 1908.

On the death of the original proprietor in 1910 the theatre was purchased by William Haggar for use as a hall giving variety entertainment including bioscopes and immediately commenced showing film presentations. Over the next eighty years the theatre was owned by a number of different proprietors and was known at various times as Haggar's, The Hippodrome and 'Argos' Bingo Hall.

It was demolished in 1977 to make way for a new Tesco store and this too has now been demolished and replaced with a new building accommodating the Tinopolis new media industries.

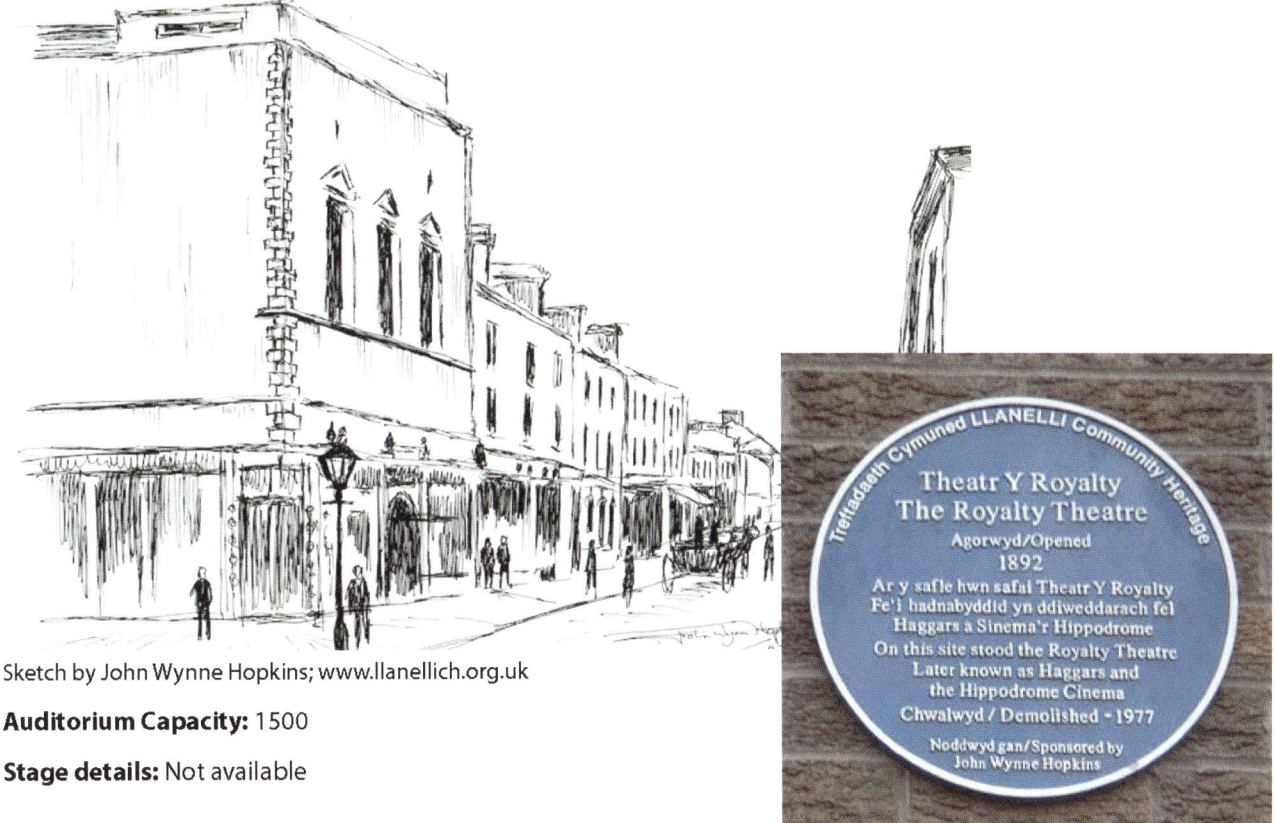

Sketch by John Wynne Hopkins; www.llanellich.org.uk

Auditorium Capacity: 1500

Stage details: Not available

Pembrokeshire

Haverfordwest
The County Theatre

County Theatre, Haverfordwest

Address: Picton Place, Haverfordwest

Construction/Opening: 1934

Architect/Builder: unknown/unknown

Demolished: 1971

History/previous names & ownership

The County Haverfordwest was a large cine-variety theatre with a tall fly tower over the stage and had an audience capacity of 1,000 seats. It was demolished in 1971.

Photograph: Stagedoor's photostream, www.flickr.com

Auditorium Capacity: 1000

Stage details: Not available

Bibliography and sources of historical information

Bibliography

Auditoria, Designing for the Performing Arts. Michael Forsyth. Published by Mitchell, London 1987

Building Wales, Monica Cherry. Welsh School of Architecture 2005

Buildings for the Performing Arts, 2nd Edition. Ian Appleton. Architectural Press 2008

The Buildings of Wales; Glamorgan; John Newman; published 1995

The Buildings of Wales; Gwent/Monmouthshire; John Newman, published 2000

The Buildings of Wales; Carmarthenshire and Ceredigion; Lloyd, Orbach, Scourfield; published 2006

Performing Architecture; Opera Houses, Theatres and Concert Halls for the 21st Century. Michael Hammond. Merrell Publishers Ltd, London. 2006

Act Now! Modernising London's West End Tehatres, A Report by the Theatres Trust, published 2003

One Wales, The Welsh Assembly Government, 2007

A Position Paper on Theatres and Arts Centres Across Wales, Elan Closs Stephens, published 2009 by Creu Cymru

Building a stronger future for the arts, Arts Council of Wales Regional Plan 2009-11

Manifesto for the Performing Arts in Wales, published by Wales Association For The Performing Arts, 2011

Capital Strategy 2012-17 (Draft for Consultation), published by Arts Council of Wales 2011

Internet sources

www.28dayslater.co.uk
www.alwynjones.com
www.archive.rhondda-cynon-taf.gov.uk
www.archiveswales.org.uk
www. arthurlloyd.co.uk/Newport
www.artswales.org.uk
www.austinsmithlord.com
www.barryarchive.zoomshare.com
www.bbc.co.uk/wales
www.blackwoodlt.org.uk
www.blackwoodminersinstitute.com
www.blaenaugwentvenues.com
www.boroughtheatreabergavenny.co.uk
www.bp-hall.co.uk
www.bridgend.ac.uk
www.bridgend.gov.uk
www.britishlistedbuildings.co.uk
www.brycheiniog.co.uk
www.btmcommunitycouncil.com
www.cadw.wales.gov.uk
www.caerphilly.gov.uk
www.capitaarchitecture.co.uk
www.cardiff.gov.uk/learn
www.cardiffians.co.uk
www.cardiffymca.co.uk
www.carmarthenshiretheatres.co.uk
www.chapter.org
www.chepstow.co.uk
www.cinema-theatre.org.uk
www.cinematreasures.org
www.ciswo-services.org.uk
www.congresstheatrecwmbran.co.uk
www.craigynoscastle.com
www.creation.me.uk
www.creucymru.co.uk
www.crosshands-hall.co.uk
www.cwmamantheatre.co.uk
www.dolmantheatre.co.uk
www.dylanthomastheatre.org.uk
www.ejhales.co.uk
www.flickr.com
www.forlornbritain.co.uk
www.fotg.org.uk
www.francisfrith.com
www.genuki.org.uk
www.geograph.org.uk
www.glamro.gov.uk
www.gtj.org.uk
www.gwenttheatre.com
www.holdermathias.com
www.huwgriffithsarchitects.co.uk
www.its4u.org.uk
www.lawray-architects.co.uk
www.llandybiepublicmemorialhall.org.uk
www.llanellich.org.uk

www.localinfohistory.moonfruit.com
www.maestegtownhall.com
www.memorialhalltheatre.co.uk
www.merthyr.ac.uk
www.monmouthsavoy.co.uk
www.monmouthshire.gov.uk
www.myglyw.org.uk
www.nationalarchives.gov.uk
www.neathlittletheatre.co.uk
www.neuaddpontyberemhall.co.uk
www.newbridgememo.com
www.newport.gov.uk/theriverfront
www.newportpast.com
www.newtheatrecardiff.co.uk
www.npt.gov.uk/theatres
www.oldtheatres.co.uk
www.oldukphotos.com/wales
www.opera-singer.co.uk/adelina5.html
www.parchall.co.uk
www.paterhall.org.uk
www.pattipavilion.co.uk
www.pavrep.org
www.pembrokeshire.ac.uk
www.pembrokeshire.gov.uk
www.penarthtowncouncil.gov.uk
www.peoplescollectionwales.co.uk
www.porttalbotopera.co.uk
www.powys.gov.uk
www.rcbi.co.uk/theatre.html
www.rct-arts.gov.uk
www.rhondda-cynon-taff.gov.uk/
heritagetrail
www.rwcmd.ac.uk
www.shermancymru.co.uk
www.smphoto.co.uk
www.smu.ac.uk
www.stdavidshallcardiff.co.uk
www.stdonats.com
www.stephenquick.co.uk
www.swansea.gov.uk/brangwynhall
www.swanseagrand.co.uk
www.swanseaheritage.net
www.swanseasgrand.co.uk
www.swanseaymca.org.uk
www.taliesinartscentre.co.uk
www.tenby-today.co.uk
www.terrynorm.ic24.net
www.the-met.co.uk
www.theatrestrust.org.uk
www.theatre-wales.co.uk
www.theblaketheatre.org
www.thegate.co.uk
www.thequeenshall.org.uk
www.thewelfare.co.uk
www.thisissouthwales.co.uk

www.toptenbingo.co.uk
www.torchtheatre.co.uk
www.torfaen.gov.uk
www.tredegar.co.uk
www.tredegar.co.uk/littletheatre
www.tredegar.co.uk/starlight
www.treharrisdistrict.tech-hosts.
co.uk
www.trinity-cm.ac.uk
www.urbexforums.co.uk
www.valeofglamorgan.gov.uk
www.wales.gov.uk
www.walesonline.co.uk
www.website.lineone.
net/~victor-morgan
www.welshicons.org.uk
en.wikipedia.org
www.wmc.org.uk

Index of Theatres and Performance Buildings

CPSIA information can be obtained
at www.ICGtesting.com
Printed in the USA
2676LVUK00009B